The ROMAN WORLD

SOURCES AND INTERPRETATION

D. Brendan Nagle
University of Southern California

PEARSON

Prentice
Hall

Upper Saddle River, NJ 07458

Library of Congress Cataloging-in-Publication Data

Nagle, D. Brendan (date)
   The Roman World : sources and interpretation / D. Brendan Nagle.
      p. cm.
   Includes bibliographical references and index.
   ISBN 0-13-110083-1
   1. Rome—History.   2. Rome—History—Sources.   1. Title.

DG209.N255 2004
937—dc22

                       2004015193

VP/Editorial Director: Charlyce Jones Owen
Executive Editor: Charles Cavaliere
Editorial Assistant: Shannon Corliss
Executive Marketing Manager: Heather Shelstad
Marketing Assistant: Cherron Gardner
Manufacturing Buyer: Ben Smith
Cover Design: Bruce Kenselaar
Director, Image Resource Center: Melinda Reo
Manager, Rights and Permissions: Zina Arabia
Manager, Visual Research: Beth Brenzel
Manager, Cover Visual Research & Permissions: Karen Sanatar
Image Permission Coordinator: Cynthia Vincenti
Production Liaison: Marianne Peters Riordan
Composition/Full-Service Project Management: Anita Ananda/Integra Software Services
Printer and Binder: Phoenix Book Tech
Cover Printer: Phoenix Color Corp.

Credits and acknowledgments borrowed from other sources and reproduced, with permission, in this
textbook appear on appropriate page within text.

Pearson Education LTD   Pearson Education North Asia Ltd
Pearson Education Singapore, Pte. Ltd   Pearson Educación de Mexico, S.A. de C.V.
Pearson Education, Canada, Ltd   Pearson Education Malaysia, Pte. Ltd
Pearson Education–Japan   Pearson Education, Upper Saddle River, New Jersey
Pearson Education Australia PTY, Limited

10 9 8 7 6 5 4 3 2 1
ISBN 0-13-110083-1

For
Mary, Dermot, Kit, Jo, Donald, Robert and James

This fine mosaic floor found in the ruins of the city of Conimbriga in central Portugal testifies to the concern Rome had for promoting urban development in its western provinces.

Contents

Maps and Visual Sources

PREFACE

The aim of this reader is to provide students of history and civilization with a balanced selection of texts illustrating the social, cultural, political, and military history of Rome from the time of the kings to late antiquity.

At times the richness of the material was overwhelming, but more often than not, the accidental survival of individual sources limited choice to a handful of texts. In selecting the documents I had the help of a large number of colleagues and friends who assisted at various stages in the preparation of the book. My thanks goes in particular to Steve Chrissanthos, Kate Porteus, Lee Reams, Chris Rasmussen, Brigette Russell, and Mehmet Yavuz, all of whom either read portions of the book, contributed suggestions or both. I am especially grateful to my son Garrett who read the entire manuscript with great care and offered many keen and helpful insights. Prentice Hall reviewers contributed numerous useful suggestions: John K. Evans, University of Minnesota; Valerie French, American University; Dave Hood, California State University, Long Beach; Fred Lauritsen, Eastern Washington University and Cheryl Riggs, California State University, San Bernadino. Finally, I would like to thank Charles Cavaliere, Executive Editor at Prentice Hall, who recommended the format for this book and helped it forward at every stage.

Unless otherwise noted the translations are my own.

D. Brendan Nagle

Chapter 1

Rome of the Kings

The Geography of Italy

Italy is divided into a number of clearly identifiable geographic regions by the switching back and forth of the Apennines, its great central mountain range. These mountains begin at the point where the Alps reach the Mediterranean coast at the Riviera, then cut all the way across Italy to the Adriatic Sea at a point below Ariminum (modern Rimini). There they begin to turn southeast and recross the peninsula until they touch the Tyrrhenian coast in Lucania. From there they continue on south through the toe of Italy, reappearing in Sicily, and again in Africa as the Atlas chain.

This zigzagging of the Apennines creates three great natural lowland regions. The first two, the Po valley in the north and Apulia in the south, open onto the Adriatic. In the west, the third, which contains the districts of Etruria (Tuscany), Latium (Lazio), and Campania, opens onto the Mediterranean proper. Between Apulia and Campania the mountains flatten out to form a large plateau, known to the Romans as Samnium, which dominates the plains on either side.

In ancient times the richest agricultural land and almost all the mineral wealth of Italy were to be found in the western lowland region. In addition, the natural lines of communication lay in this area rather than in the mountainous central highlands or on the narrow Adriatic coastal plain. Rome, with its central location astride these routes, could prevent movement north or south or from the Mediterranean into the interior. Long before there were any roads leading to Rome, all the lines of communication converged on the site where a number of hills overlooked a ford on the lower reaches of the Tiber.

In the following readings the Roman statesman Cicero praises Romulus, Rome's founder, for his choice of Rome's location (**1.3**). Romulus was inspired in his choice, Cicero thought, for

Although Italy looks like a peninsula of Europe extending into the Mediterranean, it is better to think of it as a land mass surrounded by lakes. These "lakes" are the Adriatic and Ionian Seas to the east, and the Tyrrhenian Sea to the south. Because communication by water is easier and cheaper than transportation by land, lakes traditionally have had the tendency to draw the inhabitants of their shores into contact with one another. Thus, for early Rome the Tyrrhenian Sea was as important if not more important than much of mainland Italy. Carthage lay just a few days sailing from Italy, and Rome's ultimately successful struggle with that city for dominance of the Tyrrhenian Sea, set it on the path to Empire. The Ionian Sea was the main route to Greece and the Eastern Mediterranean. The Adriatic provided Rome with access to the Danube and Central Europe.

while Rome was close enough to the coast to receive supplies from overseas, it was sufficiently far inland, eliminating the fear of surprise attacks by pirates and, more importantly, avoiding the kind of social and cultural contamination he associated with port cities and their overseas contacts.

The Peoples of Italy

The Italy of Rome's early years was a complicated mosaic of peoples, cultures, and languages. Celts began to infiltrate across the Alps in the early fifth century B.C. and then came in massive numbers around 400 B.C., settling first in the Po valley and then extending themselves southward along the Adriatic coast. Greeks had been in Italy and Sicily since the eighth century B.C. Their main concentrations were in the south along the instep of the boot, in the area known as Magna Graecia, but they also had important settlements on the Adriatic and the Tyrrhenian Sea coasts. The Phoenicians were influential in Etruria, where they found allies to support them against common enemies: the Greeks of Italy, Sicily, and Marseilles in southern France. With the exception of the late-arriving Celts, however, these peoples never ventured deep into the hinterland, and the interior of Italy remained in the hands of two groups of earlier arrivals. The first was made up of Indo-European-speaking peoples, of whom the most important were the Venetians of the Po valley, the Oscans and Umbrians of the central highlands and east coast, and the Latins of the west. The second group, which did not speak Indo-European languages, included one of the most important of the peoples of Italy, the Etruscans. Others of lesser note were the Messapians of Apulia and the Ligurians of the northwest. Italy of the early Roman phase was a babel of languages, dialects, and cultures in various stages of development, from the primitive to the most sophisticated.

Of all these peoples, the Oscans were the most widespread and the Celts probably the most dangerous. The Latins were confined to the small area between the Tiber and Campania, hemmed in by enemies on all sides. The Oscans and Celts, however, were pre-state, tribal peoples who only slowly made the transition to an urban form of life, and then only partially. Organizationally they were backward compared to the Etruscans, Greeks, and Latins, but because of their numbers, military aptitude, and raiding habits, they gave the urban-based peoples of Italy some difficult moments before they were finally overcome. Among the Oscans the Samnites were the predominant group. They were to wage generations-long war with Rome for control of the Italian peninsula. Not all the Oscans were as threatening as the Samnites. Some of the nearby Sabine Oscans participated in the founding of Rome (**1.4; 1.5; 1.7; 1.8**).

Of the peoples of Italy it was the Etruscans (and with their help, the Latins) who made the most remarkable responses to the new influences coming out of the east from the ninth century onwards. Around 700 B.C. the inhabitants of the rich area between the Arno and the Tiber created a flourishing city-state civilization that was recognized throughout the Mediterranean for its opulence and at times for its peculiar customs. To the Greeks they were Tyrsenoi (from which comes "Tyrrhenian Sea") and to the Romans Etrusci or Tusci (hence Etruscan or Tuscan). Etruscans, too, participated in the building of the Roman state (**1.10**).

Economically, the wealth of Etruria lay in its great deposits of iron, copper, tin, and zinc and in its fertile agricultural areas. Etruscan decorative bronzes and jewelry were unsurpassed in the ancient world, and Etruscan farmers achieved high levels of excellence, inventing, among other things, the *cuniculus*, or tunnel method of draining river valley bottoms. By eliminating meandering streams and marshes, this technique reduces erosion and expands cultivable land. Access to abundant raw materials in tandem with a network of trade routes linking them with the eastern Mediterranean allowed Etruscan aristocrats to enjoy unprecedented prosperity—and to supply, via their graves, the museums of the modern world with some of the greatest art of antiquity.

Etruria was at its height between 650 and 450 B.C., but repeated collisions with Greeks, Latins, Oscans, and Celts, as well as internal difficulties, shattered the military power of its city-states, and the Etruscans, like their allies, the Carthaginians, entered into a period of eclipse.

Historiography

Although the Romans were literate from the sixth century B.C., it was a long time before they felt a need to organize the chaotic mass of legends, folk tales, archaic rituals and calendars, treaties, law codes, and family histories that constituted the sources for their early history. They had no Homer to transform their folk tales into poetic legends and myths. So late were the Romans in setting about this task that no generally acceptable date for Rome's founding was available until the first century B.C., 400 years after the founding of the Republic and almost 600 years after the founding of the city. The result is that the early history of Rome is, even to the present, a quagmire of scholarly dispute. For centuries the Romans were engaged in struggles on the Italian peninsula for their bare survival and had little time to devote to the arts or literature let alone to ethnography, or history.

The impulse to construct a coherent explanation of Rome's origins came in several stages. As their power expanded, the Romans found themselves compelled to give some kind of intelligible account of themselves to their new neighbors and subjects, so by about the mid-third century B.C., when the first Punic War or war with Carthage was underway, an established version of their earliest history began to take shape.

There were two problems facing the Romans when they came to say something about their early history. The first was the sheer absence of any hard data regarding Rome's beginnings. What little may have been written down in the form of treaties and state documents was destroyed during the Gallic sack of Rome in 390 B.C.

The second problem was how to fit the strictly local Latin and Roman traditions into the wider, Greek view of things. Compared to the Greeks, the Romans came late to the game of reconstructing the past. For centuries the Greeks had plied the Mediterranean from one end to the other. By the time the Romans became conscious of the need to say something about themselves and their origins the Greeks had already worked out synchronous chronologies for the prehistories of most of the peoples with whom they came in contact, linking them with their own prehistory and such helpful but vague wanderers as Heracles, Jason, Odysseus, and Evander. The local peoples, who knew no more than their own traditions (and even these not very well), were in no position to make such complicated connections, for they lacked the information and even the interest. The Greeks, however, had a passionate need to make sense and order out of the anarchic stories of the Mediterranean and Black Sea peoples. In fact, among the peoples of this world, they and the Hebrews were the only ones to develop a full-scale, comprehensive account of the origins of all peoples.

A number of possible founders of Rome, including Odysseus, had already been put forward by the Greeks. However, because the Romans were not eager to acknowledge a Greek founder, they settled on another possibility, the Trojan hero Aeneas. Aeneas, a prominent leader and member of the Trojan royal family, had escaped from Troy at its destruction and according to one tradition established himself in Italy, where he founded the city of Lavinium near Rome. In this account his distant descendant was Romulus, a figure who may have been part of the local native legend.[1] Six additional kings were given schematic reigns to fill in the gap between Romulus and the traditional date of the founding of the Republic (509 B.C.): Numa Pompilius, Tullus Hostilius, Ancus Marcius, Tarquinius Priscus, Servius Tullius, and Tarquinius Superbus. The historical reality behind these kings is impossible to recover at this point. All we can say is that they probably represent early leaders of the developing community, of whom some were Sabine (Numa and Ancus), some Latin (Romulus and Tullus), and some Etruscan (the two Tarquins and possibly Servius Tullius, despite his Latin-sounding name).

The Romans worked these stories of their origins to their own propaganda advantage. Unlike many Greek peoples (such as the Athenians) who claimed to have been sprung from the earth (called *autochthony*)—the most noble form of origin—the Romans chose to emphasize the simplicity and heterogeneity of their beginnings. They pointed out that from the start they were an amalgam of peoples and customs. By this means they were able to emphasize the greatness of their accomplishments in building a mighty Empire from such unpromising beginnings as those suggested by the story of Romulus and Remus. Unlike the mythic founders of Greek cities these founders invited homeless peoples, shepherds, exiles, and

---

[1]Like sounding names were used throughout antiquity to identify a people with a founder of the same or similar sounding names. Such a person was said to be the eponymous ancestor of that particular people, e.g., in Greek accounts the ancestor of the Persian people was the hero Perseus. Thus Romulus is the eponymous ancestor of the Romans.

other undesirables to assist them in populating Rome. To guarantee the survival of the city, they resorted to the stealing of women from their neighbors.

The five principal sources for early Roman history are, in chronological order: Polybius, M. Tullius Cicero, Titus Livius (Livy), Dionysius of Halicarnassus and Plutarch. These writers lived from 600 to 800 years after the events they claim to describe. Since no hard data existed in their age for Roman origins, Cicero, Livy and Dionysius could construct their own versions of early Rome from differing ideological viewpoints. Their sources were the works of a series of imaginative earlier historians who initiated the writing of Roman history in the late third and second centuries B.C., which now survive only in fragmentary form.

The account of the founding of Rome provided here is taken from the writings of the great statesman, orator and intellectual, Marcus Tullius Cicero (106–143 B.C.). Despite the late date, Cicero's account is the earliest continuous account of Rome's origin. Cicero was chosen over Livy and Dionysius in part because of the brevity of his account, but mainly because his work reflects the thought of a working politician of immense stature and influence rather than the more literary or antiquarian versions of Livy and Dionysius. It cannot be overemphasized that, although Livy may be classified as an "historian," he is not an historian in the modern sense of the world. In terms of "historical accuracy" there is not much to choose between Cicero and Livy. Just as Cicero freely constructs his story of early Rome around a few basic historical events, so Livy (and Dionysius in his own way) with equal abandon develops his version of things around the same facts. The benefit of Cicero's account is that at least we get to know something about the mindset of the class that built Rome, while obtaining insight into the political, cultural and intellectual conditions in the late Republic.

The Founding of Rome

Cicero starts his tale of Rome's origins by contrasting Roman constitutional beginnings with those of Greek states such as Sparta and Athens where lawgivers played the principal role (1.1; 1.9). For Cicero what made Rome different from these and other Greek states was that it achieved the same results through practical experience over a long period of time. Rome's government was tested by practice; it was not the product of some all-important, but in the end, limited, legislator. By continually adapting to changing circumstances, and by making sure setbacks led to reforms, Rome, according to Cicero, achieved the kind of perfectly balanced constitution made up of elements of monarchy, aristocracy and democracy that was the aim of such political theorists as Aristotle (1.12). It was the application of practical reason (Latin: prudentia, *prudence) not dreaming about utopias that produced the mixed constitution that made Rome great.*

In Cicero's scheme of things, Romans were practical, hard-headed statesmen from the beginning. Romulus, for instance, as founder of Rome, immediately recognized that he could and should not govern alone. Hence he associated the leading citizens, the "good" people (in Latin, the boni*), with him in his rule, forming a kind of council or senate (1.5). The kings were not* *succeeded by their sons but by the best individual for the job. The state, Cicero suggests, was not a legacy, a piece of property, to be passed on from father to son. Numa, the second king, took Romulus' statesmanship a step farther and asked the people at large, not just the elite, to confirm his* imperium, *i.e., the power by which he ruled* (1.7). *Thus the people were given an explicit role in the constitution as early as the second king of the city. Romans, accordingly, achieved in practice what Greek political theorists had always asserted was a characteristic of legitimate government: that is, that it be: (1) conducted with the consent of the governed; (2) on behalf of the governed and not just in the interests of the ruler(s); and (3) according to established law and custom. From the start, according to Cicero, Rome conformed to the strictest standards of legitimate, enlightened government.*

Other aspects of Roman statecraft are also on display in Cicero's analysis of early Roman history. He pointedly emphasized that unlike other nations the Romans found a way to conciliate hostile or frightened neighbors. Peoples such as the Sabines and Latins were incorporated as citizens in the Roman commonwealth (respublica) *either by choice or upon conquest* (1.4; 1.8). *They were not enslaved or reduced to helotry (a form of serfdom), alternatives often pursued by other powers in the Mediterranean. This method of incorporating non-Romans in the Roman state was a technique that ultimately became the basis of the Roman empire. We have no way of knowing whether the process was developed as early as Cicero claims, but it was certainly in practice from the mid-fourth century* B.C. *onward.*

Other key points made by Cicero: Good kings always took the auspices, *i.e., they consulted the gods by ritual before engaging in any important activity* (1.3; 1.5; 1.7). *Conquered territories were made public property; they did not become the booty of private individuals, but a resource of the state* (1.6). *Wars were state enterprises not opportunities for private citizens to make money. In his description of the formation of the Centuriate Assembly (the assembly that chose the principal magistrates of Rome and had the power to declare war and make peace), Cicero emphasizes the principle that while the majority should have some power, it should not have too much power. Rome was emphatically not a democracy* (1.11). *Cicero expresses his greatest dislike for tyranny, the rule of one man who did not rule by law or with the consent of the governed nor on their behalf, but strictly in his own self-interest* (1.12; 1.13; 1.14). *Writing this dialogue in the last days of the Republic, Cicero was conscious of the danger that Rome, like many states before it, would come permanently under the control of a charismatic military commander and lose its political freedom. In fact, just a few years after the dialogue was completed in 51* B.C., *Julius Caesar began to put an end to the tottering republican government of Rome, and his successor, Caesar Augustus, became Rome's first emperor.*

Cicero's account is, in effect, an ideological construct of an ideal early Rome passed off as history. He deliberately excludes some of the most lurid and discreditable episodes found in the other sources. There is no mention, for example, of Remus, Romulus' twin brother whom Romulus murdered, after the infancy narrative. It should not be read as a factual account of Rome's beginnings but rather as an interpretative lecture on Roman statecraft written in a time of great danger to the state. The main speaker in the dialogue is Scipio Aemelianus, the general who destroyed Carthage in 146 B.C., *a man recognized in Rome not just for his generalship but for his preeminent virtue. There was a dramatic point to Cicero's choice of Scipio as chief interlocutor. At the fall of Carthage Scipio was supposed to have shed tears as he witnessed the destruction of that great city and quoted Homer on the fall of Troy. Polybius, a Greek historian and statesman, who was with Scipio at the siege, asked him what he meant by his referral to Troy and he replied that he feared for his own country.*[2]

1.1   The Superiority of the Roman Constitution

Scipio, the main speaker in the dialogue begins: Cato used to say that the constitution of Rome was superior to that of other states. The reason he gave was that the constitutions of other states were generally the work of one individual who provided the state with laws and institutions. For example Minos was credited with establishing the constitution of Crete, Lycurgus that of Sparta, and Athens, which often changed its form of government, had Theseus, Draco, Solon, Cleisthenes and others. . . . By contrast the Roman republic was shaped not by one man's genius but that of many. It was founded not in one generation but over a period of centuries. For, he said, no man existed who possessed such genius that nothing could escape him. Nor, for that matter, could the powers of all men living at any given time anticipate all the contingencies that might occur in the future without the aid of practical experience and the test of time. Therefore, following the lead of Cato, I will start from the origins of the Roman people. Unlike Socrates, who in Plato's *Republic*, devises an ideal state, I will have an easier task of it if I provide you with a description of our republic at its birth, maturity, adulthood and finally as a strong and healthy state . . .

1.2   Romulus

What state's origin is as famous or well known as the foundation of this city by Romulus? His father was Mars (we should concede this much to tradition since, not only is it ancient, but it has been wisely handed down by our ancestors that men who deserved well of the commonwealth should be considered the actual descendants of the gods and be thought to possess godlike talents). When Romulus was born it is said that Amulius, the king of Alba,[3] fearing the loss of his power [*to Romulus once he had grown up*], ordered that he and his brother Remus should be exposed on the banks of the Tiber. There he was first cared for by a wild beast of the forest and was then raised by shepherds in the lifestyle of the countryside. When he was grown he so far surpassed his peers in bodily strength and ferocity of disposition that all who lived in the territory where Rome now stands, were glad and

---

[2]*De Re Publica* 2.2–40.
[3]Alba Longa, near modern Castel Gandalfo, about 20 miles from Rome, was supposedly founded by Ascanius, son of the Trojan hero Aeneas ca. 1152 B.C.

willing to obey him. After becoming the leader of these forces, we are told (to pass from fable to fact), that he captured Alba Longa, a strong and powerful city for those times, and put King Amulius to death.

1.3 The Importance of Rome's Geographic Site

After this success Romulus thought of founding a new city if favorable auspices [*signs of divine approval*] were obtained, and establishing a commonwealth [in Latin, *res publica*, literally "the public realm"]. Now as regards the site for a new city, a matter which requires the most careful foresight if one is to create a long-lasting community, Romulus made a particularly good choice. He did not establish it on the coast which would have been easy . . . or at the mouth of the Tiber where one of his successors, King Ancus, later established a colony. With remarkable foresight Romulus recognized that a site on the coast is not the most desirable if longevity and imperial rule is an expectation. Maritime cities are exposed to dangers which are both multiform and impossible to predict. A city founded inland picks up word of the coming of a foe whether anticipated or unexpected by a variety of signs. An enemy cannot come on us by land so suddenly that we are unable to know not only that he is there but even where he came from. But an enemy that is sea borne can arrive literally without warning. When he does appear he does not reveal who he is or what he wants; there is no clue as to whether he is friend or foe.

Maritime cities are also exposed to corruption and moral degeneration because they are exposed to alien languages and customs. Inevitably with the importation of foreign merchandise they also import foreign ways. As a result, none of their traditional institutions can remain unchanged. The people who live in these kinds of cities do not stay attached to their dwellings but are constantly seduced from home by high hopes and expectations. Even if they physically remain at home their thoughts wander abroad. In fact nothing more brought about the fall of Carthage and Corinth [*both were captured and destroyed by Rome in 146 B.C.*], though they had long been tottering, than the scattering and dispersion of their citizenry in their lust for profitable trade and travel. It was this that caused them to abandon their traditional agriculture and the practice of military skills. Piracy and trade by sea generate incitements to luxury that leads to the ruin of states. The very charm of these cities provides enticements to pleasure that are extravagant and debilitating. What I said of Corinth can be said in truth of the whole of maritime Greece. . . . Surrounded as they are by waves they themselves may be thought to float along with their customs and institutions of state. . . . Clearly the cause of the evils and revolutions to which Greece is prone can be traced to the disadvantages attached to maritime cities. But despite these drawbacks these cities possess one advantage: all the products of the world can be brought by water to the city where you live and conversely your people can ship whatever their cities produce to any land they like.

Could anything demonstrate the divine wisdom of Romulus more clearly than his ability to combine the advantages of maritime location without its disadvantages? He achieved this by locating his city on the bank of a never failing river whose broad stream flows steadily into the sea. Such a river allows the city to exploit the sea both for importing what it lacks and exporting its surplus products. Finally, this river allowed the city to bring goods essential to civilized life not only from overseas but also from the interior of Italy. Consequently, it seems to me that Romulus must at the very start have had a divine inspiration that this city would one day be the seat and home of a mighty empire. No other site in Italy would have allowed a city so easily to exercise such power.

1.4   The Sabine Women

All this Romulus accomplished quickly. After founding the city which by his command was called "Rome" after his own name he devised a plan which aimed at strengthening the new commonwealth. Though novel and somewhat crude it revealed a great man whose vision extended to the future. He ordered that the Sabine girls of good family who had come to Rome for the first celebration of the Consualia [*a harvest festival*] in the circus be seized and married into the most prominent families. When the Sabines understandably retaliated by waging war on Rome and the outcome was uncertain, Romulus, at the urging of the stolen women, made a treaty with the Sabine king, Titus Tatius. By this treaty he not only added the Sabines to the commonwealth of Roman citizens, giving them a share in the religious rites of the state, but he also made their king a partner in rule.

1.5   Romulus' Governing Strategy: The *Patres* and the Auspices

After the death of Tatius all the powers of rulership reverted to Romulus. In association with Tatius he had selected the leading citizens of Rome to form a royal council. These were called "Fathers" (*Patres*) because of the affection he felt for them. He also divided the city into three tribes named after himself, king Tatius and another ally, Lucomo, who had been killed in the Sabine War. Thirty voting units called *curiae* were formed named after the stolen Sabine women who had pleaded for a treaty of peace [*when assembled together these 30 voting units were called the* Curiate Assembly].

Although these arrangements had been made during the lifetime of Tatius, yet after his death Romulus ruled with even greater deference to the influence [*auctoritas*] and advice of the *Patres*. It was as a result of this that he first discovered and approved the policy of Lycurgus at Sparta a short time earlier, namely, that a state can be better governed and directed by the authority of a single man, if the influence of the state's most eminent men (the *optimi*) is joined to the ruler's absolute power [*Cicero's point is that from the start Rome's constitution was a mix or blend of different constitutional elements. Here we have the kingly combined with the aristocratic*]. Supported and guarded by this quasi-senate he waged many successful wars against his neighbors. Though continually enriching the citizens at large, he never took any of the plunder for himself.

Romulus also gave complete obedience to the auspices [*the signs of divine approval*], a practice which we still observe to the great security of the state. He took the auspices himself when he founded the city and this was the beginning of our commonwealth [*res publica*]. Also, before the performance of any public act he chose augurs, one from each tribe to help him in taking the auspices. He divided the plebeians up among the most prominent citizens who were to act as their patrons. . . . After Romulus had ruled for thirty-seven years and had instituted those two excellent foundations of our republic, the auspices and the senate, he was so successful that when he did not reappear after a sudden darkening of the sun, he was thought to have become a god. Indeed such a view could never have become widespread about any human being unless he was preeminently renowned for his virtue.

1.6   Numa Pompilius, Second King of Rome

When the senate of Romulus, which consisted of the best men in the city (the *optimi*) . . . attempted to rule the state by itself without the benefit of a king, the people (the *populus*) objected. In their affection for Romulus they repeatedly demanded a king. At that point the senators wisely came up with a plan that was altogether novel and unheard of in any other state. This was the *interregnum*, a period during which the throne could be vacant. Until a king was chosen the state should neither be without a king nor yet have a single long-term king. The idea was that no one should become so used to power that he would be slow in surrendering it, or too interested in hanging on to it. Even in that ancient period the new nation saw something that escaped the founder of the Spartan state, Lycurgus. He thought that the king should not be selected but accepted, whatever kind of person he might be, so long as he was descended from the family of Hercules [*an essential qualification for Spartan kings*]. Yet our ancestors, rubes though they were, thought that kingly virtue and wisdom, not just royal ancestry, were the proper qualifications for a monarch.

Since Numa Pompilius had a reputation for preeminently possessing these qualities, the people themselves, on the advice of the *Patres*, passed over their own fellow citizens and invited him to Rome from Cures in Sabine territory. Thus the Romans chose a foreigner, a Sabine to rule them [*Romulus was a Latin*]. When he arrived, although he had already been chosen king in a vote of the Curiate Assembly [*see 1.5*], he had another curiate law passed to confirm his authority [*imperium*]. Seeing that as a result of their lifestyle under Romulus, the people eager for war, he thought he should to some extent curtail this propensity.

His first act was to divide up among the citizens the land which Romulus had won by warfare, giving each man a share. He showed them that by cultivating their farms they could have abundance of everything without have recourse to plunder or spoils. Thus he implanted in them a love of tranquility and peace. It is through these that justice and good faith most easily flourish and under whose influence the cultivation of the land and the enjoyment of its produce is most secure.

1.7   Numa's Religious Reforms

Pompilius also instituted what are known as the "Greater Auspices," added two augurs to the original number and put five pontiffs or priests selected from the leading citizens in charge of all religious rituals. By promulgating these laws which still are on record, he quenched the people's ardor for war to which they had been accustomed. He also added the Flamines [*priests assigned to the worship of Mars*], the Salii, and the Vestal Virgins [*who care for the sacred hearth of Rome*]. He established all the branches of our religion most devoutly. He insisted that the proper performance of the religious rituals would not be easy but the equipment for the rites would be readily obtainable. He required that much should be learned by heart and carefully done, but should not be expensive. He thus made religious observance laborious but not costly. He also established markets, games and all sorts of occasions for people to gather and celebrate festivals. By these institutions he recalled men who had become savage and inhuman through love of war to humanity and kindness. When he had reigned for thirty-nine years in complete peace and harmony . . . he died, having established the two elements which most conspicuously contribute to the stability of a state, namely religion and a spirit of mildness.

1.8   Tullus Hostilius and Ancus Marcius

After the death of King Numa the people, organized in the Curiate Assembly and presided over by the *interrex* [*i.e., the person holding the throne until the legitimate king was selected, see "Interregnum" in 1.6*], made Tullus Hostilius king. He followed the example of Numa by consulting the people in the same Curiate Assembly and asking them to confirm his *imperium*. Tullus was an outstanding military leader and achieved many successes in war. From the spoils gained on campaign he made the enclosure known as the Comitium, the meeting place for the Curiate Assembly, and built the Curia, the Senate House. He formulated laws for the dec- laration of war and sanctified this most just code by the rituals of the Fetial Priests [*a college of priests who had special ritual responsibilities in foreign affairs*]. Any war that had not been declared and announced should be considered unjust and impious. This suggests how wisely our kings saw that the people should be given some rights (and I will be saying more on that score). Tullus did not dare to assume even the insignia of royalty without the permission of the people. . . . [*At this point a page is missing from the manuscript. From another source we learn that Tullus was killed by a lightning bolt.*]

After Tullus the son of Numa's daughter, Ancus Marcius, was made king by the people. He too insisted that a curiate law be passed by the Curiate Assembly confirming his power. Ancus conquered the Latins in war and enrolled them as citizens. He added the Aventine and the Caelian Hills to the city and divided among the citizens the land he had conquered. All the coastal woodlands he conquered he made public property. At the mouth of the Tiber he founded the city of Ostia and settled it with colonists. After twenty-three years he died.

1.9 Tarquin the Elder

At this time Rome took a cultural step forward, receiving as it were a graft of a foreign system of education. It was no mere stream but a full river of culture and learning. The story is that Demaratus of Corinth, easily the most important person in his city in terms of rank, influence and wealth, fled with his riches because he could not endure the tyranny of Cypselus at Corinth. He came to Tarquinii, the most prosperous city in Etruria, and when he learned that the despotism of Cypselus was firmly established, this free and brave man became an exile and being granted citizenship at Tarquinii, made his home there. His wife, a native of Tarquinii, bore him two sons. These he raised in all the arts in accordance with the Greek educational system. [*There is another gap in the manuscript. When it resumes, one of Demaratus's sons, Lucius has migrated to Rome. The story resumes.*]

At Rome Lucius Tarquinius easily obtained the citizenship and became a friend of King Ancus because of his friendliness and learning. They were so close to each other that Lucius was thought to be involved in all the king's plans and was, in effect, the co-ruler of Rome. He was, in addition, a man of great personal charm and gave help, assistance, protection and even monetary aid to all citizens. Accordingly, when Ancus died, the people unanimously elected Lucius Tarquinius king. After having his *imperium* ratified by law he first doubled the number of senators and gave the original ones the title "Fathers of the Greater Families." These were the senators he consulted first. He gave the title "Fathers of the Lesser Families" to those whom he had added. He next organized the cavalry [the *equites*] in the way we still have it . . . adding new detachments to it, making it 1200 in all, thus doubling its number. . . . We are told that he instituted those great games known as Roman Games [the *ludi Romani*] and vowed a temple to Jupiter the Greatest and Best on the Capitoline Hill in the midst of a battle. He died after a reign of thirty-eight years.

Laelius (one of the interlocutors) adds the following comment: This proves the truth of Cato's claim that the foundation of Rome was neither the work of one period nor of one man. It is clear that good and useful institutions were made by every monarch. However, it is my opinion that the king who came next had the better appreciation of government than any of the others.

1.10   Servius Tullius

Scipio resumes: Yes, indeed, for Tarquinius was followed by Servius Tullius. According to tradition he was the first to hold royal power without being chosen by the people. It is said that his mother was one of Tarquinius' slaves and his father one of the king's clients. Although he was brought up as a slave and served the king's meals, yet the spark of genius which appeared even when he was boy, was obvious in every duty he performed and every word he spoke. Accordingly Tarquinius, whose own children were quite young, became so attached to Servius that it was generally assumed that he was actually his own son. The king took the greatest care to have Servius educated in all the arts which he had himself studied and in accordance with the highest standards of Greek practice.

After Tarquinius had been murdered by the sons of Ancus, Servius began to rule. This was done, as previously noted, not by command of the people but with their good will and consent. This came about because a false report came out that Tarquinius, although wounded, was still alive and Servius took it on himself to assume the royal regalia, administer justice and relieve debtors out of his own pocket. His affability convinced the people that he was acting on the orders of Tarquinius. He did not put the question of the succession to the senate, but after the burial of Tarquinius, brought the matter in person to the people. When they had directed him to act as king, he proposed the usual curiate law to be passed confirming his royal authority (*imperium*) . . . [*There is a gap in the manuscript. When it resumes Scipio is speaking of the constitutional reforms of Servius, especially with regard to the Centuriate Assembly.*]

1.11   The Centuriate Assembly

Servius organized the equestrian order [*the knights from whom the senators were selected*] in eighteen centuries according to grades of wealth. After having set off this large group of knights from the main body of the people, he divided up the rest of the citizens into five classes and further subdivided them into older and younger categories. He made this division so that the largest number of votes did not belong to the ordinary citizens but to the well-off, establishing the principle which ought always to be adhered to in the Republic that the majority should not have the greatest power.

If you were not already familiar with this system, I should explain it to you. You already know that the arrangement is such that if the eighteen centuries of knights (including the original six) are added to the first class centuries and supplemented by the century of carpenters who were organized as a special century because of their importance to the city, the total is 89. Therefore, if only eight of the remaining 104 centuries are added to the 89, a voting majority is achieved.

The remaining 96 centuries, which included by far the largest number of citizens, would not be deprived of their votes, for that would be dangerous and high-handed. On the other hand, they would not possess too much power, for that too would be dangerous.

Servius was careful even with the terminology used in his scheme. The wealthy were given the designation of *"assidui"*, i.e., "money givers" because they gave money.[4] Those who had less than 1500 denarii or nothing at all except their persons were given the designation of *"proletarii"* to indicate that their offspring (*proles*) were to be the progeny of the state. Therefore, a single one of the 96 centuries contained almost as many citizens as were in the entire first class of centuries. Thus while no one was deprived of the right to vote, the majority of the votes lay in the hands of those who had the principal responsibility for the well-being of the state. . . .[5]

1.12   The Balanced Constitution

I believe that the best constitution for a state is one which is made up of a combination of monarchy, aristocracy and democracy. . . . This equitably balanced system of government seems to me to have been common to our constitution as well as to that of Sparta and Carthage. I will now describe in more detail what is unique to our incomparable republic. Nothing like this quality is to be found in any other state. The elements which I have previously referred to were combined in our state during the monarchical period as in the states of the Spartans and Carthaginians, but in such a way that the balance between them was not maintained. For in a state in which a single individual holds power for life, especially if he is a king, even if there is a senate as was the case at Rome under the monarchy, and at Sparta under the Lycurgan constitution, and even if the people have some power as they did under the kings, nevertheless the royal power is bound to be supreme. Such a government is inevitably a monarchy and will be so called. Unfortunately this form of government is of all constitutional forms the most unstable. One man's vices can subvert it and easily sweep the whole state into ruin. Kingship in itself is unexceptionable, and if I had to choose among the simple forms of the constitution [*namely monarchy, aristocracy democracy*] I would choose

---

[4]"Assiduus" according to Cicero came from "as" (a coin) and "do" (I give).
[5]Cicero's version of the Centuriate Assembly differs in some important respects from the accounts of the other two main sources, Livy and Dionysius of Halicarnassus. The points are much disputed among scholars. All sources agree, however, that the total number of centuries was 193 and that the Assembly functioned on the principle that those who had the largest stake in the community and the best education and preparation for rule should have the most power. In due course this oligarchic, or timocratic principle as the Romans preferred to call it, was balanced by the more democratic Plebeian Assembly which evolved during the fifth and fourth centuries.

monarchy as long as it maintained its true character. Still, it accomplishes this only when the security, citizen rights and the peace of the community are protected by the life long authority, justice and wisdom of a single ruler.

1.13   Tarquin the Proud: The Monarchy Ends in Tyranny

[*There is a gap in the manuscript at this point, but from the other sources we know that the reigning king, Servius, was brutally murdered and his throne usurped by Lucius Tarquinius Superbus, son of Tarquin the Elder. He soon began to act tyrannically, proving Cicero's point about the instability and danger of one man rule.*] Nevertheless the people put up with the tyranny of Tarquinius, for this unjust and cruel ruler was lucky in his public undertakings. He conquered the whole of Latium and took the rich city of Suessa Pometia. With the gold and silver taken from Suessa he fulfilled his father's vow to build the Capitoline temple of Jupiter on the Capitoline hill. He also founded colonies and following the examples of his forefathers sent magnificent gifts, the first fruits of his spoils, to Apollo at Delphi.

At this point begins the change in the political cycle [*in this instance, the transition from legitimate one man rule, monarchy, to illegitimate one man rule, tyranny*], the natural course and revolution of which we need to recognize from the outset. The whole point of political science, which is the aim of our discussion here, is to understand the regular though twisting path through which the forms of government move. Thus, when we know the direction the state is evolving, we will know what actions to correct or advance the changes underway.

1.14   Lucius Brutus the "Liberator": "No One is a Mere Private Citizen when the Liberty of his Fellow Citizens is at Stake"

Now this king of whom I am [*i.e., Cicero*] speaking was from the outset stained by the blood of an outstanding king. As a result he did not begin his reign with a clear conscience. As he was in fear of the proper punishment merited by his crime, he wanted to have others fear him. Later on, relying on his victories and wealth, he let his pride get the better of him and was unable either to control his own conduct or the lusts of his own family. When his oldest son raped Lucretia, the daughter of Tricipitinus and wife of Collatinus, this modest and well-born woman committed suicide in self-punishment because of the assault. This inspired Lucius Brutus, a man of preeminent ability and courage, to free his fellow citizens from the unjust yoke of oppressive servitude. Though he was only a private citizen he sustained the whole burden of government and was the first person in our state to demonstrate that no one is a mere private citizen when the liberty of his fellow citizens is at stake.[6] Following his lead the country was moved to revolt against Tarquinius. The people, aroused not only by the charges of Lucretia's father and kinsmen, but also by their own memory of the arrogance of Tarquinius and the many wrongs committed by him and his sons, banished the king, his children and all his relatives.

Consider, therefore, how a king was transformed into a tyrant and a good form of government into the worst by the evil action of a single individual. . . . Monarchy is undoubtedly a good form of state but nevertheless it has a tendency, almost naturally one might say, to transform itself into the worst type of government. No creature more horrible than a tyrant, or more loathsome to the gods and mankind can be imagined.[7] For though he may look like a human being he in reality surpasses the most savage of wild beasts in the cruelty of his nature. How can the title of human being be given to a person who wants no community of justice and no partnership in human affairs with his fellow citizens or, for that matter, with any part of the human race?

Such, therefore is the first form, variety and origin of the tyrannical state. It came to be in our state which Romulus founded after duly taking the auspices. It did not come into existence in that commonwealth described by Socrates which Plato tells us about in his famous dialogue on the state [the *Republic*]. We have found how a man like Tarquin was able to overthrow the whole monarchical constitution not by seizing any new powers, but by his arbitrary misuse of the powers he already possessed.

▼▼▼

Questions

1. What problems did historians of Rome face in writing about early Rome? (Introduction, *Historiography*)
2. Cicero's version of early Roman history is loaded with ideological viewpoints, principally on the nature of Roman statecraft. Identify some of the elements that Cicero thought were characteristic of Rome's political behavior (Introduction)

---

[6]This question of what a private citizen was allowed to do became a major issue in Roman politics after a private individual murdered the tribune Tiberius Gracchus. Those who supported the justice of the assassination of Gracchus appealed to precedents such as this to justify the action. The problem of how a legitimately constituted officer of the state might be done away with has remained a problem for politicians and ethicists throughout history.

[7]Greeks and Romans both had strong, anti-tyrannical traditions, but here Cicero is anticipating the distinct possibility that Rome is about to fall into the hands of a tyrant. In fact, some six years after the publication of the *De Re Publica*, Gaius Julius Caesar, fulfilling Cicero's worst forebodings, had himself declared Dictator in Perpetuum, Dictator in Perpetuity. Caesar was soon murdered (to Cicero's intense satisfaction) but his successor, Gaius Octavius (Augustus) was more successful in establishing a permanent military dictatorship.

3. Cicero identified several marks of legitimate government. What were they? (Introduction)
4. Why, according to Scipio [Cicero's interlocutor], was the Roman constitution superior to Greek constitutions? (**1.1**)
5. What were the advantages of Rome's geographical location? (**1.3**)
6. What were the drawbacks to cities located on the coast? Why did Scipio object to commerce? (**1.3**)
7. According to Scipio Romulus took two steps that guaranteed that his rule was that of a legitimate monarch and not a tyrant. What were these? (**1.5**)
8. The second king of Rome, Numa, rounded out the constitution left incomplete by Romulus. How did he do this? (**1.6; 1.7**)
9. What happened to land conquered by the Romans? (**1.6**)
10. The Sabine element in the Roman population was explained by what strange event? (**1.4**)
11. The rituals of the Fetial Priests were introduced by Tullus Hostilius to govern what important activity? (**1.8**)
12. Servius Tullius made some major reforms in the voting arrangements of the Centuriate Assembly. He made sure the elite had the majority of the vote but that the rest of the electorate should not be neglected. Why did he make this arrangement? (**1.11**)
13. Scipio has some good things to say about the weakness of monarchical rule. Yet he thought such rule was good under some circumstances. What were these? (**1.12**)

Chapter 2

▼▼▼

Political Culture of the Roman Republic

At some point in the seventh century Rome followed the lead of its Etruscan neighbors to the north and accepted the constitutional form of the city-state or *polis*, a type of government found in many places in the Mediterranean, but most successfully developed by Phoenicians and Greeks.[1] The adoption was a revolutionary step for the peoples of Rome and Latium as it committed them to a way of life that was fundamentally at odds with many of the other peoples of Italy such as the Oscans who resolutely clung to non-*polis* forms of social and political organization.

The Nature of the Polis

The *polis* (plural: *poleis*) took many forms, but in its Greek shape the city-state tended to give heavy emphasis to the role of the military. A close relationship existed linking the ownership of property, almost invariably land, and the duty of participation in military and civilian affairs. Land-owning citizens fought as a unit in the military formation known in Greek as the phalanx (later, in an adapted form, the phalanx became the Roman legion). These same citizens when not under arms constituted the civilian assembly of the *polis*. The assembly, along with elected magistrates and a council of elders (at Rome the Senate), constituted the government of the community.

The *polis* form of government was enormously flexible in terms of types of constitution that were available for adoption. Legitimate constitutions of *poleis* stretched in a continuum from monarchy on the right to extreme democracy on the left. In between were oligarchies and democracies that shaded into

---

[1]It is hard to find a good translation for the term *polis*. A recent suggestion has been "citizen state," but here the traditional translation is given, "city-state."

each depending on the degree to which the members of the assembly had (or lacked) active roles in government.

Democracies were defined in terms of the large numbers of citizens who participated in assemblies, juries, councils, and commissions, and by the use of sortition or the lot, for the selection of their magistrates. Smaller landowners exercised the most power in democracies. In oligarchies fewer citizens participated, and the better off landowners had stronger representation. Election was favored over the lot by oligarchies. Too much should not be made of these distinctions as states often fluctuated back and forth over time between oligarchy and democracy. Illegitimate forms of government were tyranny on the right, and ochlocracy, or mob rule, on the left.

Poleis tended to be small. Aristotle for instance thought that the ideal recommended by Plato of about 5,000 households was far too large. Of the 1,500 or so Greek *poleis* known, the majority were in the range of about 200–700 households. Cities like Athens with 30,000 households, were exceptions. Only a few of these mega-*poleis* existed. Indeed the greatest problem faced by Greek city-states and their imitators was how to maintain their size relative to their ancestral traditions and their territories. Too small a population invited encroachment on empty farmlands by neighbors, while too large a population meant the *polis* had to expand or ship its surplus population overseas. Beyond a certain size, Athens being a good example, *poleis* found it exceedingly hard to maintain internal equilibrium. It was Rome's genius to be able for find a formula that enabled it to preserve many of the most desirable forms of the small city-state constitution with territorial and demographic expansion.

The New Constitution: The Patrician Constitution

The challenge facing Rome after the expulsion of the kings was to find a governing formula that would guarantee both order and freedom in the midst of a threatening world. The constitution that eventually emerged modified the previously adopted *polis*-style government. It evolved in several stages, the first being the emergence of the Patrician Constitution. The centralized power of the kings provided Rome with stability and guaranteed order within the state and protection from without in its early years. Unlike many Greek states during the period of their early evolution, Rome existed in a high risk environment. A powerful central magistracy of some kind was essential to its internal coherence and to its ability to defend itself against threatening enemies (**2.1**).

In the Patrician Constitution that succeeded the monarchy the Romans opted to continue the tradition of a strong executive, but attempted to guard against the dangers of its magistrates becoming too powerful by two techniques, annual rotation of office and collegiality. The former guaranteed that no matter how abusive an individual might be while in office, he would only hold power for a year, while being subject to prosecution and reprimand when out of office. Even while in office, abusers of power would be restrained by the second principle, collegiality. Roman magistracies were typically held by multiple office holders, two in the case of consuls and some other offices, but larger numbers in the case of the lower magistracies. These multiple office holders constituted a *collegium* and could be counted on to hold in check more ambitious colleagues by the exercise of veto power (called *intercessio*; the term "veto" simply means "I forbid" in Latin). Adding to their power, Roman magistrates, unlike those of Athens and other more democratically inclined *poleis*, were never formally responsible to the people who elected them. The result of these arrangements was that the Roman magistracies provided the city with a strong executive which allowed quick response to military threats, and in the case of internal upheaval the power to maintain order when it was challenged (**2.1**; **2.4**). All of this was accomplished with relatively few restraints on political freedom. It was not a compromise, however, with which thorough-going democracies such as Athens, would have been satisfied.

One of the most important strengths of the Patrician Constitution was its capacity to attach the Roman elite to the interests of the state (**2.3**). Rather than pursuing their own separate self interest, as was frequently the case in Greek states (and in modern states), the Roman elite was fully wedded to Rome. For centuries the glory of Rome trumped family issues and individual ambition. This tradition of Rome lasted down to the end of the Republic, 400 years later, at a time when the whole system collapsed. As a result Rome never had to cope with the fear of betrayal from within by its own elite. The elite's loyalty was not a form of altruism, but rather one of self-interest. At Rome the elite got what elites world wide want: power, recognition, and self-fulfillment. The very Latin terms that constantly crop up in Roman political discourse, *gloria, virtus, dignitas, fama, gravitas, industria, innocentia* (integrity), *honor, auctoritas, severitas*, all more or less translated by their modern equivalents, suggest what the elite wanted and got. First came glory, fame and honor, all the result of action in battle and or in the public arena on the home front, summed up in the all embracing term, *virtus*, weakly translated in English as "virtue." As a consequence of much state service, authority, dignity and gravity were won. Another underlying value was *fides*, dependability in relations with others of the elite and one's inferiors, and between Rome and its neighbors (**2.3**; **2.4**).

The assembly that elected, judged and passed legislation in the Patrician Constitution was the Centuriate Assembly. All citizens, including plebeians, belonged to this assembly, and were enrolled in 193 voting units called centuries. These units, however, were distributed unequally among the well-to-do and the rest of society. It was what the Greeks called a "timocratic" system, that is a system that rewarded status and gave people of high status more votes than people of low status. It assumed geometric rather than arithmetic equality. As Cicero was wont to say, "we Romans do not count votes; we weigh them." This arrangement may seem intrinsically unfair to our egalitarian sensibilities, but it guaranteed the fidelity of the elite to the state and discouraged it from going outside the state for redress of its grievances when things did not go its way. The problem of assuring the allegiance of a state's elite is not a given in any society, including our own, and Rome's solution to it was one of the most successful in world history. (For more on Cicero's version of the Centuriate Assembly see **1.12**.)

The Plebeian Constitution

Had there only been a Patrician Constitution Rome would not have looked (or fared) much differently from any of the oligarchic *poleis* that were to be found around the Mediterranean. What made Rome unique was its invention of a parallel political system that represented the majority of the population in a far more democratic way. This was the Plebeian Constitution.

Almost immediately after its founding, the Patrician Constitution came under pressure from the non-elite segment of society, the plebeians. The plebeians sought two things, protection from the power (the *imperium*) of the magistrates, and a share in political power (**2.2**). Gradually, over the following centuries, the plebeians managed to wrestle a series of concessions from the elite that in the end satisfied their sense of entitlement and fairness (*aequitas*). Just as the Patrician Constitution cemented the elite to Rome by providing the elite with what it wanted, the Plebeian Constitution cemented the remainder of society to the state by providing it with what it wanted. For the most part this was security from arbitrary interference by the governing elite in matters of property or personal rights. This form of security was achieved, over time, by the acquisition of the right of appeal, *provocatio*, and protection by tribunes, magistrates with the power of the veto, *intercessio*, elected by plebeians (**2.2**). Finally a real share in political power was achieved in the early third century B.C. when the assembly of the plebeians won the right to pass resolutions, *plebiscites*, that had the power to bind the whole state.

From a constitutional viewpoint the evolved Roman state combined the strengths of monarchy, aristocracy and democracy in a winning combination (**2.4**; see also **1.12** for Cicero's Interpretation of Rome's balanced constitution). Taken as a whole the constitution amounted to a kind of stable infrastructure which allowed the state to operate effectively in the dangerous environment of central Italy. Both rich and poor, weak and powerful, were united by a sense of shared self-interest. The antagonisms were not papered over; they were simply shunted into different venues which allowed each group to pursue its own aims. It was obviously, from a functional standpoint, a clumsy arrangement, one guaranteed to impede progress or change rather than accelerate it. But that is a characteristic of the institutions of most modern constitutional states.

From a military viewpoint the Roman constitution was enormously efficient. Because the masses were not the reluctant, coerced partners of the elite in the state, Rome was assured of a large, dependable, manpower pool for the army. Proportionate to the population Rome probably achieved a higher leverage in this regard than any other ancient state. A willingness to suffer casualties on behalf of the state on the part of both upper and lower classes provided the foundation for Rome's successful defense in its early years and later on for its ability to project its power far beyond its boundaries. A weaker constitutional arrangement would never have tolerated the losses suffered during the years of war with Carthage. Unlike Lincoln and other American presidents who had constantly to worry about the willingness of Americans to tolerate battlefield casualties, this was not an issue for Rome.

The Role of Diplomacy

Rome's strength did not depend ultimately on just the raw exercise of military power. Another element of this strength was its capacity to integrate non-Romans into its commonwealth, thereby enlarging its own population, wealth and military manpower reserves while at the same time being able to draw upon the diverse talents and enthusiasm of other peoples.

After a successful war in 340–338 B.C. against its old allies, the cities of the Latin League, Rome was faced with the traditional method of ending wars, selling off the conquered populations or reducing them to serf-status as was the practice in many Greek states. Rome opted to exercise neither alternative, and instead decided to integrate some of their defeated Latin neighbors directly into its commonwealth, conferring on them municipal status, either with the vote (*municipia optimo iure*), or without the vote (*municipia sine suffragio*), while allowing others to retain their Latin status. The newly designated *municipia*, along with the old Latin states whose status was unchanged, remained dependent on Rome for their foreign policies. The arrangement allowed the citizens of the *municipia* and of Latins states to continue to govern their own internal affairs while their elites had, at least in the case of *municipia optimo iure*, the opportunity to participate directly and fully in Rome's government, stand for office, command legions and so forth. The lower strata of the *municipia* benefited from the right to enroll in the legions as Roman citizens and share in the conquests of the Roman state. Overall, the arrangements made at the end of the Latin War were brilliantly successful. They reconciled Romans and Latins with each other and provided Rome with an efficient means of expanding and introducing new citizens into its citizen body.

Informal Political Bonds

In addition to the formal aspects of government mentioned above many (but not all) Roman citizens were politically and socially connected to each other by bonds of clientage and friendship. Patronage exercised by the powerful over the less powerful was a form of self-help that enabled many ancient societies to function without the huge apparatus of the modern welfare state which has taken its place. Patrons were expected to look out for the welfare, social, economic and political, of their clients, and vice versa. Where neither banks nor insurance companies existed, networks of patronage and friendship provided the services offered by these institutions in modern societies.

In addition to individual patronage, whole communities could look for patronage among the powerful. In the late Republic Cicero, for instance, was the patron of a large number of communities in Italy and a few overseas as a result of his governorship of the province of Cilicia in Asia Minor (**2.5**). Other even more powerful Romans such as Scipio, Pompey and Caesar had whole nations as clients.

Another form of patronage, that between freedman and his manumitter, also existed. If properly manumitted, slaves became full Roman citizens but always retained a form of dependency on their former masters. From a psychological viewpoint the position of clients tended to be one of awkwardness and at times complete humiliation. In Rome's highly status conscious society the relationship between various strata was often blurred or at best, ambiguous. But the tradition of *fides*, mutual dependability, helped mitigate some of the worst aspects of this relationship, translating it into a kind of fictitious partnership.

The republican constitution served Rome well, allowing it first to survive and then to conquer. Lessons learned during the period of the Republic (509–31 B.C.) formed the basis for Rome's success during the Empire. Roman political culture, combining elements that stimulated and rewarded ambition, while at the same time preserving political freedom and stability, had the ability to bring out the best—and sometimes the worst—in people not just from Rome and Italy, but ultimately from all over the Mediterranean as well as much of Europe and the Middle East. As Cicero liked to point out, while the Greeks spoke and wrote at great length about the possibility of creating an ideal state it was the Romans who came closest to building one (see Chapter 1, p. 6).

▼▼▼

2.1   Order and Liberty: The Monarchy and the Republic

Five centuries after the founding of the Republic, the historian Livy composed a history of Rome that began with its glorious, legendary founding and reached to "the dark dawning," as he put it, of his own day. Livy editorialized a lot, and his reflections on Roman history are colored by the events of his own times: the chaotic and bloody collapse of the Republic and the rise of a new, if veiled, monarchy under Augustus Caesar (27 B.C.–A.D. 14). Livy understood full well the difficulty of maintaining the twin ideals of freedom and order. This reading constitutes the preface to Book 2 of his history. Book 1 dealt with the kings and the overthrow of the last of them, Tarquin. Here he mulls over the problems faced by the new state.[2]

---

[2]Livy, *History of Rome*, Book 2, Preface. Translation based on D. Spillan, *The History of Rome by Titus Livius* (New York, 1867). All the readings from Livy in this chapter are based to some extent on Spillan's translation.

THE FORUM: THE NEW STATE FINDS ITS ARCHITECTURAL EXPRESSION

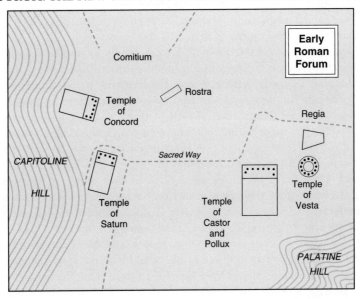

The emergence of the new Roman state, the Republic, was manifested graphically for all to see by the creation of a new civic center in the heart of Rome, the Forum. Under the kings the old space which the new Forum was to occupy had been a shapeless, indeterminate, unimportant marketplace. The power of the state was manifest elsewhere: in the palaces of the kings on the nearby Palatine Hill.

With the establishment of the Republic this was all changed. The old marketplace was reorganized and became, henceforth, the center of the Roman state. First, the king's house, the *Regia*, was moved from the Palatine Hill and became the place where the relatively unimportant *Rex Sacrorum*, the King of Sacrifices, performed his functions. The king's house was now no longer the inaccessible private dwelling of a king, but the public residence of a magistrate, located in a public place. The king himself, as symbolized in the new office of King of Sacrifices, was simply a minor priest in the Roman religious hierarchy. Monarchy was at an end.

The *Regia* was placed in calculated relationship to the Temple of Vesta, Goddess of the Hearth of Rome, and the house of her ministers, the Vestal Virgins. This dwelling was also now transferred to the Forum where the hearth of the new community was established. The King of Sacrifices and the Vestals were thought of as maintaining the offices and cults without which the state could not continue, but in a setting adjusted to the needs of the new community. In the old order the king embodied the priestly, military, judicial, and political powers of the state, and these activities were regarded as inseparable and vital to the functioning of the state. The new Republic preserved the functions but redistributed them in such a fashion as to bring about a thorough reorganization of the state without departing from its underlying religious concepts.

At the other end of the Forum from the Regia and the Temple of Vesta, the Comitium, or meeting place of the people, created. Now the Forum had two poles, the one political and secular, the other religious, giving visible evidence of the existence of a new state based on a new set of presuppositions, the most fundamental of which was that the business of the community was no longer the private affair of an individual, but belonged to all the people of Rome; Rome was to be a Republic, not a monarchy.

My theme from now on will be the civil and military affairs of the now free Roman people, their annual magistracies, and the sovereignty of their laws, which are superior in their authority over men.

The haughty insolence of the last king, Tarquin the Proud, had caused this liberty to be all the more welcome. The kings before him, by contrast, had ruled in such a manner that they all might well be regarded as successive founders of at least parts of the city, for each had developed new districts to serve as homes for the population they themselves added. Nor is there any doubt that the very same Brutus who had earned so much glory for expelling this haughty monarch would have done his country great disservice if, through an over-hasty desire for liberty, he had wrested the kingdom from any of Tarquin's predecessors.

For what would have been the consequence if that rabble of shepherds and vagrants, fugitives from their own countries, having under the protection of an inviolable asylum [*the asylum was established at Rome's founding by Romulus to attract migrants to the new city*] found liberty, or at least impunity, uncontrolled by the fear of royal authority? In such circumstances they would no doubt have been distracted by the demagoguery of tribunes and would have engaged in contests with the patrician rulers. This would have happened before the influence of wives and children, and the love of the soil, all of which take time to develop, had united their affections. The nation, not yet matured, would have been destroyed by discord. Luckily, the tranquil moderation of the government of the kings before Tarquin allowed the people, their strength being now developed, to produce wholesome fruits of liberty.

The origin of liberty may be traced to the limitation of the consuls' powers to a single year rather than to any lessening of the regal power of their office. The first consuls had all the kings' privileges and marks of power with only one exception. Instead of two bundles of rods [*the fasces*], one for each consul, with which to strike terror, there was to be only one between them both.

Brutus was, with the agreement of his colleague, first attended by the fasces. Yet he had not been a more zealous asserter of liberty than he was afterwards its guardian. First of all he bound the people, still enraptured with their newly acquired liberty, by an oath that they would allow no one to be king in Rome, lest afterwards they might be corrupted by the appeals or bribes of the royal family. Next, in order that a full-strength Senate should enjoy greater authority, he filled its depleted ranks to the amount of 300. Its numbers had been reduced by the murderous activity of Tarquin. To do so he chose men from among the principal ranks of the equestrian order [*the rank immediately below the Senate*]. From now on it is said that the custom was handed down of summoning to the Senate both those who were Fathers (*patres*), and those who were later enrolled (the so-called *conscripti*). This latter term was the designation of those who were elected into the Senate as conscripts. This measure was enormously effective in promoting the concord of the state and in attaching the affection of the plebeians to the patricians.

2.2 The Importance of Concord: Secession and Concession

The importance of concord runs as a theme throughout Livy's history of early Rome. It is emphasized at the end of the previous reading, as we have seen. The great internal social and political problem of the early Republic was the degree to which political power would be divided between the upper-class patricians and the remainder of society. Some kind of equitable solution had to be worked out or the state would not survive. In this reading Livy tells the traditional story of a major development in this process, the emergence of the plebeian branch of government, the Plebeian Assembly (the Concilium Plebis), and the office of tribune of the plebs. The event is supposed to have happened in 495 B.C.[3]

The city was in a state of internal discord. Hatred burned between patricians and plebeians, chiefly on account of those who had been forced into a kind of slavery to their creditors because of debt. These complained noisily that, while fighting abroad for liberty and dominion, they were enslaved and oppressed at home by their fellow citizens. They said that the liberty of the people was more secure in war than in peace, and among their enemies than at home.

This growing resentment was further aggravated by the striking sufferings of one individual. An old man, with all the signs of his misfortunes, flung himself into the Forum. His clothes were squalid and his body still more shocking, being pale and emaciated. His long beard and hair gave the impression of savage wildness to his face. Despite his appearance, he was still recognized as a veteran centurion. People standing around him recalled openly his military awards, and he himself showed the scars on his chest which bore witness to his honorable service in battle.

When he was asked the reason for the squalor of his dress and the condition of his body, the people now having gathered around him like a small assembly, he replied: "During the Sabine war the enemy deprived me of my crops, destroyed my home, and drove off my cattle. Then at this awful moment taxes became due. I borrowed to pay them and thus fell into debt. This debt, increased by interest, stripped me first of my father's and grandfather's farms, and then of all my other property. Finally, like a disease, ruin spread even to my body. I was taken by my creditor, not to slavery, but to prison and the rack." He then showed them his back disfigured with the marks of recent beatings. At this a great uproar resulted and spread from the Forum all over the city. Debtors who were already enslaved, and those who were still free, rushed into the streets from all quarters to beg the protection of the people. Everywhere people joined in, running through the streets to the Forum in noisy crowds.

---

[3]From Livy 2.23, 31–33. The Centuriate Assembly was presided over by consuls or praetors who had been elected by this assembly. Tribunes of the plebs presided over the Plebeian Assembly, and patricians could not attend. A later modification of the Plebeian Assembly, the Tribal Assembly, differed from the Plebeian Assembly only in so far as it was convened by consuls or praetors and patricians could attend.

The senators who happened to be in the Forum and fell in with the mob were in great danger. Nor would the crowd have refrained from violence had not the consuls, Publius Servilius and Appius Claudius, hurriedly intervened to put down the disturbance. But the mob turned on them and showed them their chains and other marks of misery. These, they said in bitterness, were their rewards for campaigns. Each recounted his individual experiences. They demanded, more with threats than requests, that the consuls convene the Senate. They then surrounded the Senate House itself so that they could both witness and direct the debate.

The Senate assembled, but its debate was interrupted by a series of invasions by neighboring peoples. People and Senate agreed to shelve the debt issue momentarily and fend off the invasion, since, as the consul pointed out, the debt issue concerned only a part of the community whereas the war threatened everyone. Nevertheless discontent continued and the people began to hold secret meetings to plan political actions to free themselves from patrician coercion. The last invasion was so serious, and the Romans so disunited, that the Senate was forced to employ the emergency powers of a dictator. By way of reassurance for the plebs, who felt even more vulnerable to a dictator than to the regular consuls, a popular figure, Manlius Valerius, was appointed to the office. Valerius promised to fix the debt issue when the war was over. The story resumes after the army returned victorious.

Although a triple victory had been won, patricians and plebeians were still uneasy about affairs on the home front. The money-lenders, with great cunning and the assistance of powerful interests, set out to frustrate not only the people, but even the dictator [*Valerius*] himself.

As soon as the consul Vetustius had returned to Rome, Valerius brought up before the Senate as the first item of business the matter of the common people who had been victorious in the recent campaign. He moved that the Senate decide on a policy regarding people who had been bound over for debt. The motion failed. Valerius then addressed the Senate: "You reject me, an advocate of concord. Yet I tell you that you will soon wish that the Roman plebs had patrons like me to deal with. For my part, I will neither further disappoint my fellow citizens, nor will I be a dictator to no purpose. Internal dissensions and foreign wars made the office of dictator a necessity. Peace has been secured abroad but aborted at home. I prefer to play my part as a private citizen when the revolution comes." Then, leaving the Senate House, he abdicated the dictatorship. It was clear to the commons that he had resigned the office because of his indignation at the treatment they had received. Accordingly, as if his commitments to them had been kept, since it was clear it had not been his fault that he had not been able to make good on his promises, the people escorted him home with applause and signs of approval.

A New Technique of Coercion: Secession

Fear seized the patricians, since, if the army was dismissed, secret meetings and conspiracies would once more occur. Accordingly, under the pretext that the Aequi had started hostilities again, they ordered the legions to be led out of the city. The army had been raised by the dictator, but the oath had been sworn to the consuls [*who were still in office*], so presumably the soldiers were still bound by their oath. This maneuver backfired and instead had the effect of accelerating the revolt. At first there was talk, it is said, of killing the consuls and by this means obtaining liberation from the oath, but being told that no religious obligation could be shuffled off by a criminal act, on the suggestion of a man named Sicinius, and without orders from the consuls, the army withdrew to the Sacred Mount across the River Anio, about three miles from the city. . . . There, without any leader, they made a camp with a rampart and trench and remained quietly for several days, taking nothing but what was necessary for their sustenance. They neither received nor gave any provocation.

There was a great panic in the city. All business came to a standstill due to fear. The plebs who were left in the city dreaded the violence of the patricians, and the patricians dreaded the people, uncertain whether they wanted them to stay or leave. The main question was how long the multitude who had left would remain quiet. What were the consequences if, in the meantime, any foreign war should break out? Assuredly, there was no hope left except concord among all the citizens. This had to be restored to the state whether by fair or foul means.

It was resolved, therefore, that Menenius Agrippa, an eloquent man and one who was a favorite with the people because he was himself of plebeian origin, should be sent as ambassador to the people. Being admitted to their camp, he is said to have simply told them the following story in the primitive style of those far-off days:

"There was a time when all the parts of the human body did not as now agree together, but each part had its own scheme and its own ideas. Some of the parts were indignant that everything was procured for the stomach by their care, labor, and service but that the stomach, remaining quiet, did nothing but enjoy the pleasures provided it. They conspired accordingly that the hands would not convey food to the mouth, nor the mouth receive it when presented, nor the teeth chew it. While they sought in their resentment to starve the stomach into submission, the members and the whole body were reduced to the last degree of emaciation. Hence it became apparent that the service of the stomach was not an idle task, that it did not so much receive nourishment as supply it, sending to all parts of the body this blood by which we live and possess vigor, distributed equally to the veins when perfected by the digestion of the food."

By comparing in this way the internal sedition of the body to the resentment of the people against the patricians, he made an impression on the minds of the multitude. Steps were taken toward concord, and a compromise on these terms was brought about:

> That the commons should have their own magistrates [*the tribunes of the plebs*], with inviolable privileges [*the tribunes were to possess* sacrosanctitas, *"inviolability"*], who should have the power of bringing aid against the consuls and that it should not be lawful for any patrician to hold that office.

Two tribunes of the plebs, Gaius Licinius and Lucius Albinus, were accordingly chosen. They in turn appointed three colleagues, one of whom was the Sicinius who had started the revolt. Who the other two were is uncertain. Some authors believe that only two tribunes were elected on the Sacred Mount and that the law of inviolability (the *lex sacrata*) was enacted there.

2.3   Values that Made Rome Great

The public realm—religion, politics, war, law, and administration—was of preeminent importance at Rome. Private affairs were supposed to be subordinate to public. The majesty of the state and its survival were paramount. Basic to the constitution was the principle, Salus populi suprema lex, *"The safety of the people is the supreme law." In this regard the first safeguard of the state was religion, the* pax deorum, *the friendly relationship between the gods and the people of Rome. Hence the central role of the rituals of the state's public religion. But the private rituals of the individual families were also thought to be vital. Other moral qualities Romans thought significant were the ability to succeed on the battlefield, in politics, and in law—generically termed "virtue" (*virtus *in Latin). However, until toward the end of the Republic, individual Romans were expected to, and largely did, seek fame and glory, dignity, honor, and wealth for the sake of the state and their families rather than for their own personal benefit. Prized above all were the values of dependability, or trustworthiness (*fides*), and bravery.*

"All Things Went Well When We Obeyed the Gods, but Badly When We Disobeyed Them": The Speech of Camillus

In 390 B.C. the Roman army was defeated and Rome itself captured and sacked by a marauding band of Celts. The traditional explanation was that the generals had not performed the proper rituals before the battle. The catastrophe was a turning point in the history of the city, psychologically and politically. However, in the aftermath of the disaster there was talk of moving to a new site, the recently captured Etruscan city of Veii. The idea was squelched by the dictator Camillus, who pointed out that Rome was forever tied by its religious connections to the site on which the city had been originally founded "with all due auguries and auspices."[4]

"When you see such striking instances of the effects of honoring or neglecting the divine, do you not see what an act of impiety you are about to perpetrate, and indeed, just at the moment we are emerging from the shipwreck brought about by our former irreligiosity? We have a city founded with all due observance of the auspices and augury. Not a spot in it is without religious rites and gods. Not only are the days for our sacrifices fixed, but also the places where they are to be performed.

"Romans, would you desert all these gods, public as well as private? Contrast this proposal with the action that occurred during the siege and was beheld with no less admiration by the enemy than by yourselves. This was the deed performed by Gaius Fabius, who descended from the citadel, braved Gallic spears, and performed on the Quirinal Hill the solemn rites of the Fabian family. Is it your wish that the family religious rites should not be interrupted even during war but that the public rites and the gods of Rome should be deserted in time of peace? Do you want the

---

[4]Livy 5.52–54.

Pontiffs and Flamens to be more negligent of public ritual than a private individual in the anniversary rite of a particular family?

"Perhaps someone may say that either we will perform these duties at Veii or we will send our priests from there to perform the rituals here—but neither can be done without infringing on the established forms of worship. For not to enumerate all the sacred rites individually and all the gods, is it possible at the banquet of Jupiter for the *lectisternium* to be set up anywhere else other than the Capitol? What shall I say of the eternal fire of Vesta, and of the statue which, as the pledge of empire, is kept under the safeguard of the temple [*the statue of Athena, the Palladium, supposed to have been brought by Aeneas from Troy*]? What, O Mars Gradivus, and you, Father Quirinus—what of your sacred shields? Is it right that these holy things, some as old as the city itself, some of them even more ancient, be abandoned on unconsecrated ground?

"Observe the difference existing between us and our ancestors. They handed down to us certain sacred rites to be performed by us on the Alban Mount and at Lavinium. It was felt to be impious to transfer these rites from enemy towns to Rome—yet you think you can transfer them to Veii, an enemy city, without sin! . . .

"We talk of sacred rituals and temples—but what about priests? Does it not occur to you what a sacrilege you are proposing to commit in respect of them? The Vestals have but one dwelling place which nothing ever caused them to leave except the capture of the city. Shall your Virgins forsake you, O Vesta? And shall the Flamen by living abroad draw on himself and on his country such a weight of guilt every night [*the Flamen was supposed to never leave Rome*]? What of the other things, all of which we transact under auspices within the Pomerium [*the sacred boundary around Rome*]? To what oblivion, to what neglect do we consign them? The Curiate Assembly, which deals with questions of war; the Centuriate Assembly at which you elect consuls and military tribunes—when can they be held under auspices except where they are accustomed to be held? Shall we transfer them to Veii? Or shall the people, for the sake of the assemblies, come together at great inconvenience in this city, deserted by gods and men? . . .

"Not without good cause did gods and men select this place for the founding of a city. These most healthful hills, a convenient river by means of which the produce of the soil may be conveyed from the inland areas, by which supplies from overseas may be obtained, close enough to the sea for all purposes of convenience, yet not exposed by being too close to the danger of foreign fleets. Situated in the center of Italy, it is singularly adapted by nature for the growth of a city. The very size of so new a city is itself proof. Citizens, it is now in its three hundred and sixty-fifth year. Throughout those years you have been at war with many ancient nations. Not to mention single states, neither the Volscians combined with the Aequi, together with all their powerful towns, not all Etruria, so powerful by land and sea, occupying the breadth of Italy between the Tyrrhenian and Adriatic seas, have been a match for you in war. Since this is so, why in the name of goodness do you want to experiment elsewhere when you had such good fortune here? Though your courage may go with you, the fortune of this place certainly cannot be transferred. Here is the Capitol, where a human head was found which foretold that in that place would be the head of the world, the chief seat of empire [*a play on words; head in Latin is* caput]. Here, when the Capitol was being cleared with augural rites, the gods Juventas and Terminus, to the great joy of your fathers, refused to be moved. Here is the fire of Vesta, here the sacred shields of Mars which fell from heaven. Here the gods will be propitious to you—if you stay."

The Glory of Rome before All Else: Mucius Scaevola

A favorite tale that showed the bravery of Roman citizens and their dedication to the state was the story of Mucius Scaevola, "Lefty Mucius." The event is assigned to the period not long after the Romans drove out the kings. Rome is under siege by the Etruscan king, Lars Porsena. His aim is to reinstall the deposed Tarquin.[5]

The blockade went on. . . . There was shortage of food, and what was available went for a very high price. Porsena's hopes began to rise that by continuing the siege he could take the city. Then a certain Gaius Mucius, a young Roman nobleman, began to think that it was a disgrace that the Roman people, who, when enslaved under kings, had never been confined within their walls in any war with any enemy, now as a free people were being besieged by these very Etruscans whose armies they had often routed in the past. He made up his mind that such an indignity should be avenged by some great and daring effort.

At first he planned, of his own accord, to make his way into the enemy's camp. However, he was afraid that if he went without the permission of the consuls or the knowledge of anyone, he might be seized by the Roman guards and brought back as a deserter. Indeed, the circumstances of the city at the time would have justified the charge. Accordingly, he went to the Senate and said: "Fathers, I intend to cross the Tiber and enter the enemy's camp if I can, not as a plunderer or as an avenger of their devastations. I have a greater deed in mind if the gods permit."

The Senate approved his plan. He set out with a sword concealed under his clothing, and when he arrived at the enemy's camp, he stood among the thickest of the crowd, near the king's tribunal. There the soldiers were receiving their pay, and the king's secretary sitting by him was dressed nearly in the same style as the king. He was very busy, and the soldiers, for the most part, seemed to talk to him. Being afraid to ask which of the two was Porsena, lest by not knowing the king he should betray himself, as fortune would have it Mucius killed the secretary rather than the king.

As he tried to escape through the frightened crowd, making a way for himself with his bloody sword, he was seized by the king's guards. They dragged him back before the king's tribunal. Though alone and in clearly desperate circumstances, yet he was one more to be feared than fearing. "I am a Roman citizen," he said. "Gaius Mucius is my

---

[5]Livy 2.12–13.

name. I am your enemy and I came to slay you. I have no less resolution in suffering death than I had in inflicting it. Both to act and endure with courage is the Roman way. Nor have I alone harbored such feelings toward you. There is after me a long line of persons aspiring to the same honor. Therefore, if you choose it, prepare yourself for this peril, to contend for your life every hour, always to have the sword and the enemy in the very entrance of your pavilion. This is the war which we, the Roman youth, declare against you. Fear not an army in array, nor in battle. It will be between you alone with each of us singly."

Porsena, angry and at the same time frightened, ordered Mucius to be flung into the flames unless he revealed the plot thus obscurely hinted at. Mucius replied, "See how cheaply men hold their bodies when they hope to gain great glory." And with that he thrust his right hand into the fire that was lighted for the sacrifice and let it burn there as though unconscious of the pain. Porsena, astonished at this surprising sight, leaped from the throne and commanded the young man to be removed from the altar. "Go free," he said, "you who have acted more as an enemy to yourself than toward me. I would encourage you to persevere in your courage if that courage were on behalf of my country. I now dismiss you untouched and unhurt, exempted from the penalties of war." Then Mucius, as if making a return for the kindness, said: "Since bravery is honored by you, in gratitude I will give you the information which you could not obtain by threats. Three hundred of us, the foremost youths in Rome, have conspired to attack you in this fashion. It was my lot to go first. The rest will follow, each in his turn, as the lot shall send him forward, until Fortune shall have delivered you into our hands."

The release of Mucius, who henceforth was known as Scaevola [*left-handed*] because of the loss of his right hand, was followed by ambassadors from Porsena to Rome. The risk of the first attempt, from which nothing but the mistake of the assailant had saved him, and the prospect of repeated encounters with more conspirators, made so strong an impression on Porsena that of his own accord he made proposals of peace to Rome. . . .

"The Laws of War and Peace": The Schoolmaster of Falerii

The incident recounted here occurred during the siege of Falerii, a town near Rome, sometime before the Gallic invasion of 390 B.C. The story gives Livy an opportunity to preach a sermon on the ideal of a just war, fair dealing, fidelity {fides}, honor, and responsibility toward conquered peoples. Despite Livy's idealization, the tale highlights a genuine principle of Roman statecraft. The survival of Rome, as well as its expansion, was as much a function of diplomacy and calculated self-interest as one of successful military campaigns. Rome needed not only to win wars but also to rule justly afterwards.[6]

---

[6]Livy 5.27.

A regular blockade of Falerii began and the usual siege works were constructed. Occasionally attacks were made by the townsmen on the Roman positions, and small skirmishes took place. Time passed and there did not seem much hope of either side prevailing. . . .

It was the custom among the people of Falerii to employ the same person as teacher and guardian for their children, as in Greece today a number of boys are entrusted to the care of one man. Naturally enough, responsibility for the children of the leading families of the city was given to the most distinguished teacher. This man, during peace, had established the custom of taking the boys out beyond the city for the sake of play and exercise, and he continued this practice after the war began. Sometimes he went a shorter distance from the gate, sometimes a longer, entertaining them with this or that game or story. Being farther away one day than usual, he seized the opportunity to bring the boys through the enemy's outposts, right to the Roman camp and to the headquarters of Camillus. There he compounded his treacherous act with an even more treacherous allegation, claiming that he had in fact delivered Falerii into the hands of the Romans when he put into their power those children whose parents were in control of affairs there.

When he heard this Camillus answered: "Unscrupulous as you are, you come with your vile proposal neither to a people nor to a commander like you. Between us and the Faliscans, it is true, there does not exist a relationship of treaties and contracts, but there does exist, and indeed always will exist, that common humanity which nature has established. There are laws of war as well as of peace, and we have learned to wage them justly not less than bravely. We carry arms not against children, who are spared even when towns are taken, but against men who are themselves armed. . . ." Then having stripped the schoolmaster and tied his hands behind his back, he gave him to the schoolboys to be brought back to Falerii. He also gave them rods to beat the traitor as they drove him to the city.

To see the sight, a crowd gathered at Falerii, and afterwards the senate of the city was convened by the magistrates to consider the strange affair. So great a change was produced in their sentiments that the entire state earnestly demanded peace from the hands of those who lately, in the fury of their hate and resentment, almost preferred the fate of Veii [*i.e., capture and destruction*] to that of Capena [*a nearby city given federate status by Rome*]. Roman trustworthiness [*fides*] and the justice of the commander were praised in the Forum and the Senate House. By universal agreement, ambassadors set out for the camp of Camillus and from there, by permission of Camillus, to Rome to the Senate to present the submission of Falerii.

When introduced to the Senate, they are said to have spoken in this way: "Conscript Fathers, you and your commander have won a victory over us with which no one, neither god nor man, could find displeasure. We surrender ourselves to you, believing that we will live more happily under your rule than under our own law. Nothing, surely, can be more glorious for a conqueror. As a result of this war, two salutary examples have been exhibited to mankind. You preferred faith in war to an opportunistic victory. We, challenged by your good faith, have voluntarily given up to you the victory. We are under your sovereignty. Send representatives to receive our arms, our hostages, our city with its open gates. You shall never have to repent of our trustworthiness [*fides*], nor we of your rule [*imperium*]."

"Thirst for Glory Filled Men's Minds"

The historian Sallust (86–35 B.C.) identified glory as the principal driving force of the Roman elite. Unfortunately when the thirst for glory became a thirst for wealth, as happened in his day, the Roman Republic began to decline.[7]

Once the state gained its liberty [*from the kings*] it is remarkable how much progress it made, such was the thirst for glory that filled the hearts of its citizens. As soon as young men reached the age of military service, they were taught the art of warfare in camp under strict discipline and took greater pleasure in fine looking arms and cavalry horses than in prostitutes and parties. For such men no undertaking was too difficult, no terrain too steep or rugged, no enemy too formidable. Courage (*virtus*) overcame all. In fact the hardest struggles for glory occurred among themselves. Each man sought to be the first to cut down an enemy, mount a wall—and to be seen publicly by all while doing these deeds. It was this they thought to be wealth and it was in this way that reputation and nobility was to be won. Covetous of praise they were lavish with money; their goal was unbounded glory and riches honorably won. . . .

In war and peace good morals were cultivated. There was the greatest harmony (*concordia*), and avarice was virtually unknown. Justice and probity were upheld not so much by laws as by nature itself. Quarrels, discord and strife were directed at their enemies, while citizens strove among themselves for honor. They were generous in their offerings to the gods, frugal in their private lives and faithful (*fideles*) to their friends. By combining boldness in war and justice in peace they guarded themselves and the republic. . . .

But when the state had grown great through hard work and the practice of justice, when great kings had been defeated in war, savage tribes and great peoples subdued, when Carthage, Rome's rival in imperial ambitions, had been destroyed, and all lands and seas lay open to them, then Fortune turned cruel and began to upset everything. Those who found it easy to sustain toil and peril, anxiety and adversity, found leisure and wealth—usually regarded as desirable—a burden and a curse. The lust for money developed first, and then the desire for power. These were the root of all evils. For avarice destroyed loyalty, integrity and every other virtue. It taught in their place pride and cruelty, the neglect of the gods, and to put a price on everything. Ambition enticed many men to become false, to have one thought in their hearts and another on their tongues, to become a man's friend or enemy not because they thought him worthy or unworthy but because it would pay off. They put more emphasis on a good front than a good heart.

---

[7]Sallust, *The War with Catiline* 7, 9, 10, 12.

Initially these vices grew slowly and at times they were corrected, but finally when the disease had spread like a plague, Rome was changed. Its rule (*imperium*) from being most justice and good, became cruel and unendurable. . . . As soon as riches came to be considered honorable, and it was found that glory, military commands and political power followed in their train, virtue became dulled, modest means were regarded as a disgrace, and a blameless life despicable . . .

Fame, Family, and Self-Promotion: The Roman Funeral

Polybius, a prominent Greek soldier and statesman, was brought to Rome in 168 B.C. as a hostage for the good behavior of his native state, the Achaean League. At Rome he was befriended by a young nobleman, Scipio Aemilianus, who later became famous for his capture of Carthage and Numantia. With a ringside seat from which to view the unfolding events of Roman history, Polybius set about explaining to the world Rome's rise to Power. In this excerpt he describes how the Roman upper-class family functioned to promote itself and socialize its younger members. It is found in the section of Book 6 that compares the Roman constitution with others, such as those of Carthage, Sparta, and elsewhere.[8]

Whenever one of their illustrious men dies, in the course of his funeral the body with all of its paraphernalia is carried into the Forum to the Rostra, as the raised platform there is called. Sometimes he is propped upright on it so as to be conspicuous, or, more rarely, he is laid flat on it. Then, with all the people of Rome standing around, his son, if he has one of full age and he happens to be in Rome, or failing him, one of his relatives, mounts the Rostra and delivers a speech about the virtues of the dead man and the successful deeds performed by him in his life.

By these means the people are reminded of what the deceased accomplished and are made to see it with their own eyes—not only those who were involved in the actual deeds, but those also who were not—and their sympathies are so deeply moved that the loss appears not to be confined to the actual mourners but to be a public one affecting the whole people.

After the burial and all the usual ceremonies have been performed, they place the likeness of the deceased in the most conspicuous spot in his house, surmounted by a wooden canopy or shrine. This likeness consists of a mask made to represent the deceased with extraordinary fidelity both in shape and color. These likenesses they display at public sacrifices, and they decorate them with much care.

Also when any notable member of the family dies, they carry these masks to the funeral, putting them on men who seem most like those whose masks they wear in terms of height and other personal characteristics. And these substitutes assume clothes according to the rank of the person represented. If he was a consul

---

[8]Polybius 6.53–54. Translation based on E. S. Shuckburg, *Polybius: The Histories* (London–New York, 1889).

or praetor, for example, a toga with purple stripes is worn; if a censor, a wholly purple toga; if he had also celebrated a triumph or performed any exploit of that kind, a toga embroidered with gold. These representatives also ride in chariots, while the fasces and axes and all the other customary insignia of the particular offices lead the way, according to the dignity of the rank in the state enjoyed by the deceased in his lifetime. On arriving at the Rostra, they all take their seats on ivory chairs in a row. There could not easily be a more inspiring spectacle than this for a young man of noble ambitions or virtuous aspirations. For can we conceive anyone to be unmoved at the sight of all the likenesses collected together of the men who have earned glory, all, as it were, living and breathing? Or what could be a more glorious spectacle?

Furthermore, as soon as the speaker who gives the eulogy over the person about to be buried finishes, he then immediately starts upon the others whose representatives are present, beginning with the most ancient, and recounts the successes and achievements of each. By this means the glorious memory of brave men is continually renewed; the fame of those who have performed any noble deed is never allowed to die, and the renown of those who have done good service to their country becomes a matter of common knowledge to the multitude and part of the heritage of posterity.

But the chief benefit of the ceremony is that it inspires young men to shrink from no exertion for the general welfare, in the hope of obtaining the glory which awaits the brave. And what I say is confirmed by this fact. Many Romans have volunteered to decide a whole battle by single combat. Not a few have deliberately accepted certain death, some in time of war to secure the safety of the rest, some in time of peace to preserve the safety of the commonwealth. There also have been instances of men in office putting their own sons to death, in defiance of every custom and law, because they rated the interests of their country higher than those of natural ties, even with their nearest and dearest. . . .

2.4   The Roman Constitution According to Polybius

Polybius (see p. 36), was present at both sieges. He was thoroughly impressed with Roman organization and military capacity. The fundamental question he asked himself was: "How was almost the whole known world conquered and brought under the rule of Rome in not quite fifty-three years? How was this done, and under what of a constitution?" (1.1.5). His answer to this question was given in a history of forty books. Only part of these books survive. One includes the following document which gives Polybius' version of the Roman constitution. For Greeks, political success could not be divorced from the kind of government a state possessed. Hence he regarded the description of the Roman constitution as an important part of his work. His description is purely formal following a convention of constitutional analysis going back in Greek intellectual history at least to Herodotus in the fifth century B.C. *His conclusion was that Rome possessed a balanced or mixed constitution, one consisting of monarchical, aristocratic and democratic elements. This was an excellent constitutional form and provided the basis for Rome's success. Fortune* (Tyche), *also had a major hand in Rome's success.*

He writes what he called "pragmatic history" (pragmatike historia). *This type of history involved the careful analysis of documents, visits to sites of battles and other events (autopsy— seeing for oneself), and the examination of eye witnesses. He claimed that "history is in the truest sense an education, and a training for political life." For him "recalling the catastrophes of others is the best way of learning to cope with the ups and downs of Fortune." Unfortunately much of Polybius' work has perished perhaps because, as the ancient critic Dionysius of Halicarnassus claimed, Polybius was "an author whom no one could bear to read to the end"* (de comparatione verborum, 4).

The influence of Polybius was immense. By the time of Machiavelli, Polybius' theory of the mixed constitution had become accepted doctrine. It influenced British constitutional development and French political thinking. Montesquieu translated Polybius' balance of monarchic, aristocratic and democratic elements into a balance of powers: executive, legislative and judicial. In this form Polybius was influential in the thinking of the Founding Fathers of the United States. John Adams constantly refers to Polybius, especially in his Defense of the Constitutions of Government (1787), *much of which is based on Book 6.*[9]

I will now attempt to describe the constitution of Rome at the period of their disastrous defeat at the Battle of Cannae (*in 216* B.C., *against Hannibal in the Second Punic War*). I am fully aware that to the people who actually live under this constitution I will appear to give an inadequate account of it by the omission of certain details. Knowing every part of it from personal experience and from having been brought up in its customs and laws from childhood, they will not be struck so much by the accuracy of the description as annoyed by its omissions. . . . But a good critic should not judge a writer by what he leaves unsaid, but from what he actually says. If he detects misstatement in the latter, he may then feel certain that ignorance accounts for the former; but if what he says is accurate, his omissions ought to be attributed to deliberate judgment rather than ignorance . . .

As for the Roman constitution, it had three elements, each of them possessing sovereign powers. However, their respective share of power in the whole state was regulated with such fairness and equality that no one, not even a native, could say for certain whether the constitution as a whole was aristocratic, democratic or monarchic. And no wonder, for if we consider only the power of the consuls, we would be inclined to regard it as royal and monarchic; if we focused on just that of the Senate, it would seem to be aristocratic. Finally, if we

---

[9]Polybius 6.11–18. Translation based on E. S. Shuckburg, *Polybius: The Histories* (London–New York, 1889).

examined the power of the people, it would seem to be democratic. The administrative responsibility of each of these parts was then, and still are, with a few exceptions, as follows.

The Consuls

The consuls, while in the city before taking command of the legions in the field, are in charge of all public business. The other magistrates, except the tribunes of the plebs, are under them and take their orders from them. The consuls present foreign ambassadors to the senate; bring matters requiring deliberation before it; and see to the execution of its decrees. If there are any matters of public business which require the approval of the people, it is the business of the consuls to attend to them. They are responsible for calling meetings of the assemblies, placing proposals before these assemblies and carrying out the decisions of the majority. In preparations for war and in the course of military campaigns they have practically absolute power. They can demand from the allies whatever levies of manpower they think are necessary. They appoint military tribunes and enroll the soldiers, selecting those they regard as suitable. In addition, they have the power to punish in the field all under their command. They can spend as much of the public funds of the state as they choose, being accompanied by a quaestor who does exactly as they command. A review of these powers would in fact justify describing this constitution as purely monarchic and royal. . . .

The Senate

Next, the Senate has first of all control of the treasury and regulates all income and expenditures. The quaestors [*officers of the treasury*] have no authority to draw on public monies for the various departments of the state without a decree of the Senate, except in the case of payments to the consuls. The Senate controls also what is by far the largest and most important expenditure, namely the one made by the censors every five years for the repair and construction of public works. This money cannot be obtained by the censors except by permission of the Senate. Similarly, all crimes committed in Italy that require a public investigation, such as treason, conspiracy, poisoning, and homicide, are in the hands of the Senate. Furthermore, if any individual or state among the Italian allies needs a controversy to be settled, a penalty assessed or help or protection to be provided, all this is in the province of the Senate. Or again, outside Italy, if it is necessary to send an embassy to reconcile warring communities or to remind them of their duties or, sometimes, to impose requisitions on them or to receive their submissions or, finally, to proclaim war against them—this too, is the responsibility of the Senate. In like manner the reception of foreign ambassadors in Rome and the answers to be returned to them are decided by the Senate. The People have nothing to do with matters like these. Consequently, if one were staying at Rome when the consuls were not in town, one would imagine that the constitution was wholly aristocratic. This has been the view taken by many Greeks and many kings as well because nearly all business they had with Rome was settled by the Senate.

The People

After this, one would naturally be inclined to wonder what part was left in the constitution for the people when the Senate has all these powers, especially the control of income and expenditures and the consuls have absolute power over military preparation and absolute authority in the field. Yet there is a share for the people and a most important one. The people are the sole fountain of honor and punishment and it is by these two things and these alone that dynasties and constitutions, and, in a word, human society are held together. For where the distinction between them is not sharply drawn both in theory and practice, there no undertaking can be properly administered—as indeed we might expect when good and bad are held to be exactly the same.

The People, then, are the only court to decide matters of life and death and those cases where the penalty is money if the sum to be assessed is sufficiently serious, and especially when the accused have held the higher magistracies. And in regard to this arrangement there is one point deserving special examination and emphasis. Men who are on trial at Rome for their lives, while sentence is in the process of being voted on, if even only one of the tribes whose votes are needed to ratify the sentence has not voted, have the privilege at Rome of departing and condemning themselves to a voluntary exile. Such men are safe at Naples or Praeneste or at Tibur, and at other towns with which this arrangement has been duly ratified by oath. Again, it is the People who have the power to bestow offices, which are the most honorable rewards of virtue, on those they think worthy of them. They also have the absolute power of passing or repealing laws. Most important of all, it is the People who deliberate on the question of peace or war. And when provisional terms are made for alliance, the suspension of hostilities or treaties, it is the People who ratify or reject them.[10]

These considerations again would lead one to say that the chief power of the state was in the hands of the People and the constitution was thus a democracy.

Analysis

Such then is the distribution of power between the several parts of the state. I must now show how each of these parts can, when they choose, oppose or support each other. The consul, when he has started on a campaign with the powers I have described, is to all appearance absolute in the conduct of the war. Yet he still has need of the support both of the People and the Senate and without them he is quite unable to bring the war to a successful conclusion. For it is clear the he must have

---

[10]Polybius does not think it worthwhile to point out that when he refers to the "People" he mostly refers to the actions taken by the Centuriate Assembly where the elite were predominant.

the supplies sent to his legions from time to time. Yet without a decree of the Senate he can get neither grain nor uniforms nor pay, so that all his plans as commander will be futile if the Senate lacks resolve in the face of danger or decides [*for other reasons*] to hamper his plans. And again, whether the consul shall bring any undertaking to a conclusion or not depends entirely on the Senate, for it has absolute authority at the end of the year to send another consul to supersede him or to continue him in his command [*as a proconsul*].

Even to the successes of the generals, the Senate has the power to add distinction and glory or, on the other hand, to obscure the generals' merits and lower their credit. The reason for this is that the high achievements of the generals are brought in tangible form before the eyes of the people in what is called a "triumph." But these triumphs cannot be celebrated with proper pomp or, in some cases, celebrated at all, unless the Senate concurs and grants the necessary funding. As for the people, the consuls are preeminently obliged to court their favor, however distant from home may be their field of operation, for it is the people who, as I have said before, ratify or refuse to ratify the terms of peace and of treaties. Most of all the people have to be considered because when laying down their office, the consuls have to give a public account of their administration to the assembled people. Therefore in no case is it safe for the consuls to neglect either the Senate or the good will of the People.

As for the Senate which possesses the immense powers I have described, it is obliged in the first place in public affairs to take the People into account and respect their wishes. It cannot investigate crimes against the state which are punishable by death unless the People first ratify the procedures. Similarly, even in matters which directly affect the senators—for instance, in the case of a law diminishing the Senate's traditional authority or depriving senators of certain dignities and offices or even actually cutting down their property—even in such cases the people have the sole power of passing or rejecting the law. Most importantly of all it is the fact that if the tribunes of plebs interpose their veto, the Senate not only is unable to pass a decree, but cannot even hold a meeting at all, whether formal or informal. Now the tribunes are always bound to carry out the decrees of the People and above all things to have regard for their wishes. Therefore, for all these reasons the Senate stands in awe of the multitude and cannot neglect the feelings of the People.

In like manner the People, for their part, are far from being independent of the Senate and are bound to take its wishes into consideration, both collectively and individually. For contracts, too numerous to count, are given out by the censors in all parts of Italy for the repair or construction of public works. There is also the collection of revenue from many rivers, harbors, gardens, mines and land—everything, in a word, that comes under the control of the Roman government. And in all these the People at large are engaged so that there is scarcely a man, so to speak, who is not interested either in a contract or as being employed in the work. For some purchase the contracts from the censors for themselves and others go partners with them. Yet others go security for these contractors or actually pledge their property to the treasury for them. Now, over all these transactions the Senate has absolute control. It can grant an extension of time and, in the case of unforeseen accidents, relieve the contractors from a portion of their obligation or release them from it altogether if they are absolutely unable to fulfill it. And there are many details in which the Senate can inflict great hardships or, on the other hand, grant great indulgences to the contractors. For in every case the appeal is to it. But the most important point of all is that the judges are taken from its members in the majority of trials, whether public or private, in which charges are serious. Consequently, all citizens are much at its mercy and, being fearful at the uncertainty as to when they may need its aid, they are cautious about resisting or actively opposing its will. And for a similar reason men do not rashly resist the wishes of the consuls, because one and all may become subject to their absolute authority on campaign.

Conclusions

The result of the capacity of the several estates [*i.e., the magistrates, the Senate and the People*] for mutual help or harm is a union sufficient for all emergencies. No better constitution could be found. For whenever any danger from without compels them to unite and work together, the strength which is developed by the state is so extraordinary that everything required is unfailingly carried out by the eager rivalry shown by all classes to devote their whole minds to the need of the hour and to make sure that any decision arrived at should not fail for want of close attention. Each individual works, whether privately or publicly, to accomplish the task at hand. As a result, the peculiar constitution of the State makes it irresistible and enables it to attain whatever it resolves upon.

Finally, when relieved of whatever is the immediate threat, and the People are enjoying their good fortune and the fruits of their victories and, as usually happens, become corrupted by flattery and idleness, showing a tendency to violence and arrogance—it is in these circumstances that the constitution is seen to possess within itself the power of correcting abuses. For when any one of the three classes gets above itself and displays an inclination to be contentious and unduly encroaching on one of the others, the mutual interdependency of all three and the possibility of the pretensions of anyone being checked and thwarted by the others, has the capacity to check this tendency. And so the proper equilibrium is maintained by the impulsiveness of the one part or class being checked by its fear of the other.

2.5   Getting Elected

Getting elected to office in Rome was as calculated a procedure as winning an election in modern times. It required visibility, a vast network of friends, money, and a good memory for names and faces. It also required a thorough knowledge of what motivated the electorate and how the electoral system worked. Rome's dual system of government, the Patrician State, and the Plebeian State, was a complicated affair. The Centuriate Assembly, which annually elected consuls and praetors, was structured in favor of the well-to-do on the principle that the rich, having more responsibilities than the poor, deserved more votes. "We weigh votes, not count them," said Cicero. On the other hand the Plebeian Assembly, which elected tribunes and passed most laws, was more democratic and tended to reflect the needs of the majority of Romans. Its officers, the tribunes, with their powers of veto and intercession, could, potentially at least, provide the masses with protection from rich and powerful interests and from an overly intrusive government. The following reading is in the form of a letter addressed to Marcus Cicero by his brother Quintus. The passage reveals the intensely personal nature of Roman politics; the practical side of Roman-style friendship; how free legal representation in court was repaid by support at the polls; the kind of open-house Romans active in the political system were expected to maintain; and the intense networking which was at the core of the political system. Tribes, it should be noted, were geographical areas, not kinship groups.[11]

Networking Relatives and Friends

Canvass for office comes down to activities of two kinds, one of which is securing the loyalty of friends. The other deals with the concerns and feelings of the People. The loyalty of friends must be secured by acts of kindness and attention, by length of time spent with them, and by an easy and pleasant temper. It is a great advantage to be popular among those who are friends on the usual grounds of blood or marriage relationships, membership in the same club or some other close tie. You must make a great effort to see that all who are close to you and your household should love you and desire your highest honor. These would be, for instance, your fellow tribesmen, your neighbors, clients, freedmen and even your slaves, for nearly all the talk which shapes public opinion about you comes from domestic sources [*i.e., if you don't run your household well your reputation is likely to be affected*].

You must secure friends in every class. Some of these will be for show such as men well known because of their office or name, who, even if they do not give any actual assistance in your electioneering, yet add some dignity to your candidature. Others again are those useful for securing the votes of the centuries, men of high popularity. Take pains to win and secure those who either have gained or hope to gain the vote of a tribe or century or any other advantage through your influence. Do your best to make sure such men are attached to you from the bottom of their hearts and with complete devotion.

In the course of a canvass you can acquire numerous useful new friendships. For among its annoyances an election has this advantage: you can, without loss of dignity, as you cannot in other affairs of life, admit whomsoever you choose to your friendship. These are the kind of people who you could not at any other time befriend without looking foolish, whereas during a canvass, if you don't befriend and take pains about it, you will be thought to be no use as a candidate at all. Moreover, I can assure you that there is no one, unless he happens to be tied by some special relationship to one of your rivals, whom you could not induce, if you made the effort, to earn your affection by his good services, and to seize the opportunity of putting you under an obligation. Let him fully understand that you value him highly, that you really mean what you say, that he is making a good investment, and that there will result from the relationship not just a brief electioneering kind of friendship, but a firm and lasting

[11]*Electioneering Handbook*, 13–55.

one. There will be no one, believe me, if he has anything in him at all, who will let slip this opportunity of making a friendship with you, especially when by good luck you have competitors whose friendship is to be neglected or avoided . . . .

Motivating the Electorate

Men are mainly induced to demonstrate good will and energy in the election process by three considerations: benefits received in the past; hope of benefits to come; and personal affection and good feeling. We should therefore examine these factors to see how we can take advantage of each of them. First, some men are encouraged by very small favors to think they have sufficient reason for supporting you at the ballot-box. Those you have actually saved by your advocacy (and their number is large) cannot fail to understand that if they fail at this critical moment to support you, they will never have anyone's confidence. However, even though this is the case, they still need to be appealed to and must be led to think it possible that whereas they have up until now been under obligation to you, they may now, as it were, put you under obligation to them.

As for your genuine friends, you will have to make them more secure by expressions of gratitude and by making your words coincide with the motives which influenced them to support you in the first place . . . In all these cases consider and weigh carefully the amount of influence each possesses in order to estimate the degree of attention needed to be paid to each, and what you can expect in return. For some men are popular in their own neighborhoods and towns and others have energy and wealth, who, even if they have not up to this point sought popularity, yet could easily obtain it for the sake of one to whom they owe, or wish to do a favor, namely, in this instance, yourself. You must make it plain in your attention to these men that you clearly understand what is to be expected from each, that you appreciate what you are receiving, and will remember what you have received.

Identifying the Voters

So see that you have the votes of all the centuries won for you by the number and variety of your friends. The first and most obvious step is to canvass senators and knights [*the second rank of the elite*], and the active and popular men in all the other orders of society. There are many hard working city men and freedmen engaged in business who are popular and energetic. You will be able by your efforts and through common friends, to win them to your side. See that they are enthusiastic about you. Work hard, seek them out, send friends to them, show them that they are putting you under the greatest obligation. After that review the entire city, all the clubs, districts, neighborhoods. If you can attach their leading men to yourself, you will through these men easily be able to keep a hold on the electorate. Next you must have in your mind a map of all Italy laid out according to the tribe of each town, and learn it by heart, so that you may not allow any municipality, colony, prefecture, or, in a word, any place in Italy, to exist in which you have not an adequate foothold. . . .

The Daily Canvass

You should be very careful to receive every day a large number of every class and order in your home, for from the mere number of these others will be guessing the amount of support you are likely to have among the electorate at large. Such visitors are of three kinds. The first are the morning callers, the second those who escort you to the forum and third those who actually attend you during your canvass. The first are a less select crowd and tend to come in larger numbers. Nevertheless you must contrive to make them think that you value even this slight attention very highly. Let them see that you notice their presence at your house; mention your appreciation to such of their friends as will be likely to repeat it to them; frequently repeat it to the persons themselves. It often happens that people, when they visit a number of candidates, and observe that there is one who above the rest notices them, then it is to this person they devote themselves. They leave off visiting the others and little by little become devoted to you rather than just being neutral.

As for those who escort you to the forum, since this is more important than the morning calls, let them know that this is still more gratifying to you. As far as possible, go down to the forum at fixed times. The daily escort by its numbers produces a great impression and confers great distinction. The third class are those who actually attend you during your electioneering efforts. See that those who do so spontaneously understand that you regard yourself as forever obliged to their kindness. As for those who owe you this attention remind them, as far as their age and business allow, that they should be in constant attendance on you. People who should be there but cannot, should find relatives to take their place. You should always be surrounded by large numbers. To be accompanied by those whom you have defended, preserved and acquitted in the law courts demonstrates the power of your reputation. Persuade this category of people by reminding them that by your efforts and without pay of any kind, some of them have retained their property, others their honor, others their civil existence and entire fortunes. Since there will never be any other time when they can show their gratitude, they should repay you now by this service.

Dangers

Deception, intrigue, and treachery are everywhere . . . your high character has made many pretend to be your friends while they are, in reality, jealous of you. So remember the saying of Epicharmus that the key to wisdom is to believe nothing too easily. When you have made sure of your friends, you must next acquaint yourself regarding what your detractors and opponents are saying. They fall into three classes, those whom you have attacked in the courts; those who dislike you for no identifiable reason; and third those who are friends of your competitors. As for those you attacked while pleading a friend's cause against them, frankly excuse yourself; remind them of the ties constraining you; give them reason to hope that you will act with equal zeal and loyalty in their cases if they become friends with you. Do your best to remove the prejudice of those who dislike you without reason by some actual service or holding out hope of such service, or by demonstrating kindly feelings to them. As for those who oppose you because of their association with your competitors, gratify them by the same means as the others, and if you can get them to believe it, show that you are kindly disposed to the very men who are standing against you.

Winning the Ordinary Folk

As for the people at large, to win them over requires a knack for remembering names, good manners, constant attention, liberality and the ability to convey a hopeful feeling about the condition of the state. Make conspicuous use of the faculty you possess of recognizing people and improve it every day; there is nothing so popular or so influential. Next, if nature has denied you some quality, make up your mind to assume it, so as to appear to be acting naturally. For though you are not lacking in the courtesy which good and polite men should have, yet there is a great need to have a flattering manner which, however discreditable it is in other transactions of life, it is essential during electioneering. Certainly were such activities to affect a person for the worse, they would be wrong; but when all they do is to make a person only more friendly, then they do not deserve to be judged so harshly . . .

Liberality is a trait of wide application. It is shown in the management of your private property, which, even if it does not actually affect the masses of the voters, yet if spoken of with praise by friends, earns their favor. It may also be displayed at banquets which you must take care to attend yourself and cause your friends to attend, whether open ones or those confined to particular tribes. It may again be displayed in giving practical assistance which you should make available far and wide. Be sure to be accessible day and night, and not only by the doors of your house, but by your expression, which is the door of the mind. If your face shows your feelings to be distant and reserved, it is of little good to have your house doors open. . . .

2.6   Techniques for Absorbing Non-Romans into the State

The sack of Rome by the Celts in 390 B.C. demonstrated the weakness of the Latin League. When the League was dissolved after the Latin War of 340–338 B.C. the Romans, instead of meting out harsh punishments to their old allies, instead found a means to take them into their commonwealth by a graded process of incorporation. The story seems pedantic and uninteresting, but this event was crucial to Rome's capacity to expand beyond the bounds that normally constrained a polis. In the speech Livy composed for Camillus the victorious general counsels mercy for the Latins remarking "The strongest government by far is the one to which men are glad to be subject." *This was an approach Rome continued to use for the rest of its history.*

All of the Latins surrendered as did the Campanians. Latium and Capua were deprived of land. . . . The people of Laurentum among the Latins, and the upper class among the Campanians were exempted from this punishment because they had not revolted . . . The people of Lanuvium receiving full citizenship. . . . The people of Aricia, Nomentum, and Pedum were admitted to citizenship with the same rights as Lanuvium. The people of Tusculum retained the citizenship which they had before. Responsibility for their revolt was shifted from the whole population to the handful of ringleaders. The Veliternians, who had been Roman citizens for a long time, were punished severely because they had revolted so often. The walls of the city were torn down and their senate deported and order to live on the other side of the Tiber. . . . Colonists were settled on the lands of the senators with the result that Velitrae looked as populous as before. A new colony was also sent to Antium, but the people of the city were allowed to enroll themselves as colonists if they wanted to. Their navy was confiscated and the Antiates were forbidden to go to sea. They were granted the full franchise. The land of Tibur and Praeneste was confiscated, not so much because of the part which they, like other Latins, had taken in the recent war, but because they had, upset by the power of Rome, sided with the Gauls (*this refers to the sack of 390 B.C.*).

The rest of the Latin cities were deprived of the rights of intermarriage, trade and holding common councils (*these were the traditional rights of the old Latin League*). Capua, as a reward for the refusal of its aristocracy to join the Latins in revolt, was granted citizenship without the suffrage (*civitas sine suffragio*), as were also Fundi and Formiae because they had always allowed a safe and peaceful passage through their territories. It was decided that Cumae and Suessula should enjoy the same rights and terms as Capua.[12]

▼▼▼

Questions

1. Despite his appreciation of the value of freedom, Livy gives some reasons why he thought Rome needed the firm hand of the kings for a period in its development. What were these? (**2.1**)
2. What techniques did the plebeians use in order to extract concessions from the patricians? (**2.2**)
3. What powers did the newly created office of tribunes of the plebs have? (**2.2**)
4. What values, according to Roman ideology, made Rome great? (**2.3**)
5. What reasons did Camillus give for the population to remain at Rome after its sack by the Gauls? (**2.3**)
6. The ceremonies associated with the Roman funeral aimed at promoting what aspect of Roman social and political life? (**2.3**)

---

[12]*Livy* 8.11, 14.

7. Polybius said the Roman constitution was a mixed government of three powers. What were these? How did they check each other (be specific)? (**2.4**; See also **1.12** for Cicero's version of the balanced constitution.)
8. According to Polybius what powers did the people have to check the Senate and the magistrates? How, in turn, were the people kept in check? (**2.4**)
9. Name three categories of voters that Quintus Cicero said should be courted by a candidate? (**2.5**)
10. How were voters to be encouraged to vote for a candidate and how was he supposed to go about his canvass? (**2.5**)

Chapter 3

▼▼▼

War and Warfare in the Republic

"No sane man," wrote Polybius, "goes to war with his neighbors merely for the sake of defeating them, just as no sane man goes to sea simply to get to the other side." Polybius, soldier, statesman, and historian (212–ca. 118 B.C.), was someone who knew: he was a confidant of one of the great aristocratic families in Rome at a time when Roman war-making was in high gear. He also saw the Roman army in action. As a friend of Scipio Aemilianus he was present at the successful sieges of Carthage (**3.7**) in Africa and of Numantia in Spain (146 and 133 B.C.). We have already seen his constitutional explanation for Rome's success in the previous chapter (**2.4**). For him, as for other Greek thinkers, the constitution was, "the most powerful agent for success or failure" (Preface to Book 6). But warfare was also an essential ingredient in an empire's success. Here we will read his account of the Roman army (**3.4**).

Rome Vulnerabilities

War was a normal feature of Roman life. When, in 235 B.C., the doors of the temple of Janus were closed, symbolizing peace, it was for the first time in 450 years. Why warfare played so large a role in Roman history is partially explained by the vulnerable position of Rome in the middle of the Italian peninsula, and the presence of warlike peoples on all sides (**3.1**).

Rome was located at a strategic crossing point in the lower reaches of the Tiber River at a site where a number of low hills offered opportunity for defense. There was another crossing point a little further up the river at Fidenae, but Rome was the ford of preference for just about all movement west of the Apennines. Whoever controlled this ford effectively controlled all movement in peninsular Italy. In turn, whoever occupied the site of Rome had to make a choice whether or not to defend the river crossing. It was a choice the earliest inhabitants of the site, and subsequently their descendants, had to make: Either defend the borders and maintain their independence or become the slaves of whoever happened by. Ultimately this choice was at the root of Roman militarism (**3.7**).

Apart from its vulnerable geographic position, Rome had other problems. The city was wedged between the advanced and powerful Etruscan confederacy to the north, the Oscan pastoralists of the mountains to the north and east, and the Latin communities and Campania to the south. Of these the most dangerous and warlike were the pastoralists of the Apennines. The Oscans pursued a way of life organized economically around the movement of their animals from lowland pastures in winter to highland pastures in summer, a system called transhumance. By contrast the peoples of the coastal lowlands, the Etruscans, Latins, Campanians and Greeks, practiced settled agriculture. Italy was thus divided by a cultural and economic fault line into two, virtually incompatible ways of life. This does not mean that the Oscans and the rest of the inhabitants of peninsular Italy were constantly at each other's throats, but rather that the possibility of conflict was built into the very structure of Italian society and economics. Even to use the term "Italian" is an anachronism. It was not until the ascendancy of Rome that any sense of a non-Roman, "Italian" identity begin to emerge among the non-Roman peoples of Italy. In the end this Italian identity was swallowed up in the more powerful Roman one.

The Advantages of Vulnerability: Central Place Location and Internal Lines of Communication

In all of its struggles Rome had the advantage of a central place location and with it, internal lines of communication. Rome was so situated that if it could succeed in holding off its enemies on one frontier while concentrating against the other, it had a good chance of winning campaigns for survival. This is reflected in the following hypothetical model:

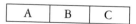

"B" represents a country with potentially hostile neighbors "A" and "C". Ideally diplomacy should enable "B" to prevent "A" and "C" from uniting and attacking simultaneously, but in a worst case scenario, with both "A" and "C" hostile, the key to "B's" survival will be its ability to move its armies rapidly from one frontier to another. With luck "B" should be able hold off one enemy while concentrating on the other. In both World Wars, Germany was in position "B" and was able to deploy its internal lines of communication and superior organization to good effect, nearly winning in both instances. Rome had to learn how to exploit its natural geographical advantages and organize its defenses accordingly. It was a process

with a short cut-and-thrust sword. This sharp, carbon steel sword, called the *gladius*, was not a long slashing sword (the kind, for instance, favored by the Celts), but a stabbing weapon of great lethality and stopping power. The long sword was a stand-off weapon which required large amounts of space between the warriors and often required multiple slashes to bring down an enemy while the *gladius* was intended to penetrate and hit an internal organ and drop the attacker with one stroke. Defensive armor was improved and throwing javelins replaced the old, phalanx style thrusting spears. The legion depended henceforth on a very flexible tactical style of fighting that required a much higher degree of coordination and experience than in the past. In battle the three lines of the legion (**3.4**) were gradually fed into combat. After the first line had thrown, on command, its javelins, it closed rapidly with the enemy and went to work with its swords, scything through the opposing forces. At a certain point, if the first line was not victorious, the second line was fed in and the first line withdrew to rest. Usually only in the most difficult battles was the third line brought into play.

Pay was introduced as part of the reforms. Another series of reforms took place in the second century B.C. when the thirty maniples were consolidated into ten larger units called cohorts. These are known as the Marian reforms, initiated by the consul Gaius Marius, to enable the legions to stand up to the mass charges of German invaders in the period 115–105 B.C. They will be dealt with in a later chapter.

Cohesion and professionalism in the legions were provided largely by the centurions. These men were drawn from the ranks, not from the elite classes. The latter provided the higher officers, the consuls, quaestors (financial officers), and military tribunes. Centurions were not officers in the traditional sense of being outsiders from a different class who represented a potentially different set of interests from those of the enlisted men. They were instead rankers promoted on the basis of competence and trust. Unlike the officers who belonged to the legion as a whole, centurions were attached directly to the individual maniples, the tactical units of the legion. The introduction of pay that accompanied these reforms made them workable. A complete break with the past was thus achieved. The new legionary army was not the equivalent of the hoplite phalanx of a Greek city, which consisted only of those who could afford the necessary equipment for warfare. Instead, the legion more accurately reflected the integrated patrician–plebeian state of Rome, where the upper classes maintained control of the higher commands while the other classes supplied the bulk of the troops and some of its most critical subofficers, the centurions. Nevertheless, the Roman army was still a militia, an army of amateur citizen-soldiers. It was recruited and dissolved annually.

Roman Values

Unlike the United States before recent times, Rome did not enjoy the luxury of distance from those who would harm it. Its values inevitably reflected military priorities. Just a list of Latin words indicate where Roman values lay: *gloria* and *fama*, glory and fame, need no translation, even if in English they lack the force that, for instance, *la gloire*, has in French. *Honor* and *dignitas* do not need translation either. *Severitas*, sternness, or seriousness was a prototypical Roman virtue. *Gravitas* and *auctoritas* mean gravity and authority not in a legal sense, as though these qualities were awards bestowed by the state. They were, rather, acquired by a lifetime of devotion to the state in civilian and military affairs. *Industria* and *innocentia* mean diligence and integrity, again in a largely public sense of hard work on behalf of the community, self-control in so far as handling of people and public funds are concerned. The overarching term *virtus*, virtue, included all of the above. A virtuous Roman was one who handled his family affairs blamelessly and served the state diligently in civilian and military capacities.

These values tell us where the center of gravity of Roman society lay. It did not lie in either commercial success or professional accomplishment. Quite the contrary. Industry, trade and the professions were largely in the hands of non-Romans, slaves or freedmen. Needless to say the values expressed by these words enshrine a good deal of ideology, but at least in the Republic there was a considerable degree of correspondence between ideology and reality. The early Roman state existed in a high-risk environment; it allowed little room for mistakes or feckless social behavior. Imagine what kind of society the US would have if its immediate neighbors were Russia and China rather than Mexico and Canada.

▼▼▼

3.1   Roman Views of their Enemies: Celts and Samnites

There were two stages of Celtic cultural development, the first known as the Hallstatt phase (ca. 700–450 B.C.) and the second the La Téne phase (450–50 B.C.) which arose in the area between the River Marne in France and the southern Rhineland. Around 400 B.C. a wave of migrations began from this area and by 300 B.C. La Téne culture had spread from the Atlantic coast of France east to Romania, and south into Spain and northern Italy. The sack of Rome in 390 B.C. was one of the ramifications of these migrations. By the first century La Téne culture had spread to Britain and Ireland. During this period the Celts, especially those in contact with the Mediterranean, began to move away from the chiefdom form of social and political organization toward an early form of urban and state culture. Some Celtic kingdoms adopted the alphabet, issued their own coinage, collected taxes and conducted censuses. Paradoxically this made them an easier target for the Romans to deal with than the more primitive Germans who maintained the chiefdom for several more centuries before they too began to adopt forms of the state.

By the first century the Romans had conquered most of the Celtic heartland. Celtic culture in these regions was essentially decapitated: Its ruling elites were either eliminated or

Romanized. Having lost their chance to evolve on their own, continental Celts became part of Roman history and their history was written for them by their conquerors. Understandably it was not written from a sympathetic viewpoint.

What follows is an accurate enough description of some types of Celtic warfare. Generally Greeks and Romans were repelled by those features of Celtic society which were unlike their own such as the use of butter, as opposed to olive oil, the drinking of beer and distilled alcohol (whiskey, "uisce" water, in Celtic), as opposed to wine, and especially by the large bodily size of the Celts, which resulted from their consumption of meat and dairy products to which Mediterranean peoples had only limited access. The Samnites (second reading), as noted in the introduction, were Oscan speaking highlanders who provided the main impetus for resistance to Rome down to the third century.[1]

Celtic Ferocity

In their wanderings and in battle the Celts use chariots drawn by two horses which carry the driver and the warrior. When they meet with cavalry in battle, they first throw their javelins at the enemy and then step down from their chariots and fight with their swords. Some of them despise death so much so that they enter the dangers of battle naked, wearing only a sword-belt. They bring to war with them their freedmen attendants, choosing them from among the poor. They use them in battle as chariot drivers and shield bearers. They have the custom when they have lined up for combat to step in front of the battle line and challenge the bravest of their enemies to single combat, brandishing their weapons in front of them in an attempt to terrify them. When anyone accepts the challenge to single combat, they sing a song in praise of the great deeds of their ancestors and of their own achievements, at the same time mocking and belittling their opponent, trying by such techniques to destroy his spirit before the fight. When their opponents fall, they cut off their heads and tie them around their horses' necks. They hand over to their attendants the blood-covered arms of their enemies and carry them off as booty, singing songs of victory.

Spoils of war they fasten with nails to their houses, just as hunters do the heads of wild animals they have killed. They embalm the heads of the most distinguished opponents in cedar oil and carefully guard them in chests. They show these heads to visitors, claiming that they or their father or some ancestor had refused large sums of money for this or that head. Some of them, it is said, boast that they have not accepted an equal weight of gold for the head they show, demonstrating a kind of barbarous nobility. Not to sell a thing that constitutes the proof of one's bravery is a noble, well-bred kind of thing, but on the other hand, to continue to ill-treat the remains of a fellow human being after he is dead is bestial.

---

[1]Diodorus Siculus 5.29.

The Samnite Enemy

The fact that the Oscans practiced a pastoral rather than a settled form of agriculture was not lost on the Romans. The first reading emphasizes the contrast between two agricultural regimes. The incident described in the first reading occurred in 320 B.C. during the longest of the wars with the Samnites, the Second Samnite War (327–304 B.C.).[2] The second reading describes an event from the Third Samnite War (298–291 B.C.).[3]

A. The second army, led by the consul Papirius, advanced along the coast as far as Arpi. Everything was peaceful on the way not because of benefits bestowed by the Roman people but because of the injuries done by the Samnites and the resulting hatred of them. The reason for this was that the Samnites at that time lived in mountain villages and used to plunder the plains and coastal areas. They despised the soft character of the settled farmers. As tends to be the case, the character of the inhabitants reflects the kind of countryside they live in. The Samnites, unlike the plain and coastal dwellers, were rugged mountain dwelling people. Had this region been loyal to the Samnites, a Roman army would never have been able to reach Arpi. It would have been cut off from its supplies and annihilated along the way because of the barren nature of the countryside.

B. The Samnites made their preparations for war [*in 293 B.C.*] with the same dedication and effort as on the former occasion and provided their troops with the most magnificent arms money could buy. They likewise called to their aid the power of the gods by initiating their soldiers in accordance with an ancient form of oath. Under this ordinance they levied troops throughout Samnium, announcing that anyone of military age who did not report in response to the general's proclamation, or who departed without orders, would be dedicated to Jupiter [*i.e., they were "sacred" to Jupiter and could be killed with impunity by anyone meeting them*]. Orders were then issued for all to assemble at Aquilonia, and the whole strength of Samnium came together, amounting to 40,000 men.

At Aquilonia a piece of ground in the middle of the camp was enclosed with hurdles and boards and covered overhead with linen cloth. The sides were of equal length, about 200 feet each. In this place sacrifices were performed according to directions read out of an old linen book. The priest performing the rituals was an old man by the name of Ovius Paccius, who claimed that he took these ceremonies from the ancient ritual of the Samnites and that these were the same rituals that their ancestors had used when they formed the secret design of wresting Capua from the Etruscans.

When the sacrifices were finished, the general ordered an attendant to summon all those who were most distinguished by their birth or conduct. These were brought into the enclosure singly. Besides the other ritual objects of a solemnity calculated to impress the mind with religious awe, there were in the middle of the covered enclosure altars around which lay the slain victims. Centurions stood round about with

---

[2]Livy 9.13.
[3]Livy 10.38.

drawn swords. Each individual was led up to the altars—rather like a victim himself than a performer in the ceremony—and was bound by an oath not to divulge what he should see and hear in this place. He was then compelled to swear according to a dreadful formula containing curses on his own person, his family, and his people if he did not go to battle wherever the commander should lead, if he fled from the field, or if he should see any other fleeing and did not immediately strike him down.

At first, some refused to take the oath and were beheaded around the altars. Lying among the carcasses of the victims, they served afterwards as a warning to others not to refuse. When the leading Samnites had been bound under these solemnities, the general nominated ten of them and made each choose a man, and so on until they had brought up the number to 16,000. This body of men was called the Linen Legion, from the covering of the enclosure wherein the nobility had been sworn. They were furnished with splendid armor and plumed helmets to distinguish them from the rest. Somewhat more than 20,000 men made up another army, which neither in personal appearance nor renown in war or in equipment was inferior to the Linen Legion. This was the size of the Samnite army, comprising the main strength of the nation, that encamped at Aquilonia.

3.2 Annoying Greeks: "Incompetent to manage their own affairs but thinking themselves competent to dictate war and peace to others."

Greeks had been in southern coastal Italy in large numbers for centuries before the Romans were drawn into the region by their wars with the Samnites. The most important settlement in this area was Tarentum, founded by Sparta in the eight century B.C. As was typical of Greek cities everywhere, including those overseas, they had difficulty maintaining internal stability and were frequently at war with each other. The event recorded here occurred in 320 B.C. when the Romans were campaigning in Apulia to the north of Tarentum.[4]

Just at that moment, as both sides were getting ready for battle, ambassadors from Tarentum arrived and ordered both Samnites and Romans to stop fighting. They threatened that whichever army was responsible for preventing an end to hostilities they would take on themselves on behalf of the other. The consul Papirius listened to the envoys as if he were persuaded by what they had to say and replied that he would have to confer with his colleague. He sent for Publilius [*the second consul commanding the other Roman force*] but went about getting ready during the interval. Then, after he had discussed the situation with Publilius, he gave the signal for battle.

---

[4]Livy 9.14.

The two consuls were involved in the usual matters that occurred before battle, both religious and practical, when the Tarentine envoys appeared again, hoping for an answer. "Men of Tarentum," Papirius said, "the keeper of our chickens [*the augur*] tells us that the auspices are favorable and that the omens from the sacrifice are also good. So, you see, the gods are with us as we go into action." With that he gave the order for the standards to advance and led out his troops, commenting on the folly of a people which was incompetent to manage their own affairs because of internal strife and discord, but thought themselves competent to dictate limits of peace and war for others.

3.3   Roman Dedication: Decius Mus at the Battle of Sentinum (295 B.C.)

Although the Romans were the champions of the more urbanized and presumably more civilized areas of Italy, they were not far removed themselves from the barbarous customs of Celts and Samnites. In the desperate battle of Sentinum in 295 B.C. against a combined army of Gauls and Samnites, one of the consuls, Decius Mus, "devoted" himself and his enemies to the gods to win victory. The fact that the act of "Devotio" was a formal state ritual, administered by a properly designated pontiff, and not a private vow, says a lot about the way warfare was waged by Rome during the early Republic.[5]

Twice the Romans compelled the Gallic cavalry to give way. At the second charge, when they advanced farther and were briskly engaged in the middle of the enemy's squadrons, they were thrown into confusion by a method of fighting new to them. A number of the enemy, mounted on chariots and wagons, made toward them with such frightening noise from the trampling of the cattle and the thunder of the wheels that the Roman horses were terrified. The victorious cavalry were scattered in panic; in blind flight men and horses fell to the ground. The disorder spread to the legions, and many of the first ranks were trampled underfoot by the horses and wagons which swept through their ranks. As soon as the Gallic infantry saw their enemy in confusion, they pursued their advantage and did not allow them time to recover themselves.

Decius shouted to his men, asking where they were fleeing to or what hope there was in running away. He tried to stop them as they turned their backs, but finding that he could not persuade them to keep their posts because they were so panicked, he called on his father, Publius Decius. "Why do I postpone any longer the fate of our family?" he cried. "It is destined for us to serve as sacrificial victims to avert dangers to our country. I will now offer the legions of the enemy, together with myself, to be immolated to Earth and the Gods of the Underworld."

Having said this, he ordered Marcus Livius, a priest whom he had ordered not to leave his side when they went into battle, to dictate the form of the ritual in which

---

[5]Livy 10.28–20.

he was to devote himself and the legions of the enemy on behalf of the army of the Roman people. He was accordingly devoted with the same prayers and in the same dress in which his father, Publius Decius, had ordered himself to be devoted at Vestris during the Latin War. Immediately after the solemn ritual prayers he added the following: "I drive away dread and defeat, slaughter and bloodshed, and the wrath of the gods, celestial and infernal; with the contagious influence of the Furies, the Ministers of Death, I will infect the standards, the weapons, and armor of the enemy. The place of my destruction will be that of the Gauls and Samnites also." After uttering these curses on himself and his foes, he spurred forward his horse where he saw the line of the Gauls was thickest, and, rushing on them, met his death.

From then on the battle seemed to be fought with a degree of force that seemed scarcely human. The Romans . . . stopped their flight . . . and were anxious to begin the fight again. Livius the priest, to whom Decius had transferred his lictors* with orders to act as propraetor, cried out aloud that the Romans were victorious, having been saved by the death of the consul, and that the Gauls and the Samnites were now the victims of mother Earth and the Gods of the Underworld; that Decius was summoning and dragging to himself the army devoted along with him . . .

3.4   The Roman Army in the Second Century B.C.

As noted in the introduction Rome modified its original tactical unit, the phalanx, at some point in the third century. The thrusting spear was replaced by the throwing javelin. This led inevitably to open order fighting since hurling a javelin requires space between each soldier so equipped. The reformed legion was drawn up in three lines of ten maniples. From front to rear these were hastati, principes *and* triarii. *Ahead of the legion was placed units of light infantry, the* velites. *The maniples were staggered to cover gaps in the line. The depth of the legion from the* velites *to the* triarii *has been estimated at about 100 yards. Its width would have been 200–250 yards. Once the javelins had been thrown the fighting continued with the* gladius, *a short cut and thrust sword (see chapter introduction under "The Legions"). Celts and Germans, by contrast, used slashing swords. Such warrior cultures generally focused on the individual warrior, and the individual warrior in turn valued his sword as a kind of special, sacred possession (think of King Arthur's* Excalibur). *The* gladius *by contrast was just a regulation issue type of weapon of purely practical significance.*

The Roman army was an engineering army. After every day's march the legions set about building a marching camp. This provided protection in hostile territory and allowed relatively few soldiers to stand guard while the rest ate and slept. This technique helped the Romans to project their power far into an enemy's territory and maintain good communications with rear

---

*Attendants of priests, consuls and some other magistrates.

areas. Supplies could be brought forward in an orderly way. The author of this reading is Polybius who had seen the Roman army in action on many occasions.[6]

The youngest soldiers, the *velites*, are ordered to carry a sword, javelins and a small shield. The shield is strongly made and large enough to protect the man, being round, with a diameter of three feet. Each man wears a helmet without a crest but covered with a wolf's skin or something of that kind, for the sake both of protection and identification, so that the officers may be able to tell whether he shows courage or the reverse when confronting dangers. The spear of the *velites* has a wooden shaft of about three feet and a finger's breadth in thickness. Its head is about nine inches, hammered and sharpened in such a way that it becomes bent the first time it strikes and cannot be used by the enemy to hurl back. Otherwise the weapon would be used by both sides.

The men next in age, the *hastati*, are under orders to wear full equipment. For a Roman this means, first, a large convex shield, four feet by two and a half feet. It consists of two layers of wood fastened together with glue. The outer surface is covered first with canvas, then with calf's skin. On the upper and lower edges it is bound with iron to resist the downward strokes of the sword and the wear of resting on the ground. It has an iron boss to deflect the blows of stones, pikes and heavy missiles. With the shield they also carry a sword [the *gladius*], called the Spanish sword, hanging down by their right thigh. The sword is especially good for cutting and thrusting. It is strong and unbending, doubled bladed and has a sharp point. In addition they carry two javelins [*pila*], a brass helmet and greaves. . . . Each man is decorated with a plume of feathers, purple or black, about a foot and a half long. The effect of these being placed on the helmet, combined with the rest of the armor, is to give the soldier the appearance of being twice his real height and to give him an impressive aspect calculated to strike terror into the enemy. The infantry men wear a small bronze breastplate over the heart. This completes their weaponry. Soldiers who have property worth more than 10,000 drachmae wear coats of mail [*loricae*] instead of breastplates. The *principes* and *triarii* are armed the same way as the *hastati*, except that instead of javelins they carry long spears [*hastae*].

The Centurions

The *principes*, *hastati* and *triarii* each select twenty centurions according to merit. All these sixty have the title of centurion alike, of whom the first man chosen is automatically a member of the council of war. The centurions in turn select a rear-rank officer called an *optio*. . . . Each maniple selects two of their strongest and best-born men as standard-bearers [*vexillarii*]. That each maniple should have two commanding officers is only reasonable. It is often impossible to know what a commander may be doing or what may happen to him. The necessities of war

---

[6]Polybius, *The Histories* 6.22–39.

allow no slip-ups and the Romans are anxious that the maniple never be without a commander. Hence, when the two centurions are both on the field, the first elected commands the right of the maniple, the second the left. If one is not there, the one who is there commands the whole unit. They want their centurions not to be so much daring and adventurous as men with a capacity for command, steady rather than showy, not prone to launch attacks thoughtlessly and open the battle but men who will hold their ground when hard pressed and be ready to die at their posts.

The Cavalry and the Allies

Similarly they divide the cavalry into ten squadrons [*turmae*] and from each they select three officers [*decuriones*], who each select a subaltern [*optio*]. The officer first selected commands the squadron, the other two having the rank of *decuriones*, a name which indeed applies to all alike. If the first *decurio* is not on the field, the second takes command of the squadron. The armor of the cavalry is very like that used in Greece . . . no nation has ever excelled the Romans in their readiness to borrow new techniques from other people and to imitate what they see is better in others than themselves. . . .

The allies are mustered along with the citizens and are distributed and managed by the officers appointed by the consuls. They have the title of Prefects of the Allies [*praefecti sociorum*] and are twelve in number. These officers select for the consuls from the whole infantry and cavalry of the allies such men as are most fitted for actual service. These are called *extraordinarii*. The whole number of the infantry of the allies is generally equal to that of the legions, but there are three times the number of cavalry.

Guard Duty

The duty of going the rounds is entrusted to the cavalry. The first prefect of cavalry in each legion, early in the morning, orders one of his rear-rank men to give notice before breakfast to four young men of his squadron who are to go the rounds. At evening this same man's duty is to give notice to the Prefect of the next squadron that it is his turn to provide for going the rounds until the next morning. This officer thereupon takes measures similar to the preceding one until the next day, and so on throughout the cavalry squadrons. The four men thus selected by the rear-rank men from the first squadron, after drawing lots for the watch they are to take, proceed to the tent of the tribune on duty and receive from him written orders stating which posts they are to visit and at what time. The four then take up their quarters for the night alongside the first maniple of *triarii*, for it is the duty of the centurion of this maniple to see that a bugle is blown at the beginning of every watch.

When the time has arrived, the man to whose lot the first watch has fallen goes his round, taking some of his friends as witnesses. He walks through the posts assigned,

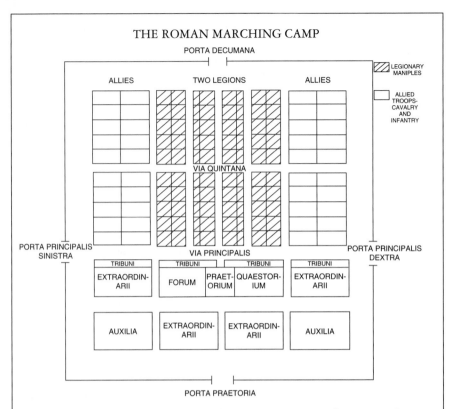

THE ROMAN MARCHING CAMP

The plan of the Roman camp described here follows, with some simplifications, the description offered by Polybius. The camp was surrounded by a ditch and a rampart on which was set a palisade of stakes. In the center of the camp was the *Praetorium*, the tent of the commanding officer. On either side of this tent were open areas, the *Forum*, a market area, and the *Quaestorium*, where the *quaestor*, a junior officer in charge of the finances of the army, had his tent. Tents of the tribunes were adjacent, located along the main thoroughfare and axis of the camp, the *Via Principalis*. The tents of the maniples of the legions and the troops of the allies were lined up in groups of five on either side of another street which ran parallel to the *Via Principalis*. This was the *Via Quintana* ("Fifth Street"). Elite groups of allies, the *extraordinarii*, were billeted on the other side of the *Praetorium*.

The construction of the camp was an integral part of Roman legionary tactics. At the end of each day's march all members of the legion pitched in to dig the ditch and rampart and set up the stake palisade. There were several aims behind this laborious undertaking. One was that it permitted Rome to project force deep into enemy territory. A line of marching camps followed the route of the advancing army and allowed for the movement of supplies forward without loss of manpower in the legions as they advanced. At night a small force could patrol the perimeter of the camp and allow the majority of the legionaries get a good night's sleep. In case of a serious attack, especially one at night, all members of the force knew exactly where their positions were.

Over time some marching camps (the kind described here) evolved into permanent bases or even cities. Camps in northern environments had to be built to withstand the rigors of northern winters. At Inchthuthil in Scotland, for example, the houses of some of the officers were equipped with central heating provided by hypocausts underneath the floors through which hot air passed, a common technique used by the Romans for heating their houses and public buildings.

which are not only those along the rampart and gates, but also the pickets set by the several maniples and squadrons. If he finds the men of the first watch awake he takes from them their *tesserae* [wooden tablets on which the watch-word was written]. If, however, he finds any one of them asleep or absent from his posts, he calls those with him to witness the fact and passes on. The same process is repeated by those who go the rounds during the other watches. The charge of seeing that the bugle is blown at the beginning of each watch, so that the right man might visit the right pickets, is as, I have said, laid upon the centurions of the first maniple of *triarii*, each one taking the duty for the day.

Each of the men who have gone the rounds at daybreak conveys the *tesserae* to the Tribune on duty. If the whole number are given in, they are dismissed without question. But if any one of them brings a number less than that of the pickets, an investigation is made by means of the mark on the *tessera*, as to which picket he has omitted. Upon this being determined, the centurion is summoned. He brings the men who were on duty, and they are confronted with the patrol. If the fault is with the men on guard, the patrol clears himself by providing witnesses whom he took with him, for he cannot do so without. If no fault is found with the guards, the inquiry turns to the man who made the rounds.

The Court Martial

A court martial made up of the Tribunes is at once convened and the accused soldier put on trial. If convicted he is flogged. The method of flogging [in Latin the *fustuarium*] is as follows. The Tribune takes a staff and merely touches the condemned man. Thereupon all the soldiers attack him with clubs and stones. Generally speaking, men thus punished are killed on the spot, but if by any chance, after running the gauntlet, they manage to escape from the camp, they have no hope of ultimately surviving. They may not return to their own country, nor would anyone dare to receive such a fugitive into their house. Those who have once fallen into this misfortune are utterly and completely ruined. The same fate awaits the Prefect of the squadron, as well as his rear-rank man [the *optio*], if they fail to give the necessary order at the right time, the latter to the patrols, and the former to the prefect of the next squadron. The result of the severity and inevitability of this punishment is that in the Roman army the night watches are kept faultlessly . . . the punishment of flogging is assigned also to anyone committing theft in the camp, bearing false witness, or acting as a male prostitute. . . . The following acts are considered cowardly and dishonorable: to make a false report of courageous behavior to the Tribunes with an eye on getting a reward; for men assigned to an ambush to quit the place assigned out of fear; for a man to throw away his weapons from fear on the field of battle. Consequently, it sometimes happens that men confront certain death at their stations but because of the fear of the punishment awaiting them, they refuse to quit their posts. Others who have lost their shield or spear or any other arm during a battle, throw themselves on their enemy in the hope of recovering what they have lost or of escaping by death certain disgrace and the insults of their relatives.

Decimation

But if it happens that a number of men are involved in these same acts—if for instance, an entire maniple has quit its position in the presence of the enemy—it is thought impossible to condemn the whole maniple to the *fustuarium* or to military execution. But a solution has been devised that is at once adequate for the maintenance of discipline and calculated to inspire terror. The Tribune assembles the legion, calls the defaulters to the front, and after administering a sharp rebuke, selects five or eight or twenty of them by lot, so that those selected should number about a tenth of those who have been guilty of the act of cowardice. Those selected are punished with the *fustuarium* without mercy. The rest are put on rations of barley instead of wheat and are ordered to take up their quarters outside the rampart and the protection of the camp.

Medals and Decorations

They have an excellent plan to encourage young men to face danger. When an engagement has taken place and any of them have shown conspicuous gallantry, the consul calls the whole legion to a meeting and calls up those he thinks have served with distinction. He first compliments each of them individually on his gallantry and mentions any other distinctions he may have earned in the course of his life, and then presents them with awards. A decoration in the form of a spear is given to any man who has wounded an enemy; a cup styled decoration to one who has killed and stripped the armor of any enemy; a horse medallion if he is a cavalry trooper. This does not take place in the case of having wounded or stripped an enemy in a set engagement, or the storming of a town, but in a skirmish or other occasion where there is no necessity for them to expose themselves to danger, but they do so anyway. In the capture of a town those who are first to mount the walls are presented with a gold crown. So too those who have protected and saved any citizen or ally are honored with presents. The person they have saved may voluntarily give them a crown, or if not, they are compelled to do so by the Tribunes. The man thus saved reverences his preserver throughout his life as his father, and is bound to act toward him as a father in every respect. By such incentives those who stay at home are stirred up to the noble rivalry and emulation in confronting danger, no less than those who actually hear and see what takes place. For the recipients of such rewards not only enjoy great glory among their comrades in the army, and an immediate reputation at home, but after their return they are marked men in all solemn festivals. They alone who have been thus distinguished by the consuls for bravery, are allowed to wear robes of honor on these occasions. Moreover, they place the spoils they have taken in the most conspicuous position in their houses, as visible tokens and proofs of their valor. No wonder that a people whose rewards and punishments are allotted with such care and received with such feelings, should be so brilliantly successful in war.

3.5 Quarreling Consuls: The Dangers of Divided Command

Rome fought two major wars with Carthage—from 264 to 241 B.C. and from 218 to 201 B.C. The second war, known as the Hannibalic War after the great Carthaginian general, stretched Roman society to the breaking point. In the early years one disaster succeeded another. Two legions were lost at Trasimene in 217 B.C., and the following year approximately 50,000 Romans and their Latin and Italian allies perished at Cannae in southern Italy.

Part of the military problem the Romans faced was of their own making. The army, as befitted a free republic, was a militia commanded by amateurs. There was no single commander in chief. Two consuls were elected annually. Consuls rose to the top on the basis of political as well military expertise, or sometimes mostly just political expertise. No Roman officers were without military experience, but the ability to exercise successful command on the battlefield has been, throughout history, a hit and miss affair. The opening years of wars frequently see the wholesale clearing out of generals until finally—or on occasion not at all—some competent commander is discovered. Consider Lincoln's problems in the early years of the U.S. Civil War. The Roman military was no exception to this general rule. It had the added disadvantage of having two, coequal commanders when the whole Roman army was assembled for a single campaign. When that occurred the command rotated on a daily basis between the two consuls present. Such an arrangement was hazardous at best; some would say idiotic, but the principles of political freedom trumped military common sense.

In the Hannibalic War the Romans had the bad luck of confronting a fully professional army led by one of the greatest generals of all time. That Rome's amateurism in the end triumphed is one of the proofs that something more than military expertise is an essential ingredient in the successful waging of war. The following reading provides a description of the lead-up to the battle of Cannae. It emphasizes the problem of divided command but also the political nature of the consulate and the degree to which ordinary Roman soldiers had a way of making their views felt. In the senatorial tradition Varro was portrayed in a very hostile manner. He was described as the son of a butcher and, therefore, a radical demagogue who managed to get himself elected with popular support. There was nothing wrong with the system of command so this explanation ran; it was the intrusion of lower class incompetence that brought disaster. In fact, Varro was probably elected with the support of the blue blooded Scipio family and their allies.[7]

When the consuls arrived at Cannae they had a clear view of the Carthaginian position. They themselves established two camps at about the same distance as had been the case in the previous encampment at Geronium. As before, their forces were divided. The River Aufidus flowed between the two camps. It could be reached from both of them as was needed, though not without opposition from the Carthaginians. It was easier to reach the river from the smaller Roman camp on the south side of the Aufidus since there was no enemy garrison on that side.

---

[7]Livy 22.44–45.

Hannibal, hoping he could persuade the consuls to engage him on ground suited to cavalry, his strongest arm, drew up his battle line and sent his Numidian cavalry to provoke the enemy. Immediately the soldiers in the Roman camps began to agitate and the consuls to quarrel. Paullus cited the reckless behavior of Sempronius and Flaminius [*two generals who had recently been defeated badly by Hannibal; Flaminius was killed*] to Varro. Varro replied by claiming that the example of Fabius [*the "Delayer," the general who counseled avoiding confrontations with Hannibal*] was a specious excuse for timid and spiritless commanders. Varro then called on the gods and mankind to witness that it was through no fault of his that Hannibal was now in possession of Italy; his hands, he claimed, had been tied by his colleague. His men, he continued, were ready for the fight but were deprived of the opportunity to use their weapons. Paullus replied that he was blameless if the legions were recklessly betrayed into an ill-considered and imprudent battle, though he would, of course, suffer the consequences. It was to be seen, he said, whether a quick and rash tongue was matched in battle by equally vigorous action.

While the Romans spent time arguing among themselves rather than getting ready for battle, Hannibal began to withdraw his troops from the position he had occupied for most of the day. At the same time he sent his Numidian cavalry to harass the watering parties sent out from the smaller camp. Almost before these disorganized groups had reached the bank they were sent fleeing in noise and confusion by the Numidians who then continued their advance right up to a guard post in front of the camp's ditch and almost to the camp's gates. The Romans were indignant that their camp should appear to be threatened by what was in reality a mere auxiliary skirmishing force. The only thing that held them back from immediately crossing the river and challenging Hannibal to battle was the fact that it was Paullus' day of command. The following day Varro was in control of the army and, without consulting his colleague, gave the order to engage the enemy. Having drawn up his battle line he crossed the river. Paullus had no choice but to follow and help though he fundamentally disagreed with his colleague's action.

Needless to say disaster followed. The Roman cavalry was defeated and driven off, the infantry was surrounded and destroyed, and the consul Paullus killed. Varro survived. Despite his rash behavior he was greeted on his return to Rome after the battle by crowds of people. The Senate thanked him publicly for "not having despaired of the Republic." Had he been a Carthaginian general in similar circumstances, Livy went on to say, he would have been severely punished (i.e., he would have been crucified). By implication, it was Rome's values that in the end enabled it to triumph over their most menacing foe.

3.6   A Draftee's Viewpoint: The Speech of Spurius Ligustinus

The steadiness of the Senate during the Hannibalic War gave that body practical control of foreign affairs. Its ideology is reflected in a speech that Livy composed and put in the mouth of a centurion, Spurius Ligustinus. The context for the speech was a protest led by his fellow

*centurions who protested the way the draft was being conducted in preparation for a cam-
paign against Macedonia (the Third Macedonian War, 171–167 B.C.). Although the
speech reflects a senatorial viewpoint some of the realities of war as seen from the viewpoint
of the ordinary draftee are also to be found in it. It is interesting to note how the draft was
conducted and how tribunes could get involved in what was essentially a military affair.*[8]

A Problem with the Draft: Tribunes and Centurions

The consuls were conducting the draft with greater care than usual. Licinius was
enrolling veteran infantrymen and centurions, but many signed up voluntarily because
they saw that those who had fought in the previous Macedonian War and against King
Antiochus in Asia had become rich. However, when the military tribunes who had been
enlisting the centurions put them down in the order in which they enlisted, twenty-
three centurions who had held the rank of chief centurion, upon being treated this way,
appealed to the tribunes of the people. Two of the tribunes, M. Fulvius Nobilior and
M. Claudius Marcellus, threw the matter back to the consuls. They claimed that the
investigation was the responsibility of those to whom the job of conducting the draft and
the war had been given in the first place. The other tribunes agreed to investigate the
case and, if injury had been done, they would intervene on behalf of the citizens injured.

The procedure took place at the tribunes' benches. Marcus Popilius, a former consul, appeared as counsel for the aggrieved centurions. Also appearing were the centurions themselves and the consul who had been conducting the draft. Licinius
demanded that the investigation take place in a public assembly, and the people
were duly gathered. Popilius, who had been consul two years earlier, spoke on behalf
of the centurions. These experienced soldiers had completed their regular military
service, he said. Their bodies were worn down by age and unremitting labor. They
had no objection to serving the state, but they requested they not be assigned to a
rank lower than they had had during their regular stint.

In response, Licinius the consul ordered the decrees of the Senate to be read, first
the one authorizing the war against Perseus, then the decree authorizing the enroll-
ment of as many centurions as he thought necessary and exempting no one under
fifty years of age. He went on to request that the people not interfere with the draft
being conducted by the military tribunes or prevent the consul from assigning the
rank to each as was in the best interest of the state. There was, he reminded them, a
new war in progress, near Italy, and against a very powerful king. Should there be
any issues in doubt, they should be referred back to the Senate.

Impasse Resolved: Speech of Centurion Ligustinus

When the consul had finished, Spurius Ligustinus, one of the centurions who had
appealed to the tribunes of the people, requested permission of the consul and the
tribunes of the people that he be allowed to speak. With their permission he began:

---

[8]Livy 42.32–5.

"Citizens, I am Spurius Ligustinus of the Crustumina tribe, by origin a Sabine. My father left me an acre of land and a small cottage in which I was born and raised. I live in it to this day. When I came of age, my father found a wife for me, his niece. She brought nothing with her except her free birth and good morals and a fertility that would have been adequate for a rich home. We had six sons and two daughters, both of whom are now married. Four of our sons are grown; two are still boys.

"I began my service in the consulship of Publius Sulpicius and Gaius Aurelius (200 B.C.). I served two years as a private in the army brought to Macedonia for the war against King Philip. In the third year T. Quinctius Flamininus promoted me to centurion of the tenth maniple of the front rank [*the lowest of the three subdivisions of the legion*] because of my bravery. After the defeat of Philip and the Macedonians, when we had been repatriated to Italy and demobilized, I went to Spain with M. Porcius Cato as a volunteer with the rank of private (195 B.C.). Of all the generals alive, no one is a shrewder observer or judge of bravery. This will be borne out by those who, through long service, have served with him as well as other commanders. This general considered me worthy to be assigned centurion of the first century of the front rank. I enlisted a third time as a volunteer and a private in the army sent against the Aetolians and King Antiochus (191 B.C.). Once again I was given the rank of centurion, this time by Manius Acilius. On this occasion, however, I was made a centurion of the first century in the second rank [*a promotion*]. After Antiochus had been driven out and the Aetolians defeated, we returned to Italy. Twice thereafter I served in single, year-long campaigns. Twice I fought in Spain, once with Q. Fulvius Flaccus when he was praetor and once with Ti. Sempronius Gracchus when he held the same office. I was brought home from Spain by Flaccus along with others for his triumph. This was because we had been distinguished for bravery.

"Four times in a few years I was Chief Centurion. I was decorated for bravery thirty-four times. I won six civic crowns [*given for saving a fellow citizen's life*]. I have served twenty-two years in the army and am over fifty years old. Nevertheless, if I had not completed all my years of service, Publius Licinius, and my age did not give me an exemption, I could still give you four soldiers in my place [*i.e., his own sons*]. I would like you to take what I have said into consideration on my side of the case.

"For my part, as long as I am considered fit for service, I will never refuse to be enrolled. I am willing to accept the rank assigned to me by the military tribunes. This is their responsibility. I will try to make sure that no one in the army exceeds me in bravery. That I have always done so my generals and those who have served with me will attest. Fellow soldiers, even though it is within your right to make this appeal, it is also right that you submit to the authority of the consuls and the Senate. When you were young, you never resisted them. Consider every rank honorable in which you will be defending the state."

When Ligustinus finished his speech, Publius Licinius the consul praised him profusely and conducted him from the meeting to the Senate. There, a motion of thanks was authorized, and the military tribunes made him Chief Centurion in the first legion because of his bravery. The other centurions gave up their appeal and responded obediently to the draft.

3.7   Roman Militarism: The Sack of Carthage

The most ghastly feature of ancient warfare was the sack of cities. Everyone—men, women, and children, old and young—suffered. Sometimes the entire population was sold into slavery. In particularly bitter wars whole populations were slaughtered. In 146 B.C. Rome destroyed two ancient cities, Corinth and Carthage, and sold their populations into slavery. For some moralists writing in the next century, 146 B.C. was taken as the moment when the Republic began to decay, not because of the awful slaughter or the destruction of two ancient and glorious cities, but because in that year Rome eliminated its last serious competitor in the Mediterranean. With no outside enemy to fear anymore, Rome was without external constraint. The key question then became: could Rome find the moral strength internally to regulate its now well-developed hunger for conquest? For centuries Rome had fought for safe frontiers; now it was poised on the brink of empire. No wonder that Scipio, commander of the Roman forces at Carthage, was said to have worried about the fate of his own city, "taking into consideration the mutability of human affairs." This eye-witness account probably ultimately derives from Polybius, who was present with Scipio at the siege. Polybius, having witnessed the downfall of Macedonia, had a special interest in the rise and fall of empires.[9]

The main object of Scipio's attack was Byrsa, the strongest part of the city, where the greater part of the population had taken refuge. There were three streets going up from the Forum to this fortress; on either side along each street there were houses built closely together, six stories high, from which the Romans were attacked with missiles. They captured the first few houses and from them moved against the defenders of the next. When they had gotten control of these, they put timbers over the narrow passageways and crossed as on bridges.

While one war was raging in this way on the rooftops, another was going on in the streets below. Everywhere there was shrieking and shouting and groans and suffering of every kind. Some were stabbed, others hurled alive from the roofs to the pavement, some of them falling on the heads of spears or other pointed weapons or swords. Until Scipio reached Byrsa, no one dared to set fire to the houses on account of the men still on the roofs, but at that point he ordered the three streets burned and the passageways kept clear of burning material so that the advancing detachments of the army could move back and forth freely.

Then came new scenes of horror. The fire spread and brought down everything. The soldiers did not pause to destroy the buildings little by little but pulled them all down together. The crashing grew louder, and many fell with the stones among the dead. Some were seen to be still alive, especially old men, women, and young children who had hidden in the inmost nooks of the houses. Some were wounded, others burned to a greater or lesser degree, and they uttered horrible cries. Still others, pushed out and falling from such a height, along with the stones, timbers, and fire, were torn asunder into all kinds of awful shapes, crushed and mangled. Nor was this

---

[9]Appian 8.128–132. Based on the translation of Horace White, *Appian's Roman History* (London: 1888).

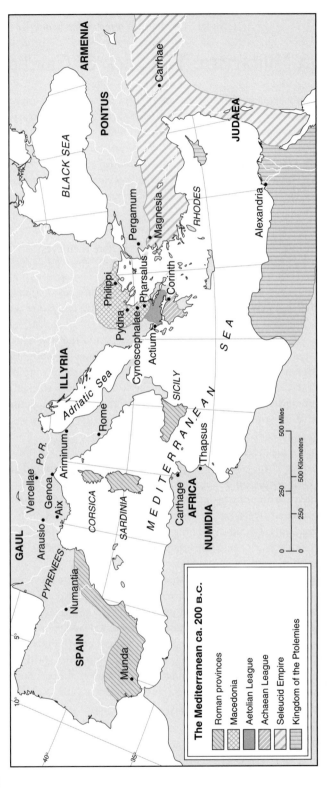

As late as 200 B.C. the Roman Empire still consisted of only a few overseas provinces: Sicily, Corsica, Sardinia, and eastern Spain. The rest of the Mediterranean lay in the hands of native peoples, a few leagues in Greece, and the three Hellenistic Kingdoms of the Antigonids (Macedonia and Greece), the Seleucids (Asia Minor, Syria, Mesopotamia), and Ptolemies (Egypt, Libya). In the second and first centuries B.C. Rome's speed of conquest increased and by 30 B.C. almost all these areas were provinces, or on the way to being provinces, of Rome.

the end of their miseries, for those who had been ordered to keep the streets clear and were removing the debris with axes, mattocks, and boat-hooks while making the roads passable tossed with these implements the dead and living together into holes in the ground, sweeping them along like sticks and stones or turning them over with their metal tools. Human beings were used to fill up a ditch. Some were thrown in head first, while their legs, sticking out of the ground, writhed for a long time. Others fell with their feet down while their heads remained above ground. Horses galloped over them, crushing their faces and skulls, not purposely on the part of the riders, but as a result of their headlong haste. Nor did the clearing parties do these things on purpose. The press of war, the glory of the approaching victory, the rush of the troops, the confused noise of heralds and trumpeters all round, the tribunes and centurions changing guard and marching units hither and thither—all combined to make everyone frantic and heedless of what was happening before their eyes.

Six days and nights were taken up in this kind of turmoil, the soldiers being rotated so that they might not be worn out by the toil, slaughter, lack of sleep, and appalling sights. Scipio alone worked without rest, standing over the soldiers or hurrying here and there, not sleeping, eating anyhow as he worked, until, utterly fatigued and worn out, he sat down on a high place from where he could overlook the work. Much remained that could be destroyed, and it seemed likely that the carnage would go on for a very long time, but on the seventh day some suppliants presented themselves to Scipio bearing the sacred garlands of Aesculapius, whose temple was the most famous and richest in the citadel. These, bearing olive branches from the temple, besought Scipio to spare just the lives of all who were willing to depart from Byrsa. He granted this request to all except the deserters. Immediately 50,000 men and women came out together through a narrow gate which had been opened in the wall. They were put under guard.

The 900 Roman deserters, despairing for their life, went to the temple of Aesculapius with Hasdrubal [*the Carthaginian commander*], his wife, and their two sons. Here they easily defended themselves for a long time although they were few in number because of the height and steep nature of the place, which in time of peace was reached by a stairway of sixty steps. Finally, worn down by hunger, want of sleep, fear, weariness, and the approach of doom, they abandoned the enclosures of the temple and fled to the shrine and its roof.

Thereupon Hasdrubal fled secretly to Scipio, bearing an olive branch. Scipio ordered him to sit at his feet and there displayed him to the deserters. When they saw him, they asked silence and, when it was granted, heaped all manner of reproaches on Hasdrubal, then set fire to the temple and were destroyed in it. It is said the fire was lighted by the wife of Hasdrubal. In full view of Scipio she presented herself as best she could in the midst of such a disaster, and setting her children by her side, said so she could be heard by Scipio: "Against you, O Roman, the gods have no cause for indignation, since you exercise the right of war. But upon this Hasdrubal, betrayer of his country and its temples, of me and his children, may the gods of Carthage take vengeance, and you be their instrument." Then turning to Hasdrubal, she said: "Wretch, traitor, most effeminate of men, this fire will entomb me and my children. But as for you, what Roman triumph will you, the leader of great Carthage, decorate? What punishment will you not receive from him at whose feet you are now sitting?" Having reproached him in this way, she killed her children, threw them into the fire, and plunged in after them. With these words it is said the wife of Hasdrubal died as Hasdrubal himself should have died.

Scipio looked at the city which had flourished for 700 years from its foundation and had ruled over so many lands, islands, and seas, as rich in arms, fleets, elephants, and money as the greatest of empires but far surpassing them in bravery and high spirit, for, when stripped of all its ships and arms, it had sustained famine and a great siege for three years. Now it came to an end in total destruction, and Scipio, beholding this spectacle, is said to have shed tears and publicly mourned for the enemy. After meditating by himself for a long time and reflecting on the inevitable fall of cities, nations, and empires as well as of individuals, and thinking of the fate of Troy, that once proud city, upon the fate of the Assyrian, the Median, and then the great Persian Empire, and most recently of all the splendid empire of Macedonia, either voluntarily or otherwise he spoke the words of Homer:

"The day shall come in which our sacred Troy
And Priam, and the people over whom Spear-bearing Priam rules, shall perish all."

In a private conversation he was asked by Polybius what he meant (for Polybius had been his tutor); Polybius says that he did not hesitate frankly to name his own country, for whose fate he feared when he considered the mutability of human affairs. And Polybius wrote this down just as he heard it.

3.8   The Triumphal Parade of Aemilius Paullus

A triumph, or its lesser form, an ovation, was awarded on the basis of the significance of the victory and the body count. A minimum of 5,000 was necessary for a triumph. Formally a triumph was the ritual purification of the army after a campaign, but it also had the effect of driving home the value of war and drawing the whole community together in a grand celebration of the state's success. It was the pinnacle of the triumphing general's career and conferred immortality on his family and on himself. The victor in this triumph was L. Aemilius Paullus, who defeated the Macedonians at the battle of Pydna in 168.[10]

The people erected stands in the race tracks (which the Romans call "circuses"), all around the Forum and at every spot in the city from which they could get a view of the

---

[10]Plutarch, *Aemilius Paullus* 32–35.

show. The spectators were dressed in white garments. All the temples were open and full of garlands and incense. The streets were cleared and kept open by numerous officers, who drove back all who crowded onto or ran across the processional route.

The triumph lasted three days. The first day was barely long enough for the presentation of the booty in the form of statues, pictures, and colossal images which were conveyed in 250 chariots. The second day the finest and richest armor of the Macedonians, both bronze and steel, all newly polished and glittering, was carried by in many wagons. The pieces were piled up and arranged artfully as though they had been tumbled in heaps carelessly and by chance: Helmets were thrown upon shields, coats of mail on greaves; Cretan light infantry targets [*small shields*] and Thracian wicker bucklers and quivers of arrows lay among horses' bits. Through these there appeared the points of naked swords, intermixed with long Macedonian sarissas [*lances*]. All these arms were attached together just loosely enough that they struck against one another as they were drawn along, making a harsh and frightening noise, so that even as the spoils of a conquered enemy they could not be seen without dread. After the wagons loaded with armor there followed 3,000 men who carried silver coins in 750 baskets, each of which weighed three talents [*roughly 180 pounds*] and was carried by four men. Others brought silver bowls and goblets and cups, all disposed in a way to make the best show, and all unusual for their size as well as the solidity of their embossed work.

On the third day, early in the morning, first came the trumpeters, who played not as they usually did in a procession or solemn entry, but the kind of martial music the Romans used when encouraging their troops to go into action. Next followed 120 oxen with their horns gilded and their heads adorned with ribbons and garlands. These were led by young men with handsomely bordered aprons and boys with basins of silver and gold for the libations. After them was brought the gold coin, which was divided into containers that weighed three talents, like those that contained the silver. There were seventy-seven of these. Next came the bearers of the consecrated bowl which Aemilius had made. It weighed ten talents and was set with precious stones. Then the cups of Kings Antigonus and Seleucus and those of Therikleius were displayed, and all the gold plate that was used at King Perseus' table.

After these came Perseus' own chariot, in which was placed his armor, and on top of that his crown. After a gap, the children of the king were led by as captives, and with them a train of their servants, teachers, and attendants, all shedding tears and reaching out their hands to the spectators. The children themselves were encouraged by their attendants also to beg for compassion. There were two sons and a daughter, whose young age made them only partly aware of their misery, to such an extent that their incomprehension of their condition made them seem the more to be pitied. At any rate, Perseus himself scarcely got as much attention when he passed by. Pity fixed the eyes of the Romans on the infants, and many of them could not stop their tears. Until the children had gone, the viewers were moved by a mixture of pain and pleasure.

After his children and their attendants came Perseus himself, clad in black and wearing the boots of his country, looking shocked and stupefied as a result of his great misfortune. Next came a great crowd of his friends and familiars, whose faces were disfigured with grief and who let the spectators see by their tears and their continued looking at Perseus that it was his fortune they lamented, not their own. Perseus had appealed to Aemilius not to be led in pomp but to be left out of the triumphal procession. But Aemilius rightly refused, reminding Perseus of his cowardice and fondness for life and saying that, as in the past, it was within his power to avoid disgrace, meaning that he could take his own life. But Perseus, relying on who knows what hopes, allowed himself to appear as part of his own spoils.

Four hundred gold crowns in honor of Aemilius' victory, which had been sent to him by the cities, together with their deputations, came next. Then came Aemilius himself, seated on a magnificently adorned chariot. Aemilius, a striking individual even without the trappings of power, was dressed in a robe of purple interwoven with gold and was holding a laurel branch in his right hand. All the army, divided into centuries and cohorts, followed in like manner, with boughs of laurel in their hands. Some sang verses mixed with jokes according to the custom; others sang songs of triumph and praise of Aemilius' deeds. He was indeed admired and regarded as happy by all men, unenvied at least by the good. It seems the responsibility of some god to lessen that kind of happiness, which is too great and disproportionate, and so to mingle the affairs of human life that no one should be entirely free and exempt from disasters. Indeed we read in Homer that those people should think themselves truly happy whom Fortune has given an equal share of good and evil.

At any rate, Aemilius had four sons, of whom Scipio and Fabius were adopted into other families.[11] The other two, whom he had by his second wife and who were still young, he brought up in his own house. One of these died at fourteen years of age, five days before his father's triumph. The other died at twelve, three days after the triumph. There was not a Roman who did not have a deep sense of Aemilius' suffering and who did not shudder at the cruelty of Fortune that had not scrupled to bring so much sorrow into a house resplendid with happiness, rejoicing, and sacrifices, and to intermingle tears and laments with songs of victory and triumph.

Aemilius, however, reasoned rightly that courage and resolution were to resist not merely arms and spears, but all the shocks of ill fortune. He so met and so adapted himself to these mingled and contrasting circumstances as to outbalance the evil with the good, and his private concerns with the public. Thus he did not allow anything either to take away from the grandeur or to sully the dignity of his victory.

▼▼▼

---

[11] The Scipio referred to here is the Scipio who was the friend of Polybius and the general who sacked Carthage (see previous section).

Questions

1. Why did the Romans think the Celts were outside the pale of normal civilized society? (**3.1**)
2. In what way did the economic foundations of Oscan society make it fundamentally different from that of the other peoples of Italy? (**3.1**)
3. The Romans did not care for Greeks meddling, as **3.2** demonstrates. What did the Greeks tell the Romans to do? How did the Romans react?
4. What did the Romans understand by the term "devotion" (*devotio*)? (**3.3**)
5. Who selected the centurions of the Roman legions? (**3.4**)
6. How was guard duty in the Roman marching camp conducted? (**3.4**)
7. What was decimation and how was it carried out? (**3.4**)
8. After the disastrous battle of Trasimene against Hannibal what were the first actions the Romans took? (**3.5**)
9. The speech of the centurion Spurius Ligustinus reflects the elite's expectations of ordinary draftees. What were some of these? (**3.6**)
10. How did Hasdrubal's wife handle her husband's treachery at the end of the siege of Carthage? (**3.7**)
11. Why did Aemilius Paullus deny King Perseus' request that he be left out of his (Aemilius') triumphal parade? How did Aemilius cope (according to Plutarch) with his own personal losses?

Chapter 4

▼▼▼

Roman Society and Culture in the Republic

Society and the State

No great divide existed between "society" and the state, or between the Roman people and the Roman government in the period of the Republic. Society and the state intermingled in intimate and surprising ways. Size had something to do with this situation. It would not be an exaggeration to say that in the early period of the city everyone knew everyone else (or at least *about* everyone); gossip kept everyone in Rome informed about what was happening in the community—thus the authorities learned of the conspiracy of the Bacchanals (**4.4**) through word of mouth. But the formal structure of the state also contributed to this state of affairs. The way the Romans went about their public affairs, passing laws, making decisions, judging, electing, and so forth, involved more people directly and intimately *with each other* than does any modern democracy. And this was the case despite the fact that Romans did not think of their constitution as being democratic, or at least not democratic in the way, for instance, Athens was democratic.

This kind of interpenetration of society and the state created a very unusual, by modern standards, kind of state. For us there is government that is distinct and apart from "us" who make up society. In contemporary popular rhetoric the government is often cast as the adversary of the "People." It would have been difficult for Romans to have shared this attitude since so much of what the "government" of Rome did was done by the people themselves directly. All aspects of life were affected by this close integration of society and the state. Children were raised first and foremost as citizens with obligations to family and society, not as individuals in search of self-fulfillment with careers or jobs in the private sector. In terms of occupations, few choices were available in any case. Professionals—physicians, musicians, actors, craftsmen, etc.—were almost always slaves, freedmen, or foreigners. Most Romans had only one job opportunity: farming.

Religion

Romans thought of themselves as a family and the city of Rome as their family home. A designated state "family" hearth burned in the Temple of Vesta in the Forum, and a group of housekeepers, the Vestal Virgins, had responsibility for seeing that it never went out (**4.2**). Just as Roman families were sustained by the rites special to each family, so was the state sustained by the observance of rites proper to it. The maintenance of proper relations with the gods and goddesses, the *pax deorum*, was of fundamental importance throughout Rome's history. Imported rituals were allowed to be practiced only under very special circumstances, usually state emergencies. Foreign rites performed secretly or without proper authorization were regarded as highly dangerous (**4.4**).

According to ancient tradition the religion of Rome was given permanent form by the second king of Rome, Numa Pompilius (**4.2**). According to this tradition, Romulus, the first king, had made Rome capable of defending itself and had infused the population with a warlike spirit. Numa, however, was supposed to have thought that warlike capacities and values were not a sufficient basis for the lasting success of the city. While making the city effective in self-defense and conquest, these warmaking qualities were not of much use in times of peace. Besides, whether at war or peace, Romans needed to be sure that the gods were properly honored (**1.7**; **1.8**). Accordingly, he set about providing the city with the means of living at peace with both the gods and their neighbors. So successful was he in this undertaking that in the words of the historian Livy "Rome's neighbors who once thought of Rome, not as a city but an armed camp disturbing the general peace, now came to revere it as a city wholly dedicated to honoring the gods. Hence, the very idea of doing Rome violence came to be regarded as nothing other than sacrilege."[1]

As is clear, this tradition, like the one represented by Cicero in Chapter 1, is nothing more than a later, ideological, reconstruction of the past. We have little knowledge of what Roman religion was actually like in the Regal Period, and scholars debate how much of the religion of the Republic, of which we know quite an amount, was a carryover from the monarchy or a product of the Republic itself. Livy, the author of the reading on Numa's religious reforms and innovations, represents the intellectually fashionable, late Republic intellectual's viewpoint that

---

[1] Livy 1.21.

religion was originally devised by the elite to keep the ordinary people in line (**4.2**). It was felt that for that reason, if for no other, religion deserved to be cultivated. Setting aside the elite's self-congratulatory view of themselves and their condescending view of religion, we should note that throughout history, with or without the consent of the elite, religion has been the principal means by which ethnic, national, and state identities have been achieved and maintained.

The Institutions of the State Religion (4.2)

There were four major colleges of priests: the Pontiffs (*pontifices*), the Augurs (*augures*), the Ten Men (originally two) for the Performance of Sacred Actions (*Xviri sacris faciundis*), and the Fetials (*fetiales*). There were originally three Pontiffs, but the number later rose to nine. Beginning in the third century, the chief of the pontiffs, the *Pontifex Maximus*, was elected by the people, rather than being chosen by the members of the college, as had been the case in the past. Incidentally, one of the most famous of the Chief Priests was Julius Caesar, which goes to show how thoroughly politics and religion intermingled. The College of Pontiffs also included the three major priests or *Flamines*, those of Jupiter, Mars, and Quirinus, and fifteen minor *flamines*. There was also the King of Rites, the *Rex Sacrorum*, who seems to have been some kind of holdover from regal times and kept his name despite the abolition of the title "king" (*rex*). All these priests held their positions for life. The twelve (originally four) Vestal Virgins served Vesta, the hearth goddess of Rome. They lived in a house beside the Temple of Vesta in the middle of the Forum. They were in some way associated with the College of Pontiffs and came under the jurisdiction of the *Pontifex Maximus*. The general responsibilities of the Pontiffs included the maintenance of the calendar (which tended to get out of step with the solar calendar), the interpretation of the sacred formulae and rules of sacrifice, and the oversight of festivals. When consulted by magistrates they could offer opinions, *decreta* (decrees), but they depended on the officials to put them into force. They had special responsibility for laws relating to burials, adoption, and the inheritance of religious duties.

Every important act, civilian or military, had to be preceded by the taking of auspices or signs from the gods as to the rightness or wrongness of the proposed act. The right to take the *auspices* was reserved to the senior magistrates, but they were assisted by a body of experts, the augurs, who were learned in the interpretation of the will of gods, as revealed by, for example, the flight of birds, how the sacred chickens behaved when feeding, and thunder and lightning.

The Augurs and Fetials (4.3)

The regular taking of the *auspices* (signs) was reserved to those elected magistrates of the Republic who possessed *imperium* (the authority conferred on magistrates by the Roman people), assisted if necessary by the College of Augurs, which consisted of distinguished political figures, usually former magistrates, not professional priests. Cicero, for instance, was an augur; Julius Caesar, was both an augur and a pontifex. The *auspices* had to be taken before any major decision was made, and there was a special spot on the Capitoline Hill, the *auguraculum*, reserved for this purpose. All this was taken so seriously that in the first century B.C., when a Roman noble built a house that blocked the view of the magistrate looking for signs in the sky from the *auguraculum*, the house had to be torn down.

The fetial priests, the *fetiales*, a college of twenty priests, were responsible for the *ius fetiale*, the Fetial Law, which governed Rome's international relations. These priests, like all the other religious functionaries in Rome, had at one and the same time religious, political, and judicial responsibilities reflecting ancient times when the king was the priest, judge, and chief political and military officer of the state. The fetials were on hand to perform rituals involved in the reception of ambassadors, the declaration of war, and the making of treaties. In the case of a declaration of war, for example, a fetial priest entered the territory of the enemy and declared Rome's grievance and demanded a settlement. He called on Jupiter to witness the event and the justice of the Roman claim. If satisfaction was not offered in thirty-three days, the Senate and the People could declare war. This declaration would then be conveyed by the fetial priest to the enemy's frontier where he read the declaration of war. He then, as part of the ritual, hurled a spear across the frontier. This done, the Romans could fight a just war, a *bellum justum*. In the course of time when it became impractical for the priests to travel great distances to perform the spear-throwing ritual, a section of the Forum near the temple of Bellona was set aside ritually as foreign territory, making it easy for the *fetiales* to perform the necessary rituals. Whether the rituals for declaring a just war actually restrained Roman war making is debated. The necessity of performing the rituals had, at least minimally, the effect of making Romans pause long enough to address the issue of whether the gods might or might not approve of the war being contemplated. Given Roman *pietas*, devotion to the gods, this was not an inconsiderable deterrent.

The Family

Throughout most of the Republic, as much as 90 percent of the population was directly involved in agriculture. Most Roman children, male and female alike, were raised with the expectation that they would assist their parents in running the family farm. In due course the children would take over the farm and support their parents in their old age. There were no 401ks, no state-supported health programs, and no Social Security. The property of the family was the sole means of economic sustenance for its members. Only by keeping this property intact and within the family could it hope to survive from one generation to the next. In case of disaster or mismanagement, the members of the family might turn, for temporary assistance, to patrons, neighbors, or kinsmen, but there was no safety net provided by the state.

As the basic unit of Roman society, Roman households were far more powerful institutions than modern families, in terms of both self-policing and economics. Unlike the Roman household which was to a considerable degree autarkic or self-sufficient economically, modern households almost exclusively depend for their existence on the flourishing of the national economy and on services, such as education, provided by the state. In place of the modern term "family," it is more appropriate to use the term "household" to describe the basic unit of the Roman state. A conjugal family unit (a CFU as social scientists call it) of husband, wife, and children, without the accompanying means of support, would not be a true family at all. It is true that the household incorporated a CFU, but other family members—widows, for example, or unmarried relatives—for a period of time during the life cycle of the family, might be members of the household. The household always included a property component that consisted of land, buildings, tools, animals, and, possibly, but not always, slaves. Slaves were fully members of the family. It might include, in addition, *liberti*, freed slaves, and their families. Slaves often had *de facto* (i.e., not *de iure* or recognized by the law) marriages, and so a Roman household could include, in addition to all of the above, the children of slaves, some of whom might be slave and some free. Adding to these complications was the fact that slaves could purchase other slaves, accumulate property, and purchase their own freedom and yet still have obligations to their original masters. Obviously, such situations were characteristic only of elite households, not the households of the majority of Romans.

The Roman family was well equipped by tradition and law to accomplish its tasks. Its heads, the *paterfamilias* and the *materfamilias*, had great power over their offspring (**4.6**). Fathers had legal power vested in them by long tradition, *patria potestas*, but mothers—and grandmothers—also were influential as a result of their positions as matrons in the community. Authority of this kind was something accumulated by years of experience raising children and running households. In some respects, *materna auctoritas* was socially and practically more important than the formal legal power fathers possessed. It has often been said that while the males of a community may make the laws, it is the older females of the community, its matrons, who enforce them. Individually and collectively, the matrons kept their daughters in line and supervised the education of their sons before the father's responsibility of initiating them into public life began. Given the late age at which men married (late twenties and early thirties), the length of time Roman heads of household spent away from home on campaigns or in the forum, and the high numbers lost in battle, the real influence of the senior female members of the household may have been much greater than the strict letter of the law recognized. Many women who were supposed to be under the control of a guardian must have de facto been free to do what they wanted.

The power of the father (*patria potestas*) in a Roman family was unique, unlike that in any other Mediterranean land. The head of the household, i.e., the oldest living male (*paterfamilias*), had literally the power of life or death over his children, although in practice custom placed restrictions on its exercise. This power extended beyond the usual decision as to whether newborns should live or be exposed. In certain circumstances (e.g., in the case of serious sexual offenses such as adultery) the *paterfamilias* could execute his own adult children; in fact, it was his responsibility, not that of the state, to do so. Even married daughters who had committed serious offenses, but whose marriages were of the non-*manus* type (see below under "Marriage"), were handed over to him for judgment. The severity of family discipline should be seen, however, in the context of a society that not only had no police force but actively rejected the idea of one. Policing society was first and foremost a private, family matter, and failure to control one's children was considered shameful to the family as a whole. It was regarded as one of the parents' obligations to the state. Technically it was possible to escape *patria potestas* by a roundabout process called emancipation (*emancipatio*), but this could be done only with parental cooperation, obviously limiting its usefulness.

The *paterfamilias* could decide who his children should marry and, more interestingly, whether they should stay married or get divorced. He owned all the family property; so even his grown sons and grandsons could not, technically, own anything until he died. However, he had no control over the public life of his sons, who might hold higher offices than he had attained. His responsibilities were heavy, for he ruled the household and owned its property not so much for his own gratification as for the benefit of the family, which was regarded as an independent corporate entity with its own traditions, history, religious rituals, and protective deities. The *paterfamilias* was the religious head of the household, as well as its property owner and ruler. He was responsible for the continuity of the family, its name, its burial places, and the cult of its ancestral spirits.

On serious family matters the *paterfamilias* was expected to consult the family council (*consilium*) made up of his wife and senior members of the family. He ran the danger of societal disapproval if he neglected to consult it or went against its recommendations. This was not an insignificant restraint since for Romans respect and family honor were all important. Hence, although technically and legally he had enormous powers, he could exercise these powers only within certain prescribed limits.

Marriage

In the strict (*manus*) form of marriage, the bride was inducted fully into the husband's family and escaped her father's control and came fully under her husband's power (his *manus*, his hand). She worshiped the guardian spirits of his family, and his ancestors became hers. Whatever property she brought with her became his, and if he died, she came under the guardianship of one of his male relatives. This system had a significant impact on the transmission of property. Technically a husband did not owe his wife maintenance; that was the point, among other things, of the dowry. Although a married woman could not own land or property in Italy, she could buy and sell personal goods (such as clothes and jewelry) and land and property as long as they were *outside* Italy.

If the commoner, non-*manus* form of marriage was followed, the wife remained legally within her own family and under the power of her own *paterfamilias*. In this instance, any property she brought with her by way of dowry was hers, and in the case of a divorce or the death of her husband, the property remained hers and reverted to her family. The guardian (the *tutor*), in this instance, would be one of her own kin. Women, unlike men, never escaped guardianship and at least theoretically could never control or dispose of property without the guardian's approval.

The kind of marriage chosen contributed to the degree of a wife's independence. In the second century B.C., the non-*manus* form became more common. This meant that wives remained in control of their own property, which could be quite substantial, especially after they received their share of their paternal inheritance. Husbands would have to think twice before engaging in any action that might bring down on their heads an irate father-in-law or an energetic, well-connected brother-in-law. This legal situation may not have been regarded as an intolerable intrusion in a man's private affairs. Marriage was regarded primarily as the source of legitimate children, and once this function had been served, a husband in an unhappy marriage had plenty of socially tolerated alternatives for his sexual energies. Concubinage was not considered wrong or sinful; slave women and women of lower social status were also available, and liaisons with them were not regarded as threats to the marriage. On the other hand, such associations were not considered wholly proper and a man's reputation could suffer accordingly. Faithfulness to one's wife was always held up as an ideal (**4.7**). For wives, dalliance with male slaves or lower-class males would not be tolerated because it raised the possibility of spurious children and serious challenges to the family name, property, and, most important of all for the upper classes, reputation. The only solution for a wife who found her husband's neglect or philandering intolerable was divorce, which was easy enough. A wife's ability to remedy a problem through the influence of her own family should not be underestimated, however. Seduction of the wives of other citizens always had the potential for serious social disruption and the creation of feuds that passed over into the political arena. Adultery was a serious and dangerous business in such a powerfully structured institution as the Roman household.

Roman Families and Their Slaves

The Roman family often included not just parents and their unmarried children but also their slaves, their freedmen, and the offspring of both. The Romans were liberal in their manumission policies; so in many households, slaves had a good chance of winning their freedom (or, at times, of purchasing it) and becoming Roman citizens. However, even after manumission, family ties persisted. In the eyes of the law, a slave had no father, and on manumission, the freedman took the name of the former owner. For example, when Tiro, the slave of the famous orator M. Tullius Cicero, was freed, he became Marcus Tullius Tiro. Sometimes, the only surviving member of a particular Roman family was a freedman and on him devolved the responsibility for maintaining the family graves and the cult of the ancestral spirits. Often the family burial plot contained the remains of the original family and their freed slaves, all bearing the same family name.

All of this made for great confusion in familial relations. Marriage relations between husband and wife were complicated by the presence of male and female slaves. Slave marriages existed but were not recognized as legal; they had their own complications, which only added to the muddle. There was always the danger that the owner of a slave couple would sell (**4.9**) one of the members of the slave marriage or one of their children, thus creating emotional havoc for the slaves (and possibly also for the master himself or his wife and children). The status of the offspring of such slave relationships was also highly complicated because during the marriage one of the partners might be manumitted. Then what was the status of the children born after that point? What of those born earlier? Or a freedman in a household might begin to consort with a slave woman in a stable relationship and have children by her, leading to yet more legal tangles. The complexities do not end here. Slaves could purchase other slaves. When a male purchased a female slave as a wife, she actually had the status of being a personal slave to her husband, though strictly speaking she belonged to his master because everything a slave owned belonged to the slave's owner. In practice this tactic could have the effect of reducing the likelihood of the slave wife being sold off into another household.

These examples suggest only some of the legal, emotional, and social headaches in Roman families that possessed slaves—a fairly large segment of the population because not only the rich but even the middle classes owned slaves. Also, to balance this fairly benign picture of domestic slavery, it should be added that slavery in rural areas, especially on large estates or in the mines, could take a much harsher form. In the countryside, where slaves worked in chain gangs, there must have been little chance of manumission (**4.9**). There slaves were exploited to the maximum and were often treated with great cruelty, from which there was no escape except flight, death, or, very rarely, revolt.

Clients, Patrons, and Fides (4.5)

Given the importance the Romans attached to the family and the power of the head of the household, it is not surprising that paternalism prevailed throughout the state and greatly influenced political and social relations.

From ancient times certain families and individuals considered themselves the clients (*clientes*) of other families and regarded the heads of these houses as their patrons (*patroni*), with whom they had special ties of a nonlegal, fiduciary kind. Freedmen automatically became the clients of those who had manumitted them, and in a less precise way, great noble households acquired patronship relations with non-Roman communities, cities, and even states, such as those the Sempronii possessed with Spain or those the Fabii possessed with the south of France.

A complicated network of mutual duties and obligations expressed by the Latin term *fides*, or "trustworthiness," bound clients and patrons together and, though not expressed in the terms of formal law, possessed great moral weight.

Patrons had comprehensive obligations toward their clients and were expected to supply such things as legal advice, representation, and, when necessary, political protection. Clients responded appropriately, aiding their patrons in whatever way they could, usually and most conspicuously by their political support and their votes. Neither patron nor client could give evidence against the other in court.

Of all qualities that Romans liked to think were most characteristically Roman, *fides* was probably the most important. The term had broad connotations of credibility and dependability and wide applicability to all Roman social relations. It existed between a man and his friends (*amici*), between upper and lower classes, and even between Rome itself and its various allies and friends. The very word was connected with the term for treaty, *foedus*, from which our own word federal comes, and with belief. *Fides* was one of the abstract deities, like Concord and Piety, that the Romans so liked to venerate and had a temple in the city going back to the most ancient times. It was not a legal but a moral and social concept. It could not be enforced in the courts, and like so much else in the Republic, it depended on custom and the opinion of the community for its enforcement. Understandably, *fides* was an essential aspect of any noble's dealings with his clients or his equals, and Roman self-identity, both individual and national, was closely connected with this concept. Foreign nations or their leaders were criticized for their lack of it, and to impugn a person's *fides* at Rome was very serious business. The strength of the Republic was seen as flowing from the commitment of the different groups of society to this ideal rather than from any formal, legal, or constitutional structure. Obligations and duties (*officia*) were not spelled out in elaborate, ironclad contracts but rather were left to the interpretive moral sensibilities of the parties involved and depended on the changing conditions of day-to-day life.

▼▼▼

4.1   The Twelve Tables: Rome's First Law Code

According to tradition the Twelve Tables, Rome's first law code, was the product of plebeian agitation (2.2) against patrician domination of the judicial process. It was enacted in 451/450 B.C. by a commission of ten men, the decemvirs. *From its content it is clear that what the commission did was codify into statutes existing customary law, but what its aim was is unclear. It may have been an attempt at self-regulation by the elite as much as the result of plebeian pressure for legal equality. In any case, the newly enacted laws constituted the basis for the development of Roman law.*

Whatever the original motivation for the issuance of the laws, the mere fact of their publication was in itself important. Indeed in any society, the first appearance of a code of laws available to the whole community for consultation is usually regarded as a huge leap forward toward the ideal of transparency from a time when the law was the secret possession of an elite class and administered exclusively by that class. The emphasis in the Twelve Tables is on the relations among individuals and reflects a time when Rome was predominantly agricultural and pastoral. Although parts became gradually obsolete, the Twelve Tables were regarded with reverence by later generations of Romans and, according to Cicero, Roman boys were expected to memorize them as part of their education. The original text of the code was destroyed in 390 B.C. at the time of the Celtic invasion. What we have is a version constructed from quotes found in the works of later writers. What follows is not the whole surviving code but selections from it.[2]

Table 1: Rules for Trial

If a plaintiff summons a defendant to court, he is to go. If he refuses to go, the plaintiff shall obtain witnesses to the refusal. Only then shall he take the defendant by force.

If the defendant behaves deceitfully or flees, the plaintiff shall lay hands on him.

If the defendant be impeded by age or disease, the plaintiff shall provide him a means of transportation; if he is unwilling, he does not have to provide a covered carriage.

For a landowner, a landowner shall be a guarantor [*vindex*]; for a proletarian [*a non-landowner*] let anyone who is willing be his *vindex*.

After the parties have arrived at a settlement, the judge shall announce it publicly. If an agreement is not reached, the parties to the case shall present an outline of the issues in the Forum before noon.

Table 2: More Trial Rules

Action under solemn deposit is 500 *asses* when the object of the dispute under solemn deposit is valued at 1,000 *asses*; 50 when less. When the dispute concerns the liberty of an individual, 50 pieces shall be the solemn deposit under which the dispute is to be undertaken.

Whoever needs evidence is to go every third day and shout before the witness' door.

Table 3: Debt

After a debt has been acknowledged or a judgment handed down in court, thirty days' grace is allowed for payment. After that the debtor may be arrested by the laying on of hands. The debtor is to be brought into court. If the debtor does not satisfy judgment in court, or no one offers to stand guarantor [*vindex*] on his behalf, the creditor may take the debtor with him. He may commit him to the stocks or bind him in fetters with weight not more than 15 pounds or with less if he wishes. The debtor may live off his own resources but if he does not the creditor shall give him one pound of wheat per day, or more if he so desires.

Unless a settlement is made the debtor is to be held in bonds for sixty days. He is to be produced before the praetor's court in the meeting place [the *comitium*] on

---

[2]Latin text in E. H. Warmington, *Remains of Old Latin*, Cambridge: Harvard UP, 1937, 3, 424–515.

three successive market days [i.e., every eight days] and the amount he has been judged liable shall be announced. On the third market day the debtor is to be executed or delivered for sale across the Tiber.

On the third market day the debtor' property is to be divided up.

Table 4: *Patria potestas*: Rights of the Father

A badly deformed child shall be killed quickly.

If a father sells his son three times, the son shall be free [of his father's *patria potestas*].

Table 5: Guardianship, Inheritance

Females are to remain in guardianship [in *tutela*] even when they have attained their majority.

Vestal Virgins are exempted from *tutela*.

As a person directs regarding his household goods or guardianship of his estates, this shall be binding.

If a person dies intestate and has no self-successor [*suus heres*],[3] the nearest agnate kinsman shall inherit the deceased's household.

If there is no agnate kinsman, the dead man's clansmen [his *gentiles*] shall inherit.

If a man is a lunatic, his agnates or *gentiles* are to have power over him.

Debt that comes by inheritance is divided proportionally among each heir. Each coheir has the right to sue the debtor automatically after the details have been investigated.

Table 6: Acquisition and Possession

Manumission by testament: A person who has been declared a free man [in a will] on condition that he pay the heir 10,000 pieces, even though he has been sold by the heir, shall obtain his freedom by paying the money to the purchaser.

Acquisition by long time use [*usucapio*] of movable things requires one year's possession for its completion; but *usucapio* of a farm and buildings requires two years.

Marriage by *usucapio*:[4] Any woman who does not wish to be subjected in this manner [i.e., if she does not wish to leave her father's *patria potestas* and come under her husband's jurisdiction, "under his hand, his *manus*"] shall be absent for three nights in succession each year; this interrupts the *usucapio* of each year.

---

[3]A *suus heres* is a person who had been under his father's power (*patria potestas*) until his father's death. Such a person was not regarded as a successor but rather as holding his father's property in common with him. On the death of his father this dormant right becomes active and the *suus heres* is eligible to inherit. The case here is if there is no *suus heres*.

[4]What we would call common law marriage, i.e., the state of marriage is deemed by law to exist after a certain period of cohabitation has elapsed. In the case of *usucapio*, the woman after one year's cohabitation is transferred to her husband's household from her father's.

Table 7: Land Ownership

A five foot strip of land between properties shall not be acquired by long usage [*usucapio*].

The width of a road is to be eight feet except at a bend where it is to be sixteen.

If rainwater does damage it must be contained according to the arbitrator's [*arbiter*] order.

Overhanging branches of a tree may be cut off to a height of more that 15 feet.

It is permitted to collect fruit that has fallen down [off one's own tree] on another man's farm.

Table 8: Torts

If the defendant has broken the bone of a free man the penalty is to be 300 *asses* [a copper coin]; if a slave's, 150 *asses*.[5]

If a four-footed animal has caused loss, legal action may be taken. Either the animal which did the damage shall be surrendered or else compensation for the damages shall be provided.

Anyone who burns any building or heap of grain along side it shall be bound, lashed, and burned to death if the act was done with malice aforethought. If the act was committed by negligence, the offender is to repair the damage; if he is too poor to do this, he is to be assessed a lighter penalty.

If the defendant has cut down a fruit tree, the penalty is 25 *asses*.

A person found guilty of giving false testimony shall be thrown down from the Tarpeian Rock.

No person shall hold meetings by night in the city.

Table 9: Public Law

Laws of exception[6] [*privilegia*] are not to be proposed. Cases in which the penalty affects the person or privileges of a person [the *caput*, the "head" of the individual] are not to be decided except as a result of the deliberation of the full assembly.

A legally appointed judge or an arbiter who is convicted of having taken a bribe shall be put to death.

A person who has not been convicted shall not be put to death.

---

[5]Coinage was not used by Rome to any extent until the third century B.C. The original *as*, a bronze coin, weighed a pound. It was gradually reduced in size, until toward 200 B.C. it weighted only 2 ounces and became the subunit of the silver denarius which was worth 10 *asses*. The denarius remained the coinage of Rome for the next 400 years. The 2 oz. *as* ceased to be produced after 157 B.C. In its place were smaller bronze coins, sixteen of which made up a denarius. Each of these coins, known as a *sestertius*, was equivalent to 2.5 *asses*.

[6]This is an important civil right. These laws are also known as bills of attainder. Such laws referred only to a specific citizen (whether in his favor or not) and not the whole community.

Table 10: Sacred Law

A dead man shall not be buried or cremated within the city.

Women are not to tear their cheeks or keen at a funeral.

There is to be no expensive sprinkling at funerals [e.g., with wine], no drinks spiced with myrrh, no long garlands, and no incense boxes.

A person may bury or cremate a person whose teeth were fastened together with gold without penalty.

Table 11: Additional Laws

There shall be no intermarriage between plebeians and patricians.

Table 12: Additional Laws

If a slave has committed theft or done injury with his owner's knowledge, the action for damages will be in the name of the slave.

In the case of damages committed by children or the slaves of a household, actions for damage [*actiones noxales*] allows the father or slave owner to either undergo assessment for damages or hand over the offender [*noxa*] for punishment.

If someone has acquired something by a false claim, he may request that three arbitrators be appointed; by their judgment the defendant must pay double the usufruct of the item.

4.2   Roman Religion

According to ancient tradition, the second king of Rome, Numa Pompilius, 715–673 B.C., was the framer of the religion of the state, instituting reforms of the calendar and founding cults, rituals, and priesthoods. He claimed to have received direct instructions on these activities from the nymph or water goddess Egeria whom he met in a grove sacred to the Muses. According to this tradition Numa thus became a cofounder with Romulus of Rome or a second founder. Romulus, Livy points out in this reading, provided the necessary state institutions that enabled Rome to wage war successfully; Numa equipped the Romans to be also able to keep the peace: "Thus two successive kings, one by one method, the other by another—the one by war, the other by peace—magnified the city. . . . Having mastered the twin arts of war and peace, Rome was as eminent for self-mastery as for military strength."[7] *The warlike character of Rome needed to be restrained by a healthy fear of the gods—a trait that characterized Roman culture throughout its history. Hence, although Livy's stories about Numa are fictions, the substance of what he has to say about Roman religion was factual.*[8]

---

[7]Livy 1.21.
[8]Livy 1.19–21.

Romulus had founded Rome by violence and arms; Numa now gave it a fresh start, a second founding on the basis of law and customs. He saw, however, that these reforms could never take hold as long as the people were accustomed to constant warfare, for war generated passion and the high spirit of the Romans could only be tamed by the setting aside of arms. He therefore built a temple to Janus at the foot of the Argiletum to serve as a sign of peace and war. When the temple was open this indicated that the city was at war; when it closed, it indicated that all the surrounding people had been pacified. Since the time of Numa the temple has been closed twice, once during the consulship of Titus Manlius at the end of the first war with Carthage [241 B.C.], and again in our time when the gods allowed us to witness the event. This was after the battle of Actium [31 B.C.] when Augustus Caesar brought peace both on land and sea. Numa himself closed the temple after securing peace by means of good will and treaties with Rome's neighbors.

Now that the dangers of attack from without had been averted Numa was concerned that with the fear of enemies removed moral flabbiness, which had been restrained by military discipline, might flourish. Hence he decided that the inculcation of fear of the gods would be the best way to keep the rough and ignorant people of those times in line. Such an endeavor was not likely to be successful unless it was accompanied by something spectacular, and so he gave out the story that he met with the goddess Egeria by night. It was her authority that guided him in the creation of the kinds of rituals that would be acceptable to the gods, and the types of priests needed to serve individual gods.

He first divided the year into twelve lunar months. . . . Secondly, he determined what days would be lawful [*dies fasti*] and which should be unlawful [*dies nefasti*] for the conduct of public business, for he saw that it would be good policy to have some days when no measures could be brought before the people.

Next he turned his attention to the appointment of priests although most of the ceremonies, especially those now presided over by the Flamen Dialis [*priest of Jupiter*], he kept in his own hands. He anticipated that a warlike people like the Romans would more often have kings like Romulus than himself and that such kings would be often away from home on campaign. Hence he appointed a permanent Priest of Jupiter and invested him with special robes and allowed him the use of the royal curule chair [an ivory inlaid chair restricted to the highest magistrates such as consuls]. This guaranteed that the sacred rituals of Jupiter would not be neglected. In addition to the Flamen Dialis, two other Flamines or priesthoods were created, one to Mars and the other Quirinus.

He instituted the Vestal Virgins, a cult familiar to Numa, that originated in Alba [a nearby town]. These priestesses were supported out of public funds so that they could devote full time to the temple service. He made these services holy and venerable by imposing virginity on the priestesses and by attaching other rituals. Numa introduced the twelve Salii or Leaping Priests in honor of Mars Gradivus. They were wore an embroidered tunic and a bronze cuirass over it. Their special duty was to carry the sacred shields (called *ancilia*) through the city chanting hymns in a leaping dance. These shields were supposed to have fallen from heaven.

Next Numa appointed the patrician Numa Marcius, son of Marcus, as Pontifex [priest]. He gave him complete instruction in writing on all matters sacred. These included instructions on what, when and where the various sacrifices should be conducted. He also specified how the sacrifices were to be paid for. He made all public and private sacred observances subject to the dictate of the Pontifex so that there should be someone for ordinary people to consult if they had need. He also wished to avoid the confusion that might result from the neglect of native Roman rites and the importation of foreign ones. The Pontiff was made responsible not only for divine rituals but also such matters as the proper forms for the burial of the dead; how to placate the spirits of the departed; and how to identify what portents [*prodigia*] manifested by lightning and other signs were to be recognized and acted upon. In order to obtain divine guidance on this subject, he consecrated an altar to Jupiter Elicius ["*Jupiter from whom signs can be elicited*"] on the Aventine Hill, and consulted by augury this deity on what signs should be noted and observed.

Having to think of and take care of so many new things, the multitude was distracted from their military preoccupations. They now had something else to occupy their minds, namely responsibility for divine worship. And since they had come to believe that the heavenly powers were involved in human affairs they became imbued with religious concern [*pietas*]. As a result, the trustworthiness [*fides*] and the holiness of an oath began to have more influence on the city than the laws and punishment for crime. Men took the king as their only model and reformed their habits, so much so that neighboring people who once thought of Rome, but not so much as a city as a threatening armed camp in their midst, inciting against the general peace, now came to see the city as one dedicated to the worship of the gods. To attack it would be unholy [*nefas*].

Thus two successive kings, Romulus by one method and Numa by another—the one by war, the other by peace—had magnified the city. . . . Having mastered the twin arts of war and peace, Romans were as eminent for self-mastery as for military prowess.

4.3   Augury in Action: The Choice of Numa

Cicero, himself a member of the college of augurs, wrote that "the highest and most important authority in the state" was that of the augurs (Laws 2.12). Numa was the first king approved by the taking of auguries whose rituals were performed at the Auguraculum, on the summit of the Capitoline Hill. The generic term templum *was given to a place set aside and marked out by ritual formulas for the purpose of taking auguries, i.e., signs indicating the will of the gods. Originally, these signs were the flight of birds, but later, thunder and lightning, the feeding behavior of the sacred chickens, and the behavior of four footed animals were considered acceptable.*[9]

When summoned to Rome, Numa ordered that the gods be consulted on his selection just as Romulus had originally consulted them on the inauguration of the city. He was led accordingly by an augur to the citadel and made to sit on a stone facing south. Thereafter, the augurate was made a permanent priesthood as a mark of honor.

---

[9]Livy 1.18.

With head covered, the augur seated himself to the left of Numa. In his right hand he held the *lituus*, a staff without a knot in it. Looking over the city and the countryside beyond he prayed to the gods and marked off the heavens by a line from east to west. The regions to the south were designated "right" and those to the north as "left." He fixed his eye on a distant point and noted it mentally. Then, transferring the *lituus* to his left hand, he put his right hand on Numa's head and offered this prayer: "Father Jupiter, if it be right [*fas*] that this man, Numa Pompilius, on whose head I have my hand, should become king of Rome, give us certain signs within the boundaries I have set." He then spoke the auspices [*auspicia*] which he desired and, on being granted them, declared Numa king and descended from the augural station [the *templum*].

4.4 "Secret Rites Performed at Night": The Bacchanalian Conspiracy

The separation of church and state is regarded as a characteristic of the modern secular state. For the Romans, however, as for all ancient peoples, such an idea was unthinkable. Indeed, the practice of private rituals not approved by the state or ancient tradition was thought to undermine family tradition, weaken the state, and offend the established gods. The historian Livy provides the following account of a crisis in 186 B.C. over the introduction of the cult of Dionysus. In trying to save his hero Aebutius' reputation while at the same time turning the prostitute Hispala Faecenia into a model Roman, Livy engages in some twisted and unconvincing logic.[10]

In the next year the consuls Spurius Postumius Albinus and Quintus Marcius Philippus were distracted from their military and administrative duties in the provinces by the need to put down an internal conspiracy. . . . [The movement began with] a lowborn Greek, who first appeared in Etruria. He had none of the culture that the Greek people—that most gifted nation—brought to us for the cultivation of mind and body, but was a mere manipulator of sacrifices and prophecies. Nor was he the kind that fill men's minds with error by publicly announcing their beliefs, but rather an initiator into secret rites, performed at night.

At first the rituals were known only to a few, but then they began to spread widely among both men and women. The pleasures of drinking and partying were added to religion to attract a larger number of people. With the people inflamed by drink and darkness, and the mix of men and women, of young and old, every moral scruple disappeared. All sorts of evils began to be practiced since each had the opportunity to do what he or she was most prone by nature to do. There was not just one kind of vice; free men and women had promiscuous sex; perjured witnesses forged seals and wills and evidence; from the same source came poisonings and secret murders, such that at times not even the bodies were to be found for burial. . . .

---

[10]Livy 39.8–12.

This evil spread from Etruria to Rome like a contagious disease. Early on, the size of the city, with its anonymity and tolerance for such evils, hid it, but eventually the consul Postumius caught wind of the evil. It happened this way.

Publius Aebutius, whose father had been a knight, was left in the care of guardians, but when they died he came under the guardianship of his mother, Duronia, and his stepfather, Titus Sempronius Rutilus. His mother was captivated by her husband Titus, Aebutius' stepfather, but Titus so completely mismanaged Publius' estate that he was unable to give a proper account of it to the court, and he decided he had to either get rid of his ward Publius or attach him to himself in some compromising way. He settled on the method of the Bacchanalian rituals.

Duronia claimed to her son that when he was sick she had vowed that if he recovered she would initiate him in the Bacchic rites. Now, since by the kindness of the gods he had recovered, she wished to fulfill her vow. . . .

Duronia's Plot, However, is Foiled.

There was a well-known prostitute, a freed woman by the name of Hispala Faecenia. She was really much better than a prostitute, but as a slave she had been initiated into the profession and after manumission continued to support herself in this way. She and Aebutius became lovers, since they lived in the same neighborhood. This did no damage to either his reputation or his possessions: he had been loved and sought out, and since his relatives provided so poorly for him he was maintained by the generosity of Hispala. Hispala went further: after the death of her patron, because she was under no one's legal control, she requested a guardian from the tribunes and praetor and, impelled by her love for Aebutius, she made him her sole heir.

Aebutius tells Hispala of his mother's plans to have him initiated into the Bacchic rites. She warns him not to let this happen. When she had been a slave, she explains, she, together with her mistress, had been initiated into the cult and had seen the horrible things the Bacchants did to new members. He agrees with her and refuses to be initiated. The plot thickens. His mother and stepfather become enraged, and in order to protect himself against reprisals, Aebutius seeks help from his aged aunt Aebutia. On her advice he goes to the consul Postumius and tells him everything. The consul is unsure whether he can trust Aebutius' fantastic story.

The consul dismissed Aebutius and told him to return three days later. In the meantime he asked his respected mother-in-law Sulpicia if she knew the elderly lady Aebutia, Aebutius' aunt, who lived on the Aventine. She replied that she did: Aebutia was a good, old-fashioned woman. Postumius then decided he needed to meet with Aebutia and asked Sulpicia to invite her to her home. Aebutia came and then, as if by chance, the consul also came by and inquired casually about Aebutius, her nephew. She broke down in tears and began to bewail the young man's fate. He had been robbed of his inheritance, she said, by those who, least of all, should have treated him this way. He had then been driven from his home because this upstanding young man—may the gods be forgiving—had refused to be initiated into what were said to be immoral rites.

Postumius, thinking that he could now trust Aebutius' story, has his dependable mother-in-law Sulpicia arrange a meeting with Hispala. After a certain amount of arm-twisting the consul gets the whole story of the Bacchanalia out of Hispala, who, though afraid to reveal the sacred mysteries of Bacchus (another name for the god Dionysus), was (rightly) even more afraid of the consul's power. The consul prudently had Hispala, her slaves, and her household gods moved into Sulpicia's house and had Aebutius move into the house of one of his own clients. With his key witnesses in safety, Postumius was now free to go public with the problem. First the Senate was informed. After debate it decided to investigate the matter and, in the meantime, to end new initiations, to stop celebrations of the rituals, and to keep the priests under surveillance. Next the consuls called an informal meeting of the people (a contio) to tell them of the affair and to give the official line on the practice of Roman religion. What follows is part of Livy's version of the speech of one of the consuls. The speech follows the usual invocations and prayers.

"Citizens: Never in any meeting has the solemn prayer to the gods been not only so suitable but also necessary. This prayer reminds us that these are the gods our ancestors appointed to be worshipped, venerated, and prayed to; they are not the kinds of gods who would lead our befuddled minds with their vile and alien rituals, as though stimulated by the furies, to commit every crime and indulge every lust. I do not know how much I should keep secret and how much I should reveal to you. On the one hand, if you are left ignorant of anything, I may be being neglectful. On the other, if I tell you all, I fear I may excite excess terror. Whatever I say, be sure that my words are less than the awfulness and seriousness of the situation. It is our job to take sufficient precautions.

"Both from rumor and from the shouts and howlings you have heard throughout the city, you know that the Bacchanalia has been celebrated all over Italy and even in Rome. Nevertheless, I feel certain you do not know what the Bacchanalia really is. Some regard it as a cult of the gods; others believe that it is an acceptable kind of play and sport, and that in any case, it concerns only a few. As regards this last point, if I were to tell you there were thousands of them, you would be terrified, unless I were to tell you what kind of people they are.

"First, many of them are women, and they are the source of the evil. But there are men who are as bad as the women, debauched and debauchers, fanatical, with their senses dulled by partying and wine, and with the noise and shouts of night. At this point the conspiracy has no strength, but it grows significantly day by day. Your ancestors did not wish that even you should casually assemble unless the emergency signal was displayed on the citadel and the army gathered for a meeting, or the tribunes had called the Council of the Plebs, or some magistrate an informal meeting. Our ancestors thought that wherever there was a crowd gathered, there should also be a legitimate leader present. What kind of meetings do you think these nightly gatherings are? What of the meetings of men and women?"

The speech goes on at length to reveal the supposed evils of the Bacchants and to excite the fears of the people by claiming that the real intent of the practitioners of the new cult was the take-over of the state. However, the main point of the speech was to assert traditional aristocratic ideological claims and convince the people to accept without debate the Senate's decree suppressing and controlling the Bacchanals.

"How often in the time of our fathers and grandfathers was the responsibility given to the magistrates of forbidding foreign cults, keeping manipulators of sacrifices and prophets away from the Forum, searching out and destroying books of prophecies, and suppressing all sacrificial rituals except those performed in the Roman way. Men most skilled in divine and human law judged that nothing was so destructive of religion as sacrifices performed according to alien, not native practice.

"I considered that this warning should be given to you so that you will not be concerned by religious scruples when you see us suppressing the Bacchanalia and breaking up their nightly meetings. All these things, the gods being kind and willing, we will do. It is because the gods are indignant that their majesty was being contaminated by crimes and acts of lust that these matters have been dragged out of darkness into the light of day. . . ."

The "conspiracy" was in due course brutally repressed with out-of-hand executions in Rome and Italy. Regulations were laid down for the future practice of the cult. Special permission for its practice had to be obtained, and it was then allowed only under certain restrictive conditions. The hero and heroine of the event, Publius Aebutius and Hispala Faecenia, were rewarded with large amounts of money and special legal privileges. Livy leaves it to the reader to decide whether Publius and Hispala got married, though he does give a hint by saying that one of the privileges accorded to Hispala was the decree that no disgrace would be incurred by a freeborn man should he marry her.

4.5   Patricians and Plebeians, Patrons, and Clients

Dionysius of Halicarnassus, a contemporary of the historian Livy (ca. 30 B.C.), gives the following rosy account of Romulus' creation of the institutions of patricians and plebeians, patrons, and clients. The latter institution still functioned in his day as an important aspect of Roman social life.[11]

[Romulus] divided those who were distinguished by birth, virtue, and wealth (at least to the extent it was possible to speak of wealth in those simpler times) . . . from the obscure, the humble, and the poor. Those who belonged to this latter group he called "plebeians" . . . and those of the higher rank "fathers" . . . and their descendants "patricians." After Romulus had divided higher from lower ranks, he established laws specifying the responsibilities of each. The patricians were to be priests, officeholders, and judges and to help him in the running of the state, devoting themselves to the city. The plebeians were freed from these responsibilities, because they were inexperienced

---

[11]Dionysius of Halicarnassus, *Roman Antiquities*, 2.8–10.

in these affairs and because their lack of means did not give them the free time to devote to them. They were to work the land, herd, and engage in useful trades. . . .

He [*Romulus*] gave the plebeians as a trust to the patricians, allowing each plebeian to choose for his patron any patrician he wanted. . . . He promoted the relationship by giving it a proper name, calling the protection of the poor and humble a "patronage." By assigning useful mutual services to each he made the coupling of the two both friendly and political. . . .

It was the duty of patrons to their clients to explain the laws of which they might not have knowledge; to care for them whether they were themselves absent or present, doing everything for them that fathers do for their children in business affairs and contracts; to bring suit on behalf of clients wronged in matters of contracts, and to defend them against those who brought charges against them. In brief, it was the duty of patrons to obtain for their clients in both private and public affairs all that security they most needed. Clients in turn were supposed to help their patrons in providing dowries for their daughters at marriage time if the fathers lacked the means; to pay ransom to an enemy if they or their children were taken prisoner; to pay out of their own resources the losses of their patrons in private as well as public suits, not as loans but as gifts; to share, as though they were family relatives, the costs involved in their public offices and positions and other state-related expenditures.

For patrons and clients alike it was sacrilegious as well as against tradition to accuse each other in lawsuits, to testify or vote against each other, or to be counted with each other's enemies. . . . As a result, the coupling of clients and patrons continued over generations, being no different from the ties of blood relations. The bonds were handed down to their children's children. It was a matter of great renown for the famous families to have as many clients as possible, to preserve the succession of hereditary patronages, and to acquire others by their own merit. It is amazing how great a contest in good will there was between patrons and clients, each striving not to be outdone by the other in kindness. . . .

4.6 *Patria Potestas* and *Materna Auctoritas*: The Power of Fathers and Mothers over their Children

Dionysius also ascribes the institution of patria potestas *to Romulus. Although considerably softened by the passage of centuries, the power of fathers over their children was still enormous. Dionysius begins by criticizing Greek lawmakers for the "mild punishments which were not adequate to restrain the foolishness of youth" and noting by contrast the sternness of Romulus' legislation in this area.*[12]

But the Roman legislator [*Romulus*] gave, so to say, all power to the father over his son, and this power continued throughout the son's life. The *paterfamilias* could

---

[12]Dionysius, *Roman Antiquities* 2.26.

imprison his son, whip him, put him to work in chains in the fields, execute him. This was true even when the son was already involved in politics, even if he had held the highest magistracies and was honored for his services to the state. . . . [*Romulus*] allowed the *paterfamilias* to sell his son. . . . For anyone educated in the loose ways of the Greeks the following would seem harsh and tyrannical: he permitted the father to make a profit by selling his son as often as three times! In this way he gave greater power to a father over his son than to a master over his slaves, for a slave once sold, and then obtaining his freedom, is his own master thereafter. . . .

This law was observed by the kings in the beginning, though whether it was written or unwritten I cannot say. They thought it was the best of laws. And when the kings were overthrown and the Romans first decided to make public in the Forum for the review of the citizens all the ancestral customs and laws . . . they recorded it among the rest. It now appears in the fourth of the so-called Twelve Tables which they set up at that time in the Forum.

In the absence of a father, however, the mother's authority, materna auctoritas, was an important substitute. An example of this was the role played by Cornelia, after the death of her husband, in the education of her sons, the famous revolutionary tribunes Tiberius and Gaius Gracchus. She was so popular with the people that after her death a bronze statue of her was erected with the inscription: "Cornelia, Mother of the Gracchi."[13]

[*After her husband's death*] Cornelia took charge of the children and the household and showed herself so sound and affectionate a mother and so constant a widow . . . that when King Ptolemy offered to share his crown with her and wanted to marry her, she refused and chose rather to live as a widow. In this state she continued and lost all her children except one daughter, who was married to Scipio the Younger, and two sons, Tiberius and Gaius. . . . Cornelia raised these sons with such care that although they were indisputably first among their peers in terms of natural endowments, they were thought to owe their excellence more to her education than to nature.

It is reported that Cornelia bore the loss of her two sons with a noble and undaunted spirit. She said of the sacred places where her sons had been slain [*Tiberius was assassinated on the Capitoline Hill of Rome, and Gaius in the grove of the Furies across the Tiber from the city*] that their dead bodies were worthy of such tombs. She moved afterwards and lived near the place called Misenum but made no change in her usual way of living. She had many friends and hospitably received many strangers at her house; many Greeks and learned men were continually about her. All the kings exchanged gifts with her. Her visitors and those who lived with her were entertained by her stories about her father, Scipio Africanus, and his way of life, but they were moved to admiration when she reminisced with inquirers about her sons without grief or tears and spoke of their deeds and sufferings as though she were narrating the history of some ancient heroes.

---

[13]Plutarch, *Tiberius Gracchus* 1; *Gaius Gracchus* 19.

4.7   Marriage: Legalities and Realities

The legal complications of marriage forms, especially where they concern property, are revealed in the following glowing encomium, recorded as an inscription put up by a husband to honor his wife, Turia, after the civil wars at the end of the Republic. The inscription also says much about the relationship between husband and wife among the upper classes at the end of the Republic.[14]

Before the day of our marriage you were suddenly left an orphan when your parents were murdered in an isolated country district. It was, however, principally through your efforts that your parents' deaths did not remain unavenged. Indeed, I had already left for Macedonia and Gaius Cluvius, your brother-in-law, was on his way to Africa. You were so vigorous in pursuing this holy duty . . . that even if we had been present ourselves we could not have done any more. . . .

While you were attending to these affairs, and after the murderers had been punished, you left your father's house to protect your reputation. You went to my mother's house where you waited for me to return. At that time you were pressured to declare that your father's will, in which we were both named as his heirs, was invalid. The alleged grounds were that he had taken his wife in the strict form of marriage (*manus*) by the process of fictitious sale (*coemptio*).

This would have necessitated that you and all your father's property revert to the guardianship (*tutela*) of the people who were making this claim (*presumably kin on her father's side*). Nothing would have been inherited by your sister because she had gone from the control of her father to that of her husband, Cluvius. Although I was not there at the time, I heard about the courage with which you listened to their proposals and the circumspect way in which you rejected them.

The aim of the litigants was to get control of the sizable fortune Turia inherited by forcing her into a guardianship (tutela) where she would have been under their thumb. She resisted vigorously, threatening to include her sister in the estate and claiming that, legally, she could not be forced into the proposed guardianship. The claimants backed off. The inscription continues.

Marriages of such length, broken by death rather than divorce, are truly unusual. Our marriage lasted for forty-one years in true happiness. My only wish is that our union had come to its final end through *my* death. It would have been more just for me, as the older partner, to have yielded to fate.

Do I need to recall your special qualities? You were chaste, deferential, sociable, easy to get on with, faithful to your wool-working. You respected the gods without being too devout. You dressed well, being elegant rather than fussy. . . . By our common household management we kept the whole of the inheritance you got from your parents. You gave it all to me, not being concerned with the care of increasing

---

[14]*Inscriptiones Latinae Selectae* 8393.

it. We thus shared the task of administering our property in such a way that I protected your fortune and you guarded mine. . . .

You were generous toward your many relatives. . . . You brought some of your worthy female relatives up in our home. So that they might maintain a social status appropriate to the rank of your family, you gave them dowries. . . .

You helped me to escape by selling your jewelry and giving me all your gold and the pearls you had on your person. . . . I was saved by your advice. You did not allow me to face danger recklessly through overly bold plans, but discreetly provided a safe house for me, choosing as your helpers . . . your sister and her husband, Gaius Cluvius. Were I to go into all these matters, I would go on forever. It is sufficient to say that your plans ensured my safety.

When the world was once again at peace and the Republic restored, we in turn enjoyed peaceful and happy times. We longed for children, which envious Fate had denied us. If Fortune had smiled on us in the ordinary way, what would we have lacked? But age put an end to these hopes. . . .

Despairing of your own fertility and distressed at seeing me without children, you spoke of divorce . . . offering to hand over your house to another, fertile, spouse. . . . You said you would consider the children as shared, and as if they were your own; there would be no division of property, which up until now had been shared in common. . . .

I must admit that I was so angry that I was beside myself, so horrified at your suggestion that I could scarcely control myself. The idea that divorce could have been discussed before Fate had intervened, or that while you were still alive you could think of anything that would have made you cease to be my wife!

But by Fate's decree your course was run before mine. You left me the grief, the longing for you, the sad fate to live alone. . . .

4.8   "A Wife without a Dowry is Under her Husband' Thumb"

The comedies of the playwrights Plautus and Terence are major sources of information about family life in the Republic. Although the original models were Greek, much of the detail, color, and emphasis are Roman. Dowries had many functions. Marriages were often used to solidify alliances among families; so the giving of a dowry was an important part of political and economic as well as social life. Dowries also helped to ensure that the bride would be properly treated in the new household and, in the event of divorce, would have something to fall back on. But there were other, less obvious effects. Here, Euclio overhears the soliloquy of Megadorus (his future son-in-law) on the subject of dowries and their effect on marriage.[15]

MEGADORUS: I've disclosed my marriage plans to all my friends. They're full of praise for Euclio's daughter. Great idea! Smart move! they say. And they're right. Indeed, if the rest of our well-heeled population would follow my example and

---

[15]Plautus, *Pot of Gold* 375–535.

marry poor men's dowry-less daughters, there would be a lot more peace in the city. For one, we would be less envied by the poor—and our wives would respect us a bit more! It would be cheaper too. Most people would welcome the idea; the only opposition would come from that greedy handful who are so grasping and insatiable that neither law nor custom can control them. If you ask, however, "Who are the rich women *with* dowries going to marry if the poor are to have this right?" the answer is: "Let them marry whom they please, *provided the dowry doesn't go with them!*" In that case they'll bring better morals than they do now, instead of money. . . .

EUCLIO: Incredible! How well he speaks of thrift!

MEGADORUS: Then you'd never hear a wife saying: "I brought you a dowry larger than all your property, so I have a right to fine clothes, jewelry, maidservants, mules, coachmen and footmen, errand boys, and carriages to ride in.

EUCLIO: Ah, well he knows society wives! I'd like to see him made censor of women's morals.

MEGADORUS: Nowadays, wherever you go there are more carts in front of town houses than you'd find in a farmyard! And that's nothing compared to what you'll see when the bill collectors show up! Here's the dry cleaner, the embroiderer, the jeweler, the wool merchant; the dealer in flounces, underwear, bridal veils, violet and yellow dyes. There are muff makers and makers of perfumed foot gear; lingerie merchants, shoemakers, slipper makers, sandal makers, and leather stainers, all waiting to be paid. And when you've paid these, another three hundred show up: weavers and lace makers, cabinetmakers and bag makers—all wanting you to settle up. You pay them—is that the lot? What more?

EUCLIO: I'd interrupt him but I'm afraid he'd stop talking about the ways of women. I'll let him go on.

MEGADORUS: When all this rubbish has been paid off, in comes the soldier, demanding the army tax. You consult with your banker while the soldier stands by, missing his lunch; unfortunately, you find you owe the banker money—you're overdrawn! . . . These are just some of the problems and expenses that go with large dowries; and there are others. On the other hand, a wife without a dowry is under a husband's thumb; it's the ones with dowries that make their husbands' lives miserable with their squandering.

4.9 "Sell Worn-Out Oxen . . . Old and Sick Slaves"

Like all ancient societies, Romans accepted slavery as an inevitable aspect of life. People became slaves because the economy was bad, or because they ended up on the wrong side of a war, or just through bad luck. Because it was an accepted part of life, Roman society developed ways of dealing with it on a day-to-day basis that in some ways lessened its most awful features. On manumission, for instance, a slave received citizenship, and within a generation, his or her descendants could have become indistinguishable from the rest of Roman society. Race was not a factor. Slaves could make money and purchase their freedom. Rich masters showed their liberality by freeing slaves. Not that these events changed the nature of slavery itself. Slaves in mines or on ranches had little chance of manumission and were often treated brutally. Shepherd slaves, on the other hand, had more freedom (of a sort) than did most other kinds of slaves. Obviously, much (if not every-thing) depended on what kind of masters or mistresses slaves had. A slave who had the bad luck to draw the profit-motivated Cato as a master would not have had much to look forward to.[16]

After the owner (the *paterfamilias*) has arrived at his ranch and prayed to the god of the household, he should make a tour of the farm, if possible that very day; if not, the next. After he has learned how the farm has been worked and knows what has been done and what hasn't, he should call the slave foreman of the farm and ask what jobs are finished and how much remains, and whether they were done on time, and whether it is possi-ble to finish the rest, and what's the situation with the wine, grain, and other products.

When he knows all this he should make a calculation on the amount of labor and time involved. Then, if the amount of work doesn't seem satisfactory, and the man-ager claims that he tried his best but that the slaves were no good, the weather was bad, the slaves had run away, he had work to do for the state—when he has given all these excuses and many others, produce *your* estimate of the amount of work done and the workers involved. Remind him what kind of work could have been done on rainy days: storage jars could have been washed and tarred, the farm buildings cleaned, grain moved, manure cleared out and a manure pit made, the seed cleaned, the ropes fixed and new ones made . . . on festivals they might have cleaned out old ditches, worked on the public highway, cut brambles, dug a garden, cleared a meadow. . . .

The owner should check the herd and hold a sale. If the price is right, sell the oil; surplus wine and grain should also be sold. Sell the worn-out oxen, the sub-par cat-tle and sheep, wool, hides, the old wagon, worn-out tools, the old slave, the sick slave, and anything else that is superfluous. An owner should be a seller, not a buyer.

4.10   The Economics of Farming

By the late Republic, a sophisticated agricultural economy had developed in Italy. It contrasted sharply with the old system of self-sufficient small farming that preceded it. In this reading the author, a contemporary of Julius Caesar, offers common-sense advice to well-to-do Romans looking for respectable but profitable investments.[17]

Farms that have suitable means of getting their products to the markets and obtain-ing in return the things they need are profitable for these reasons. Many landlords, for instance, have farmsteads which, because they do not themselves produce grain and wine, need to import these commodities; on the other hand, some have estates that produce goods that need to be exported. Hence, it is profitable to have large-scale

---

[16]Cato, *On Agriculture* 2.
[17]Varro, *On Agriculture* 1.16.

gardens near a city, producing, for instance, violets and roses and many other products for which there is a demand in the city. On the other hand, it makes no sense to grow these items on a distant estate, far from any suitable market.

Likewise, if there are towns and villages nearby, or even well-cultivated lands and estates of rich owners, from which you can buy at reasonable prices whatever you need for your own farm, and to which in turn you can sell your surplus, such as poles or reeds, the farm will be more profitable than if you had to import them from a distance. It may even be cheaper to do this than to produce them yourself. It is for this reason that small farmers like to have in their neighborhood people such as doctors and fullers and other skilled tradesmen with whom they have a yearly contract. This is better than having these skilled people on their own farms, for the death of one such craftsman can wipe out the farms' profitability. . . .

Access to transportation makes a farm more profitable, such as roads suitable for carts or a river navigable by boats. Goods are brought to and from many estates by both these methods. The way in which your neighbors maintain the land on your common boundary is also important. For example, if he has an oak grove along the boundary, you cannot plant olives alongside it since the two do not get along.

▼▼▼

Questions

1. If a defendant in a trial failed to show up in court, did the plaintiff have any recourse? (**4.1**)
2. In case a person died without designating an heir, who could succeed to the estate? (**4.1**)
3. How did a wife avoid coming under the strict (or *manus*) form of marriage? (**4.1**)
4. What compensation was available in the case of personal injury? (**4.1**)
5. The second king of Rome, Numa, is credited with making some key additions to Roman constitutional and cultural practices. What were these and why did he devise them? (**4.2**)
6. The Romans were highly suspicious of meetings held in secret (or at night) as we learn both from the twelve tables and the Bacchanalian Conspiracy. Why do you think this was the case? (**4.4**)
7. What were the reciprocal obligations of patrons and clients? (**4.5**)
8. How long did a father's power (*patria potestas*) continue over his children and in what did it consist? (**4.6**)
9. What was *materna auctoritas* and how did it differ from *patria potestas*? (**4.6**)
10. How would you characterize the marriage described in 4.7 "Marriage Legalities and Realities."
11. What power did a dowry give to a wife? (**4.8**)
12. According to Varro, writing in the late Republic, what were some of the conditions necessary for a farm to be successful in a market economy? (**4.10**)

Chapter 5

▼▼▼

The Roman Revolution

Just at the moment that the Romans had eliminated all threats to themselves in the Mediterranean, their own social, cultural, and political system began to disintegrate. Beginning in 133 B.C. with the murder of the tribune Tiberius Gracchus, Rome went through a century of civil and military turmoil. Modern historians have called the period the Roman Revolution. Perhaps the event is best explained generically as the painful—but interesting—transition of a city-state to a world-state. If this is an accurate description of the event, it is also a measure of the greatness of Rome that even in the midst of its disintegration it managed to find the necessary resources to make the successful passage from Republic to Empire. It might be said that the most significant aspect of this so-called revolution is that Rome survived its own transformation.

Modern and Ancient Versions of the Transformation

The Romans themselves were well aware of what was happening, if not its full dimensions. Of course that is true of any period in history. Nevertheless, the surviving accounts exhibit a rather narrow understanding of what went wrong. These sources speak mostly of moral decay among various segments of society which they saw beginning at different moments in the past. The politician, soldier, and historian Sallust, a supporter of Julius Caesar, looked back to the fall of Carthage in 146 B.C. as the moment the rot began (**5.2**). The historian of Augustus' time, Livy, saw the collapse starting somewhat earlier—when the army of Manlius Vulso returned from Macedonia in 187 B.C. with an unRoman appetite for dancing girls, good food, and comfortable living (**5.6**). Some blamed everything on the reforming activities of the brothers Gracchi, Tiberius, and Gaius. In any case, the end result was that Rome ceased, by 30 B.C., to be a free Republic, choosing its leaders on an annual basis by elections, and became a military autocracy ruled by the general who commanded the loyalty of the Roman army.

While the Roman writers saw the fall of the Republic in moral terms, modern historians see fundamental changes in Roman social, cultural, political, and

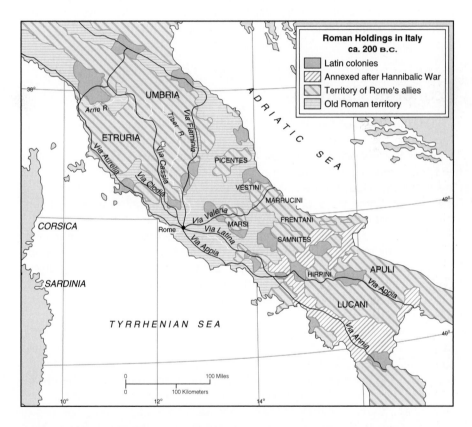

It was strange that while Rome in 200 B.C. had control of large overseas provinces such as Sicily and Spain, most of Italy remained in the hands of its native peoples. By and large they were not Roman citizens, but allies of Rome, socii. Romans were mostly confined to a stretch of territory reaching from coast to coast in central Italy, and in scattered colonies elsewhere on the peninsula. One of Rome's greatest challenges during the Roman Revolution was the integration of these peoples within the Roman commonwealth. Had Rome failed in this enterprise there would have been no Roman Empire. The process was slow, but by the end of the Revolution (around 30 B.C.), task had been accomplished and a new ruling class made up of Roman and Italian elites provided the basis for the government of the Roman Empire.

economic life, beginning with the Hannibalic War (218–202 B.C.). In their eyes, these changes were so fundamental that the old system was doomed. The result, however, was something less than a thoroughgoing transformation of all aspects of Roman life. Perhaps for that reason, the term "Revolution," although commonly used, is not altogether appropriate. Essential aspects of Roman society such as economic relations, social hierarchy, personal patronage, traditional gender relations, and so on were not greatly altered—at least not in the long run. What did change was the constitution and the way Romans governed themselves or, as some of them thought, ceased to govern themselves, for in the end, political freedom was abandoned in exchange for personal security and the security of property.

Economic Changes

One of the results of the conquest of the Mediterranean was the flow of booty into Italy in the form of looted works of art, cash, and slaves that followed the return of Rome's victorious armies. This booty was followed by war indemnities and, more importantly, permanent revenue streams in the form of annual tribute. It is not always clear, however, that these taxes paid for the cost of administering the empire. Some parts of the empire were less cost-effective than others. Although most of the money coming into Rome stayed at the top, some trickled down to the masses in various forms, such as improved services and communications, a share in war booty for soldiers, and, most important, the elimination in 167 B.C. of the *tributum*, the principal tax to which Romans were subject. Eventually, the people of the city of Rome acquired entitlements to subsidized grain or, later, bread—the "bread and the circus" entitlement (*panem et circenses*), sneered at by the satirist Juvenal.

In an underdeveloped economy with no industry and relatively little commerce, there were only a few places for the new wealth to go. Most went into the basic source of well-being in the ancient world, land. Much of it found its way into public building programs and items of conspicuous consumption in the private realm such as spectacular town houses and villas. Throughout Italy in the second century B.C., a great network of trunk roads was constructed, linking one end of the country with the other and tying distant colonies directly to Rome. New colonies were established in strategic locations, and on occasion, individual grants (*viritim*) of public land were made to attract migrant peasants from the overcrowded parts of central Italy. The slow process of clearing the forests and draining the swamps of the Po valley was begun, making this immensely fertile region available for cultivation.

Under these influences, the character of Italian agriculture began to change. The peasant subsistence farmer, the backbone of the army, began to give way to the long-term volunteer, whose loyalty was more likely to be to his commander—or at any rate to the person who could pay his wages—than to the state (**5.5**). New types of cash-crop farming were introduced, taking different forms in different parts of Italy. In the south, giant ranches (*latifundia*) were devoted to the raising of huge herds of cattle and sheep, watched over by slave herders (**5.3**). Although road construction was not undertaken with economic objectives in view, it had the effect of opening up previously inaccessible and unprofitable Roman landholdings to Roman farmers, large and small. Archaeological surveys show that land use intensified during the second century B.C. in many parts of Italy, as the primeval forest was cut down and new land came under cultivation for the first time. Northeast of Rome, for example, was a large area in which specialized farms produced vegetables, poultry, fish, and all sorts of luxury items (flowers, snails, boars, stags, and thrushes, for example) for the Roman market.

The impact of the wealth of the Mediterranean was soon felt in other ways. Rome went on a building spree that continued, on and off, for 500 years, leaving the huge monuments of brick and concrete so much admired by visitors to Rome over the centuries. Two new aqueducts, the Aqua Marcia and the Aqua Tepula, were constructed and the older aqueducts repaired, with the result that the water supply of Rome was more than doubled. The censors of 184 B.C., Cato and Flaccus, spent huge sums improving the drainage and sewage systems of the city. Over the years additional sums were poured into new bridges (the Mulvian and Aemilian), basilicas (Sempronian, Aemilian, and Opimian), a dozen or more temples, and half a dozen shrines, in addition to warehouses, porticoes, granaries, sidewalks, shopping areas, arches, and statues. The first marble buildings were constructed in the second century B.C., and a gilded ceiling was seen for the first time in Rome in the Capitolium. Elsewhere in Italy, similar building projects embellished towns with baths, forums, basilicas, and temples, some funded by the central treasury in Rome, others by local notables or municipal councils. L. Mummius, who sacked Corinth in 146 B.C., adorned the towns and provinces of Italy with looted art, as his surviving inscriptions proclaim. Huge private fortunes were accumulated, and villas and town houses, in the past marked by simplicity of style and construction, were now built with all the luxurious embellishments that eastern architects and artists could devise.

Social Changes

Although not the only cause, the shift in the structure of the Roman economy brought with it sweeping social changes. In the past the vast majority of Romans were almost exclusively rural. They were small, independent landowners who fitted into a very stable economic and social environment (**5.3**). Almost all were connected in some way with the elite through social and political ties. Some undoubtedly were the actual clients of the great families of Rome, but the majority were free, independent proprietor farmers. Either way, the social structure was geared to a very predictable economy and the unchanging, though complex, relationship of mass and elite.

All this began to change rapidly under the new conditions of the second century B.C. First, there were the enormous manpower losses of the Punic Wars and subsequent wars of conquest in Spain, Greece, and North Africa. Peasant citizens, who, in the early Republic, could readily take time from their work to repel raiders or engage in summer campaigns in Italy, now often found themselves assigned to quasi-permanent armies in provinces overseas (**5.5**). It could be years before they returned home, and their farms inevitably suffered. Throughout the first half of the second century B.C., a considerable body of men, estimated at close to 50,000, was annually in arms. But this was not the only force that transformed the peasant subsistence farmer of Italy.

With growing markets in Italy and the introduction of new cash-crop-farming techniques, peasant farmers found themselves with yet another alternative to their previous economic modes of existence. With the capital acquired in the form of war booty, they could transform their holdings into profitable enter-prises based on slave labor, granted the right conditions of access to trans-portation and a good market. Probably not many small farmers achieved this transformation, and intensively exploited farms were more likely to represent the investments of senators and members of the equestrian class. Nevertheless, with much new land coming into production in various parts of Italy, especially in the north, there were new possibilities and new incentives to move, further weakening the old social system, which had been based on the long-term occu-pation of the same farmstead and the hereditary mass–elite relationship. With-drawal from this relationship, either by emigration or by its transformation, had not occurred on such a scale before. In addition, uprooted peasants and veter-ans flowed to Rome and to the towns of Italy, where they found partial employ-ment in the great houses of the nobles and the huge (and growing) building programs and service industries, thus creating a true urban proletariat for the first time in Roman history.

Liberated Women and Men

The women of the late Republic, at least the members of the elite class, were a good deal freer than their ancestors at the height of the old order. With the liber-alization of society (on one reading), or the disintegration of it (on another), many well-to-do women were able to escape the power of the patriarchy, *patria potes-tas*, and enjoy a relatively independent life-style (**5.11**). Formally and legally, they were still under the control of some *tutor*, a male relative, but practically speaking, this did not translate into real subordination as it had in the past. Much the same could be said of elite males. Many of them cast off the restraints of the past and acted in ways that would have shocked their ancestors (**5.9**). It is less clear that either men or women escaped *materna auctoritas*, the influence of their mothers. Caesar, a poster child for the liberated males of Rome, was supposed to have told his mother on the day of the election to Pontifex Maximus, head of the Roman state religion, that he would either return as Pontifex Maximus or he would not return at all—his debts were so huge that he would have to leave Rome. At the time the Triumvirs—Antony, Lepidus, and Octavian—were trying to raise money to continue war against the murderers of Julius Caesar, they were stymied by the public action of a number of aristocratic women who publicly confronted them and challenged their assessments and were supported by the crowd when the Triumvirs ordered the women to be removed (**5.10**). Elite Roman women had always been self-assertive, but this was extreme.

How liberated non-elite women were is, as usual, impossible to determine. The sources have little to say about the life of ordinary people. It is a good guess, however, that they, too, were liberated to some extent because so many of their husbands were overseas in the military for long periods of time and, naturally, many of them never returned at all. Some of the general Lucullus' legions had been away from home for twenty-four years (**5.5**). Whether the absence of husbands was "liberation" or just more work for these women is another question.

Slaves and Freedmen

Not all the wealth that flowed to Rome was in the form of cash or movable property. Huge numbers of slaves accompanied the returning conquerors and were put to work in various segments of the economy—in agriculture, industry, the mines, and the home. No one knows the numbers, but the impact was sufficient to jolt the entire economic structure of Italy out of its traditional ways and to introduce a completely new factor into the Roman society (**5.3**). Because Roman masters had a propensity for manumission, and slaves, when manumitted by Romans, acquired the franchise (unlike their Greek counterparts), the existence of a large servile population guaranteed Rome large numbers of new Roman citizens from the second century B.C. onward. The freedman class was generally made up of former domestic or urban slaves engaged in skilled and professional activities. In comparison with the average freeborn Roman, these people were well-to-do. Some came to constitute a wealthy urban elite different from the traditional leisurely upper-class and the small proprietor majority. As in the case of the urban proletariat, there was no pre-existing, defined place for them in the Roman society.

Equestrians and Publicans

Another significant development of the second century B.C. was the increased importance of the equestrian class, the *equites*. This general term was applied to individuals outside the Senate who possessed a high census rating because of their wealth, as well as other qualifications. Since senators were barred from contracting, banking, and trade, and because manufacturing was looked down on by the elite, the equestrian class was able to exercise a near-monopoly in these increasingly important areas. One group of equestrians (called *publicani*, or publicans, because they served the public sector) was organized into small companies, *societates*, that contracted with the state for the lease of mines, the construction of roads and public buildings, the manufacture of arms, the supply of food and clothing for the armies, and so on. Because the second century B.C. was a particularly lucrative period for building contracts and arms supply, the influence of the publicans increased proportionately, although it was some time before they attempted to translate this new-found power into direct political influence in opposition to that of the Senate.

Military and Constitutional Changes

From the time of the early Republic, the Roman army was a militia. When needed it was drafted from the ranks of its small landowners who were, at least initially, expected to supply their own weapons, food, and clothing. They were commanded by amateur officers who served a year and then returned to private life. For centuries, military campaigns were local and brief. Rome's territory initially did not extend much more than 50 or so miles south of the Tiber, and threats came from their nearby neighbors, the Etruscans to the north, the Sabines to the east, and the Latins to the south. As in all *polis*-type states, there was an expectation that all citizen landowners would attend regular meetings of the assemblies and courts and, when needed, serve in the army. Only property owners had these responsibilities, but non-property owners constituted a very small percentage of the population. Only reluctantly did the state begin to supply its soldiers with arms, food, and clothing and even then made deductions for their cost from the soldiers' meager allowance. Service in the army was seen as a duty and privilege of full citizens only, and those lacking the requisite amount of property, which constituted their "stock" in the corporate state, were excluded from this privilege.

By the second century B.C., all of this had changed. Rome now had the responsibilities of a world-state while remaining a city-state. Its institutions, ideology, machinery of government, army, and assumptions were all wrong for its new obligations, especially the primary one of providing security to the Mediterranean region. Its population was too scattered to attend civic affairs in the city on a regular basis. From a security viewpoint, what was needed was a professional standing army, not a short-term militia. There were additional reasons for Rome's dysfunctional state. Its policies of weakening or destroying regional powers had short-term benefits but, in the long run, had the effect of making Rome responsible for the regions once ruled by these powers. Carthage, for instance, had maintained order in the western Mediterranean and north Africa; Rhodes, Pergamum, and the Seleucid empire did the same in the east. But with their elimination, or weakening, the forces for disorder in these parts of the world gained the upper hand. Eventually, Rome found itself, for example, with a huge piracy problem which at one point threatened to disrupt the food supply of Rome itself. Small wars in distant parts of the empire threatened the stability of Rome itself—not militarily—but in terms of the political impact they had on Rome's dysfunctional government.

Peasant soldiers who could find time for short campaigns now found themselves overseas for years at a time (**5.5**). In the past, generals were under the scrutiny of the senate and usually on campaign fairly close to home. Now they operated in distant provinces—in Spain or Macedonia, for instance—with no immediate supervision (**5.4**). Newly conquered and incorporated territories had to be governed, and here again Rome had a problem with supervising governors in provinces too far away for the kind of control they needed. The possibility of provincial armies turning into private armies and being used against the state gradually became a threat to the control of the Senate. Soldiers began to recognize the power they had to dictate events by refusing the commands of their officers. One of the earliest mutinies, that against Scipio in Spain in 206 B.C., was put down by the resolute action of Scipio and his officers, but by the first century, soldiers time and again were able to force their commanders to do their will either by actual mutiny or by the threat of mutiny. Lucullus had to give up a campaign in Armenia in 67 B.C. (**5.5**), and even Caesar, who traditionally had a good relationship with his troops, was forced to make concessions in a mutiny in 43 B.C. in Italy itself.

The ruling class divided itself between two modes of political action and formed factions known as the *populares*, the Popular Party, and the *optimates*, the Best People. These were not parties in any modern sense of the word, though the term tends to get used for them. Rather, they represented methods of political action, techniques for achieving political goals by manipulating the complicated—and now disorderly—Roman political system. The *populares* claimed to speak for the "people" at large, while the *optimates* spoke for the elite and generally those who favored the status quo. In both instances the leaders were members of the upper classes, either long-time members of famous families, such as the Gracchi brothers and their helpers, or "new men" (*novi homines*), i.e., individuals who were ennobled by being the first members of their families to hold the consulship. Just because they were "new" did not make them members of the Popular Party, as might be expected. In fact the opposite was often the case. Cicero, for instance, was a new man and a staunch supporter of the *optimates*. Julius Caesar on the other hand, a member of one of the most ancient of Roman aristocratic families, acted as a *popularis*.

The division reflected an old split in the Roman political system. The early Republic engineered a clever compromise between narrow elitism and democracy by creating, in effect, two states, the Patrician and the Plebeian (see Chapter 2, Introduction and **2.4**). The former rested on an anti-egalitarian, geometric system that apportioned more votes to the better-off class than everyone else. The main organs of the Patrician state were the Senate and the Centuriate Assembly, which elected the principal officers of the state. The Plebeian state found its expression in the Assembly of the People and its officers, the Tribunes of the Plebs. For centuries these two potentially competing states worked well side by side, but in the second century, a split occurred between them, reflecting the changed situation of the

Republic in the Mediterranean. Disaffected members of the elite such as the Gracchi made use of the popular assemblies to advance their own goals independent of the wishes of the Senate and the elite at large (**5.3**). They began to act in a "popular manner," hence the term *popularis* to describe this kind of politician. Eventually, the split became deadly when ambitious dynasts ("power wielders") like Caesar appealed directly to the people over the heads of the elite and the Senate. Working in tandem with popular leaders in Rome, dynasts of this type overtaxed the finely balanced, and now badly weakened, system of government at Rome.

Cultural Transformation

In the second century B.C., in addition to other problems brought on by its military successes, Rome had to face and cope with the encroachment of a powerful higher culture, that of Greece. In some respects this challenge of Hellenization was the most powerful of the many challenges Rome had to face during the period of the Roman Revolution.

It would not be an exaggeration to say that Romans were culturally illiterate in the fields of poetry, drama, and history before the second century B.C., although some efforts were being made in the direction of the first two at this time, chiefly by outsiders. Philosophically or scientifically, Rome never challenged Greek supremacy (**5.7**). In art and architecture, Romans were not quite so backward but still had a long way to go for a people who now claimed to be, and were in actuality, the rulers of the Mediterranean. It took time for the cultural revolution to take hold. Latin was still too rough in the third century B.C. for prose writing and was only slowly being made suitable for poetry and drama. Yet it was at precisely this time that Rome had the greatest need to communicate with the rest of the world and explain its institutions and politics to the educated classes of the Mediterranean. Public opinion was important in the Greek-speaking world, and it was essential for the Romans to respond to questions being raised throughout the Mediterranean about where Rome had sprung from; what enabled it to conquer Pyrrhus, the Gauls, and the Carthaginians (the last two ancient enemies of the Greeks); and, especially, what justification, if any, it had for possessing an empire.

The first answers to such questions were supplied by Greeks writing about Rome from a distance, such as Timaeus of Tauromenium in Sicily, who lived in Athens in the early third century B.C. Not until the end of the Second Punic War were Romans able to give an account of their institutions and history. Writing in Greek, Fabius Pictor wrote a history of Rome that emphasized its strength, moderation, tenaciousness, and good faith as well as the wisdom of its Senate and its strict moral code. With Cato the Elder, in the first half of the second century B.C., Latin history writing first came into existence, representing a new level of self-confidence on the part of the Romans, who now rose to the challenge of Greek letters by composing a literature in their own language. This was an achievement matched by no other people with whom the Greeks came into contact. For Cato, in fact, the Greeks no longer counted; the Romans and the Italians had nothing of which to be ashamed. On the contrary, he believed that they had incorporated the best of the Greek world with the best of their own rich heritage—a pardonable exaggeration with which many Greeks in the second century B.C. must have agreed. From this time on, numerous accounts in Latin by members of the senatorial class provided the growing reading public of Rome and Italy with suitably patriotic, moralizing histories, often laced with polemic tracts from the internal political battles of the century. There were few qualms about adapting history to the political needs of the Roman upper classes, and history was seen as a means of glorifying one's achievements and the achievements of one's family, as well as propagandizing for further advancement.

In Cato's younger days, Roman poetry and drama were rudimentary, with Livius Andronicus and Naevius providing translations of Greek poems and plays, but the first half of the second century B.C. saw the full flowering of Latin in the works of Ennius, Pacuvius, Plautus, Terence, and others. Epic poems glorifying Rome's past and its destiny were produced, and Ennius' aphorisms, which reflected the nobles' vision of Rome, became commonplaces quoted throughout subsequent Roman history. Plays celebrating Roman historical events were written but never became popular. Comedies, especially those of Plautus, were always popular, although the settings and the stock figures were Greek for fear of offending conservative Roman tastes. There was no place for Aristophanic humor in Rome, where the aristocracy took its role as a governing class seriously and unquestioningly. Mime and farce, which were native to Italy, were the popular fare of the lower classes and eventually displaced the plays of Roman comedy altogether.

Religious Innovations

Roman religion showed the effects of the upheavals brought about by the acquisition of an empire. Traditionally, Roman religion had been an integral part of state affairs. Of course, there was a private religion or devotion practiced within families and by individuals, but the state was involved with religion as part of its proper function. Political figures held religious offices as a matter of course, and the maintenance of the peace of the gods (*pax deorum*) was as much a part of the functioning of the state as fighting wars or hearing legal cases—the other two primary duties of Roman magistrates, who had inherited the triple roles of priest, general, and judge from the Etruscan kings. However, after the expansion of Rome, the old system was clearly inadequate, and the very localized character of the religion made it impossible to export. Religious functions were to be performed in Rome, and various figures who were priests as well as consuls or praetors were hindered in the performance of their duties and in some instances could not leave Italy at all. As Rome grew and the bonds of clientship (*clientela*) dissolved, the confinement of religion to the higher officials of state and to state functions created a vacuum. Eastern religions moved in to fill the void. The worship of the Great Mother

(*Magna Mater, Mater Deorum,* or Cybele) was introduced officially in 205 B.C., and unofficially, the worship of Dionysus crept into Italy and was savagely repressed as being dangerous to Rome both politically and morally (**4.4**). However, the two religions remained as the forerunners of many others, including the one that was ultimately to triumph: Christianity.

▼▼▼

5.1   A Survey of the Revolution

The Greek historian Appian was born in Alexandria toward the end of the first century A.D.*, gained the Roman citizenship, and moved to Rome where he devoted his life to writing a comprehensive history of Rome from its founding to the second century* A.D. *His usefulness derives from the fact that in writing his history he borrowed from a number of important Roman historians such as Asinius Pollio whose works are now lost but even more importantly from the fact that he represents a provincial's view of the Roman Empire. Provincial "voices" are hard to come by, so it is good to have as comprehensive a document as we have from Appian, even if what comes down to us is only a portion of what he actually wrote. The fact that he belongs to the elite may be dismissed as the "false consciousness" of an upper-class provincial buying into the view of the masters of the world. Unfortunately, we only hear from the elite. The peasantry of the empire was either illiterate or mute.*

In the following reading, Appian presents a very simplified view of the Roman Revolution. He reduces this complicated event to the breakdown of consensus and respect for each other among the various segments of Roman society. Incorrectly, he makes anarchy prevail from 133 B.C. *until finally, the great Augustus, rescued Rome from chaos in 31* B.C. *A convinced monarchist, he has no sympathy for the Liberators, Brutus and Cassius, who murdered the tyrannical Julius Caesar because they thought, quite rightly, that he was converting the Roman Republic into a monarchy. He sheds no tears for the passing of the free Republic. In the end, the only thing that mattered for Appian was tranquilly and peace. He concludes his introduction happily with the comment:* "Thus the Roman state passed into harmony and monarchy."[1]

The Plebeians and the Senate of Rome were often at odds with each other concerning the enactment of laws, the cancellation of debts, the division of land, and the election of magistrates. Internal discord did not, however, bring them to actual blows. Their confrontations were merely dissensions and contests that occurred within the bounds of the law, and they settled them by making mutual concessions and by retaining respect for one another. Once, for instance, when the plebeians were about to march on campaign, one of these controversies arose, but they did not make use of the weapons in their hands. Instead they withdrew to the hill which from that time on was called the Sacred Mount. Even then there was no violence,

---

[1] Appian, *The Civil Wars* 1.1–6. Translation based on that of Horace White, *Appian's Roman History* (London, 1913).

and they created a magistrate for their protection and called him the Tribune of the Plebs. His function was to serve as a check upon the consuls who were chosen by the Senate [*Appian has this wrong; the consuls were elected by the people in the Centuriate Assembly*], so that political power should not be exclusively in their hands. From this arose even greater bitterness, and the magistrates were arrayed in stronger animosity against each other from this time on. The Senate and the plebeians took sides with them, each believing that it would prevail over the other by augmenting the power of its own magistrates. It was in the midst of contests of this kind that Marcius Coriolanus [ca. 490 B.C.], having been banished contrary to justice, took refuge with the Volsci and levied war against his homeland.

This is the only case of armed strife that can be found in the ancient seditions, and this was caused by an exile. The sword was never carried into the assembly, and there was no civil butchery until Tiberius Gracchus [*133 B.C.*], while serving as Tribune of the Plebs and bringing forward new laws, was the first to fall a victim to internal dissension. With him, many others who were crowded together on the Capitol around the temple of Jupiter were also slain. Sedition [*stasis* in Greek] did not end with this abominable deed. Repeatedly the parties came into open conflict, often carrying daggers; and from time to time in the temples, or the assemblies, or the forum, some tribune, or praetor or consul, or candidate for those offices, or some person otherwise distinguished, would be slain. Unseemly violence prevailed almost constantly [*a large exaggeration*], together with shameful contempt for law and justice. As the evil gained in magnitude, open insurrections against the government and large warlike expeditions against their country were undertaken by exiles, or criminals, or persons contending against each other for some office or military command. There arose chiefs of factions [*in Greek*, dynasts] quite frequently, aspiring to supreme power, some of them refusing to disband the troops entrusted to them by the people, others even hiring forces against each other on their own account without public authority. Whenever either side first got possession of the city, the opposition party made war nominally against their own adversaries, but actually against their own country. They assailed it like an enemy's capital, and ruthless and indiscriminate massacres of citizens were perpetrated. Some were proscribed, others banished, property was confiscated, and prisoners were even subjected to excruciating tortures.

No unseemly deed was left undone until, about fifty years after the death of Gracchus, Cornelius Sulla, one of those chiefs of factions, doctoring one evil with another, made himself the sole master of the state for a very long time [*actually only 2 years, 81–79 B.C.*]. Such officials were formerly called dictators—an office created in the most dangerous emergencies for six months only, and long since fallen into disuse. But Sulla, although nominally elected, became dictator for life by force and compulsion. Nevertheless he became satiated with power and was the first man, so far as I know, holding supreme power, who had the courage to lay it down voluntarily and to declare that he would render an account of his stewardship to any one dissatisfied with it. . . .

Thus there was a cessation of factions for a short time while Sulla lived and a compensation for the evils which he had done, but after his death similar troubles broke out and continued until Gaius Caesar [*i.e., Julius Caesar*], who had held the command in Gaul by election for some years, when ordered by the Senate to lay down his command, excused himself on the ground that this was not the wish of the Senate, but of Pompey, his enemy, who had command of an army in Italy, and was scheming to depose him. So he sent proposals that either both should retain their armies, so that neither need fear the other's enmity, or Pompey also should dismiss his forces and live as a private citizen under the laws in like manner with himself. Both suggestions being refused, he marched from Gaul against Pompey into Roman territory, entered Rome, and, finding that Pompey had fled, pursued him into Thessaly [*in Greece*] and won a brilliant victory over him at the battle of Pharsalus [*48 B.C.*]. He then followed him into Egypt, and after Pompey had been slain by agents of King Ptolemy XIV, Caesar then took control of Egypt and remained there until he could settle the dynastic dispute over the throne [*eventually putting Cleopatra VII on the throne*]. He then returned to Rome having defeated his principal rival who had been surnamed the Great on account of his brilliant military exploits. He now ruled without disguise, nobody daring any longer to dispute with him about anything, and was chosen, next after Sulla, dictator for life [*44 B.C.*]. Again all civil dissensions ceased until Brutus and Cassius, envious of his great power and desiring to restore the government of their fathers, slew in the Senate house one who had proved himself truly popular and most experienced in the art of government [*44 B.C.*]. The people certainly mourned his death greatly. They scoured the city in pursuit of his murderers, buried him in the midst of the forum, built a temple on the site of his funeral pyre, and offered sacrifice to him as a god.

And now civil discord broke out again worse than ever and increased enormously. Massacres, banishments, and proscriptions of both senators and equites (knights) took place straightway, including great numbers of both classes, the chiefs of factions surrendering their enemies to each other, and for this purpose sparing not even their friends and brothers; so much did animosity toward rivals overpower the love of kindred. So in the course of events the Roman empire was partitioned, as though it had been a private property, by these three men [*the Triumvirs*]: Antony, Lepidus, and the one who was first called Octavius, but afterward Caesar [*Augustus*] from his relationship to the other Caesar and adoption in his will. Shortly after this division they fell to quarreling among themselves, as was natural, and Octavius, who was the superior in understanding and skill, first deprived Lepidus of Africa, which had fallen to his lot, and afterward, as the result of the Battle of Actium [*31 B.C.*], took from Antony all the provinces lying between Syria and the Adriatic Gulf. Thereupon, while all the world was filled with astonishment at this wonderful display of power, he sailed to Egypt and took that country, which was the oldest and at that time the strongest possession of successors of Alexander and the only one wanting to complete the Roman empire as it now stands. In the immediate consequence of these exploits, he was, while still living, the first to be regarded by the Romans as "august" and to be called by them "Augustus." He assumed to himself an authority like Caesar's over the country and the subject nations, and even greater than Caesar's, no longer needing any form of election, or authorization, or even the pretense of it.

His government proved both lasting and masterful, and being himself successful in all things and dreaded by all, he left a lineage and succession that held the supreme power in like manner after him.

Thus, out of the multiplicity of civil commotions, the Roman state passed into harmony and monarchy. To show how these things came about I have written and compiled this narrative, which is well worth the study of those who wish to know the measureless ambition of men, their dreadful lust for power, their unwearying perseverance, and the countless forms of evil.

5.2   Greed Unlimited and Unrestrained Corrupted and Destroyed Everything

Sallust, an ambitious careerist, a gifted writer, and a corrupt provincial governor, was one of the new types of Romans who became prominent in the late Republic. Like Marius and Cicero, he was a "new man" from the Italian municipal aristocracy. Like them, he lacked the "right" family background for a straightforward political career at Rome and had to struggle to make his way. Although not as able as either Marius or Cicero, he was lucky in that the conditions of the time favored people like him. Just as Sallust's career had reached something of a dead end, the charismatic Julius Caesar began to unite new men from Rome and the Italian cities, some members of the old aristocracy, the people, and the army in a coalition that effectively challenged the control of the senatorial oligarchy. This new coalition spelled the end of the old order of the Senatus Populusque Romanus (the Senate and the People of Rome, or, in abbreviated form, SPQR).

Although expressed in traditional moralistic terms, Sallust's brief survey provides a synoptic view of most of the factors that went into the making of the Roman Revolution.[2] He has a quite different take on these events than does Appian in the previous reading.

The system of parties and factions, with all their corresponding evils, developed at Rome some years before this war, as a result of peace and the kind of material prosperity that all people prize highly. For prior to the destruction of Carthage, the People and the Senate of Rome ran the government peacefully and with consideration for each other. Citizens did not struggle among themselves for glory or domination. Fear of enemies preserved the good morals of the state. But when this fear was removed, the vices of prosperity, licentiousness, and arrogance arose. Thus the peace the Romans sought in times of adversity, after they had obtained it, turned out to be harder and more bitter than the adversity itself. For the nobles began to abuse their dignity and the people their liberty; each began to look out for its own advantage, to squander and to grab. Accordingly, everything was split between the two. The republic, trapped between the factions, was torn apart.

The nobility had the more powerful faction. The people's power, being divided and scattered among so many, was less effective. Domestic and military issues were

---

[2]Sallust, *The Jugurthine War* 41–42.

decided by a tiny handful of nobles who had control over the treasury, the provinces, the magistracies, and all distinctions and triumphs. The people were burdened by military service and poverty. The generals seized the spoils of war and shared them with their friends. Meanwhile, the parents and small children of the soldiers were driven from their homes if they happened to have powerful neighbors.

Thus the possession of power led to the rise of greed; unlimited and unrestrained, it corrupted and destroyed everything. Nothing was respected, nothing held sacred. Eventually this greed brought about its own downfall, for as soon as representatives of the nobility were found who preferred true glory to unjust power, the state began to be shaken, and civil dissension began like an earthquake. For after Tiberius and Gaius Gracchus, whose ancestors had contributed much to Rome during the Carthaginian and other wars, began to assert the freedom of the people and expose the crimes of the oligarchs, the guilty nobles were terrified. They opposed the Gracchi, now through the allies, now through the Knights. These latter they won away from the commons by holding out the hope of sharing their special privileges. First Tiberius, then a few years later Gaius, who had followed in his brother's footsteps, were slain, although one was a tribune and the other a member of a commission for the founding of colonies.

5.3   Social and Economic Conditions: The Gracchi

Roman writers such as Sallust (above) were not much given to the kind of economic and social analysis that is characteristic of modern history. They wrote about people, not about "movements" or "forces." Social and economic explanations have to be pieced together from scattered accounts. Often these accounts are fragments of political tracts or propaganda speeches. Each side, popular or oligarchic, tried to give its own "spin" to its particular account of the issue in question.

Of these issues, none was more inflammatory than the matter of land, poverty, and the army. By the middle of the second century B.C., Rome had become the preeminent military power in the Mediterranean. As a consequence, wealth poured into Italy and undermined the traditional style of family farming, and with it the military basis of the draft. Writing over 200 years later but using earlier sources, the biographer Plutarch gives the following sketchy account of how the problem originated and the efforts of one member of the senatorial class, the tribune Tiberius Gracchus to address it.[3]

Of the land which the Romans won in war from their neighbors, some they auctioned publicly. The rest they turned into public land and assigned to the poor and needy, for which the latter were to pay a small rent to the state treasury. But when the rich began to offer more by way of rent and drive out the poor, a law was passed that restricted the holding of public land by one person to no more than 500 acres.

---

[3]Plutarch, *Tiberius Gracchus* 8; 9; *Gaius Gracchus* 3–7 (selections).

For a while this law restrained the greed of the rich and helped the poor. They were able to remain on the land they rented, and they continued to occupy the allotment they had from the outset. But then the rich of the neighborhood managed to transfer these rentals to themselves by means of fictitious names. Finally they openly took possession of most of the land in their own names.

The poor who were forced off the land were no longer enthusiastic about military service, or even about raising children. The result was that in a short time there was a distinct manpower shortage of freeborn men all over Italy. In their place, gangs of foreign slaves filled the land. The rich used these to cultivate the lands from which they had driven off the free citizens. . . .

On being elected tribune of the plebs, Tiberius took the matter in hand. Most writers say he was encouraged in this plan by Diophanes the rhetorician and Blossius the philosopher . . . but some say that Cornelia, the mother of Tiberius, was partly responsible. She often reproached her sons with the fact that the Romans still called her the daughter of Scipio [*i.e., Scipio Africanus, the conqueror of Hannibal*] rather than the mother of the Gracchi. . . . [However] his brother Gaius claimed in a propaganda tract that when Tiberius was passing through Etruria on his way to Numantia [*in Spain*], he saw for himself that the countryside had been stripped bare of its native inhabitants and that the farmers and the tenders of the flocks were imported, barbarian slaves. It was this experience that first led him to develop the policies which were so fatal to the two brothers. Most of all it was the people themselves who excited Tiberius' energy and ambition. By means of messages and appeals written on public porticoes, walls, and monuments, they called on Tiberius to recover the public land for the poor.

And so Tiberius proposed a law for the redistribution of publicly owned land to the landless. By this means he hoped to restore the traditional basis of the draft and so restore the Roman army. Plutarch preserves a fragment of one of his speeches drumming up support for his program.

The wild animals that wander over Italy have dens and lairs to hide in, but the men who fight and die for Italy have only air and light—and nothing else! Houseless and homeless they wander the land with their wives and children. And when their generals appeal to them before a battle to defend their ancestral tombs and shrines from their enemies, they lie: Not one of them has a family altar; not one of these Romans possesses an ancestral tomb. Instead they fight—and die—for the wealth and luxury of others. They are said to be the masters of the world, but they do not have so much as a single clod of earth they can call their own.

Although the law passed, Tiberius was assassinated by his enemies while still in office. His opponents tried to make a case for the legitimacy of his murder, but the killing of a tribune, protected by sacrosanctitas, *the inviolability and holiness of his office, made a mockery of the traditions of the ancient social pact between rich and poor and patricians and plebeians, that for so long had undergirded the state. More blows to social concord were delivered in the next round of the Gracchan crisis, 123/121 B.C., when Tiberius' brother Gaius took up the cause. Having been elected tribune, he proposed another, much more comprehensive round of reform legislation.*

After Gaius entered office, he instantly became the most prominent of all the tribunes. He was incomparably the best orator, and the passion with which he still lamented his brother's death made him all the more fearless in speaking. He used every occasion to remind the people of what had happened to Tiberius, and he contrasted their cowardly behavior with that of their ancestors. . . . "Before your eyes," he said, "these men beat Tiberius to death with clubs. They dragged his body from the Capitol through the streets and tossed it into the Tiber. Moreover, those of his friends who were caught were put to death without trial. And yet it is the ancient tradition of our fathers that if anyone is accused on a capital charge and does not make an appearance in court, a trumpeter shall go to the door of his house and summon him to appear. Until this is done, the judges may not vote on his case. These were the kinds of safeguards and protections our ancestors believed necessary in capital cases."

After he had stirred up the people with words of this type—and he had a power-ful voice and spoke with great conviction—he proposed two laws. One provided that if the people had deprived any magistrate of his office he should be disbarred from holding any future office. The second law made a magistrate who had banished a citizen without trial to be liable himself to prosecution by the people. The first was obviously aimed at disqualifying Marcus Octavius, who had been deposed from the tribunate by Tiberius. The other targeted Popillius, who as praetor had banished the friends of Tiberius. Without waiting for trial, Popillius fled from Italy. The other law, however, was withdrawn by Gaius himself, who said he spared Octavius at the request of his mother Cornelia. This pleased the people and they agreed to its with-drawal, honoring Cornelia no less on account of her sons than of her father. Later on they erected a bronze statue of her with the inscription: "Cornelia, Mother of the Gracchi" . . .

He now introduced a number of laws to flatter the People and undermine the power of the Senate. The first regarded public land which was to be divided up among the poor. The next stipulated that soldiers were to be equipped at public cost without any deduction being made from their pay for this and that nobody under seventeen should be drafted. A third law proposed to extend the franchise to the Italians. A fourth lowered the price of grain for the poor. The fifth had to do with the appointment of jurors.

It was this law that did more than any other to cut down the power of the Senate. They alone served as jurors in criminal cases, and this privilege made them feared by the people and the knights alike. Gaius' law added 300 knights to the 300 senators to create a pool of 600 from which the jurors would be drawn. . . . The People not only passed this law but also allowed Gaius to choose the jurors, who were to come from the equestrian order, so that he found himself invested with something like monarchical power. Even the Senate agreed to accept his advice. When he did coun-sel them, it was always in support of some measure that brought credit to that body. For instance, there was the case of the very equitable and ethical decree concerning the grain which the propraetor Fabius sent to the city from Spain. Gaius persuaded the Senate to sell the grain and to send the proceeds back to the cities of Spain. He had Fabius censured for making the administration of the province intolerably burdensome to the inhabitants. This brought Gaius a great reputation in addition to making him popular in the provinces.

He also introduced legislation for the founding of colonies and the building of roads and public granaries. Although he himself undertook the management and direction of all these projects, he showed no signs of being worn down by these different and demanding tasks. On the contrary, he carried each one out with amazing speed and application as if it were the only one he was doing. Even those who hated and feared him were struck by his efficiency and his ability to get things done. As for the people, they were thrilled to see him surrounded by a mob of contractors, craftsmen, ambassadors, magistrates, soldiers, and scholars. He was on familiar terms with all of these. Yet, while showing kindness and the kind of consideration that was due to each, he was able to preserve his dignity. In this way he was able to demonstrate that those who cast him as intimidating, overbearing, or violent were envious detractors. . . .

His greatest enthusiasm was reserved for the building of roads. These he made beautiful and graceful as well as useful. Made of quarried stone and tamped sand, they were laid out straight across the countryside. Depressions were filled in, and watercourses or ravines were bridged. Both sides of the road were leveled or raised to the same height, so that the whole project had everywhere an even and attractive appearance. . . .

Unfortunately for Gracchus, the office of tribune was a weak base on which to try to carry out such an ambitious, independent program. The Senate outbid him in crowd-pleasing legislation and was able to undermine his support. When he ran for a third term as tribune, he was defeated. Then, when the Senate proceeded to take apart his legislative program, Gaius' followers were provoked into a confrontation. In the riot that ensued, violence resulted and the oligarchs in the Senate had the excuse to declare an emergency. Gaius and his followers were slaughtered and their property confiscated. To crown their triumph and rub salt in the wounds, the temple of Concord, which had been built centuries earlier as a monument to the establishment of understanding between plebeians and patricians, was refurbished by Opimius, one of the prime instigators of the emergency decree.

5.4 Politicians and Generals Out of Control

In 88 B.C., L. Cornelius Sulla was sent out as commander against the king of Pontus, Mithridates VI, whose generals had invaded the Roman provinces of Asia Minor and the mainland of Greece. One of the events of the campaign was the siege of Athens. Plutarch, after narrating the barbarous cutting down of the groves of the Academy and Lyceum gymnasia (the locations of Plato's and Aristotle's schools) for lumber for the siege, and detailing Sulla's demands for money, contrasts the behavior of the generals of the past with those of the present. It was precisely the transformation of the generals of Rome from servants of the state to independent dynasts that illustrates the distance between the late Republic and the earlier Republic. In a trenchant comment he says: "In order to become the masters of those better than themselves they made themselves the slaves of the worst." *This is an apt description of how the dynasts—and their opponents—of the Late Republic often behaved.*[4]

Since he [*Sulla*] needed a great deal of money for the war, he helped himself to the treasures in the sanctuaries of Greece, taking some from Epidaurus and some from Olympia, sending for the most beautiful and valuable objects deposited there. He also wrote to the guardians of Delphi saying that it was better to send the possessions of the god to him: either he would protect them more safely, or, if he used them, he would give back as much. . . .

Accordingly, the treasures were shipped out; most of the Greeks did not know about this. But the great silver wine cask, the last of the royal gifts [*of Croesus, king of Lydia*], was too large and heavy for transportation, and the guardians of Delphi were forced to cut it into pieces. As they did so, they recalled first Titus Flamininus, then Manius Acilius and Aemilius Paulus. Manius had driven Antiochus [*King of Syria*] out of Greece, and the others had conquered the Macedonian kings. Not only did these men leave untouched the sanctuaries of Greece but they even made gifts to them and honored them and increased the general veneration felt for them.

These were lawful commanders, they reflected, of well-disciplined men who had learned to serve their leaders without question. The consuls themselves were men of kingly souls and simple in their personal expenses, keeping their costs within the fixed allowances of the state. They thought it more shameful to seek popularity with their men than to fear the enemy. But now the Roman commanders rose to the top by force, not worth, and because they needed armies to fight each other rather than enemies of the state, they were forced to be both demagogs and generals. In order to pay for the gratifications with which they purchased the loyalty of their soldiers, before they knew it, they had sold off the fatherland itself.

Thus, in order to become the masters of those better than themselves they made themselves the slaves of the worst. These kinds of activities drove Marius into exile and again brought him back against Sulla; these made Cinna the murderer of Octavius and Fimbria of Flaccus. And not least, Sulla led the way. For to corrupt and win over those under the command of others, he made lavish expenditures on his own soldiers. As a result of making traitors of the soldiers of other generals and profligates of his own soldiers, he had need for a great deal of money, especially for this siege.

The breakdown of the old system of senatorial control was complete by 60 B.C. Although Roman politics was always characterized by political factions and deal-making, nothing was quite so brazen (at least to that point in time) as the so-called "First Triumvirate" of Pompey, Crassus, and Caesar. The complaints of Cato (the Younger) about the use of women for political purposes do not mean that marriage was not used for this end in the past but merely that it had become part of a larger process of "new politics" in which the traditional restraints were gone.[5]

---

[4]Plutarch, *Sulla* 12.
[5]Plutarch, *Caesar* 14.

Caesar, shielded by the friendship of Crassus and Pompey, launched his campaign for sthe consulship and was triumphantly elected with Calpurnius Bibulus. As soon as he entered his office, he immediately began to legislate, but more in the style of a demagogic tribune of the people than a consul. Thus, to please the mob he proposed a variety of laws for the establishment of colonies and the division of land.

In the Senate he was opposed vigorously by the traditional power wielders. But this was just the opportunity he had been seeking for a long time, and so, complaining loudly that the Senate's insolence and stubbornness left him no alternative, he took himself off to the Forum. Then, with Crassus on one side of him and Pompey on the other, he asked the people if they approved his laws. When they said they did, he asked them for their help against those who were threatening to oppose him with their swords. They promised him their help, and Pompey added that if it came to swords, he would come with both sword *and* shield. The aristocracy was offended by this crazy and childish talk; they thought that it was degrading to Pompey's own dignity and lacked the respect due to the Senate. The people, however, were delighted by it.

Caesar tried to make still greater use of Pompey's power. He had a daughter named Julia, who was engaged to Servilius Caepio. He now engaged her to Pompey, saying that he would give Pompey's daughter to Servilius, although she too was engaged, having been promised to Faustus, the son of Sulla. A little later Caesar married Calpurnia, the daughter of Piso, and had Piso made consul for the next year.

Thereupon Cato violently objected, protesting that it was unbearable that the power of government be bargained away by marriage alliances and that these men should advance each other to the commands of provinces and armies and other positions of power by means of women. Caesar's colleague in the consulship, Bibulus, finding he was unable to obstruct Caesar's legislation and that, along with Cato, he was in danger of being killed in the Forum, shut himself up at home for the rest of his time in office.

Right after his marriage, Pompey filled the Forum with his veterans and helped the people pass Caesar's laws as well as securing for him as his consular province Gaul on both sides of the Alps, along with Illyricum and four legions. The governorship was to last five years. Cato tried to speak against these measures. Caesar, thinking he would appeal to the tribunes, ordered him off to prison. But Cato, without saying a word, went off to jail. Caesar, seeing that both the nobility and the people were displeased, and out of respect for his good character were following him in silence dejectedly, secretly asked a tribune to release him.

5.5   Soldiers Out of Control

Threats posed to the state by generals with too much unsupervised power, operating at great distances from Rome for long periods of time, are illustrated by the following reading. The reading also illustrates the indiscipline of the officer class and the ordinary Roman draftee soldier. Lucullus, whose full name was Lucius Licinius Lucullus, was a well-connected member of the

THE SECRET BALLOT AT ROME

The Roman constitution was not a democracy but it did have certain democratic features. The illustration shows a voter bending down to receive a ballot from a man standing on the ground. The voter has already climbed onto the voting *pons* or bridge by means of a ladder (not shown). Another voter is shown at the other end of the *pons,* depositing his ballot in the *cista* (ballot box). The point of the elevated bridge was to make sure that everyone could see what was going on and that no ballot-stuffing took place. The ballot used was a wax tablet on which the voter made a mark with a stylus, a "V" for "yes" and an "A" for "no." Other marks were "A" and "C" (*Absolvo/Condemno*) or "L" and "D" (*Libero/Damno*).

The secret ballot was introduced by a series of plebiscites (popular votes) in the second century B.C. Elections were covered in 139 B.C.; non capital trials in 137; legislation in 131; and capital trials in 106. The elite, according to Cicero, regarded the introduction of the secret ballot as a serious blow to their influence since they could no longer tell how their clients and supposed friend and allies voted. Judges in the courts that tried cases of extortion in overseas provinces were also required to vote secretly. These jurors had to cast their ballots with a bare arm, demonstrating they were casting only one ballot. (With their fingers they concealed the mark on the ballot that indicated their choice.)

Even this system was not wholly tamper proof. In the first century B.C. Cato the Younger had an election of aediles cancelled because he found a number of ballots written in the same hand. Nevertheless every effort was made to keep the election system honest. Special ballot watchers, *custodes,* were appointed from a list of well know people. These *custodes* also had the responsibility of counting the ballots and reporting the vote to the presiding magistrate. The secret ballot appeared in U.S. elections only in the 1880s.

*elite in Rome and a close associate of the revolutionary general Sulla (see previous reading).
Lucullus succeeded to the unfinished war against Mithridates (previous introduction) in 74 B.C.
Without much difficulty he had Mithridates on the run, but at this point, Tigranes II,
king of Armenia, intervened on behalf of Mithridates and Lucullus turned his attention to
him. He captured and plundered his capital Tigranocerta (69 B.C.). Tigranes himself escaped,
and Lucullus launched an invasion of Armenia in pursuit of the fleeing king. At this point
things began to go wrong for Lucullus. His troops mutinied, and he was forced to withdraw
and spend the winter in Syria. His brother-in-law, who was one of his officers, conspired with
the mutinous troops and in Rome public opinion turned against him. Things went from bad to
worse, and eventually Lucullus was superseded by his arch enemy, Pompey "The Great."*

*The main point of this story, however, is not the personal disasters Lucullus suffered but
rather the picture it paints of the power of the ordinary soldiers in the Roman army, the lack
of unity in the officer class in the field, and the political divisions in Rome itself. Mutinies
occurred earlier in Roman history (for example, soldiers mutinied against the great Scipio
Africanus in Spain in 207 B.C.), but these previous mutinies were crushed because the officer
class was united behind the general and at home the Senate backed the general. The soldiers
in these situations were always punished and discipline restored. Not so by the first century
B.C. This weakening of the power of the senate and indiscipline of the armies in the field are
symptoms of the collapse of the old system of the Republic. Lucullus was a brilliant general
who won major victories but also tried to treat the provincials well by not quartering his
soldiers on them. It was not the first time in history that a conquering army came to regard
conquered territory as a resource to be plundered and then turned on the person who tried to
stop them.*[6]

Lucullus, flushed and emboldened by his victory over Tigranes, determined to
march on into the interior and there complete the conquest of the Armenians.
But, contrary to expectations, winter came on early at the time of the autumnal
equinox, with storms and frequent snow falls. Even on the most clear days, hoar
frost and ice made the water barely drinkable for the horses and made it hard to
pass through without the ice breaking and cutting the horses' sinews. The country for the most part was dark and gloomy, with difficult passes and much forest.
It kept the soldiers continually wet, with the snow falling thickly on them as
they marched by day. At night the ground they slept on was sodden. It was not
long after the battle, as they followed Lucullus, that they began to complain.
First they appealed to him by sending the military tribunes to him, but after a
while they gathered threateningly together and shouted all night long in their
tents, a characteristic sign of a mutinous army. Lucullus earnestly entreated
them, asking them to have patience until they captured the Armenian Carthage
and overthrow the work of their great enemy, meaning Hannibal. Since he was
unable to persuade the mutinous troops to go forward, he led them back and
crossing the Taurus mountain range entered the sunny country of Mygdonia

---

[6]Plutarch, *Lucullus* 32–34.

where there was a great and populous city called Nisibis by the natives and Antioch of Mygdonia by the Greeks.

Lucullus captured the city, but this did not satisfy the now thoroughly aroused troops

Sallust says that the soldiers were not well disposed to him from the beginning of the war because they were forced to stay in the field for two winters, once at Cyzicus and the other at Amisus. Their other winters also annoyed them because they either spent them in enemy territory or were confined to their tents in the open field among their allies. Not so much as once did Lucullus enter a Greek-allied town with his army [*Lucullus was trying to protect the provincials and allies against the rapacious soldiers*]. To this disaffection in the army, the Tribunes of the People at home contributed, invidiously accusing Lucullus as one who for the sake of empire and riches was prolonging the war . . . This is what we are told was said by Lucius Quintius, one of the praetors, at whose insistence, in particular, the people determined to send a replacement for Lucullus in his province and also to relieve many of the soldiers under him from further service.

Besides these evils, the one that most affected Lucullus' undertakings was the activity of Publius Clodius, a man of unrestrained violence, full of arrogance and bravado. He was the brother of Lucullus' wife, a dissolute woman with whom Clodius himself was suspected of having intercourse. At this time he was on Lucullus' staff but not as highly honored as he thought was his due. He thought that he should have been chief-of-staff, but when others were preferred before him because of his bad behavior, he ingratiated himself secretly with the troops of Fimbria. He stirred them up against Lucullus, using persuasive speeches on men who were used to being flattered in this manner. These were the men whom Fimbria had persuaded to kill the consul Flaccus and choose him as their leader. [*Flaccus had been sent out earlier against Mithridates; Fimbria was one of his officers.*] Accordingly, they listened willingly to Clodius and called him the "Soldiers' Friend" for the concern he professed for them and the indignation he expressed at the prospect, as he said that

> There will be no end of wars and hard labor, but only continual fighting with all nations. Wandering throughout the world you will wear out your lives receiving no other reward for your service than the privilege of guarding the carriages and camels of Lucullus, laden as they are with gold and precious vessels. Meanwhile the soldiers of Pompey, now demobilized and living a private life, are safe at home with their wives and children, in possession of fertile lands and cities. And this was not after driving Mithridates and Tigranes into wild deserts and demolishing royal cities in Asia as you did, but after having clashed with exiles in Spain or fleeing slaves in Italy. Why then, if our campaigns are never to end should we not rather keep what is left of our bodies and souls for a general who will reckon his chief glory to be the wealth of his soldiers?

Being persuaded by these pretexts the army of Lucullus was demoralized and refused to follow him either against Tigranes or against Mithridates, who had once more come back into Pontus from Armenia and was trying to recover his kingdom. Using winter as an excuse they sat idle in Gordyene, every minute expecting Pompey or some other general to succeed Lucullus.

After more mutinous behavior on the part of his troops, Lucullus was forced to sit by and watch Tigranes plunder at will and Mithridates resume power. As an added extra to his embarrassment, the commission that had been sent out from Rome to organize the supposedly pacified province of Pontus arrived and discovered that Lucullus was not even in control of his own camp, let alone the territory of Mithridates. Finally, Pompey came to take command and Lucullus went home (66 B.C.). This was not the end of the story. The optimates, *the traditionalists, were outraged. Pompey, they thought, had won his command by his flattery of the people and its leaders. It was a bad precedent. Neither the mutinous soldiers, the colluding officers in the field, nor the intriguing factional heads in Rome were punished or even shamed. The episode was yet another of the many nails being hammered in the coffin of the Roman Republic.*

5.6 Social and Cultural Changes: "The Beginnings of Foreign Luxury"

By the time Livy set about writing his story of the rise and decline of the Roman Republic, he had plenty of evidence of what looked like moral decay all around him to explain the decline. How much of this was real moral decay and how much was just an aspect of the change from city-state to world-state is a complicated issue. An additional factor that needs to be emphasized is that Livy was the heir to a long literary tradition of viewing the present in terms of the failure of contemporaries to live up to the glories of their virtuous ancestors. However, if we set aside Livy's complaints about the awful present, we can see some of the changes that really did take place—for instance, the introduction, along with new wealth, of a generally higher standard of living than the puritanical past of the "ancestors" allowed.

The following is a particularly good example of Livy's taking shots at the present in the guise of analysis of the past. Manlius Vulso returned to Rome in 187 B.C. to celebrate his triumph over the Gauls of Anatolia. His enemies spread the rumor that he had relaxed the old-fashioned discipline of Roman commanders and let his troops run riot in his province. Livy uses the opportunity to preach a little sermon.[7]

The origins of foreign luxury were brought to Rome by the returning army [of Manlius]. They were the first to introduce into Rome bronze couches, expensive rugs as covers, curtains, and other elaborate woven fabrics, and—what *then* were thought to be exotic pieces of furniture—tables with a single leg and marble-topped sideboards. To banquets were added women lute and harp players and other pleasures of the feast. The banquets themselves began to be prepared with greater care and

---

[7]Livy 39.6.

expenditure. Then the cook, for our ancestors the lowest of slaves in terms of both actual worth and use, began to have real value. What had been regarded as a mere labor now became an art! Yet these things, which at the time were thought to be remarkable, were merely the seeds of the luxury to come.

5.7   "He Mocked All Greek Culture and Learning"

Prolonged contact with the Hellenistic world made the Romans conscious of their cultural backwardness. They also discovered that there were life-styles other than the rather narrow one that all Romans had been forced to accept to that time. One of the key aspects of the Roman Revolution was the rapid and self-assured response of the Roman elites to the challenge of Greek culture, though, understandably, the guardians of traditional values at Rome regarded this response as evidence of moral decadence.

From approximately 200 B.C. onward, Romans began first to dabble in, and then become serious practitioners of, many, though not all, aspects of Greek high culture. In due course the Romans would have attractive private alternatives to service to the state, something the shrewd Cato anticipated when an embassy came to Rome in 153 B.C. from Athens to plead against a judicial decision and stayed to "infect" the youth of the city.[8]

Cato was already an old man when a delegation came from Athens to Rome. Carneades the Academic philosopher and Diogenes the Stoic came to beg that the people of Athens be released from a fine of 500 talents that had been imposed on them. The Oropians had brought suit, the Athenians failed to appear, and the Sicyonians had judged against them.

As soon as the philosophers arrived the most intellectual among the younger Romans rushed to see them and listened to them with pleasure and wonder. Most of all they were impressed by the grace and power of Carneades' oratory whose performance did not fall short of his reputation. His speeches attracted a large and sympathetic audience, and the city was filled with his praises as if by a great, roaring wind. The word spread all over that a Greek of astonishing ability had come who could overwhelm all opposition by his eloquence. He had so entranced the youth of the city that they had abandoned their pleasures and pursuits and had become enthused with philosophy. The majority were pleased with this and were glad to see their youth involved with Greek culture and associating with such distinguished men. But Cato, when passion for words first manifested itself in the city, was much upset, fearing that the younger generation's ambition would be deflected to the glory of mere words rather than military exploits.

---

[8]Plutarch, *Cato* 22–23.

Accordingly, when the reputation of the philosophers continued to increase in the city, and no less prominent a man than Gaius Acilius volunteered to act as their interpreter for their first meeting with the Senate, Cato determined to find some plausible excuse to clear all the philosophers out of the city. So, he came to the Senate and proceeded to blame the current magistrates for keeping the embassy in such long suspense although they were men whose powers of persuasion were so great that they could obtain anything they wanted. "We ought," he said, "to decide one way or the other on this issue and to vote on what the embassy proposes so that these distinguished men may return to their own schools and lecture the youth of Greece while the young men of Rome may, as in the past, pay attention to their own laws and magistrates."

He did this not as some think because of personal hostility to Carneades but because he was entirely opposed to philosophy and mocked all Greek culture and learning out of patriotism. . . . In order to discredit Greek culture in the eyes of his son, he spoke too loosely for his years, predicting that the Romans would be destroyed when they became infected by Greek learning. But time has shown how empty this prophecy was, for while the city was at the height of its powers, it embraced every form of Greek learning and culture.

5.8   In Defense of Public Service

A century later, Cato's presentiments had become reality. By the first century B.C., *the Roman upper class discovered pleasures—and ideals—other than service to the state. In 56* B.C., *Cicero felt the need to defend the old system in his tract.* On the Commonwealth (De Re Publica) *and to attack those who proposed the ideal of leisure as an alternative way of life, as it was found in some Greek philosophical systems. Although Cicero cannot avoid giving himself a pat on the back for his service to the state (see especially the closing paragraph), there is a great deal of truth in his eulogy of the old Republican ideal.[9]*

It is not enough to possess virtue as if it were an art of some kind; it must also be applied in real life. While it is true that an art, even if never used, can still be retained in the form of knowledge, virtue, on the other hand, depends entirely on use. And its highest use is in the government of the state and the actual performance in deeds, not words, of those principles with which the philosophers make their ivory towers resound.

No principles worked out by philosophers . . . have not also been discovered and put into practice by those who draw up law codes for states. What is the source of our sense of moral obligation and our duty to the gods? What is the source of the law of nations or our own civil code? Whence justice, dependability, fair dealing? From where comes our sense of shame, self-restraint, fear of disgrace, desire for praise, and honor? Whence courage in the face of toil and

---

[9]Cicero, *De Re Publica* 1.2.

danger? Where else but from those men who have developed these qualities by a system of education and then either confirmed them by custom or enforced them by laws. Xenocrates, one of the foremost philosophers, was asked, so it is said, what his students learned from him. He replied: "To do of their own free will what the law required them to do." Therefore, the individual who compels *all* men by the authority of the magistrates and the penalties of law to follow a way of life that the philosophers by persuasion can convince *only a few* to follow is to be held superior. . . .

Against these well-founded and sound arguments, those who take the opposite view allege first the amount of work involved in the defense of the state . . . then the grave risks involved in a political career. . . . They say that the most worthless men are attracted to public life. To be compared with them is degrading, to quarrel with them, especially when the mob is worked up, wretched and dangerous. Therefore, it is claimed, the wise man should not get involved in government since he cannot restrain the mindless and untamed furies of the crowd. Nor does a freeman struggle with vile and savage opponents or submit to the scourgings of abuse. . . .

They hold up before the brave man the dishonorable fear of death. Brave men, however, are more likely to regard it a greater disaster to be wasted by the natural processes of aging than to have the opportunity, in preference to all else, of giving up their lives for their country—lives which, in any case, must be surrendered to nature. . . . In truth, our country did not bear us or educate us without expecting some kind of service in return. It has not been only to serve our convenience that it has provided us with a safe refuge for our leisure and a quiet place for our moments of tranquility. Rather, our country has given us these opportunities so that it may take advantage of our most important powers of mind, our talents, and our wisdom, leaving only for our private use what it did not need. . . .

I see that nearly all of whom the Greeks called the Seven Wise Men spent their lives in public service. For there really is no other occupation in which human excellence nearly approaches the divine than the founding of new states or the preservation of those already in existence.

5.9   Cicero on the Decadence of the Roman Elite

The previous reading was Cicero in his philosophic mode. As Cicero well knew, however, the kind of leisure activities enjoyed by Romans of the new age did not involve much philosophizing. This is clear in the following brief extract from a letter to his friend and confidant, Atticus.[10]

---

[10]Cicero, *Letter to Atticus* 2.1.

Our leading men think they have transcended the summit of human ambition when the bearded mullets in their fish ponds eat out of their hands while letting everything else go to hell.

5.10   Women of the Late Republic: Standing Up to the Triumvirs

The soldier and senator Velleius Paterculus made the following sardonic comment about family loyalties during the murderous proscriptions of the Triumvirs Antony, Octavian, and Lepidus: "Toward the proscribed {i.e., those who ended up on the death lists} their wives showed the greatest loyalty; their freedmen quite a lot; their slaves some; their sons none." We have already seen a proof of this in the Turia inscription in Chapter 4 (4.7). Another example follows, not so much of the loyalty of wives to husbands, as of how women felt that they had the right (and the duty) to protect what was theirs and that they could depend on popular support for their position.

The background of the story is this. After the murder of Caesar his avengers needed money to pursue their campaign against the assassins Brutus and Cassius. First the Triumvirs proscribed the property of their enemies, but when they found that they were still short, they decided to tax the property of the female family members of their enemies. Note how the women first try to handle the matter privately but, when that does not work, they go public. Aristocratic ideology is heavily emphasized.[11]

The Triumvirs addressed the people on this subject and published an edict requiring 1,400 of the richest women to make a valuation of their property and to furnish for the service of the war an amount the Triumvirs would see fit. It was provided further that if any should conceal their property or make a false valuation, they should be fined, and that rewards would be given to informers, whether free or slave.

The women decided to approach the womenfolk of the Triumvirs. With the sister of Octavian and the mother of Antony they did not fail, but they were repulsed from the doors of Fulvia, the wife of Antony, whose rudeness they could scarcely endure. They then forced their way to the tribunal of the Triumvirs in the Forum, the people and the guards dividing to let them pass. There, through Hortensia, whom they had delegated as their representative, they spoke as follows:

"As befitted women of our rank addressing a petition to you, we had recourse first to the women of your households. But having been treated with discourtesy by Fulvia, we have been driven to come to you in person publicly. You have already deprived us of our fathers, our sons, our husbands, and our brothers, whom you accused of having wronged you. If

---

[11]Appian, *Civil Wars* 4.32–34. Translation based on that of Horace White, *Appian's Roman History* (London, 1913).

you take away our property also, you reduce us to a condition unbecoming our status, our manners, and our gender. If we have done you wrong, as you say our husbands have, proscribe us as you do them. But if we women have not voted any of you public enemies, have not torn down your houses, destroyed your army, or led one against you, if we have not hindered you in obtaining offices and honors—why do we share the penalty when we did not share the guilt?

"Why should we pay taxes when we have no part in the honors, the commands, the politics for which you fight against others with such dreadful results? 'Because this is a time of war,' do you say? When have there not been wars, and when have taxes ever been imposed on women, who are exempted by their gender among all humankind?

"Our mothers did once rise above their gender and made contributions when you were in danger of losing the whole empire and the city itself during the Carthaginian Wars. But then they contributed voluntarily, not from their landed property, their fields, their dowries, or their houses, without which life is not possible to free women, but only from their own jewelry, and even these not according to fixed valuation, not under fear of informers or accusers, not by force and violence, but what they themselves were willing to give. What alarm is there now for the empire or the country? Let war with the Gauls or the Parthians come, and we shall not be inferior to our mothers in zeal for the common safety. But for civil wars may we never contribute, nor ever assist you against each other! We did not contribute to Caesar or to Pompey. Neither Marius nor Cinna imposed taxes upon us. Nor did Sulla, who held despotic power in the state, do so, whereas you say that you are reestablishing the commonwealth."

While Hortensia was giving her speech, the Triumvirs were angry that women should dare to speak publicly while the men were silent and that they should demand reasons for their acts from the magistrates. . . . They ordered the lictors to drive them away from the tribunal, which they proceeded to do until cries were raised by the people outside. Then the lictors stopped and the Triumvirs said that they would postpone consideration of the matter until the next day.

On the following day they reduced the number of women who were to present a valuation of their property from 1,400 to 400 and decreed that all individuals who possessed more than 100,000 drachmae, both citizens and strangers, freedmen and priests, men of all nationalities without a single exception . . . should lend them at interest a fiftieth part of their property and contribute one year's income to the war expenses.

5.11   Sempronia: A Woman of the Late Republic

Sempronia was a member of one of Rome's most distinguished families, the gens Sempronia. She was the wife of Decimus Junius Brutus and the mother of the Decimus Brutus who was one of the assassins of Julius Caesar. The story told here by Sallust concerns her role in 63 B.C. at the time when the alienated aristocrat Catiline was trying to launch a coup d'état. Her role, not related here, involved providing cover at one point during the plot for some of the conspirators. Catiline, however, failed in his plans due to the vigilance of the consul Cicero. His coconspirators were caught and executed, and a short while later Catiline fell in battle.[12]

When the elections took place, Marcus Cicero and Gaius Antonius were elected consuls. This alarmed at first the conspirators, but Catiline's furor did not abate. On the contrary he became even more active, establishing caches of weapons at convenient places throughout Italy, raising money on his own credit or that of his friends, sending it to Fiesole [near Florence] to a man named Manlius who was afterward the one who first took the field. About that time Catiline was said to have gained the support of many people of every background, including some women who, while younger, had lived extravagantly on the money they obtained by prostituting themselves. Later, when their age had stopped this activity but not their taste for luxury, they contracted large amounts of debt. These women, Catiline thought, could bring the slaves of the city over to him and organize acts of arson. Their husbands could either be won over to his side or murdered.

Among these women was Sempronia. She had in the past committed crimes of masculine daring. By birth and beauty, in her husband and children, she had been favored by Fortune. She was well educated in Greek and Latin literature and could play the lyre and dance more skillfully than any respectable woman should. She had many other accomplishments in decadence. She set no value by modesty and chastity. It would be hard to say whether she was less prodigal with her money or her honor. Her desires were so strong that she more often made advances to men than they to her. Even before the time of Catiline's coup, she had broken her word, repudiated her debts, and been an accomplice to murder. Luxury and poverty combined to drive her over the edge. Yet she was a woman of many endowments. She could write poetry, exchange jokes, or converse modestly, tenderly or wantonly. She was a woman of wit and charm.

▼▼▼

Questions

1. Why do you think such detailed information is available in this chapter, whereas so much of the information we have about early Roman history is so obviously concocted?
2. Sallust and Livy each give different dates for the beginning of the fall of the Republic. Each also gives a different interpretation of what went wrong. Analyze. (**5.2**; **5.6**)

---

[12]Sallust 24–25 *B.C.*

3. Plutarch makes a list of what Tiberius Gracchus and his followers thought was wrong with Rome. What were the main items? Do you suspect that there might be some spin in the stirring speech Tiberius gives? (**5.3**)

4. Gaius Gracchus went beyond his brother in proposing reform measures. Name some of these. Do you think he was a demagog? (**5.3**)

5. Plutarch makes a comparison between the behavior of different generations of Roman generals. Which did he prefer and why? (**5.4**)

6. An officer in Lucullus' army by the name of Clodius gives a speech in which he lists the grievances of the ordinary Roman soldiers. What were these? What impact did the speech have? (**5.5**)

7. Why do you think Cato (and others) were nervous about the impact Greek culture was having on the young people of Rome? (**5.7**)

8. Cicero argued strongly in defense of service to the state. What were some of his main points? How did his opponents argue? (**5.8**)

9. Why were the Triumvirs particularly vexed at the elite women who confronted them in public? (**5.10**)

10. What were Sempronia's "accomplishments in decadence"? Why was Sallust so critical of her and others like her?

Chapter 6

▼▼▼

Augustus and the Principate

With the disintegration of the old political order of the Republic in the first century B.C. (the "Fall of the Republic"), under which Rome acquired most of its empire as well as its military reputation, there was a high likelihood that what had been laboriously cobbled together over the centuries would fragment into regional power centers, each governed by its own independent army commander. Under one such conjectural scenario the fragmentation of the empire would have followed the lines of the geographical arrangement worked out by the Triumvirs Antony, Lepidus, and Octavius (later known as Augustus) after the murder of Julius Caesar in 44 B.C.

This division gave Antony the eastern Mediterranean with Egypt as his main base. Lepidus had Africa, and Octavius Italy and the western provinces. Over the years these might have become permanent divisions, paralleling what actually happened centuries later at the time of the fall of the Roman Empire. That the disintegration did not occur in the first century B.C. was due to the dogged, and sometimes inspired, efforts of one member of the Triumvirate, Julius Caesar's adopted son, Gaius Octavius.

The story begins with the fact that Caesar did not have a son and, as a result, had some freedom in selecting an heir. He could have chosen some promising young man from among the Roman nobility, as sonless Romans of the past had done. There were, however, a number of alternatives. He had two sisters, one of whose daughters had a son named Gaius Octavius, a sickly but energetic young man. Another sister, by different husbands, had two sons, Pinarius and Q. Pedius. Pinarius never seems to have made Caesar's short list of potential heirs, but Pedius was a legate with Caesar during his campaigns in Gaul and later, during the civil wars, fought with him in Spain. Following his return, Pedius was allowed a triumph. Nevertheless, Caesar passed him over and instead chose the much younger Gaius

Octavius as his heir. This was clearly a well thought out selection so that when Caesar was assassinated in 44 B.C., provision had been made for the continuation of his legacy. Theoretically, at least, there was not to be a free for all among the potential heirs for Caesar's mantel. Perhaps he learned from the bad example of Alexander the Great who, despite repeated urgings, failed to appoint an heir and left chaos behind him when he died.

The selection of an heir was, however, only the first step in a very long process of knitting the broken parts of the Republic into a single whole again. Octavius was only nineteen years of age when he accepted his adoptive father's inheritance. Against him were pitted the older, hardened and more experienced leaders of the Caesarian party among whom he initially had to struggle merely to survive. He may have had the name of Julius Caesar as the result of his adoption, but this was not sufficient to guarantee his success even within his own faction. Then there were his even more numerous republican opponents, the enemies of everything Caesar and his followers stood for. But by adroit and often ruthless maneuvering, Octavius managed, over the following years, first to dispose of the most dangerous of the anti-Caesarians, republican die-hards such as Brutus, Cassius and Cato the Younger, and such moderates as Cicero. Then he was able to turn against the senior leaders of his own faction, Lepidus, Antony and the rest. Antony was the most difficult to defeat, but a series of disastrous campaigns against the Parthians, his association with Cleopatra, queen of Egypt, and his natural indolence, helped Octavius. Finally, at Actium in 31 B.C. Octavius defeated the combined forces of Antony and Cleopatra. Both subsequently committed suicide and Octavius was left alone upon the Roman stage.

The Political Issues

Despite his victories over his opponents for the control of Rome, Octavius had his hands full. A century of civil disturbances, assassinations, and civil wars had left the Roman governing apparatus a shambles. Even the brilliant and energetic Caesar did not seem to have any better idea on how to rescue Rome from anarchy than to turn it into some kind of monarchy. The republican opposition had even less credible solutions. A number of things were clear. Neither the Senate nor the Assemblies could govern under the old system of mutual deference and cooperation. The consensus of the Republic was broken forever. What was to replace it was not, however, clear to anyone. Cicero had proposed a blueprint in his *De Re Publica*, a tract on government laying out a possible scenario (see Chapter 1) for a revived Republic, but it was no more than a dream.

At least one thing favored Octavius. This was a general feeling of exhaustion on the part of all parties in the civil wars leading up to Actium. Besides, almost no one knew what the old Republic had been like. As Tacitus, the great historian of the early Empire put it: "Actium had been won before the younger generation was born. Even most of the older generation had come into a world of civil wars. Practically no one

had seen a truly Republican government. Thus the state was revolutionized."
(*Annals* 1.3). Both elite and people recognized the need for a new regime. The
people, in particular, were clear on that point. They wanted stability at any cost.
Whatever he did, Octavius had to find a political and constitutional formula that
would embrace the whole state—the people, Senate, equestrian order, and army
alike—in a new and lasting relationship. In addition, the system of imperial government, so haphazard and irresponsible in the past, badly needed to be overhauled
and made responsive to the needs of the provincials. The formula would have to
contain elements of the old and the new, but no one knew the correct proportions.
Some of the components were already to be found in the faction of Caesar, but the
task confronting Octavian was that of making faction and state coincide.

By 30 B.C. Octavius, although only thirty-three years old, was a hardened veteran, a pragmatist willing to experiment like FDR did with various programs during
the Depression era. If a program worked, fine; keep it; if it failed, discard it and try
again. He surrounded himself with an excellent cadre of talented people, not car-
ing, in Caesarian fashion, whether they were from the nobility, the common people or the Italian municipal elites. His most trusted henchman, Marcus Vipsanius
Agrippa, came of humble origins, as did Quintus Salvidienus Rufus, who started
out as a shepherd. There were bankers and men of affairs like Balbus, Oppius,
Matius and Rabirius Postumus. Of his inner circle, however, the most important
was his wife, Livia, a brilliant and powerful personality in her own right, whom
many thought was the real brains and driving force behind Octavius.

It does not matter who, individually, deserves the credit, even supposing we
could penetrate the inner workings of Octavius' government. What counted was
that this gifted group found a way to fix what seemed unfixable. Their work was to
constitute a new foundation for Rome and the basis for centuries to come for the
Roman Empire. It was an intricate balance of military power and freedom built on
the foundation of the old Republic. The government created by Octavius and his
helpers bears no resemblance to modern military autocracies which, for the most
part, exist in places which have no prior experience of the rule of law and no
traditions of liberty on the part of either elite or populace at large, let alone both
as was the case of Rome. By the time Octavius began to refound the Republic, he
was dealing with institutions and a culture that already had 500 years of experience of freedom and the rule of law.

The Army, the Senate, and the People

The most pressing problem was that of the army. Between 31 B.C. and 13 B.C.
Octavius reduced it from 60 to 28 legions, in the process settling over 100,000
veterans in colonies in Italy, Africa, Asia, and Syria. Under Sulla resettlement had
been financed by a bloody proscription; fortunately, the means for accomplishing
Octavius' enormous resettlement were supplied by the treasures of Egypt, which
Octavius seized after the defeat of Antony.

The matter of imperial defense was resolutely faced by making the permanent legionary forces in the provinces large enough to cope with the problems of the frontiers without having to raise emergency armies and by regularizing length of service, pay scales, and discharge benefits. Regular pay came out of the old Republican treasury, and in A.D. 6 a special military treasury, funded by a sales tax and death duties, was set up to pay retirement bonuses to the 9,000 or so veterans who were discharged annually.

The political problem of the army was not so easily solved. Somehow Octavius had to discover a legally acceptable means of keeping control of the legions, or Rome would once more be plunged into the horrors of civil war.

Having held the consulship continuously from 31 B.C., Octavius suddenly renounced his powers in 27 B.C. and declared the reestablishment of the Republic. In recognition of his restoration of the Republic he was given the cognomen "Augustus," which had religious connotations and suggested he had the blessings of the gods for what he was doing. Pressed by the Senate, he retained the consulship and also proconsular control of the legions. Although this solution had at least constitutional form, it was not completely satisfactory. For example, it halved the number of consular positions available to the nobility and saddled Augustus with many routine duties. After a serious illness and an attempted coup, he resigned the consulship in 23 B.C. but was compensated by being given special proconsular power (*maius imperium*), greater than that possessed by any other proconsul, which allowed him to intervene in the provinces wherever he thought it necessary. This proved to be a generally satisfactory solution to the problem of how to control the legions and became one of the pillars of the new constitution.

Relations between Augustus and the upper classes were considerably eased by his concern for constitutional formalities, but he exploited other, less formal approaches with great ingenuity and apparent genuineness. For example, whereas Caesar had little patience with the Senate and offended it unnecessarily, Augustus went out of his way to be deferential. He did not flaunt his power, and maintained a simple and modest standard of living. He wore homespun togas and lived in a dwelling that any of the nobles might have possessed. In the matter of titles, which were so important at Rome, his preference was for the informal *princeps*, or "elder statesman." In the Republic this term had been applied to ex-consuls whose prestige and authority were such that they were able to dominate the Senate and the government, though not in any formal or legal sense. Augustus' use of the title implied that he ruled in a similar traditional way, by his authority (*auctoritas*) and not by virtue of any alteration in the constitution. Although no one could overlook the fact that Augustus' influence went far beyond his *auctoritas*, after fifty years of bloodshed the upper classes were willing to close their eyes to the reality of his power as long as they did not also have to face the external trappings of an autocracy.

In other respects, Augustus managed relations with the Senate with tact and dignity. Its numbers were gradually reduced from 1,000 to 600, and membership was made hereditary, although Augustus retained the right to nominate new members.

The census qualification was put at 1 million sesterces, but special emphasis was placed on integrity and capacity for public office.

The powers and jurisdiction of the Senate and of Augustus tended to overlap in a number of areas, and the lines of demarcation were left deliberately vague. Both made appointments to the provinces, but the Senate sent governors to the peaceful, senatorial provinces, whereas Augustus sent his governors to the remainder, the imperial provinces where the legions were stationed. Imperial governors were now paid regular salaries, and their terms were extended from one year to three to five years. The temptation to exploit their positions was thus reduced, and their lengthened tenure allowed them sufficient time to acquire expertise in the exercise of their duties. By these means and by the judicious reform of the tax-collecting system, Augustus was able to establish the provinces on a sound administrative basis.

In the course of seeking suitable legal forms for his extraordinary powers, Augustus selected one constitutional form from the old patrician state and one from the plebeian. The first was *proconsular imperium*, which gave him control of the army, and the second was tribunician power, which was voted to him in 23 B.C. Together they were to be the real foundation of the new state. The choice of tribunician power was particularly popular with the people. For centuries they had turned to their tribunes for the redress of all kinds of grievances, and now they could turn to their tribune–emperor. It was also a good choice from a purely practical, constitutional viewpoint. As tribune, Augustus could veto or enact legislation, intervene on behalf of individuals, hold court, or call the Senate into session, yet the office had none of the tyrannical connotations of the kingship or even, from the people's view, of the consulship. By the same willing oversight by which the Senate and the upper classes came to accept Augustus' perpetual proconsular power as the price of peace, the people were willing to acquiesce in their loss of power by accepting Augustus as their permanent tribune.

Religious and Social Reform

Augustus attempted to stem the rising tide of moral change that had developed in the late Republic by enacting a comprehensive program of social, religious, and moral reform. Because many men and women of the upper classes preferred to remain celibate and regarded the raising and education of children as too much trouble, Augustus enacted penalties for childless couples while creating special benefits for those with children, although later he was compelled to reduce or even remove the penalties and increase the benefits. To cope with adultery, which was widely condoned among the elite, and to extend the power of the state over the family, Augustus made the act a public crime to which severe penalties were attached. Existing sumptuary laws were strengthened to curb luxury, and attempts were made to control the haphazard manumission of slaves and the number of the poor eligible for free grain.

The idea that prosperity and peace in the state depended on the pious fulfillment of religious duties to the gods was an ancient one in Rome, and in the Republic the magistrates had taken particular responsibility for maintaining the *pax deorum*, the peace between gods and men. Augustus made a point of stressing his concern for this traditional belief by restoring temples—82 by his own account—and becoming a member of the sacred colleges of pontiffs and augurs. He revived many cults and ancient practices, and in 12 B.C., when Lepidus died, he became *pontifex maximus*. From this date he was not only the secular but also the religious head of the state.

Control of the Media

The peace and tranquility that Augustus' rule introduced were deeply felt by all of Italian society, not least by its literary figures and artists. Augustus had the good fortune of finding in Virgil, Horace, and Livy spokesmen for the regime who were in genuine accord with its goals.

Both Virgil and Livy were inspired by the epic rise of Rome, its sufferings, its piety, and its great destiny. In the hero Aeneas, Virgil discovered the ideal figure of the Augustan Age: sober, tenacious, pious, a slave to duty. Livy, as has been noted, traced the history of Rome from its meager beginnings to his own day, filling it with patriotic and moral examples, and Horace elegantly expounded in his *Odes* the virtues of the Romans, their frugality, hardiness, and simplicity. However, Ovid failed to adjust himself to the new current of morality and was banished, for instead of writing elevating moral tales, he produced the *Art of Love*, a humorous sexual handbook that was not taken well by the reform minded Augustus, whatever he might have thought of it in private.

More directly Augustus used the coinage of the Empire to herald his achievement in bringing peace to the world. The plastic arts, too, were made to reflect this theme. One of the best-preserved monuments of the age is the Altar of Peace (the *Ara Pacis*), a simple structure surrounded by walls decorated with friezes whose serenity and order are immediately striking, and which to this day convey a profound sense of the Augustan peace (See next page).

Order in the City

The reign of Augustus also brought other, more tangible benefits to the Roman people. For the first time in its history the city of Rome was provided with a proper urban administration. In addition to Augustus' personal bodyguard, the Praetorian Cohorts, a police force of 3,000 men (*Cohortes Urbanae*) was created, as well as a firefighting force of 7,000 (*Vigiles*). New aqueducts were built, and the sewage system was thoroughly overhauled. A permanent board of commissioners (*Curatores Aquarum*) was

THE AUGUSTAN PEACE

One of the great monuments of the Augustan Age was the Altar of Peace located between the banks of the Tiber and the mausoleum Augustus constructed for himself and his family. Both monuments still stand.

The Altar is placed on a podium flanked by tall screens carved on the outside with life size figures representing Augustus, the Imperial Family, magistrates, senators, members of religious confraternities and representatives of the Roman people. The carvings are intended to convey a message of a state restored to political tranquility, and society to its proper order after over a century of civil and military turmoil. The correct social hierarchy has been reinstated, the old morality renewed and religion reinvigorated. But beyond the restoration of public order there is also a message regarding the fertility and material well being that accompanied the restored state. This is what the goddess portrayed here is intended to convey.

She can be identified as Mother Earth, Venus, Italia, or just generally, Peace. She is a dignified, motherly deity holding two children who reach towards her. Her lap is filled with fruit and her head is adorned with wreaths of grain and poppies. More grain and poppies grow behind her. At her feet are a seated an ox and a grazing sheep, symbols of the increase of the herds. Two figures flank the goddess. These are the land and sea breezes which bring moisture to the land. Seated on a goose and a sea monster respectively, they are intended to convey to the viewer the sense that even wild creatures have been tamed in the new age of peace and prosperity.

On the reverse side (not shown here) the goddess Roma is depicted seated on a mound of armor. This is a reminder that ultimately the blessings of peace and material well being rest on military might, a suitable symbol of the restored Roman state.

The state, restored by Augustus, needed new imagery to express its message of political tranquility and moral renewal. The Ara Pacis symbolized the new golden age that had been inaugurated by Augustus after his reform of the state.

appointed to maintain the supply of water. Similar commissions were created to look after flood control (*Curatores Riparum Tiberis*) and the food supply (*Cura Annonae*). Entertainment was not neglected, and the first permanent amphitheater in Rome's history was erected. Only a century later the satirist Juvenal was to use the bitter epithet "bread and the circuses" to describe the imperial people of Rome.

The Succession

Augustus rose to power as the adopted son of Caesar and maintained himself as *princeps* (elder statesman) by his careful management of the constitution and his sensitivity to the residue of republican feelings among his subjects. These were the essentials of his rule: his personal and dynastic popularity with the people and the army, and his acceptance by the Senate as the "best man" in the state. The appearance of a monarchy was avoided, and technically all the emperor's powers were conferred on him by the Senate and people, and would cease to exist when he died. Therein lay the problem. How could power be passed on in an orderly way, without civil strife, after his death?

The problem nagged at Augustus, and at some point he made up his mind that the stability of the state could be maintained only if power were to be transmitted to an heir who bore his name. Unfortunately, Augustus had no sons, and his daughter Julia's sons, Gaius and Lucius, died young. That left Tiberius, his wife Livia's son from a previous marriage, and it was this man, already in middle age, whom Augustus finally adopted and associated with himself in the ruling of the Empire in A.D. 4. In turn, Tiberius was forced to adopt as his heir his brother's son, Germanicus, whose mother had been a daughter of Antony and Augustus' sister Octavia. Thus, when Augustus died in A.D. 14, Tiberius succeeded as the son of Caesar to the loyalty of the people and the army, having already been constitutionally invested with most of the powers of the *princeps*.

This solution to the problem of succession recurred throughout the subsequent history of the Empire. For some years the imperial office remained within the family of Augustus, the Julio-Claudian dynasty. An army rebellion followed by the suicide of Nero in A.D. 68 brought an end to the Julio-Claudians and revealed to all what Tacitus called the *arcana imperii*, the secrets of empire, namely that it was on the armies that the emperor's power ultimately rested. The Flavian dynasty ruled from A.D. 69 to 96 and was succeeded by the so-called "Five Good Emperors" (Nerva, Trajan, Hadrian, Antoninus Pius, and Marcus Aurelius) each of whom, with the exception of the last named, picked as their successor someone who was not their son. From the time of Commodus, Marcus Aurelius' son, this system broke down, and with the Severan dynasty the military aspect of the emperor's power became more and more pronounced. The chaos of the third century A.D. continued this trend, and the elaborate pretences of political freedom woven by Augustus were gradually eroded away nearly completely.

▼▼▼

6.1   A Contemporary's Estimate of the Young Octavius

*In the chaos following the murder of Caesar, Octavius arrived in Rome to contend with the other Caesarian leaders such as Antony and Lepidus for control of Caesar's faction and legacy. Most contemporaries gave him little chance of success. How wrong they were. Here Cicero scornfully refers to him as a "*puer*", a mere boy, not a man. Cicero paid for his arrogance when Octavius sacrificed him to the vengeance of Antony during the proscriptions of the Triumvirs. The reading comes from one of Cicero's letters to his good friend and confidant, Atticus.*

Octavius was here with me recently; very complimentary and friendly. His friends refer to him as "Caesar", but Philippus [*prominent senator, ex-consul, stepfather of Octavius*] did not, so neither did I. My feeling is that he is not a reliable citizen: there are too many people who threaten our friends about him with death [*the friends referred to are Brutus and Cassius and the other assassins of Caesar*]. They say the situation is intolerable. What do you think they will say when the boy [*i.e., Octavius*] comes to Rome, where our liberators cannot be safe? . . . . (Cicero, *Letters to Atticus*, 14.12.2).

A second reading is from Decimus Brutus, one of Caesar's assassins, in a letter to Cicero. He, too, paid a price for underestimating the young Octavius.

The young man (*adulescentem*) is to be praised, honored—and removed (Cicero, *Letters of his Friends* 11.20.1).

6.2   The *Res Gestae*: What Augustus Wanted Posterity to Think of Him

The Res Gestae Divi Augusti, *the* Acts of the Divine Augustus, *give us Augustus' view of the events of his life from the time he became Julius Caesar's adopted son after the dictator's assassination in 44 B.C. They are not an autobiography (which he also wrote, but which has not survived), but a picture of himself as he wanted to be remembered by posterity as statesman and general. They were also statements of the ideology of the new state that Augustus wanted to be widely disseminated. The best surviving copy, for instance, was chiseled into the walls of the temple of Rome and Augustus at Ancyra (in modern Turkey), though fragments of other copies are known. We know that the* Res Gestae *was also inscribed on bronze pillars, now long since melted down, set in front of Augustus' mausoleum in Rome. At Ancyra the text was carved on the inner walls of the vestibule of the temple. It was intended to be read as one moved around the temple, from left to right.*

Although technically a truthful documents it leaves out much. Nothing, for instance, is said of Antony and Cleopatra. Augustus gives a great deal of emphasis to providing legal justifications for all of his actions from the time he accepted the will of his great uncle Julius Caesar and formally became Caesar's adopted son. He is at pains to point out that he settled demobilized soldiers legally by compensating the landowners, but omits to mention the confiscation of land from those who chose the wrong side. The document testifies to the touchiness of his situation as First Man in Rome—Princeps—and the need to reconcile various constituencies to his rule. These included various factions among the Roman and Italian elite, the army, the rural populations of Italy, the urban plebs of Rome, provincial elites and many others. As such the Res Gestae provides a justifying ideology for the first several centuries of the early Empire that modern historians call the Principate.

1. When I was nineteen, on my own initiative and at my own expense, I raised an army to restore the liberty of the Republic. At that time it suffered under the tyranny of a faction (*that of Mark Antony*). For this deed, during the consulships of Hirtius and Pansa, I was enrolled in the senate by honorary decrees. At the same time I was given consular precedence in voting (*i.e., in the proceedings of the Senate he spoke and voted with the consuls*). I was also decreed the right to command soldiers as propraetor with *imperium*. As propraetor the Senate ordered me to see that no harm came to the *res publica*. After the consuls died in battle that same year, the people elected me consul (*but in fact only after Octavian marched his army on Rome and intimidated the Senate into acting*). I was also elected Triumvir for Establishing the Constitution (*along with Antony and Lepidus*).

2. I drove into exile the murderers of my father (*i.e., his adoptive father, Gaius Julius Caesar*), punishing them by due process of law. Afterwards when they waged war on the Republic I twice defeated them in battle (*the double battle of Philippi; Octavian was sick on both occasions and Antony was the real victor*). 3. I undertook wars on land and sea, both domestic and foreign, throughout the world. I spared all citizens who sued for pardon (*only partially true*). Those foreign peoples who could safely be pardoned I chose to save rather than destroy. Half a million citizens were bound to me by military oath. Of these I settled 300,000 in colonies or sent back to their hometowns after their term of service was complete. To all I assigned land or money as a reward for their service. . . .

4. I triumphed twice with an ovation (*a minor triumph*). Three times I celebrated curule triumphs and was hailed as *imperator* (*i.e., commander, for military victories by his troops*) twenty one times. . . . In my triumphs nine kings or children of kings were led before my chariot. At the time of this writing I have been consul thirteen times and held tribunician power for the thirty-seventh time (*in A.D. 14, the year of his death*). 5. I did not accept the dictatorship which was offered to me once in my absence and later in the consulships of Marcus Marcellus and Lucius Arruntius by the Roman Senate and People. At a time of great scarcity I accepted the responsibility for the grain supply. I so administered it that within a few days

I freed the entire people from the fear and danger to which they were exposed.
This was done at my own expense.

Augustus' Concern for Legality

I did not accept the consulships, either on an annual basis or for life then offered to
me (*i.e., after the threat of famine had been removed*) 6. When the Senate and the Roman
people unanimously agreed that I should be elected overseer of laws and morals without a colleague and with full power (*in 19 and 18 B.C.; most Roman offices were collegial,
i.e., they were shared offices, and power was usually restricted in various ways*) I refused to
accept any power contrary to the traditions of our ancestors. The matters the senate
wanted me to enact at that time I did in virtue of my tribunician power. . . . 7. I was
one of the Triumvirs for the Reestablishment of the Constitution for ten years in succession. Up to the time of this writing I have been *princeps senatus* for forty years (*this
traditional honor gave him the right to speak first at meetings of the Senate*). I have been
pontifex maximus; augur; a member of the board of fifteen commissioners for sacred
rites; a member of the board of seven for sacred feasts; an Arval Brother; a Sodalis
Titius; a fetial priest.

8. . . . In my sixth consulship with Marcus Agrippa as colleague, I conducted a
census of the people (*28 B.C.*). I performed the sacrifices at the close of the census
(*known as the* "lustrum") after an interval of forty-one years. In this census 4,063,000
Roman citizens were entered in the census rolls. A second time in the consulships of
Gaius Censorinus and Gaius Asinius, I conducted the *lustrum*, this time alone, with
consular *imperium*. In this census 4,233,000 citizens were entered in the census rolls
(*8 B.C.*). For a third time, with consular *imperium* and with my (*adopted*) son Tiberius
Caesar as my colleague, I performed the *lustrum*. This was in the consulship of Sextus
Pompeius and Sextus Apuleius (*in A.D. 14, three months before his death*). In this census
4,937,000 Roman citizens were counted (*the increase in population demonstrates the success of Augustus' stewardship of the state*).

I restored many of the traditions of our ancestors by means of new laws. I myself set
precedents in many things for subsequent generations to imitate. . . . 10. . . . I refused
the office of Pontifex Maximus while my colleague (*Lepidus*) was still alive, although
the people offered it to me and it had been an office my father had held. . . . 11. The
Senate erected in honor of my return (*from tours of Sicily, Greece, Asia Minor and Syria*)
an altar to "Fortuna Redux" at the Porta Capena. . . . 12. . . . When I returned from
Spain and Gaul after conducting affairs there successfully, during the consulships of
Tiberius Nero and Publius Quintilius, the Senate voted in honor of my return the dedication of an altar to the Augustan Peace (*the famous* "Ara Pacis" *or Altar of Peace, which
is still extant*). 13. Our ancestors had ordered that the temple of Janus Quirinus should
be shut whenever there was peace secured by victory throughout the whole *imperium* of
the Roman people, both on land and on sea. Before I was born there is record that it
was closed only twice since the foundation of the city. It was closed three times when I
was *princeps senatus*.

Imperial Good Works: Augustus' Euergetism

15. I paid 300 sesterces to each of the Roman plebs in accordance with the will of my father (*44 B.C.*). Similarly in my own name in my fifth consulship I gave 400 sesterces from war booty individually to the plebs (*in 29 B.C.*). For a second time in my own name in my tenth consulship I distributed 400 sesterces out of my inheritance to each individual by way of a gift (*24 B.C.*). In my eleventh consulship I made twelve distributions of grain bought at my own expense (*23 B.C.*). When holding tribunician power for the twelfth time I gave 400 sesterces to each of the plebs (*12 B.C.*). This was for the third time. The number of persons affected by these donations (*congiaria*) was never less than 250,000 people . . . (*the list of Augustus' donations continues down to 2 B.C.*).

16. I recompensed the municipalities for the land I assigned to the demobilized soldiers in my fourth consulship and later in the consulships of Marcus Crassus and Gnaeus Lentulus the Augur (*after the battle of Actium in 30 B.C. and in 14 B.C. when he settled 100,000 veterans on confiscated or purchased land in Italy and the provinces*). The amount I paid for land in Italy was about 600,000,000 sesterces. In the provinces I paid for land worth 260,000,000. I was the first and only one to do this of all those who up to my time settled soldiers in colonies in Italy or in the provinces. . . . Later I paid cash gratuities to soldiers I settled in their hometowns at the end of their terms of service. For this purpose I spent 400,000,000 sesterces as an act of bounty (*in the years 7–2 B.C.*). 17. I helped the treasury four times out of my own resources to the amount of 150,000,000 sesterces. In the consulships of Marcus Lepidus and Lucius Arruntius I contributed 170,000,000 sesterces out of my own patrimony to the military treasury which had been established at my recommendation so that payments should be made from it to soldiers who had given twenty or more years of service (*A.D. 6*). 18. From the year of the consulships of Gnaeus and Publius Lentulus (*18 B.C.*). I supplied from my own resources and patrimony whenever taxes fell short, tickets for grain and cash to as many as 100,000 citizens, sometimes many more. 19. I built the Curia (*the Senate meeting house*); the Chalcidicum beside it; the temple of Apollo on the Palatine with its porticoes; the temple of the deified Julius; the Lupercal; the portico at the Circus Flaminius which I allowed to be called "Octavia" after the man who built an earlier one on the same spot; the state box at the Circus Maximus; the temples on the capitol of Jupiter Feretrius and Jupiter Tonans. . . . 20. At great expense I rebuilt the Capitolium (*the temple of Jupiter Optimus Maximus on the Capitoline Hill*), and the theater of Pompey without putting up an inscription in my name. I restored the channels of the aqueducts which in many places had fallen into disrepair through old age. I doubled the capacity of the *aqua Marcia* by adding a new source. I completed the Forum of Julius Caesar and the Basilica Julia located between the temples of Castor and Saturn, works begun by my father and well in progress (*the list of temples and sacred sites goes on; 82 were claimed to have been restored by Augustus*). . . .

22. On three occasions in my own name, and five times in the name of my sons or grandsons, I gave gladiatorial shows (*munera*). About 10,000 men fought in

these shows. I gave an exhibition of athletes from all over the world twice in my own name and once in that of my grandson. I gave games four times in my own name and twenty three times in the names of other magistrates. . . . On twenty-six occasions I staged wild beast hunts of African animals for the people. In these about 3,500 animals were slain. 23. I gave the spectacle of a naval battle on the other side of the Tiber to the people. . . . There a basin eighteen hundred by one hundred and twenty feet was excavated (*the water was supplied by an aqueduct, the* Aqua Alsietina, *constructed for this purpose as well as to supply the people living in the area*). In this event thirty beaked ships, either triremes or biremes, and a large number of small vessels fought. About 3,000 men, exclusive of rowers, were involved.

Miscellaneous—But Important

25. I freed the sea from pirates and returned to their masters for punishment about 30,000 slaves who had been captured in the war. These were runaways who had taken up arms against the republic (*they had joined Sextus Pompey, son of Pompey and one of the challengers of Augustus and the other triumvirs. The fleet commanded by Pompey was based in Sicily and raided the grain fleets supplying Rome*). All of Italy took an oath of loyalty to me and demanded me as leader in the war which ended in the victory of Actium (*31 B.C.*). The provinces of the Gauls and Spains, of Africa, Sicily and Sardinia took the same oath of allegiance. Those who fought under my standards included more than 700 senators. Among them were 83 who had previously or have since been consuls up to the day on which these words have been written. About 170 of them have been priests (*Augustus is making a case for the legitimacy of his war with Mark Antony*).

Campaigns and Additions to the Empire

26. I increased the boundaries of all those provinces of the Roman people which were adjacent to peoples not yet subject to our *imperium*. I pacified the provinces of the Gauls, the Spains and Germany from Gades (*Cadiz*) to the mouth of the Elbe, bounded by Ocean. I pacified the Alps from the area closest to the Adriatic to the Tyrrhenian Sea. None of these peoples were subjected unjustly. My fleet sailed through Ocean from the mouth of the Rhine eastwards to the land of the Cimbri (*northern Germany close to Denmark*) which, up until then, no Roman had ever reached either by land or sea. The Cimbri, the Charydes and the Semnones and other German peoples through their envoys sought out my friendship and that of the Roman people. On my command and auspices two armies were led into Ethiopia and Arabia which is called "Blessed or Happy." Huge numbers of the enemy of both peoples were slain in battle and many towns were captured. . . . 27. I added Egypt to the empire of the Roman people. Although I could have made Greater Armenia a province after the killing of Artaxes, I preferred, on traditional precedent, to hand the kingdom to Tigranes, son of King Artavasdes. . . .

28. I settled colonies of soldiers in Africa, Sicily, Macedonia, the two Spains, Achaia (*Greece*), Syria, Gallia Narbonensis (*Southern France*), and Pisidia (*in modern Turkey*). There are twenty-eight colonies I founded in Italy under my auspices. In my lifetime they have become noted and well populated. 29. I recovered many military standards lost by previous commanders. This occurred after successful campaigns in Spain, Gaul and Illyria. I forced the Parthians to restore the spoils and standards of three Roman armies (*those of Crassus lost at Carrhae in 53 B.C., and by Antony in 40 and 36 B.C.*). . . . 30. I brought under the *imperium* of the Roman people the tribes of Pannonia (*parts of modern Austria and Hungary*) into which no army of the Roman people had penetrated before my principate. . . . I advanced the frontier of Illyria to the banks of the Danube. . . . 31. The kings of India sent me embassies frequently. Prior to this no Roman general had received such embassies. The Bastarnae, the Scythians and the kings of the Sarmatians (*peoples living in what is now Romania, Ukraine and southern Russia*) sought our friendship through embassies. These people live on either side of the River Tanais (*the Don*). So did the king of the Albani (*living on the Caspian Sea*), the Hiberi (*in modern Georgia*) and the Medes (*of Iran*). . . .

The Restoration of the Republic

34. In my sixth and seventh consulships (*28–27 B.C.*), after I had put an end to civil war and by universal agreement had obtained control of affairs, I transferred back the Republic from my control to the will of the Senate and the Roman people. For this I was given the title "Augustus" by decree of the Senate. The doorposts of my house were garlanded with laurels, a civic crown placed above my door, and a golden shield put up in the Curia Julia with an inscription which testified that the Senate and the Roman people granted me this honor in acknowledgement of my bravery, clemency, justice and religiosity (*virtus, clementia, justitia, pietas; these titles appear on coins and inscriptions and sum up the message of this document*). From that time on I took precedence in rank but possessed no more power that those of my colleagues in any magistracy.

35. While in my thirteenth consulship (*2 B.C.*) the whole Senate and People of Rome gave me the title of "Father of my Country" (*pater patriae*). They ordered that this title should be carved on the vestibule of my houses, of the Senate House, and in the Forum of Augustus under the quadriga (*a four-horse chariot in bronze*) erected there by decrees of the Senate. At the time of writing this I was in my 76th year.

6.3   A Senator's Estimate of Augustus

With biting irony the senatorial historian Tacitus (d. ca. A.D. 120) gives his version of how the Roman Republic ended. He gives scant credit to the overwhelming nature of the problems facing Octavian after a century of upheaval, let alone his adroitness and general success in solving them. His account is more a commentary on the morally compromising situations in which senators found themselves under despotic rulers. Tacitus had to suffer through the bad times of the emperor Domitian and his experience forever warped his view of human nature and history. It was a view congenial to historians such as the famous Edward Gibbon, author of The Decline and Fall of the Roman Empire, *who did not have to live with the real dilemmas of public life. Gibbon's one act of independence, his conversion to Catholicism, was speedily abandoned when his father threatened to cut off his financial support.*[1]

When after the destruction of Brutus and Cassius there was no longer any army of the Republic . . . and when with Lepidus pushed aside and Antony slain . . . then dropping the title of Triumvir and giving out that he was a consul and was satisfied with a tribune's authority for the protection of the people, Augustus won over the soldiers with gifts, the populace with cheap grain, and all men with the attractions of peace. So he grew greater by degrees while he concentrated in himself the functions of the Senate, the magistrates, and the laws. He was wholly unopposed, for the boldest spirits had fallen in battle or in the proscription, while the remaining nobles, the readier they were to be slaves, were raised the higher by wealth and promotion, so that, aggrandized by revolution, they preferred the safety of the present to the dangers of the past. Nor did the provinces dislike this condition of affairs, for they distrusted the government of the Senate and the People, because of the rivalries between the leading men and the rapacity of the officials, while the protection of the laws was unavailing, as they were continually upset by violence, intrigue, and finally by corruption. . . .

At home all was tranquil, and there were magistrates with the same titles; there was a younger generation, sprung up since the victory of Actium [*the battle in 31 B.C. that eliminated Octavian's last rival, Antony*], and even many of the older men had been born during the civil wars. How few were left who had seen the Republic! Thus the state had been revolutionized, and there was not a vestige left of the old-style virtue. Stripped of equality, all looked up to the commands of a sovereign without the least apprehension for the present.

On the death of Augustus, Tacitus reports various opinions about his accomplishments. Intelligent people . . . spoke variously of his life with praise and blame. Some said that dutiful feeling toward a father [*the duty to avenge the murder of his adoptive father, Julius Caesar*], and the necessities of the state in which laws had then no place, drove him into civil war, which can be neither planned nor conducted on any right principles . . . the only remedy for his distracted country was the rule of a single man. Yet Augustus had reorganized the state neither as a monarchy nor as a dictatorship but as a principate [*the rule of the first man in the state, the* Princeps]. The ocean and remote rivers were the boundaries of the Empire; the legions, provinces, fleets—all things were linked together; there was law for the citizens; there was respect shown for the allies. The capital had been beautified

---

[1]Tacitus, *Annals* 2, 3, 4, 9, 10. Based on the translation of A. J. Church and W. J. Brodribb, *The Annals of Tacitus* (London: Macmillan & Co. 1906).

on a grand scale; only in a few instances had he resorted to force, simply to secure general tranquility.

It was said, on the other hand, that filial duty and state necessity were merely assumed as a mask. His real motive was lust for power. Driven by that, he had mobilized the veterans by bribery and, when a young man with no official position, had raised an army, tampered with a consul's legions, and pretended attachment to the faction of Sextus Pompey. Then, when by a decree of the Senate he had usurped the high functions and authority of praetor . . . he at once wrested the consulate from a reluctant Senate and turned against the Republic the arms with which he had been entrusted for use against Antony. Citizens were proscribed and lands divided. . . . Even granting that the deaths of Cassius and Brutus were sacrifices to a hereditary enmity (though duty requires us to ignore private feuds for the sake of the public welfare), still Sextus Pompey had been deluded by the phantom of peace, and Lepidus by the mask of friendship. Subsequently, Antony had been lured on by the treaties of Tarentum and Brundisium and by his marriage with the sister of Augustus, and he paid by his death the penalty of a treacherous alliance. No doubt there was peace after all this, but it was a peace stained with blood.

6.4   Reaction to Augustus' Moral Reforms

Most of Augustus' energies were directed towards solving political and military problems, but he was also confronted with the moral decay of the upper classes where adultery was common and marriage was infrequent along with childlessness among those who did marry. The marriage laws of Augustus of 18 B.C. and A.D. 9 attempted to do something about this state of affairs. They encouraged marriage and having children, made adultery a crime and prohibited marriage between freeborn citizens and members of disreputable professions. Augustus, however, was not exactly a model for others to imitate as the following reading demonstrates.[2]

In the meanwhile there was a ruckus in the senate over the disorderly conduct of young men and women. It was alleged that this was the reason for their reluctance to marry. When the senators urged Augustus to do something about this problem, making ironical allusions to his own philandering, he at first replied that the necessary restrictions had already been laid down and that nothing further could be regulated by decree in a similar way. When driven by his questioners into a corner he said, "You yourselves ought to lay the law down to your wives as you wish; that is what I do." When the senators heard this they questioned him even more, asking to know what admonitions he claimed to give to Livia [*his wife*]. Reluctantly he made a few remarks about women's dress and their adornment, about their going out and their modest behavior, not a bit concerned that his actions did not conform to his words.

---

[2]Dio Cassius 54.16.3–5.

6.5 The Succession

The problem of how one emperor was to succeed another plagued the Principate from the start. Augustus, having no son, hoped to see the imperial office pass to his sister Octavia's son, Marcellus, and after he died, to his grandsons. But with their premature deaths, in which Tacitus suspected the hand of Livia "who had the aged Augustus firmly under control," the title went to her own son by a previous marriage, Tiberius. He in turn was succeeded by his unstable great nephew Gaius (Caligula) and Gaius, haphazardly, as is described in this reading, by Claudius. It is with the accession of Claudius that we first see the direct hand of the military who, with the help of the people, were determined not to have the Senate regain control.

The story begins with the assassination of Gaius. When word reached Claudius of the emperor's death, he tried to hide fearing that the conspirators were out to eliminate the entire imperial family.[3]

Soon after hearing that Gaius had been killed Claudius crept onto a balcony and hid himself behind the hangings of the door. But a soldier passing by saw his feet and wanting to find out who it was, dragged Claudius from behind the curtain. Recognizing him, he threw himself in fear at his feet, saluting him as emperor. He then led Claudius to his fellow guardsmen who were all in a rage and uncertain what to do. They put Claudius in a litter and because the slaves of the palace had all fled, took their turns in carrying him to the camp. Looking melancholy and in great consternation, Claudius was pitied by the people who met him on the way, thinking of him as an innocent man being led to execution.

Claudius was brought within the ramparts of the camp [*the camp of the Praetorian Guards*] and spent the night with the watch. He gradually recovered from his fright, but did not have much hope of the succession. The reason for this was that the consuls, the Senate and the Urban Cohorts had taken possession of the Forum and the Capitol with the intention of proclaiming liberty [*i.e., restoring the Republic and the power of the Senate*]. A tribune of the plebs was sent to bring Claudius to the Senate to provide it with advice on what should be done under the present circumstances. He replied that he could not come because he was under duress.

The following day, the Senate, being divided, was slow to follow up on its proposed restoration of liberty. The people at large also slowed down deliberations because they insisted on being governed by one man, naming specifically Claudius. As a result Claudius allowed the Praetorians to assemble under arms and swear allegiance to him after promising them 15,000 sesterces per man. He was the first of the Caesars to purchase the fidelity of the soldiers with money.

---

[3]Suetonius, *Claudius* 10.

6.6   Imperial Women

Cleopatra VII

Cleopatra VII (69–30 B.C.) was the last of the Ptolemies, the Macedonian monarchs who ruled Egypt from shortly after the death of Alexander the Great in 323 B.C. Her skill at manipulating first Julius Caesar, and then Mark Antony, enabled her to maintain the independence of Egypt from Rome to the time of the battle of Actium in 31 B.C.

This short, recently discovered document, an official decree of the queen dating from 33 B.C., shows her at work building up her support from one of Antony's most important commanders, Publius Canidius. The document, which bears the original signature of Cleopatra, reveals a side of the queen obscured by the propaganda of Octavius and the romanticization of popular tradition. Cleopatra was a highly competent ruler. During her reign she must have dealt with thousands of ordinances similar to this one. By her command Canidius and his descendants were given a lucrative, tax free import–export license, an exemption from taxes on land possessions in Egypt, and other important privileges.

We have granted to Publius Canidius and his heirs the annual exportation of 10,000 artabas of wheat and the annual importation of 5,000 Coan amphoras of wine without anyone exacting anything in taxes from him or any other expense whatsoever. We have also granted tax exemption on all the land he owns in Egypt on the understanding that he shall not pay any taxes, either to the state account or to the account of me and my children, in any way in perpetuity. We have also granted that all his tenants are exempt from personal liabilities and from taxes without anyone exacting anything from them, not even contributing to the occasional assessments in the nomes or paying for expenses of soldiers or officers. We have also granted that the ships used for the transportation (down the Nile) of the wheat are likewise exempt from "personal" liabilities for taxes and cannot be commandeered. Let it be written to those to whom it may concern so that knowing it they can act accordingly.

[Subscription by Cleopatra in her own hand]: Make it happen.[4]

Agrippina

Towards the end of the Republic, women, at least of the elite class, had begun to acquire a considerable amount of freedom, in their ability to dispose of their own properties, but also to influence political events, sometimes directly. Fulvia, the wife of Antony, went on a military campaign against Octavius with her brother-in-law when Antony was off in the eastern Mediterranean. Octavius' sister Octavia was a significant figure in the maneuvering leading up to the battle of Actium. Tacitus saw the "stepmotherly malevolence" of Livia (Annals 1.6) at work in the disposal of the direct heirs of Augustus and the accession of her own son

---

[4]Translation by Peter van Minnen, *Ancient Society* 30 (2000), 34. By permission of *Ancient Society*.

Tiberius. Agrippina, the sister of Caligula, inveigled the aging Claudius into marrying her
and adopting her son Nero from a previous marriage. He was three years older than Claudius's
own son Britannicus and so took precedence over him. When Claudius died in A.D. 54 *Bri-*
tannicus was pushed aside and Nero became emperor. In due course Britannicus too was
removed. For some years, Agrippina, his tutor Seneca and the Prefect of the Praetorian Guard,
Burrus, managed to keep the unpredictable Nero in line. Finally the emperor turned on his
handlers and eliminated them all, beginning with his mother. This, it turned out, was a more
difficult task than Nero imagined.[5]

Nero finally came to the conclusion that wherever Agrippina was she was a menace
to him. He decided to kill her. His only question was whether to use poison, a dagger or violence of some other kind. His first choice was poison but he realized that
death at his table would not look accidental after Britannicus' murder in this fashion. Further, Agrippina's alertness to plots stemming from her own criminal mentality, made it impossible to subvert her household. Furthermore, she had
strengthened her body by a preventive course of antidotes. As for stabbing her to
death, no one could think of doing so without being detected. Besides, there was
always the danger that the selected assassin might shrink from executing his orders.

Anicetus, a freedman who commanded the fleet at Misenum, came up with a plan.
He had been Nero's tutor during his boyhood and he had a personal vendetta against
Agrippina. The plan was to have a ship made so that a section of it would come loose
at sea. Agrippina would be thrown into the water without warning. Anicetus com-
mented that sea faring is full of surprises so that if Agrippina died in a shipwreck, no
one would think that humans, rather than wind and waves, were responsible.
Besides, after her death, the emperor could dedicate a temple to her and altars and
other proof of his filial responsibilities.

Nero accepted the clever plan. The time of year too was right since he regularly
attended the festival of Minerva at Baiae. Now he enticed his mother there. . . . When
Agrippina arrived from Antium, Nero met her at the shore. He welcomed her with out-
stretched arms and hugs and led her to Bauli, a mansion on the bay between Cape Misenum and Baiae. Some ships were anchored there and one, more magnificent than the
others, seemed to be intended as a compliment to his mother who was used to being
conveyed by warships of the imperial navy. She was invited out to the ship for dinner
where the murder was to take place under cover of darkness. It is said there was an
informer and Agrippina got wind of the plot. She could not decide whether or not to
believe the story and decided to go on to Baiae by litter. There her fears were allayed by
Nero's attentions. He received her kindly and gave her the place of honor next to himself. They talked a great deal. At times Nero was boyish and at times serious and confidential. The meal went on for a long time. When she left he saw her off and looked into
her eyes and clung to her. This may have been pure acting but perhaps Nero's brutal
heart was affected by the thought of seeing his mother for the last time.

---

[5]Tacitus, *Annals* 14.3–9.

The gods, however, seemed determined to reveal the crime. The night was quiet, the star light bright and the sea clam. As the ship began to move Agrippina was being looked after by two of her attendants, one of whom, Crepereius Gallus, stood near the tiller and the other, Acerronia, leaned over the feet of her resting mistress, talking happily about Nero's remorseful behavior and Agrippina's reestablished influence. At that moment the signal was given and under the pressure of heavy lead weights the roof collapsed. Crepereius was crushed and killed instantly, but Agrippina and Acerronia were saved by the raised sides of the couch which were strong enough to sustain the weight. The ship did not sink as planned and in the confusion those in on the plot were hampered by the many who were not. Some of the oarsmen tried to capsize the ship by putting their weight on one side, but it took them too long to work out their plan and in the meantime others brought their weight to bear on the other side. This allowed the ship to go down on a more even keel. Acerronia started to cry out "I am Agrippina, help the emperor's mother." With that she was struck dead by blows from poles and oars and whatever else was available from the ship's gear. Agrippina kept quiet and avoided recognition. Though she had a shoulder injury she managed to swim until she came to some small sail boats which took her to the Lucrine lake and from there to her home.

There she realized that the invitation and the special attentions she had received had all been part of a plot. The shore was close. The ship had not been driven by the wind and did not strike a rock. The top part of the ship had collapsed like a piece of machinery on land falling over. Reflecting on Acerronia's death and her own wound she decided that the only way to escape was to profess ignorance of the plot and so she sent the freedman Agermus to tell Nero that by the mercy of the gods and his good fortune she had survived a serious accident. The messenger was told to add that despite his concern for her dangerous experience he was not to visit her since what she needed now was rest. Pretending unconcern she had her wound cared for. . . .

To Nero came the word that Agrippina had escaped with a slight injury. . . . Half dead with fear he insisted she might arrive at any moment with vengeance in mind. "She may arm her slaves or whip up the army or gain access to the Senate or to the People and incriminate me for shipwrecking her and wounding her and killing her friends! What can I do to save myself?" What about Burrus and Seneca? They were awakened and immediately fetched. Whether they knew of the plot ahead of time is uncertain. For a long time neither said anything for fear of inciting Nero if they came up with a plan contrary to what he wanted. Or they may have felt that things were already so far advanced that unless they anticipated Agrippina, Nero would be finished. Finally Seneca turned to Burrus and asked if the soldiers could be ordered to kill her. Burrus replied that the Praetorian Guardsmen were devoted to the whole imperial family and remembered Germanicus [*Agrippina's popular father*]. They would commit no violence against his offspring. Anicetus, the original deviser of the plan, he said, must take responsibility. Without hesitation Anicetus volunteered to complete the crime. . . .

Meanwhile Agermus, Agrippina's messenger, arrived but was summarily arrested. Word of the supposed accident spread among the local population and they gathered to inquire into Agrippina's state of health.

But Anicetus' armed band arrived and scattered the well-wishers. The house was surrounded and broken into. The slaves who were encountered were arrested until Anicetus came to Agrippina's bedroom door. Here a few servants stood, the rest having been frightened away by the invasion. In the dimly lit bedroom only a single maidservant waited with Agrippina whose alarm increased as nobody, not even her messenger Agermus, came from her son. If things were going well there would not be this isolation nor the sudden uproar and signs of extreme danger. Her maid vanished. "Are you leaving me, too?" she called out. As she spoke she saw Anicetus and behind him the naval commander Herculeius and Obaritus the fleet centurion. "If you have come to visit me," she said, "you can say I am better. But if you are assassins, I know my son is not responsible. He did not order matricide." The assassins closed around her bed and the naval commander first hit her on the head with a club. Then as the centurion, his assistant, was drawing his sword to finish her off Agrippina cried out: "Strike here!" pointing to her womb. She was finished off with many blows.

So far accounts agree. Some add that Nero inspected his mother's body and praised her figure. That however is contested. She was cremated that night on a dining couch with little ceremony.

6.7   Augustan Literature

The reign of Augustus coincided with the Golden Age of Latin literature. It seems odd that an age of such vicious turmoil could have fostered such development, yet it may be that it was precisely the chaos of the period that assisted its cultural florescence. The old social and cultural norms that restrained the creative minds of the past were shaken during the last century of the Republic, providing an opportunity for the leisured class to engage in literary endeavors without fear of criticism. To this development it must be said that Augustus himself gave some support. Suetonius said that Augustus "fostered the talent of his age in every way. He listened to recitations kindly and patiently, not only of poetry and history, but also of speeches and dialogues" (Aug. 89.3). His court included the Alexandrian Greek philosopher Arius with whose assistance he collected useful examples and precepts from philosophical and moral writers that he could send as useful messages to provincial governors and army commanders.

Although his own literary interests tended to the practical he encouraged many of the writers of his time. Livy, the historian, was an intimate friend of the imperial family although his political viewpoints were known to be republican. Maecenas, one of the princeps' *inner circle, had an eye for talent and introduced many of his finds to Augustus. These included Propertius who hailed from Umbria; Cornelius Gallus from Gallia Narbonensis (Provence, southern France, an old province of Rome); Virgil, from Mantua and Horace, the son of freedman from southern Italy. The poet Ovid was a friend of Horace and Propertius and so may be presumed to have been in Maecenas' circle also. Augustus took an interest in all of these poets. He offered Horace the post of private secretary and made Gallus prefect of Egypt. He followed with interest the progress of Virgil's great epic, the Aeneid, and stopped the poet, who was unhappy with its unfinished state, from destroying it on his deathbed. The senatorial historian Messala Corvinus was another patron in whose group the poet Tibullus was found. Although Virgil and Livy pursued public themes of politics and war, most of the other poets wrote of private affairs.*

Horace

Don't ask—besides its not right to know,
What ends the gods intend for you and me, Leuconoe;
Do not fool with astrological charts.
Better to endure what is to come,
Whether Jupiter allots us winters or
Has given this one as the last which now wearies the Tyrrhenian Sea
dashing it against the opposing rocks.

Be wise; drink wine; since life is short
Cut short far reaching hopes.
Seize the day (*carpe diem*);
Trust as little as possible in tomorrow.

Odes 1.11

The man who wants only what he needs
is not deterred by the turbulent seas
nor the furious storm winds
when Arcturus is setting or Haedus is rising. . . .

If Phrygian marble or purple garments
brighter than the stars, or wine from Falernum,
or the perfumes of the east
cannot comfort the troubled man,
why should I build a palace in the latest style
with pillars that generate envy?
Why would I trade my Sabine glen
for the burdens of wealth?

Odes 3.1

Plenty of times even a confident poet is thrown into a panic when the mob in the cheap seats, ready to brawl if opposed, superior in numbers but inferior in everything else, calls for a bear or a prize fight in the middle of his play. But this is exactly what the mob wants! Nowadays all pleasure, even among the upper class, has fled from the ear to the eye—everyone wants to SEE something!

Epistles 2.1.183–201

Vergil

In book 6 of his great epic poem the Aeneid, *the hero Aeneas makes a journey to the under world (Hades) where he has an opportunity to query the dead about his own destiny. He encounters his father, Anchises, who reveals to him the glorious future of Rome. In the small section provided here Anchises warns against civil war and insists that if Rome is to govern it must do so with justice.*[6]

My children, do not accustom your spirits to civil warfare,
Nor turn those overmastering forces against the heart and soul of your fatherland.
You who are sprung from Olympus—be first in mercy!
O blood of mine, cast down your weapons!

Remember, O Romans, your charge is to rule the nations with power (*imperium*),
To establish the practices of peace, to spare the conquered,
And to put down the arrogant: These shall be your arts.

▼▼▼

Questions

1. In the *Res Gestae* Augustus is at pains to prove he acted legally. Give some examples. (**6.2**)
2. We also learn in the *Res Gestae* of Augustus' pride in his euergetism or the good works he did on behalf of the state. List some of them. What does this activity have in common with that of Pliny in 7.13? (**6.2**)
3. Tacitus reports various estimates, pro and con, regarding Augustus' character and accomplishments. What were some of these? (**6.3**)
4. Apparently some people thought Augustus' moral reform may have involved hypocrisy. What do you think? Were his critics endangering themselves by their comments? (**6.4**)
5. Claudius was a kind of accidental emperor. How did he make it to the imperial throne? (**6.5**)
6. In what way does the decree of Cleopatra VII prove that she was a hands-on ruler? (**6.6**)
7. What was Nero afraid that his mother would do after his initial failure to assassinate her? (**6.6**)
8. Vergil famously stated the norms and goals of Roman rulership. What are they? (**6.7**)
9. Horace seems more laid-back, less interested in public affairs than Vergil. Is that true? (**6.7**)

---

[6]*Aeneid* 6.832–835; 851–853.

Chapter 7

▼▼▼

The Roman Peace

The Roman Empire was one of the great multicultural, multilingual empires of all time. It was also one of the most successful. Geographically the empire stretched from Scotland to Sudan and from Morocco to Ukraine. It embraced most of Western Europe, all of the Mediterranean, and large portions of the Middle East. Before the coming of Rome these regions had never formed a single state. After the collapse of the Roman Empire they were never united again.

Ethnicity in the Empire

Generalizations about the Empire should take these factors into account. For instance, one way of looking at the Roman Empire is to see it simply as the sum total of its myriad peoples, nations, tribes, temple-states, chiefdoms, independent cities, and petty kingdoms. Over this amalgam presided a handful of Romans who themselves became less and less "Roman" and more and more provincial as the centuries passed.

Yet it would be a mistake to assume that the diverse peoples of the Empire possessed the kind of strong ethnic self-consciousness that is found in modern times and is often associated with the formation of states. Greeks, for instance, while identifying each other as sharers in a common culture spread throughout the Mediterranean and Black Sea areas, never recognized a common "Greek" government or state. Apart from their utopian dreamers, they never demonstrated any great desire or capacity for coming together to form a self-governing nation. Among the peoples of the Empire, Jews were exceptional in that they had both a state, Judaea, and a self-conscious culture that extended outside the narrow borders of Judaea. A more common state of affairs was the picture sketched by the Scots chieftain Calgacus, who depicts the Roman army as a rabble of peoples from everywhere in the Empire, even, to his regret, from his own land (**7.2**).

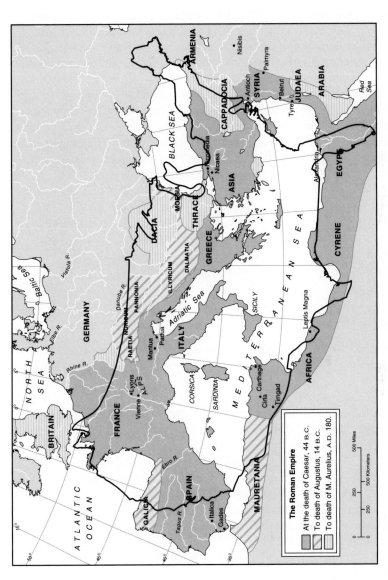

Distance and time were the secret enemies of the Roman peace. The continental size of the Roman Empire (which was, as can be seen, slightly larger than that of the U.S.), made communication among its scattered provinces difficult and slow. Interestingly, the imperial Roman road system of around 50,000 miles was close to that of the present 55,000 miles of the U.S. interstates. Despite the generally fine quality of Roman roads, moving contingents of troops from say, Britain or Germany to Syria, took months and the costs were enormous. The roads helped the transportation of bulk goods, but it was still cheaper to ship grain from one end of the Mediterranean to the other by ship than to send it 75 miles overland.

Despite its multi-ethnic character, we have little information about what ordinary people of the Empire thought about it or even what they knew of it. Did the peasants who constituted perhaps 90 percent or more of the population care much who governed them as long as the government was beneficial to them in some way? We do know, however, a lot about how the Roman upper classes felt about the Empire, and especially what they *thought* was appropriate for their subjects to feel. We also know how some Romans, such as the poet Juvenal, felt about Greeks and other foreigners (**7.9**) and what, at least for public consumption, a provincial such as Josephus had to say about Rome (**7.1**).

That the Empire ultimately fell is no surprise; that it survived for as long as it did is astonishing. What held it together was a complex web of institutions. The army and its great reputation, won primarily in the Republican period, was clearly one, if not the principal factor, as the survey by Josephus (**7.1**) demonstrates. The emperors were generally hardworking, intelligent men who dealt in person with great as well as very ordinary matters. The system was open enough to allow provincials to make their way in it, as did the forebears of the great African Septimius Severus, as well as Septimius himself. The ancient practice of extending the franchise and involving non-Roman elites in the governing system was practiced to great effect. In general, the case for the Empire is summed up by the clear-sighted historian Tacitus in the blunt speech of Cerialis to the rebellious Gauls: the only alternative to Rome, he said, "was chaos" (**7.3**).

The Cement of Empire

The cement that held the Empire together for as long as it did was social, cultural, political, and military in character. Of these four elements, the military component was the most important or, at least, the most fundamental. On it rested the security of the Empire. Ultimately the fate of Rome depended on the ability of the army to intimidate or, at times, inspire, the inhabitants of the Empire and those outside it who might threaten it. The army in turn depended on the willingness of the people of the Empire to foot the bill for its expenses. It was a simple enough equation, amounting to a tacit understanding between the elites of the Empire and the imperial government that costs would not exceed benefits, or at least not for long periods of time. When they did, as began to happen in the third century A.D., the foundations of the Empire were shaken.

Although the army was ultimately the bedrock of imperial rule, Rome did not govern by force alone. Far from it. Without the ability to build some kind of consensus among the heterogeneous and competing elites of the Empire, there was no way that the army could have ensured Roman overlordship for very long. Rome had no systematic ideology of Empire nor any strong belief in the power of bureaucracy to govern. Instead, Romans used in the task of ruling what they knew best, their own relatively open social system with its hierarchical organization of society on the basis of wealth and public service. Personal patronage allowed connections to be established across class and cultural lines. At the core of this network of patronage was the Emperor (**7.11**). Careers in the army and civil service encouraged the able and the ambitious of the Empire to rise to high office. At the local level, Rome's key to success was its ability to involve the elites of the Empire in the basic day-to-day tasks of maintaining order and collecting taxes. Based on Rome's uniform socio-political system, Syrians were able to mingle with Africans, and Spaniards with Italians in the imperial army and administration in the task of maintaining the power of Rome. Indeed, some of the most successful imperial dynasties, such as those of the Severans from Leptis Magna, an old Phoenician city in Libya, were not even from Italy, let alone from the old Roman heartland of Latium (**7.7**).

The Emperors

Roman emperors were not kings. They could not rely on anything like the sentiment that medieval or modern monarchs inspired in their subjects. Indeed, the very idea of being the subjects of anyone was at odds, especially among the upper classes, with ancient traditions of freedom, dignity, and honor (**7.17**). The emperor as chief patron of the Empire could, however, be dealt with without total humiliation. In the Republic, friends were forever doing favors for each other. In the Empire the same reciprocities were expected of emperors who had an enormous range of benefits at their disposal. They could, for instance, allow favored households to tap into the public aqueducts or use the public transportation system. On request, they granted citizenship and exemptions from marriage and the raising of children, or from military service (**7.11**). They could bestow freedom on slaves or grant promotions to equestrian, senatorial, or military ranks.

Although the emperors usurped the kind of patronal resources the famous families of Rome used to dispense in the Republic, their trusted inner circles were allowed to build up clientships of their own. In this way, in addition to ensuring the loyalty of their closest adherents, the emperors bound to themselves, through them, their clients throughout the Empire. Consequently, numerous provincial elites were brought within the web of imperial patronage. Everyone benefited. Senators acted as brokers of imperial favors and themselves benefited. As Pliny put it when requesting a promotion for his client Rosianus Geminus: "Sir, I ask you that you please me by increasing the *dignitas* of my former quaestor. I mean to say you will increase my *dignitas* by showing your favor to him" (*Letters* 10.26). By this system, generation after generation of provincials were co-opted, tutored, and brought into the imperial system.

If the emperor's power was significant, his responsibilities were overwhelming. Any administration, ancient or modern, stands or falls by the qualities of its appointees, and it was the emperor's main job to find the right governors, legionary commanders, financial administrators of imperial possessions, and military officers down to the level of centurion.

The first and foremost responsibility of the emperor was the defense of the Empire against outside aggression and internal disorder. For this the army had to be maintained in constant readiness over thousands of miles of frontier. New recruits, armaments, and supplies had to be shipped to the farthest corners of the world in a regular, dependable fashion. Suitable officers from generals to centurions had to be selected, trained, and appointed—no easy task in an army of 350,000–400,000 men spread over forty-five provinces. The military responsibilities alone would have taken all the time of an emperor, as in fact they did in times of invasion or civil war. Military responsibilities, however, were only part of the emperor's responsibilities. He had to maintain peace within the Empire as well as without, peace within his own family, with the senate and with elites throughout the Empire and with the ordinary people, especially of Rome and the cities of the Greek East.

In the Republic it was evident that the senate was in control of foreign affairs even though governors had considerable freedom in their provinces. In the Empire, the emperor, through his coins, statues, inscriptions, and the imperial cult, made it clear that he was in charge, with the result that the people of the Empire, when dissatisfied with the treatment they received from local governors, city councils, and the like, felt that they could turn to the emperor directly and personally for help. They did this by sending or sometimes delivering in person petitions, *libelli*, which the emperor in fact received, read, and replied to in a note at the bottom of the petition. Cities and villages sent delegations, but sometimes individuals sought the emperor out, such as did a fisherman from a small town in Africa who traveled to meet Augustus in 29 B.C. to seek relief from tribute. Sometimes, swamped by the mountains of correspondence, emperors delegated others to reply. Caracalla asked his mother, Julia Domna, to fill in for him while he was on campaign in Syria. She did so, and a recently published inscription contains a letter from her to Ephesus in Asia Minor. Governors, either at a loss for what to do in a particular case or covering themselves in case they made a mistake, sent letters asking emperors for advice. In irritation, the emperor Trajan replied to a request from his governor Pliny in Bithynia for an architect: "You can have no lack of architects; every province has experienced and talented people. Don't assume it is easier to send to Rome for one" (*Letters* 10.40).

Imperial Governors

At the beginning of the Principate, the main personnel resources of the emperor were a handful of senatorial governors, equestrian legates, and financial agents (procurators), members of his own family and close personal friends (his *consilium*, or council, **7.17**), and the freedmen and slaves of his household. To a surprising degree, the emperors ran the Empire the way a Roman *paterfamilias* ran his family. Government tended to be informal and personal, characterized by exchanges of letters (which the emperor himself read), recommendations by friends, and purely personal choices and decisions arrived at in consultation with the *consilium*. The early emperors had no alternatives. It would have been unseemly for a senator or a knight to be thought of as working for, or employed by, the emperor. The emperors could not turn senators or knights into the kind of office managers and accountants they needed to enact their policies. Nor could the emperor be sure of the loyalty of such men whose commitment was to their careers and the institution to which they belonged, the senate. Hence the real professionals who managed the Empire were the freedmen and slaves of the emperor's household, and to a large extent, even with the later development of the equestrian civil service in the second century, this remained true to the end of the Principate.

This accounted for the inner workings of the administrative system, all held in the family, but the Emperor still needed to find the forty or so legionary commanders and governors he needed to command the legions and govern the provinces and the hundreds of junior positions he needed to fill. For this he relied on the recommendations of his friends among the elite. There were no official personnel files. The future emperor Vespasian owed his advancement to the fact that the powerful freedman in the imperial household, Narcissus, brought Vespasian to the emperor's attention. Pliny's many recommendations were not based on an impartial evaluation of his candidates' qualities (**7.11**). Instead he touted their *probitas*, their uprightness, their *industria*, the fact they were not slackers, and their *humanitas, innocentia* (integrity), and *modestia*. Irrespective of the office, the same virtues were repeated in the letters of commendation. Essentially, what men like Pliny were saying in their testimonials was: "This person is a friend of mine and hence a worthy character. Trust my judgment." Unlike other empires which established schools to train professional administrators or held standardized examinations, Rome relied on its ancient patronage system, which it knew well. Character, in Roman eyes, counted for more than technical competence or cleverness.

As a consequence, the Empire was not overburdened with bureaucracy. The principal work of administration was done at the local level. Even the initial steps of collecting the taxes were left to the individual city councils or senates of the Empire. According to one calculation, 100 elite Romans (army commanders, governors, etc.), in the first century, and about 160 in the second, not counting their small staffs, ran the entire Empire, with an estimated population of 50 million. Rome was a libertarian's paradise. Senators and knights who held the highest offices remained, as they were in the Republic, amateurs, who devoted a good part of their lives to public service. They received no specialized training outside their experience in the offices they held. Gradually, however, as the administration stabilized over the years, and the vast amount of power wielded by freedmen and slaves became clear and the institutional character of the senate declined, the beginnings of a kind of a civil service began to emerge and be given definite form under Hadrian in the second century.

Governors of the frontier provinces had the double task of ruling the civilian population and commanding whatever armed forces happened to be there. These might consist of only a few auxiliary units, as in Austria, or two or three legions, as in Syria or the Rhine area. As chief administrator, judge, and general, the governor needed as much political ability as military.

In the peaceful provinces the prime responsibility of the governor was to maintain order. He had to do this without the assistance of the legions or even of a well-developed bureaucracy. His staff was minute. At most he was allowed three or four assistants, and beyond that he had to round up his own staff among his friends in Rome and the provinces and among his own servants. When Fronto, a close friend of Marcus Aurelius, was appointed governor of Asia in the mid-second century A.D., he asked friends from Cirta, his hometown in Africa, to come along, as well as some literary figures from Alexandria and a military expert from Morocco. Some other individuals from Cilicia were also invited.

The Army

According to the dictum of the historian Michael Howard "The military system of a nation is not an independent section of the social system but an aspect of it in its totality." This was certainly the case with the Roman army during the Empire. It was the lineal descendant of the army of the Roman Republic, and just as that army was shaped by the society from which it sprang, so the army of the Empire was shaped by, and in turn shaped, imperial society. Apart from its obvious military role the army of the Empire had important social and political functions. It had a major role to play, for example, in the romanization of the Empire and in bringing local provincial elites into the imperial aristocracy.

The Roman Empire had over 6,000 miles of frontier to defend, from Hadrian's Wall in Britain to the deserts of North African and Arabia. Some of the frontiers were rivers, such as the Rhine and the Danube, along which the army had constructed an elaborate chain of fortress towns, watch posts, palisades, ditches, walls, and military roads. In Syria, another network of fortresses existed to defend the eastern half of the Empire against Parthia, the only major organized state with which Rome had to contend. Nevertheless, we should not think of the Roman frontiers as we do of frontiers between modern nation states which clearly demark one culture and state from another.

The bulk of the frontiers, whether in Europe, Africa, or the Middle East, were simply zones of supervised contact between the peoples of Roman provinces and peoples who lived beyond them. Many of the transfrontier peoples did not recognize settled boundaries and with good reason. For millennia, Celts in Britain, Germans and Dacians in central Europe, Berbers in north Africa, and Arabs throughout the East had moved freely in response to seasonal pastoral needs, population pressures, or natural catastrophes such as famine or flooding. From the viewpoint of these peoples, the provinces of the Empire were artificial obstacles having no intrinsic legitimacy. Needless to say, the Roman authorities and the bulk of the provincials took a different view.

As a practical matter the frontiers were set up mainly to channel the movements of transfrontier peoples in ways that would create the least disturbance for the settled provinces of the Empire. Walls, ditches, palisades, roads, and bridges were used as means of directing and moving populations to where they could be supervised and counted, since one of the key elements in the Roman defense of Empire was the possession of accurate information. Frontiers were thus supervised corridors or regions of economic and social exchange, not fortified, exclusionary zones. Nor did the Romans think that the frontiers restricted their ability to move beyond them. They expected to use the frontier areas as jumping-off points in periodic campaigns of intimidation or conquest. Hadrian's Wall in Britain, for instance, was a lightly held chain of fortresses, walls, and ditches, while the main legionary forces were encamped at York a hundred miles to the south. Roman power extended for, perhaps, a hundred miles to the north of the wall.

The Genius of the Roman Military

The Roman army consisted of about 350,000–400,000 men, divided almost equally between citizen legionaries and noncitizen auxiliaries. The citizen soldiers were grouped in legions of some 5,500 men each. The auxiliary units were much more varied, consisting of cavalry units (*alae*) of 1,000 each and cohorts of 500 that could be either all infantry or part infantry and part cavalry. Serving among the auxiliaries were other, more barbarous units recruited outside the Empire called *numeri*. A Roman army could thus consist of a legion or a number of legions with whatever number of auxiliary units and borrowed legionary cohorts were deemed necessary for the campaign. Without changing the basic commitment to heavy infantry, the Roman army was able to find flexibility by employing the special skills of the auxiliary units, which were commanded by Roman officers but fought according to their own style (**7.6**).

The cement that held this heterogeneous army together was the Roman officer corps. Legions were commanded by senatorial legates who had under them six tribunes, one of senatorial birth; the others were of the equestrian class. The mixture of civilian and military experience that Roman officers of senatorial and equestrian rank possessed seems strange to modern eyes, which at least in peacetime regard the two careers as separate. However, from the viewpoint of Romans of the upper and middle classes, there was a self-evident connection between civilian and military life. From the viewpoint of military cohesion, it was the influx of educated civilians from the towns of Italy and the provinces that provided much of the talent necessary for the proper operation of the army.

The army was concerned primarily with maintaining peace, and it performed a great number of civilian functions in addition to its military duties. It was the single greatest reserve of technically trained people in the Empire—engineers, surveyors, builders, and administrators of all kinds. It was principally from this source that the emperors drew their technical staffs, judges, governors, and legionary commanders. Far from being a peripheral element in the Empire, the army had a much more central role than most modern armies.

The constant movement of officers and the promotion of ordinary soldiers guaranteed a unity to the scattered legions and auxiliary units (**7.6**). The civilian character of the equestrian officers was an unusual feature that opened the army to whole classes of people whose careers would otherwise have terminated with a minor office in a provincial town. Men of talent could transfer their expertise to the army and find a whole new world of imperial service opened to them. The close connection between military commands and civilian administration made the army an integral part of Roman life and guaranteed that it would not become overly professionalized. This also had its weaknesses, but at least in peaceful times it proved a brilliant solution to the problem of integration of such a diverse region as the Empire. Although not intended as such, the Roman army was the prime agent of social unity and mobility in the Mediterranean world (**7.5**).

Roman Society

It would be misleading to talk about *the* society and culture of the Roman Empire as though the Empire were some kind of modern homogeneous nation-state, a France or a Japan, which possessed a single dominant culture and society. Analogies with multinational empires—Ottoman, Habsburg, or Russian/Soviet—are more helpful but still misleading because of their huge centralized administrative systems, something Rome completely lacked. Yet the Empire did have a dominant culture and society: a mix of Greek and Latin elements at one level, and local, combined with Latin *or* Greek, at another. Multiple empires coexisted: A developed, urbanized, culturally dominant Greek east was wedded to a more rural, less-developed, Latin-dominated west. At the same time, most of the Empire, east as well as west and north, operated at the level of a Third World society: primarily rural, with a small urban population. The hundreds of local and regional cultures were united only to the extent to which they had a connection with one of the dominant cultures.

Rome had no plan, ideological or otherwise, to knit all of these heterogeneous bits and pieces of society into a coordinated whole. Acknowledgment of diversity came naturally, if unavoidably, to the Roman mentality. The only really major issue for Rome was how to maintain order and thereby preserve its privileged position in the chaotic cultural geography Romans called their Empire. This was accomplished by a variety of means. Local elites were tied to the administrative and military system and to each other by patronage and opportunity (see *The Emperors*), but they also found cohesion through religion; common forms of leisure; similar expectations of each other on the part of rich and poor alike (**7.13**; **7.14**); a common high culture including art, literature, and philosophy; the extension of uniform urban forms of life into areas of the west and north which had never experienced them before; and a legal system (**7.17**). Daily life was altered for millions just by the possibility of easy travel between one part of the Empire and another, as well as by the presence almost everywhere of temples, baths, theaters, aqueducts, amphitheaters, and impressive public buildings of all kinds.

Cultural and social diversity, of course, lay close to the surface, and Greco-Roman culture was always wafer-thin. The frontier with the barbarian world existed not only along the great rivers of northern Europe and the deserts of Africa and the East, but within the Empire itself. Nevertheless, despite its apparent brittleness, Greco-Roman culture was remarkably vital and enormously elastic. It had great depth and richness. To the end, it managed to attract and hold significant numbers of outsiders. Its ability to cope with diversity has hardly been matched before modern times.

The complexities of ethnicity, language, culture, and religion of the Empire were further confused by a bewildering variety of constitutional and legal systems. Almost all the old legal classifications of the Republic continued during the Empire. First, there was the complication of citizenship, because one could have Roman, Latin, or simply native (peregrine) status. Of course, Roman citizens were potentially capable of a full political life at Rome, but in addition they had certain rights in criminal law not possessed by anyone else. In cases in which the charge was capital, they could appeal from a local court to Rome, and often the mere status of an individual as a Roman would deter local authorities from dispensing summary justice. It was not that Roman citizens were exempt from the local laws of provinces but that as members of the ruling power, their political standing was something a local magistrate needed to take into account. Saint Paul, who had Roman citizenship, made good use of this during his travels in the Roman world, where he often came into conflict with local ruling bodies. Even within the citizenship, there were gradations, as some Romans belonged to immune cities and so escaped the standard forms of taxation, or were Romans with freedman (ex-slave) status and so had other built-in restrictions, such as the inability to serve in the legions or hold public office. Then there were persons of the Latin Right, which entitled them to practically the same legal but not the same political privileges as Romans. Being married or single, old or young, independent (*sui iuris*) or under guardianship, or male or female also had important legal consequences. Moreover, there were slaves, whose only rights were vaguely defined in the Law of Nations (*jus gentium*) and in some specific enactments handed down by the emperors.

To the extent that the privileges of citizenship were thought to have been watered down by the increase in numbers, there developed another system of classification that counteracted this and ensured the preservation of the traditional system based on wealth and public esteem. This was the distinction between high-status individuals (*honestiores*) and low-status individuals (*humiliores*). By the second century A.D., the distinction between high- and low-caste inhabitants of the Empire, regardless of their citizenship, was an established fact of law. *Honestiores* could claim special treatment under the law and were subject to much less stringent criminal punishments than *humiliores*. For example, a provincial governor could not execute persons of high status and could exile them only after consultation with the emperor, whereas *humiliores* received summary judicial treatment and punishment. This distinction cut across citizenship bounds, so that ultimately it was more advantageous to be a member, especially a powerful member, of the upper classes with high status than to be a poor citizen with low status.

Those who belonged to the *honestiores* included first of all senators and equestrians, then decurions (local senators), soldiers, veterans, and some professionals. The scramble for citizenship became a scramble for inclusion in one of the higher classifications. Such inclusion was one of the ways the Romans could ensure their continuing interest in local administration and the army because service in either brought membership in the higher caste. This was not quite as discriminatory as it seems because those who scrambled hardest also needed the higher status the most. These were the property owners of moderate holdings whose material goods made them targets for exploitation by tax collectors, soldiers, and imperial administrators. The lower classes, as always, had little to protect them beyond public opinion, their membership in some organization patronized by the powerful, such as burial societies, or direct dependence on some powerful individual. Toward the end of this period, even this system of privilege failed to protect the middle class property owners from the exactions of the tax collectors, and there was a great deal of pressure either to move up to such a high status, either equestrian or senatorial, as to be out of reach, or to stop such attempts altogether and become the client of someone powerful enough to offer adequate protection.

7.1   "Nations by the Thousands . . . Serve the Masters of the Entire World": What Held the Roman Empire Together

One of the most comprehensive overviews of the geographical extent of the Roman Empire and its military power appears in the form of a speech the Jewish historian Josephus attributes to King Herod Agrippa, who was trying to restrain Josephus' countrymen from revolting. Judaea had suffered at the hands of some particularly poor Roman governors, the last of whom, Gessius Florus, was one of the worst. The country boiled with plots for rebellion. Although Herod does the speaking, the substance of the speech probably reflects the speech Josephus himself gave at the beginning of the war when he found himself in similar circumstances and had to try to dissuade the countrymen of his district from rebelling.

The speech reveals the kind of knowledge of the Romans a provincial upper-class individual such as Josephus possessed at the time of the Jewish Revolt (A.D. 66–70). It also reveals the kinds of predicaments people in the provincial upper classes could find themselves in vis-à-vis their hotheaded countrymen. Josephus rather readily went over to the Romans and, as a result, was hated by his countrymen who joined the revolt.

He begins by reminding his hearers that their forebears, although much better organized, had not resisted the Romans effectively in their first encounter with them in 63 B.C. While Josephus/Herod's knowledge of geography and the battle order of the Roman army is impressive, it is hard to believe that people set on revolt would be impressed by this kind of academic approach.[1]

"Your ancestors . . . , the Athenians . . . , the Spartans . . . , the Macedonians—nations by the thousands, who had greater passion for liberty than you, have yielded. Will you alone refuse to serve the masters of the entire world? What troops, what weapons do you rely on? Where is your fleet to sweep the Roman seas? Where are the financial resources for your revolt? You must think you are going to war with Egyptians or Arabs! Are you blind to the magnitude and extent of Roman power? Why do you refuse to weigh your own weakness? Our forces have often been defeated even by our neighbors, while theirs are undefeated throughout the world! Indeed, they want even more. They are not content with the Euphrates as a frontier in the east, the Danube in the north, Libya and the desert beyond to the south, and Cadiz on the west. They have sought a new world beyond the Ocean and fought the previously unknown Britons!

"Face up to it! You are not richer than the Gauls, stronger than the Germans, smarter than the Greeks, more numerous than the people of the inhabited world. What gives you the confidence to tackle the Romans? 'It is cruel to be enslaved,' someone will say. How much more so for the Greeks, who are the most talented of peoples and occupy such a vast territory. Yet they must obey the six fasces [*the bundle of rods symbolizing authority*] of a Roman magistrate! A similar number control the Macedonians, who, more justly than you, are due their liberty. What of the five hundred cities of Asia? Without a garrison they prostrate themselves before a single governor and his consular fasces. Is it necessary to speak of the peoples around the Bosporus, Black Sea, the Sea of Azov . . . ? Previously these peoples did not recognize a ruler even from among themselves, but now they are subject to three thousand legionaries. Forty war ships keep the peace in that formerly unnavigable, dangerous sea. What powerful claims to freedom might be made by the peoples of Anatolia; yet they pay what they owe without the compulsion of arms.

"Then there are the Thracians, a people spread over a country [*Bulgaria and part of Greece*] five days' march in width and seven in length. Their land is more rugged and much more easily defended than yours. Its icy cold repels invaders, but do they not obey two thousand Roman guards? Their neighbors the Illyrians, who live in the land stretching from Dalmatia to the Danube frontier [*i.e., Yugoslavia*], yield to two legions and even cooperate with the Romans to repel the raids of the Dacians [*from Romania*]. . . .

"But if any nation might be excited to revolt by its natural advantages it is surely the Gauls. Nature provides them with the ramparts of the Alps to the east, the River Rhine in the north, the Pyrenees mountains in the south, and the Ocean in the west. Although surrounded by these defenses, with a population of three hundred and five tribes, and prosperity welling as it were from the land and flooding the rest of the

---

[1]Josephus, *Jewish Wars* 2. 358–388.

world with its products, they nevertheless allow themselves to be treated by the Romans as a source of taxes. They have their own good fortune served back to them by their conquerors. And they accept this, not because of weakness of will or meanness of spirit: they fought for their freedom for eighty years. But they are overawed by the power of the Romans and their good fortune which wins them more victories than their arms. That is why the Gauls are enslaved to twelve hundred soldiers—hardly more than the number of their cities!

"As for Spain—neither the gold from its mines nor the vast stretch of land and sea which separates it from the Romans were sufficient to protect it in its struggle for freedom. Nor for that matter did the Lusitanian and Cantabrian tribes with their passion for war, nor the neighboring Ocean, whose tides terrify even the native, make any difference; the Romans, advancing beyond the Pillars of Hercules and traversing the cloud-capped Pyrenees, enslaved all these peoples. The guard for this remote nation of hard fighters is a single legion!

"Who among you has not heard of the populous German nation? You have seen their huge and powerful figures on many occasions since everywhere the Romans have them as their captives. This people occupies a vast territory. Their spirit surpasses the size of their bodies and disdains death. Enraged they are fiercer than wild beasts. Yet the Rhine stops their expansion. Tamed by eight Roman legions, those captured are enslaved and the whole nation seeks safety in flight.

"You who put your trust in the walls of Jerusalem consider what a wall the Britons had! The Ocean surrounds them; they live in an island as big as our whole Mediterranean world. Yet the Romans crossed the Ocean and enslaved them. Four legions now secure that vast land. But why say any more when the Parthians, the most warlike of peoples, rulers of so many nations and secure by the possession of such great power, send hostages to the Romans? Under the pretext of seeking peace, the elite of the East may be seen in Italy bowing in submission.

"When almost every nation under the sun prostrate themselves before the arms of Rome will you alone make war against them? Consider the fate of the Carthaginians, who boasted of the great Hannibal and the nobility of their Phoenician origins. They fell to the hand of Scipio. . . . This third part of the whole inhabited world [i.e., North Africa], whose peoples are hard to enumerate, bounded by the Atlantic Ocean and the Pillars of Hercules and stretching to the Indian Ocean, supporting as it does the countless Ethiopians—they have it all under their thumb. Besides their annual harvest, which feeds the Roman people for eight months, these peoples over and above pay tribute of all kinds. Unlike you, who see outrage in the demands of Rome, they readily contribute to the needs of the Empire, although only a single legion is garrisoned among them.

"Why look so far afield to demonstrate the power of Rome when we can find it in Egypt, our closest neighbor? Egypt stretches as far as Ethiopia and Arabia Felix and is the point of departure for India. It has a population of seven and a half million, not counting the inhabitants of Alexandria. This is shown by the individual tax returns. Yet this country does not spurn the rule of Rome. What an incentive to revolt it has in Alexandria, with its huge population, its great wealth and size! . . . The tribute

Egypt sends to Rome exceeds in one month what you send in a year! The land is protected by impassable deserts, seas without harbors, rivers, and swamps. Yet none of these assets were sufficient to resist the Fortune of Rome. Two legions stationed in Alexandria curb the remotest parts of Egypt and the proud Macedonian elite to boot.

"What allies do you hope for in the coming war? You must expect them from the uninhabited wilds, for the inhabited world is all Roman. . . . "

7.2 "They Make a Desert and Call It Peace": A View of Rome from the Provinces

Britain was added to the Empire in the first century A.D. *One of the principal architects of the conquest was Agricola, the father-in-law of the great senatorial historian Tacitus. The following reading is found in a eulogy composed by Tacitus in honor of Agricola's accomplishments. The speech is attributed to the Caledonian (Scottish) chieftain Calgacus, who is trying to rally his troops against the Romans. The sentiments are conventional Greco-Roman projection—that is, they express what they thought would or should be the appropriate sentiments of barbarians. Tacitus' intent was not so much to provide historical insight into the mind of a Scots chieftain egging on his reluctant followers to fight as it was to berate contemporary Romans for their lack of spirit. Although they thought of themselves as masters of the world, Romans, Tacitus is saying, were in reality the slaves of the emperors.*

The picture he paints of the Empire is a bleak one. While it is undoubtedly true that a percentage of Rome's subjects would have shared these sentiments, the opinion that states were nothing but organized robberies was an old one. This speech should not be interpreted as though it were based on a poll of Rome's subjects. Calgacus despairingly suggests that there is some hope in the heterogeneous ethnicity of the Roman army.[2]

"Whenever I review the causes of this war and our present desperate situation, I have great confidence that today our united efforts will be the beginning of Britain's liberty. The reason is that all of us are united. We are free of the effects of enslavement. There is no other land beyond us. Indeed, not even the sea is secure, for Rome's fleet threatens us from that quarter. Thus battle and arms will offer for the brave the most glory, and for the coward the greatest safety.

"Previous battles against the Romans, although fought with varying outcome, have left us the hope of success. We, the best people in Britain, living in the country's inner recesses and never having any contact with the conquered, have, as a result, preserved ourselves unpolluted from the contagion of enslavement. Here at the world's end, we, the last unenslaved people, have preserved our liberty to this day because of our remoteness and our obscurity. Now, however, the farthest parts of Britain lie open and all the unknown is wondered at. But there are no peoples beyond us, nothing but

---

[2]Tacitus, *Agricola* 30.

the waves and the rocks—and the even more cruel Romans. Their arrogance you cannot escape by obedience and submission. Robbers of the world, having exhausted a devastated earth, they now try the oceans! If the enemy is rich they are avaricious; if he is poor they lust for power. Neither East nor West has satisfied them. Alone among humankind they covet with equal rapacity rich and poor. Plunder, slaughter, and robbery they falsely call empire; they make a desert and call it peace.

"Children and kin are by nature our dearest possessions. Yet these are carried off from us by levy to be slaves in other lands. Our wives and sisters, even if they escape the lust of our enemies, are seduced by men pretending to be friends and guests. Our goods and possessions are collected for tribute, our land and harvests for grain requisitions. Our very bodies and hands are ground down by the lash, making roads through marsh and forest. Slaves born into slavery are sold once and for all and are at least fed by their owners; but Britain daily purchases her own enslavement—and to boot, feeds what she has purchased! Just as in the slave-gang the most recent addition is the butt of the jokes of his fellow slaves, so in this worldwide slave-gang we, the most recent and most dispensable, are marked for elimination, for there are no lands or mines or harbors in our land for whose exploitation we might be preserved.

"Bravery and independence of spirit on the part of subject peoples are unpalatable to their masters. Remoteness and isolation, to the degree they provide safety, provoke suspicion. Accordingly, since there is no hope of mercy, even at this late hour take courage, whether it is safety or glory that is most precious to you. The Brigantes under the leadership of a woman were able to burn a colony, storm a camp, and if their success had not made them careless, they might have thrown off the Roman yoke altogether. Therefore, we who are untouched and unconquered, who were bred for freedom not regrets, let us show them at the first battle what kind of men Caledonia has been keeping in reserve.

"Do you imagine that the Romans will be as brave in war as they are lustful in peace? It is our own disputes and feuds that bring them fame; the mistakes of their enemies become the glory of their army. That army, made up of different peoples, is held together by success and will fall apart when things go badly for them. Unless of course you suppose that Gauls and Germans and even, I am ashamed to admit, many Britons, having loaned their support to an alien tyranny of which they have been enemies longer than subjects—unless you think they are attached to Rome by loyalty and affection. Fear and terror are weak ties of attachment; take them away and those who have ceased to fear will begin to hate.

"All the incentives to victory belong to us. The Romans have no wives to inspire them, no parents to reproach them if they run away. The majority have no fatherland at all or at best one very far away. Few in number, uneasy because of their lack of knowledge of the country, looking around at an unknown sky, an unknown sea and forest—they have been delivered by the gods to us like caged prisoners.

"Do not be frightened by their outward show; the flash of gold and silver neither helps nor hurts. We shall find help in the very battle lines of the enemy. The Britons will recognize their own cause, the Gauls will remember their former liberty; the rest of the Germans will desert them just as the Usipi did recently. Behind them there is nothing to fear: empty forts, colonies of old veterans, weak and quarreling towns with their disloyal subjects and unjust rulers. Here in front of you are the general and his army; there on the other side you have taxes and mines and all the other punishments suffered by the enslaved. Whether you endure these forever or avenge them at once rests upon this field. Therefore, as you go into battle, think of your ancestors and your descendants."

7.3 The Alternative: "If the Romans Are Driven out What Else Can There Be Except Wars Among All These Nations?"

Calgacus' despairing words in the previous reading and his description of the Empire as a "desert" was echoed by later writers, including the great Edward Gibbon, author of the monumental The Decline and Fall of the Roman Empire, *who characterized the Empire as a "dreary prison."*

Realistically, however, what was the alternative? In this reading Tacitus puts the case for Rome. It comes in the form of a blunt speech given by the Roman commander Cerialis to a number of Gallic tribes who had revolted against Rome and had just been reconquered. It is as plain and straightforward as the speech of the barbarian chief Calgacus was florid and bombastic, a supposed characteristic of Celtic rhetoric to which Cerialis refers.[3]

Cerialis called an assembly of the Treveri and Lingones and spoke as follows:

"I am not one for words; instead I have always maintained the power of Rome by force of arms. But since words mean a great deal to you people, and you judge things to be good or evil not as they really are but as agitators say they are, I have a few things to say. As the war is over, you may get more benefit from hearing what I have to say than I will get from having to speak.

"Gaul always had its petty kingdoms and wars until you submitted to our power. Although often provoked, we have used the right of conquest to burden you only with the cost of keeping the peace. For peace among nations cannot be maintained without armies; armies cost money, and money can be raised only by taxation.

"We hold everything else in common. You often command our legions; you rule these and other provinces; you are not segregated or excluded by us. You benefit from good emperors though you live far away, while we who live close by suffer from evil ones. Accept the extravagance and avarice of your masters just as you put up with bad harvests and floods and other natural disasters. There will be vices as long as there are men. But they are not eternal, and they are counterbalanced by better times—unless

---

[3]Tacitus, *Histories* 4.73–74.

of course you think you will be better off under Tutor and Classicus [*the rebel leaders*], or that the armies to protect you from the Germans and Britons will cost less!

"If the Romans are driven out—Heaven forbid!—what else can there be except wars among all these nations? Eight hundred years of the divine fortune of Rome and its discipline have produced this federal empire and it cannot be pulled apart without the destruction of those attempting to do just this.

"You are in the most dangerous situation. You have gold and wealth—the main causes of war. Therefore, love and care for peace, and also love and care for that city which victors and vanquished alike share on an equal basis. Learn the lessons of fortune for good or evil: Do not choose obstinacy and ruin in preference to submission and safety."

7.4   Training Soldiers

In his description of the Roman army, the historian Josephus noted that the legionary was equipped with breastplate, helmet, sword, and dagger. In addition, he carried a javelin, an oblong shield, a saw, a basket, a shovel, an ax, a leather strap, a scythe, a chain, and three days' food supply. "As a result," Josephus goes on to say, "the legionary soldier differs little from a loaded pack mule." (Josephus, A History of the Jewish War, *3.107–108). The fourth-century military writer Vegetius describes how recruits were trained.*[4]

The Romans have subjugated the whole world by no other means than through training in the use of weapons, strict discipline in camp, and experience in warfare. From the start of their training new recruits must be taught the military pace. Keeping their ranks while moving must be carefully checked whether on the march or in battle. This cannot be done except by constant practice, for an army which is broken up and lacks orderly ranks is always in danger from the enemy. Therefore twenty Roman miles (i.e., about 18–19 U.S. miles) at the military pace should be completed in five hours during summer time. At the quicker full pace twenty four Roman miles should be completed in the same time.

The recruit must be trained to jump ditches . . . he must learn how to swim for there are not always bridges over rivers, and in retreat or in pursuit an army is frequently forced to swim. In sudden rainfalls or snowfalls, streams become torrents and dangers arise from not knowing how to swim . . . vaulting onto horses should be practiced strictly and constantly, not only by recruits but also by trained soldiers . . . young soldiers must be frequently required to carry loads up to 60 pounds and to march at the military pace . . . every recruit must know how to construct a camp. Nothing else is more advantageous and necessary in war. If a camp is built correctly, the soldiers spend their days and nights securely inside the rampart, even if the enemy besieges them. It is like carrying a walled city around with you wherever you go.

---

[4]Vegetius, *Epitoma rei militaris* 1.

7.5   Foreigners in the Roman Army

Calgacus, the Scottish chieftain, claimed that if the Roman army suffered a defeat it would quickly fall apart because it was made up of foreigners (7.2). There was some truth to this. Although the legions were recruited from among citizens, these recruits came from widely scattered parts of the Empire. In addition, the auxiliary units which supported the legions were drawn wholly from the noncitizen population of the Empire. The following are memorial inscriptions put up by legionary and auxiliary soldiers serving in the Roman army in Britain. Avitus' monument, the second below, is elaborate. It shows the deceased in military dress holding his will written on wax tablets in his left hand.[5]

To the spirits of the dead. Marcus Aurelius Alexander, prefect of camp of the Twentieth Legio Valeria Victrix, a Syrian of Osroene. He lived seventy two years. His heirs set up this monument. To the spirits of the dead. Caecilius Avitus of Emerita Augusta [modern Merida in Spain], centurion's second-in-command, member of the Twentieth Legio Valeria Victrix. He served for fifteen years and lived thirty-four years. This inscription is set up by his heir.

As Calgacus noted to his shame, even Britons served in the Roman army. A degree of Romanization can be inferred from the fact that the father of the dead soldier in the next inscription goes by a Roman name, Vindex.

To the spirits of the departed. Nectovelius, son of Vindex, aged twenty-nine with nine years' service. He was a Brigantian [the Brigantes were a tribe in northern England] by tribe and served in the Second Cohort of Thracians [an auxiliary unit made up of volunteers from the Balkans].

7.6   Making It in the Ranks

Marcus Vettius Valens rose through the ranks, beginning as a private in the Praetorian Guard at Rome and ending up as procurator, or personal agent and representative of the Emperor Nero in Portugal. He probably got his first appointment as the result of the recommendation of a patron, but thereafter, his own abilities and the opportunity to "network" at Rome advanced his career smoothly. The Praetorian Cohorts were elite peacekeeping forces at Rome. The Vigiles served as firemen, and the Urban Cohorts also contributed to maintaining the peace.[6]

This inscription is set up to honor Marcus Vettius Valens, son of Marcus of the Aniensis tribe, patron of the colony of Ariminum [*in Italy*]. He began his career as a private in the 8th Praetorian Cohort [*at Rome*] and was clerk of the Praetorian Prefect. He was

---

[5]R. G. Collingwood and R. P. Wright, *The Roman Inscriptions of Britain* (Oxford, 1965), #490; 492; 2142.
[6]*Inscriptiones Latinae Selectae* 2648.

recalled for the campaign in Britain [*under Claudius*] and was decorated for bravery. He was then promoted centurion of the 6th Cohort of the Vigiles; next, centurion of the 16th Urban Cohort; next, centurion of the 2nd Praetorian Cohort; enrolled as a member of the Emperor's special escort; centurion, Legio XIII Gemina in Pannonia; First Centurion [*with equestrian rank*], Legio VI Victrix in Spain; decorated for successfully waging war against the Asturians; Tribune, 5th Cohort of Vigiles; Tribune, 12th Urban Cohort; Tribune, 3rd Praetorian Cohort; First Centurion for the Second Time, Legio XIV in Pannonia; Procurator of Nero Caesar Augustus at the ducenarius level in the Province of Lusitania [*Portugal*].

7.7   Making It at Rome The Career of an Emperor: Septimius Severus

Since the first century of the Empire, provincials in increasing numbers entered the Roman Senate. There was nothing unusual about the process itself. For centuries in the Republic there had been a steady, if unspectacular, movement of outsiders into the ranks of the ruling elite. They came first from the immediate areas around Rome, then from farther afield in Italy. Julius Caesar was supposed to have outraged the Senate by introducing trousered Gauls. The rise of the great emperor Septimius Severus followed a predictable pattern. His ancestors pioneered the way, though not much is known of their rise to prominence from the out-of-the-way Punic town of Leptis in Libya.

Septimius' own career was as ordinary as the style of the author who relates it. Following a fairly typical career pattern, he moved from one post to another over much of the Empire—from Italy to Spain, to Sardinia, to France, to Hungary, to Sicily. Finally, as luck would have it, he ended up in a major military command in Hungary and was there when the current emperor was killed and his own troops took it upon themselves to proclaim him emperor. A bloody civil war followed from which Severus emerged victorious, establishing a dynasty that lasted from 193 until A.D. *235. When the Severan dynasty ended, Rome was plunged into half a century of even more violent civil war.*[7]

After Didius Julius had been assassinated, Severus, who hailed from Africa, became emperor. His home town was Leptis Magna. His father was Geta, and his ancestors were Roman knights even before the citizenship had been extended to everyone in the Empire. Fulvia Pia was his mother, and his great-uncles were the consulars Aper and Severus. Macer was his father's father, and his mother's father was Fulvius Pius. He himself was born six days before the Ides of April in the second consulship of Erucius Clarus and the first consulship of Severus (A.D. 146).

When still a child, and before he began his Greek and Latin studies (in which he was highly educated), he would engage only in the game of "Judges" with the other children. When he played this game he would have the rods (the *fasces*) and axes carried in front of him and, surrounded by the other children, would sit and pass

---

[7]Augustan History, *Septimius Severus* 1–5.

judgment. At eighteen he gave a speech in public, and after this came to Rome to continue his studies. With the help of his relative [*of the same name*] Septimius Severus, he petitioned and received the broad senatorial purple stripe from the Deified Marcus [*the Emperor Marcus Aurelius*].

On his arrival at Rome he met a man—not someone he knew—who at that very moment was reading the *Life* of the Emperor Hadrian. He took this as an omen of success in his career. . . . He performed the duties of quaestor diligently, having skipped the military tribunate. After the quaestorship he was assigned to the province of Baetica [*southern Spain*] by lot, and from there went back to Africa to settle the affairs of his family, his father having died. But while he was in Africa he was reassigned to Sardinia in place of Spain, which was being ravaged by the Moors. Having served his quaestorship in Sardinia, he was appointed legate to the proconsul of Africa. . . .

He was promoted to tribune of the plebs by the Emperor Marcus Aurelius and executed his responsibilities with great strictness and vigor. It was at this time he married Marciana, although he says nothing of her in the story of his life as a private citizen. When he was emperor, however, he put up statues in her honor. He was designated praetor by Marcus [*Aurelius*]. . . . After he had been sent to Spain he dreamed that he should restore the temple of Augustus at Tarraco, which was in a state of ruin. Then he dreamed that he saw from the top of a very high mountain Rome and the whole world while the provinces sang in harmony to a lyre or flute. Although absent from Rome, he put on the usual games in the city.

He was then put in command of Legio IV Scythica, stationed near Marseilles. After this tour of duty he went to Athens to continue his studies, to perform some religious functions, and to see the public buildings and the ancient monuments. . . .

Next he was appointed legate to the province of Lyons [*in France*]. Meanwhile, since his wife had died and he wished to marry again, he made inquiries into the horoscopes of possible brides, being himself an expert in this field. When he heard there was a certain woman in Syria whose horoscope predicted she would marry a king [*Julia Domna*], he asked her to become his wife and with the aid of friends succeeded. He soon became a father. He was loved by the Gauls as no one else because of his strictness and his sense of honor.

Next he ruled the two provinces of Pannonia [*parts of modern Austria, Hungary, and Yugoslavia*] with proconsular power. After this he was selected by lot to govern the proconsular province of Sicily. Meanwhile another son was born at Rome. While he was in Sicily, he was indicted for consulting soothsayers or Chaldaean astrologers regarding the future of the emperor but was acquitted by the judges because Commodus [*the reigning emperor*] was already hated. His accuser was crucified. He was consul for the first time with Apuleius Rufinus as his colleague [A.D. *190*] among a very large group appointed by Commodus. After the consulship he spent a year without an official posting. Then on the recommendation of Laetus [*another general*] he was given the command of the army in Germany. . . . In Germany he conducted himself in the legateship in such a way that he was able to increase his reputation, which was already significant.

Thus far he pursued his military career as a subject. But when it was learned that Commodus had been assassinated and that Julianus had taken his place amid universal hatred, he was proclaimed emperor, though against his will, by the German legions at Carnuntum.

7.8   A Celt Makes Good

Another example of provincials rising in the Roman administration is the career of Gaius Julius Severus. A descendant of Celts who invaded Anatolia {Turkey} in the third century B.C., *Severus rose to prominence as a magistrate in his home town Ancyra {modern Ankara}. As such he was in a position to benefit both his own people and the Romans during the transfer of Roman troops from the western to the eastern frontier in* A.D. *113–114 in preparation for a war against the Parthians. Throughout history the movement of troops through a civilian population has been a cause of hardship for the latter. In this instance, Severus buffered the local population by supplying the needs of the troops in transit out of his own pocket. For this he was rewarded at Ancyra with an inscription and most likely a statue. Beyond that, however, he attracted the attention of the emperor Trajan, and Trajan's successor, Hadrian, appointed Severus to the Roman Senate. From there on he led a glittering career. He represents a good example of the Roman capacity to find and exploit talent no matter where it was found.*[8]

Gaius Julius Severus, the descendant of kings and tetrarchs [*the old rulers of Galatia*]. Having held all the key offices in his own nation, he was admitted to the rank of tribune of the plebs by the divine emperor Hadrian. He then served as legate of the governor of Asia, and next, by appointment of Hadrian, he was made commander of Legio IV Scythica and administrator of Syria when Publius Marcellus left because of the revolt in Judaea [*the second Judaean revolt,* A.D.*132–135; Marcellus took a legion with him*]. He was proconsul of the province Achaea [*in Greece*] with five fasces. Hadrian sent him to the province of Bithynia as curator of accounts. He was prefect of the Treasury of Saturn [*in Rome*], consul, priest, superintendent of Public Works in Rome, and propraetorian legate of Lower Germany. . . . Marcus Julius Euschemon erects this inscription in honor of his benefactor.

7.9   A Roman View of Foreign Competition

Juvenal (ca. A.D. *55–ca.130) is the author of some of the best vignettes of Roman social life. In sixteen satires he denounces women and men, rich and poor, Romans and foreigners, the corruption of wealth, and the abuse of freedom, with an invective seldom rivaled. He works an old theme that we also encountered in the writings of Livy and Sallust (see Chapter 5).*

In this particular reading, Juvenal is pursuing one of his favorite targets: "Greeks"—that is, just about anyone from the Mediterranean area who spoke Greek (or perhaps just Latin

---

[8]*Orientis Graeci Inscriptiones Selectae* 544.

with an accent).[9] *Over the centuries of their interaction, the Greek–Roman relationship had its ups and downs, somewhat like that of the U.S. and Europe. Romans clearly had the upper hand. They were the ones in charge, militarily predominant, and far more adept in practical politics than the Greeks. The Greeks tried to bolster their sagging self-esteem by emphasizing their presumed cultural superiority and the glories of their now somewhat distant past.*

Now let me talk about that race with which our rich is so much enamored but which I cannot abide. Not to put too fine a point upon it, I can't stand a Rome that is Greekized. Yet what fraction of these supposedly Greek dregs actually comes from Greece? Syrian Orontes [*the main river in Syria, a Hellenized province in the Middle East*] has for years deposited its verbal and cultural sewage into our very own Tiber. These Greeks worm their way into our great houses with the aim of becoming their masters. Quick of wit, unrestrained in nerve, they have the gift of the blarney to a degree that outstrips even professional word slingers.

What do you think that fellow's profession is? Actually he has any character you like—schoolmaster, orator, expert in geometry, a painter, an athletic coach, a diviner, a doctor, an astrologer—he's all of these professions in turn if he's hungry enough. If your order him to fly, there, off he goes, airborne. . . . Greece is a nation of actors. If you smile, your Greek friend will explode with laughter; if he sees a friend weep, he weeps—not of course that he feels anything; if you say you're cold, he puts on his cloak; if you say you're hot, he sweats. So you see, we don't share a level playing field. The Greek always has the advantage of being ready night or day to borrow his mood from somebody else's.

7.10   Provincial Administration: Hands-On Style

There is a tendency to think of Roman emperors at best in terms of distant autocrats acting through faceless bureaucrats and at worst as crazed pleasure-lovers acting out their fantasies in gaudy palaces. The reality was much more prosaic, as the following exchange of letters between the Emperor Trajan and his governor in Bithynia [northwestern Turkey], *C. Plinius Secundus, shows. Pliny tended to err on the side of caution, forever sending cases to the emperor which a more resolute (or perhaps unscrupulous) governor might have settled on the spot, in consultation with his consilium.*

The case reveals a lot about life in the provinces, at least among the upper classes. Flavius Archippus, a philosopher of somewhat dubious reputation, had ingratiated himself with the previous emperor Domitian, but when Domitian was assassinated, his enemies, led by a woman named Furia Prima, got busy and tried to have him condemned to hard labor in the mines. Archippus had kept good records and was able to fight back effectively. Clearly, he had been a strong supporter of the previous Flavian regime (as his name suggests) and had cashed

---

[9]*Satires* 3.58–107.

in on his position, alienating and victimizing in the process a number of his fellow townsmen.
Furia Prima had evidently suffered in some way at his hands. Pliny takes no chances and lets
the emperor handle the situation.

The styles of the Emperors Domitian and Trajan contrast with the pomposity of Nerva, who
reigned briefly after the death of Domitian. The shrewd reading of the evidence by Trajan and
his laconic comment regarding Furia Prima's complaint are of interest. His message to Pliny
was: "Tell Furia I've read her letter, and I don't want to hear any more on this subject."[10]

Letter of Pliny to the Emperor Trajan

Sir: When I called the jurors to attend the hearings, Flavius Archippus claimed to be
exempted because he was a philosopher. However, some people present said that
indeed, not only should he be freed from jury service, but his name should be
removed altogether from the jurors' list and that he should be shipped back to
the prison from which he had escaped, to complete his sentence. In support of this
the judgment of the proconsul Velius Paullus was read. According to this document
Archippus had been condemned to the mines for forgery. While Archippus could
not prove that the sentence had been reversed, he produced as evidence of his rein-
statement a petition he had submitted to the Emperor Domitian along with letters
from Domitian honoring him, and a decree in his honor from the people of Prusa. To
these he added a letter written by you to him as well as an edict and a letter of our
father [*the Emperor Nerva*] confirming the grants made to him by Domitian.

Accordingly, although such charges have been made against him, I thought nothing
should be decided until I had first consulted with you. The case seemed to deserve
your special attention. I attach to this letter the documents cited by the two parties.
The documents are as follows:

1. The Letter of the Emperor Domitian to Terentius Maximus [*the emperor's agent in*
Bithynia]
In response to the request of Flavius Archippus the philosopher I have ordered that up
to 100,000 sesterces be made available to purchase land for him near Prusa, his native
town. The income from this land is for the support of his family. I wish this to be done
for him. The full amount is to be written off as an expression of my generosity.

2. The Letter from the Emperor Domitian to L. Appius Maximus [*proconsul of*
Bithynia under Domitian]
My dear Maximus, I recommend Archippus the philosopher to you as a good person
whose character is in harmony with his calling. Please show him every kindness in
granting the small requests he may make of you.

3. The Edict of the Emperor Nerva
Citizens: There are some matters in which in happy times like ours there is no need
of an edict, and equally other matters in which the intentions of a good emperor

---

[10]*Letters of Pliny* 10.58; 59; 60.

cannot but be clearly understood. I want every one of my citizens to know that I gave up my private life in response to the needs of all. I did so in order to dispense gladly new benefits, and to confirm those of my predecessor.

In order that your public rejoicings may not be spoiled by the misgivings of those who received favors, or because of the memory of the emperor who bestowed them [*the assassination of Domitian had apparently raised fears that Nerva might rescind his acts*], I thought it necessary and agreeable to dispel these doubts by a manifest act of kindness: No one is to think that I will withdraw any of the benefits, either public or private, bestowed by other emperors in order to claim the credit of restoring them for myself. They are fully ratified. Let no one on whom the Good Fortune of the Empire has smiled think his joy needs to apply for a renewal of petitions. On the contrary, give me the opportunity to bestow new favors; let it be known that I need only to be asked for those benefits which have not already been granted.

4. Letter of Nerva to Tullius Justus [*proconsul of Bithynia under Nerva*]
The governmental regulations, whether merely initiated or completed under previous regimes, are to be observed. Accordingly, the letters of Domitian remain valid.

Pliny's Covering Letter to the Emperor Trajan

Flavius Archippus has asked me, by your prosperity and immortality, to forward the petition which he has presented to me. I thought I should do this though I should also let his prosecutor [*Furia Prima*] know I was doing this. She has also given me a petition which I am attaching to this letter. This way, by hearing each side, you might be better able to decide what should be done.

Response of Trajan to Pliny

It is possible that Domitian might not have known the status of Archippus when he wrote all those letters in his favor. However, I think it more reasonable to believe that Archippus was in reality restored to his former status by Domitian's intervention. This is especially likely since the people of Prusa, who could not have been ignorant of the sentence against him by the proconsul Paulus, so often voted him the honor of a statue. But I do not mean to suggest, my dear Pliny, that if any new charges are brought against him, you should be slow to hear them.

I have read the petitions of Furia Prima, his accuser, as well as those of Archippus, which you sent me with your second letter.

7.11   How Patronage Worked

Pliny cultivated his patron Corellius Rufus when he entered public life and in turn supported Rufus, helped defend his family and relatives, and worked to protect his reputation. When Rufus died, Pliny took up the defense of his daughter, Corellia, who had some legal problems and continued to work on her behalf for the rest of his life. These actions were the typical response of a good and faithful client to a good and faithful patron. The following is from a letter to a friend about the upcoming case of Corellia. Roman friendship had a strongly instrumental side to it. Romans were users and expected to be used. Such relationships were not thought to be dishonorable.[11]

How can I hesitate to defend a daughter of Corellius?. . . . When I ran for public office [*her father*] Corellius gave me his support as my patron. He introduced me and attended me when I entered upon my duties. . . . What a reputation in both the private and public realms he built up for me until finally my reputation even reached the ears of the Emperor. The reason this happened is that there was an occasion when discussion arose in the presence of the Emperor Nerva about the promising young men of the time. A number of people were saying good things about me, but Corellius kept silent. This had the effect of giving his words greater weight when he did finally speak. As you will recall he said, "I must be restrained in my praise of Pliny because he has had my advice for everything he does." With these few words he paid me a tribute far beyond what I could have hoped for since his comment suggested that I did nothing that fell short of his high standards and that I did everything with the advice of the wisest of men. As he was dying he told his daughter (it is she who tells the story) that he made many friends for her in the course of a long life, but none like Pliny and Cornutus Tertullus.

7.12   Slaves Running the Empire

The early emperors ran the Empire the way the great nobles of the Republic ran their great estates. They did this with the assistance of their family, friends, freedmen, and slaves. The following inscription suggests how important slaves could be in the running of the Empire and what influence they wielded, not to mention what kind of households they themselves had.[12]

To Musicus Scurranus, slave of Tiberius Caesar Augustus, manager of the Gallic treasury in the province of Lyons. This monument is put up by his slaves who were with him in Rome when he died. He was a worthy master.

Venustus, agent	Epaphra, butler	Facilis, footman
Decianus, accountant	Primus, valet	Anthus, butler
Dicaeus, secretary	Communis, steward	Hedylus, steward
Mutatus, secretary	Pothus, footman	Firmus, cook
Creticus, secretary	Tiasus, cook	Secunda?
Agathopus, doctor		

---

[11]*Letters of Pliny* 4.17.
[12]H. Dessau, *Inscriptions Latinae Selectae* (Berlin, 1892), 1514.

7.13   Obligations of the Rich: The Philanthropy of Pliny

While the rich had clearly defined privileges in society, they also had some well-defined obligations. These included, first and foremost, personal service to the local municipality and then to the imperial government. They were expected to stand for election to local offices, serving in the local senate or council; perform the duties of patron (which included handing out cash); and serve in the legions. For some, service in the imperial administrative system and the Roman Senate was a tradition.

In the first inscription below, Pliny, the Roman senator whom we encountered in Section 7.10 ("Provincial Administration") and earlier in this chapter (also see "Imperial Case-Work" below), serves as an illustration of a fairly typical career pattern. Among other things, his career reflects the role local aristocrats were expected to play in relationship to their home towns, in this case the city of Como in northern Italy. The inscription works back and forth chronologically, starting with Pliny's highest offices, then going back to earlier ones, and ending with his benefactions to Como.[13]

Gaius Plinius Caecilius Secundus, son of Lucius, of the Oufentina tribe, consul [A.D. 100]; augur; legate with propraetorian power of the province of Pontus and Bithynia [*parts of modern Turkey*], having been sent there by decree of the Senate with consular power, and by the Emperor Caesar Nerva Trajan Augustus Germanicus Dacicus, Father of the Fatherland. [*He was*] Curator of the Course and Banks of the Tiber and of the Sewers of the City of Rome; Prefect of the Treasury of Saturn; Prefect of the Military Treasury; Praetor; Tribune of the Plebs; Imperial Quaestor; President of a Squadron of Roman knights; Tribune of the Soldiers of Legio III Gallica; member of the Commission of Ten for Decisions on Civil Status.

He ordered by his testament the construction of baths for the municipality [*of Como*] costing . . . [*the amount is lost through a gap in the inscription*], with a further 300,000 sesterces for their decoration . . . [*another gap*] and 200,000 sesterces for their upkeep; likewise he bequeathed 1,866,666 sesterces to his city for the support of his 100 freedmen. The interest on this amount he directed to be afterward devoted to the feeding of the plebs of Como . . . [*another gap*]; likewise, during his lifetime, he gave 500,000 sesterces for the support of the boys and girls of the urban plebs; he also gave a library and 100,000 sesterces for its upkeep.

7.14   The Contributions of Freed Slaves

Freed slaves were also expected to make contributions to their community and were often glad to do so, as it gave them a certain visibility and respectability. The subject of this inscription, Decimus Eros, had clearly made a success of his life. That his master and patron (of the same name, less

---

[13]H. Dessau, *Inscriptions Latinae Selectae* (Berlin, 1892), 2927.

the "Eros," a Greek name) belonged to the Roman upper classes and was very wealthy is clear from the fact that he could afford his own private physician. But Decimus Eros himself must have been a good doctor and surgeon so that others in the Roman upper classes appealed to Decimus (the master) for Decimus' (the slave's) services. This work in turn added to the wealth and, especially, the prestige of the master. In the end, as custom dictated, Decimus Eros obtained his freedom by purchase, and he went on to a career as a municipal patron at Assisi in central Italy.[14]

Publius Decimus Eros Merula, freedman of Publius, clinical doctor, surgeon, ophthalmologist, member of the Board of Six. For his freedom he paid 50,000 sesterces; for the membership of the Board of Six he gave 2,000. He gave 30,000 sesterces for statues in the temple of Hercules. For paving public roads he gave 37,000 sesterces. On the day before he died he left an estate of 100,000 sesterces . . . [*the rest of the inscription is missing*].

7.15   Getting Along Together: The Role of Citizenship

From earliest times the Romans had used the conferral of citizenship as a technique for winning over, or at least neutralizing, the elites of neighboring peoples. In this reading the historian Tacitus has tidied up a much longer, rambling speech given by the Emperor Claudius urging the Roman Senate to admit Gauls from across the Alps into its ranks. (Claudius' actual speech, in the form of an inscription, is also extant.) In making his case, Claudius responds to arguments that plenty of excellent candidates were to be found in Italy; he indicates that Gauls from the Italian side of the Alps had already been admitted—wasn't that proof enough?—and finally, answers the objection that the admission of rich Gallic provincials would block the careers of the native-born Italians.[15]

These and similar arguments failed to impress the emperor. He immediately refuted them and, after calling the Senate, spoke as follows:

"The earliest of my ancestors, Clausus [*in Latin, Claudius*], a man of Sabine origins, was made both a citizen and a patrician at the same time. This experience encourages me to proceed by the same principle of bringing to this city the best talent from wherever it is found. I am not unaware that the Julii came from Alba Longa, the Coruncanii from Camerium, and the Porcii Catones from Tusculum [*all these cities were close to Rome and the first to be incorporated in Rome's early expansion*]. But not to spend too much time on antiquity, we are well aware that men from Etruria, Lucania, and all Italy have been admitted to the Senate and that in the end Italy itself was extended to the Alps, so that not only individuals but whole regions and peoples were joined together with us as Romans. With the enfranchisement of Italy beyond the Po [*i.e., Cisalpine Gaul*] and the enrolling of the best of the provincials in

[14]H. Dessau, *Inscriptions Latinae Selectae* (Berlin, 1892), 7812.
[15]Tacitus, *Annals* 11.24.

the legions, we revived an exhausted military and had unshaken peace at home and good relations with the rest of the world.

"Are we sorry that the Cornelii Balbi came to us from Spain and other equally distinguished men from southern Gaul? Their descendants are still with us; in their love for Rome they do not yield to us. What proved fatal for Sparta and Athens, no matter what their military strength, was the fact that they treated the people they defeated as aliens. Our founder Romulus, on the other hand, had the wisdom to convert on the same day enemies into Roman citizens. Foreigners have ruled us. The admission of the sons of freedmen to the magistracies is not, as many think, something new. It was a common practice in early times.

"It will be said: We fought against the Senonian Gauls. If that's the case then the Italian Volsci and Aequi never were arrayed against us! 'The Gauls sacked Rome.' Well, yes, but we also gave hostages to Etruscans and went under the Samnite yoke. If you review all our wars, you will see that the Gallic War took the shortest time of all. Since then we have had unbroken peace and trust with them. Now that they have assimilated our customs and ways and have intermarried with us, let them bring us their gold and their wealth rather than leaving them keep it to themselves.

"Senators, all our institutions, however ancient they now seem, were once new. Plebeian magistrates followed on patrician, Latin on plebeian, Italian on Latin. This proposal now being considered will in its turn become established practice. What we are today justifying by precedents will itself become a precedent."

The Senate approved the emperor's speech and passed the appropriate decree. The Aedui were the first Gauls to become Roman senators. This was given in recognition of their ancient alliance with Rome and the fact that they alone enjoyed the title of "Brothers of the Roman People."

7.16   The Role of Law

One of the great achievements of Rome was the expansion of what had been the law of a single polis to a world empire. As we see in the following reading, even when the power of the emperors was indisputably autocratic, the ideal of the rule of law remained intact. The Institutes of Justinian were published in A.D. *533 as an introductory textbook for law students at the same time that Justinian published his monumental codification of Roman law, The Digest.[16] For more selections from the Digest, see Chapter 9, "Daily Life as Seen through the Law Codes."*

Imperial Majesty should not only be distinguished by arms, but also protected by laws, so that government may be justly administered in time of both war and peace. The Roman Princeps [*i.e., the emperor*] may then not only stand victorious in battle with [*exterior*] enemies but also, by legitimate measures, defeat the evil designs of wicked men [*within the state*]. He can then triumph as much for his administration of justice as for his victories over his foes.

---

[16]From the Preamble of Justinian's *Institutes*.

7.17   The Law in Action

The emperor had his hands full dealing with an interesting collection of problems that came his way on a daily basis. Some problems were generated by the army, a huge force of over twenty-eight legions scattered from Scotland to Egypt. Others originated among the diverse populations of the Empire. Some were unnecessarily passed on to the emperor by nervous governors afraid to make decisions themselves. From the picture provided by the letters of the complacent Pliny, the emperor looks more like a shrewd although hard-working bureaucrat than a despot who commanded armies, a terror to those around him.[17]

To Cornelianus:

Lately I had the satisfaction at Centumcellae (as it is now called) of being summoned there by Caesar [*the Emperor Trajan*] to attend a council. Could anything be more pleasing than to see the emperor exhibiting not only his affability but his justice and wisdom, even in private, where those virtues are most observable?

The matters brought before him were a mixed bag. They tested in many instances his abilities as a judge. The affair of Claudius Ariston came up first. Claudius is a nobleman of Ephesus, of great generosity and unambitious popularity. His virtues, however, have made him obnoxious to a kind of people of very different character. These people instigated an informer against him, of the same stamp as themselves. But he was honorably acquitted.

Next the charge against Gallitta, accused of adultery, was heard. Her husband, who is a military tribune, was on the point of standing as a candidate for certain offices in Rome, but she disgraced him and herself by an affair with a centurion. The husband complained to the consul's aide, who in turn wrote to the emperor. Caesar, having examined the evidence, demoted the centurion and banished him. It remained only for some punishment to be inflicted on Gallitta, as it was a crime of which both must necessarily be equally guilty. But her husband's affection for her motivated him to drop this part of the prosecution, though not without some suspicion of connivance. Indeed, he had continued to live with her even after he had started his prosecution, contenting himself, it seemed, with getting rid of his rival. But he was ordered to proceed in the suit. He complied with reluctance. Although her accuser was unwilling, it was necessary that the defendant be convicted, and so she was. She was sentenced under the Julian Law. In his decree the emperor specified the name and rank of the centurion so that it was clear that this was a matter of military discipline. He did not want all cases of this kind to be referred to him.

The third day was devoted to the examination of Julius Tiro's will, a case that had caused a good deal of speculation. Part of the will was clearly genuine, but part of it, it was alleged, was forged. The persons accused of the fraud were the Roman knight Sempronius Senecio and one of the emperor's freedmen and procurators, Eurythmus.

---

[17]Pliny, *Letters* 6.31.

The heirs had jointly petitioned the emperor when he was in Dacia, asking him to conduct the inquiry himself. He agreed to do so and, on his return from the expedition, set a day for the hearing. Then, when some of the heirs, out of consideration for Eurythmus, thought of dropping the case, the emperor insisted, saying: "He is not Polyclitus, and I am not Nero."[18]

He had, however, given the petitioners an adjournment, and now that the time had elapsed, he took his seat to hear the case.

Only two of the heirs were present. They petitioned that either all of the heirs should be compelled to appear, as they had all joined in the prosecution, or the case should be dropped. Caesar delivered his opinion with great dignity and restraint, and when the counsel for the defendants Senecio and Eurythmus claimed that unless they were heard their clients would remain under suspicion, the emperor said: "I am not so much concerned with the fact that they are under suspicion but that I am left under suspicion." He then turned to us who made up his council. "Advise me," he said, "how to act in this matter. They complain that I don't let them drop the suit." Finally, on the advice of the council, he ordered that all the heirs were to be called to carry on the case or else each one individually had to justify his withdrawal from the case. Otherwise he would declare them guilty of bringing false charges.

Thus you see the honorable and important way we spent our time at Centumcellae. In the evenings, however, we were able to relax. The emperor invited us to dinner every day, not very grand meals when you consider his position. Then we were entertained by recitations or else passed the night in pleasant conversation. On our last day the emperor, in his usual thoughtful way, sent us presents. As for myself, I was pleased not only with the dignity and wisdom of the judge, the honor of being on his advisory council, the ease and unreserved freedom of the conversation, but also with the attractiveness of the place itself. The delightful villa is surrounded by green meadows and commands a fine view of the sea, where a spacious harbor is being carved out in the shape of an amphitheater.

▼▼▼

Questions

1. Identify five of the nations Josephus names in his list of those who had been subdued by the Romans. (**7.1**)
2. Do you think many of Rome's subjects shared the view of Calgacus the Scottish chieftain cited by Tacitus? (**7.2**).
3. Cerialis paints a different picture of the Empire from that of Calgacus. In what way do the two views diverge? (**7.2** and **7. 3**)

---

[18]Polyclitus was one of the notorious Emperor Nero's freedmen and a man to be feared.

4. According to Vegetius what kind of training enabled the Romans to "subjugate the whole world"? (**7.4**)
5. Analyze the career path of Marcus Vettius Valens. What parts of the Empire did he visit during his various tours of duty? (**7.6**)
6. What positions did Septimius Severus hold before becoming the emperor? (**7.7**)
7. What kind of qualifications do you think the Celt Gaius Julius Severus had that enabled him to transition into the Roman imperial administration? (**7.8**)
8. Outline the case against Flavius Archippus. How was he able to defend himself against his accusers? (**7.10**)
9. List the gifts that Pliny gave to his home town. What do you think motivated him? (**7.13**)
10. What problems did the will of Julius Tiro generate? (**7.17**)

Chapter 8

▼▼▼

Religion and Culture in the Roman Empire

Religions of the Empire

The great cultural diversity of the Empire was reflected in the chaotic variety of religions, cults, philosophies and theosophies that offered themselves to the inhabitants of the Roman world. They ranged from the austere, ascetic monotheism of Judaism and Christianity and some of the moral philosophies, to the flamboyant and bloody rituals of Cybele. There were officially sanctioned and supported state cults that functioned openly and splendidly, and small, private groups that met and worshiped in secret. Every taste and class was accommodated. The emperors, although tolerant, tried to maintain some kind of order by putting down practices that did not fit in with their idea of an orderly society or seemed to represent some kind of political threat. Human sacrifice was stopped in Gaul and North Africa, Druidism was stamped out in Celtic lands, and even astrology and magic captured the emperor's attention at times. Simultaneously, the emperors tried to boost the civil religions of the Empire.

Every city, town, village, and rural community had its own set of deities and cults and a corresponding calendar of holy days and festivals. The celebration of these festivals was considered essential to the community's survival and prosperity. Rules regarding appropriate rituals, how they were to be performed, and who was to perform them were prominent in municipal law codes (**8.1**). Most of these civic religions, as they are called, were low in doctrinal and ethical content, but high in local appeal and personal satisfaction. When there was money available for sacrifices, banquets, games, and other entertainment, the ritual of the civic religions could be very impressive indeed and served to bring all members of the community together in the worship of the special gods who looked after that particular community. On the other hand there were the simple rituals of the countryside (**8.4**). Mystery religions offered alternatives of a different kind involving initiation into secret rituals and the consolations of such appealing goddesses and gods as Isis and Mithra. Magic and superstition flourished. Holy men performed miracles and exorcised demons (**8.5**). Unlike its portrayal by Hollywood, paganism was an intrinsically coherent moral system.

Emperor Worship

The emperor was the high priest and head of the Roman state religion, and as such was responsible for maintaining right relations between the gods and humankind. While alive he was a semi-divine intermediary between human beings and the gods, and when dead he was a god himself.

In the east, rulers had long been worshiped as being more clearly sources of divine power than the remote deities of traditional belief, although they too were worshiped. It made good sense politically to honor a man-god, for this conveniently combined cult and homage in a single act. In the Republican period the Greeks had identified the goddess *Roma* as the source of Rome's power and worshiped her, sometimes along with an individual Roman general. Thus the cult of *Roma* and the general T. Quinctius Flamininus, who "liberated" Greece from Macedonian domination in 197 B.C., was established at Chalcis, where it survived for more than 300 years. During the Principate the cult of Rome and Augustus, replete with temples, altars, and priests, spread throughout the eastern provinces and eventually, following prodding by the emperors, to the west as well (**8.3**). In Italy and Rome homage was paid to the genius, or "spirit," of the emperors following the tradition of the cult of the genius of the paterfamilias (the head of the Roman household) within his own family. Logically, other members of the imperial family were incorporated in the cult of the reigning emperor. Thus, all the peoples of the empire could be viewed as being members of a single family, with the emperor as their kindly but firm *paterfamilias*.

Civil Religions and Cults

The imperial cult was not intended to replace the traditional civil religions or cults that flourished in profusion all over the empire. Most of the cults of the Hellenistic period continued into Roman times. Under the pax Romana the worship of Isis spread to the west, where she won thousands of new adherents. An Iranian religion, Mithraism, was popular in the army and offered an attractive combination of doctrine, ritual, and ethical practice. Its adherents believed that the cosmos was in constant tension between the forces of good and evil, light and darkness, life and death. The soul, although immortal, is contaminated by association with the body and must be liberated by an ascetic struggle in which Mithras, who has already conquered death and ascended into heaven, assists. A high level of ethical behavior was expected, but psychological support was supplied by the regular meetings of the Mithraic community, which took place in small, cavelike chapels and included a sacred meal. However, the appeal of Mithraism was limited because it excluded women.

Syncretism and fusion, as in Hellenistic times, was common. In North Africa, Saturn was associated with Jupiter; in Gaul, Mercury was identified with the native Celtic deity Lug and Jupiter with Taranis. At Bath in Britain, Minerva was identified with the local spring goddess, Sulis. Everywhere the ancient festivals and sacrifices continued to require, as always, the financial support of the cities and the upper classes for their suitable enactment. Thousands of people sat or stood in theaters, amphitheaters, town squares, or temple doorways to witness religious spectacles of one kind of another. The shrine of the healing god Asclepius at Epidaurus in Greece had a theater that could accommodate 15,000, and in other parts of the Empire, theaters were specially built adjacent to temples to accommodate worshipers at festival times. The celebrations included sacrifices, banquets, dancing, music, games, and processions. At times there were theatrical reenactments of religious or mythological events. Many of the mystery cults, such as those of Eleusis, also staged large-scale, dramatic affairs attracting thousands. Religious festivals were widely publicized outside individual cities in the hope of attracting worshipers (or just tourists, because both would pay). The more magnificent the celebration, the larger the crowds. Pilgrims and tourists alike carried the word of these religious celebrations far and wide.

The Health of Paganism

The strength but also the weakness of the cults and civil religions of the Empire lay in their close ties with the communities in which they were embedded. When their fortunes rose, so did those of the cults: the temples were maintained or embellished, the festivals were splendidly celebrated. The reverse was also true. When cities and communities declined, so did their ability to maintain the cults, which, unsustained by public support, faded. Gods not worshiped ceased to be gods at all or degenerated to the level of local superstitions (**8.10**). Nevertheless, there is little evidence that in the early Empire the traditional cults did not satisfy the religious needs of the people. At least in the cities, if the local cults did not appeal or were not conducted according to one's tastes, there were always other choices. The unity and relative peacefulness of the empire promoted the spread of religions and made exotic alternatives available everywhere. Among those that benefited from these conditions and found a secure niche throughout the Empire were the ancient national religion of Judaism, an approved cult, and its recent, heretical offshoot Christianity, which took centuries before it, too, was approved.

Judaism and Christianity

Judaism and Christianity were both exclusive in their membership and both placed emphasis on the close adhesion to strict ethical practices and dogmatic beliefs. Judaism, in addition to the attractiveness of its high moral standards and its lofty monotheism, was one of the most ancient religions of the Empire. It possessed an important collection of religious books, which propounded in organized fashion its history, laws, and philosophy. It offered a coherent account of the origin of human beings and their history from the earliest times. Its liturgy had the advantages of both the philosophers' lecture hall and the sense of community and brotherhood of the mystery cults (**8.11**; **8.12**).

Christianity borrowed these traits from Judaism but dropped the more extreme demands of the law such as circumcision and the laws of purification. To the Jewish belief that God was the Lord of History, Christians added the assertion that history had found its culmination in the lowly person of Jesus of Nazareth, who was executed by the imperial prefect Pontius Pilate during the reign of the emperor Tiberius.

The message and mission of Jesus emerge out of the world of late Jewish eschatology. Like many of his contemporaries, Jesus believed that the world was enthralled to demonic influences and that liberation would come through the intervention of God, who would overwhelm the forces of evil and set up his own kingdom over which sin and death would have no power. In the past, God had acted in a preliminary way to deliver his people from bondage in such events as the call of Abraham, the Exodus from Egypt, and the end of the Babylonian captivity; now, however, he was preparing to act in a final, decisive manner.

Jesus did not proclaim a new ethical or moral system. He was not primarily a teacher, and his message was not startlingly original; much of it was to be found in traditional Jewish or even pagan ethics. He viewed his mission, rather, as the proclamation of the coming of a new period of history, the Kingdom of Heaven. This he believed was to be brought about not by human means, such as the violent overthrow of governments, or by the observation of laws or ethical rules, but by the active intervention of God in human affairs. Moreover, Jesus' ministry was intended, somehow, to inaugurate the new age. Reaching back to the prophet Isaiah, he identified himself with the servant figure, whose sufferings would atone for the sins of Israel, a scapegoat whose death would usher in the Day of the Lord. Again drawing on the symbolism of Israel's past, Jesus described his death during the Last Supper discourse in terms of the symbols of the Passover. Just as the Exodus was a mighty act by which God had freed the Israelites from Egypt and made them his people, so Jesus' death, his "passover," or passage to the next world, would be the means by which a New Exodus leading to a New Covenant would be brought about. By means of this New Covenant (or Testament), the reign of God was to be initiated, freeing humankind from sin, death, and the power of the demonic world (**8.6**; **8.7**).

For the earliest Christians the kingdom was inaugurated not only by Jesus' death but also by his miraculous resurrection from the dead and his ascension to heaven.

New members were brought into the community by the ritual of baptism, which identified them symbolically or sacramentally with the key events of Jesus' life, his death and resurrection. Christian life itself revolved around common worship, preaching, and exhortation (**8.9**). Collections of the sayings and deeds of Jesus were made and told and retold. The common meal shared by early Christians took on the overtones of Jesus' Last Supper with his apostles and became the setting for discussions, readings, and interpretations of Jesus' life and actions. Among the major issues settled in the early years of the Christian community was the question of whether Jesus' message was to be limited to Jews or could be extended to gentiles as well. One of the principal figures in this momentous debate was a Hellenized Jew, Paul of Tarsus (**8.7**). The decision in favor of a wider audience had vital implications for the future of Christianity, the Greco-Roman world in which it came to maturity, and even the world outside the frontiers that was ultimately to achieve a triumph of sorts over Rome.

Rabbinic Judaism

During the first century A.D. there were many competing—though interacting—forms of Judaism in Judaea and among Jews outside Palestine (the Diaspora). In Palestine, two schools, the Sadducees and the Pharisees, differed over doctrinal issues such as the immortality of the soul and punishment after death. In interpreting scripture and the law Sadducees took a literal approach, insisting that only the written scriptures were acceptable sources of revelation, whereas Pharisees were more flexible. The latter claimed that the Torah (the law) came in two forms, the one written and the other oral, each necessary and complementary to the other, each God given. Besides these two main schools (further divided into subsects), there were numerous other groups of Jewish ascetics, revolutionaries, mystics, and believers in apocalyptic restoration. Of these the most important were the Essenes and the Qumran or Dead Sea community (whose library was discovered in caves above the Dead Sea in 1947). The communities of the Diaspora possessed yet another variant of Judaism.

The destruction of the Temple in Jerusalem by the Romans in A.D. 70 and further devastation following the Bar Kochba Rebellion of A.D. 132–135 resulted in a spiritual upheaval in Judaism comparable to the one that followed the destruction of the Temple of Solomon (the First Temple) by the Babylonians in 587–586 B.C., and led directly to the flowering of Rabbinic Judaism. With the elimination of the Second Temple the influence of the Sadducees faded, the Qumran and Essene sects were destroyed or scattered, and the apocalyptic movements discredited. Now, in the absence of the Temple, the synagogue became the vital focus of Jewish religious life. The rabbi as interpreter and wise man replaced the priest, and prayer became a surrogate for animal sacrifice. Of the many traditions of Judaism, Pharisaism proved to be the most vital and capable of responding to the needs of post-revolt Judaism, and it was from this root in particular, though not exclusively, that Rabbinic Judaism developed.

Philosophy, Religion, and Magic

By the time of the Roman peace, philosophy had long since given up its meta-physical search for knowledge and instead devoted itself to the humbler, more practical questions of human conduct. It did not even concern itself with theories of morality but instead sought to give concrete answers to pressing questions of daily life. What is virtue? How should wealth and power be used? How should people cope with change and loss? How involved should a citizen be in civic life? What is human happiness?

All the great schools of philosophy of the past were ransacked to provide answers to these questions. Philosophy was converted into religion and made to reply to questions that the old philosophies and religions had not even raised. It was as though it had been decided that what was needed was not new knowledge but practical answers to pressing moral issues. It was not theoretical information about the nature of human life that was sought but rather instructions on how to conduct one's everyday life: art not science, salvation rather than wisdom, revealed truths in the place of reasoning and speculation. The ability of reason to give secure answers was questioned, and more definitive sources of authority were sought. Syncretism was in the air, and the boundaries between philosophy, science, magic, and religion became blurred to the point where all of these terms became interchangeable. Even Christianity could claim to be a philosophy, meaning a way of life or a way of ascending to God.

For the middle and upper classes, Seneca, Musonius, Epictetus, Plutarch, and others provided examples, sermons, and exhortations to virtue. Seneca turned Stoicism into a religion and criticized abuses of wealth and pleasure, including cultural pursuits, argu-ing that the true objective of philosophy was to live well (**9.3**). He urged people on, somewhat cheerlessly, in the struggle against evil and developed such a high concept of God that some Christians later concluded that he must have been a convert.

Musonius, who was exiled by Nero, preached gentleness to wrongdoers and forgiveness of injuries, and argued against the double standard for men and women (**8.15**; **9.6**). Apollonius of Tyana taught brotherly helpfulness, courage, and temperance. He spoke against the luxury of the baths at Antioch and the frivolity of the Athenians. He criticized Nero as an effeminate tyrant and encouraged rebellion. Demonax successfully argued the Athenians out of staging gladiatorial contests by saying that they would first have to give up the Altar of Pity in the city before they could introduce such contests. Dio Chrysostom denounced both the sensuality of the rich and the selfishness of the mob. For him the true community was one from which greed, intemperance, and violence were banished and in which everyone lived under law. He glorified the simple life of the peasants and preached moderation to the emperor Trajan. Plutarch's vast knowledge was used in a lifetime devoted to the moral education of his contemporaries. Unlike so many of his gloomy, moralist friends, who viewed life with a deep pessimism, Plutarch cheerfully emphasized the power of positive thinking. People, he said, should think of the good things they have and look for the hidden hand of God in the disasters that befall them. Most of the bitterness of calamities comes from their own doing, he argued, not from events outside themselves.

The masses sought answers to the same kinds of questions that plagued the educated and received answers from hosts of prophets, preachers, oracle mongers, and magicians. The higher speculations of the moral theologians were put into handbook form or popularized by street preachers. Unwashed and rude Cynic philosophers disdained convention and harangued the passers-by, preaching renunciation of all social ties and responsibilities. Proteus Peregrinus, one of the more flamboyant of the Cynics, criticized the emperor Antoninus Pius at Rome and the powerful Herodes Atticus at Athens. Herodes, he said, merely gratified his vanity by his huge benefactions in Greece and elsewhere. Proteus committed ritual suicide in A.D. 165 and was hailed as a holy man throughout Greece. Apollonius of Tyana lived as an ascetic, performed miracles, and so impressed his contemporaries that after his death, his cult spread widely (**8.5**).

Others were not so reputable. Alexander of Abonoteichos deliberately set out to mine the potential of the superstitious age. Selecting an out-of-the-way town with a gullible population, he planted a newly hatched snake in a goose egg and then substituted a fully grown snake with a false head. Thus established, he proceeded to hand out answers to sealed questions, which he claimed he never opened. The fraud was attacked by Lucian of Samosata, one of the few disbelievers in an age of credulity.

▼▼▼

8.1   Civic Religion

The Empire was a patchwork of self-governing cities and their attached local villages or, where they existed, tribal communities. It was taken for granted in all of them that the gods, goddesses, heroes, and ancestral spirits would be worshipped at appropriate times of the year and with suitable rituals. During the early Empire the Romans attempted to bring order to this process of honoring the gods if for no other reason than to be sure that the gods always got their due. The pax deorum, the existence of good relations between gods and humans, had been part of the Roman sense of due order from earliest times. When the Romans came to rule their empire, they continued to promote this simple but vital idea of a tangible, manageable—and therefore legally prescribable—connection between earth and heaven.

The first reading is from the municipal charter of a Roman colony in southern Spain bearing the name "Colonia Genetiva Julia" (modern Osuna). The texts are from the regulations governing the religious obligations of the colony's annually elected magistrates, the duoviri and aediles. The magistracies of municipalities could be expensive propositions for the individuals concerned. Although they dispensed public funds, they also were expected to make significant contributions themselves to the running of the community. Note the way the ordinance is phrased in regard to public and private disbursements. The magistrates' compensation was the public recognition of their generosity by their fellow citizens (who could also choose to withhold this recognition if they thought the magistrates were being cheap).[1]

LXX. All duoviri, except those first appointed after this law, shall during their magistracy at the discretion of the decurions celebrate a gladiatorial show or dramatic spectacles to Jupiter, Juno, and Minerva and to the gods and goddesses, or such part of the said shows as shall be possible, during four days, for the greater part of each day, and on the said spectacles and the said shows each of the said persons shall expend of his own money not less than 2,000 sesterces, and out of the public money it shall be lawful for each several duovir to expend a sum not exceeding 2,000 sesterces, and it shall be lawful for the said persons so to do with impunity. Always provided that no person shall expend or make assignment of any portion of the money, which in accordance with this law shall be properly given or assigned for those sacrifices which are publicly performed in the colony or in any other place. LXXI. All aediles during their magistracy shall celebrate a gladiatorial show or dramatic spectacles to Jupiter, Juno, and Minerva, or whatever portion of such shows shall be possible, during three days for the greater part of each day, and during one-day games in the circus or forum to Venus, and on the said spectacles or shows each of the said aediles shall expend out of his own money not less than 2,000 sesterces, and from the public funds it shall be lawful to expend for each several aedile 1,000 sesterces, and a duovir or praefectus shall see that the said money is given and assigned, and it shall be lawful for the aediles to receive the same without prejudice.

8.2   The Ideology of Paganism

A statement of the ideology of the civic religion is to be found in the dialogue entitled Octavius, written by the advocate Minucius Felix sometime in the early third century. The dialogue is presented as a debate between a Christian, Octavius Januarius, and a pagan, Q. Caecilius Natalis. Part of Caecilius' side of the debate is given here. After arguing that the world is not governed by providence, he concludes that it is better to hold on to the traditional forms of religion.[2]

Since, then, because either chance is blind or nature uncertain, how much more reverent and better it is . . . to accept the teaching of our ancestors. We should cultivate the religions handed down to us and adore the gods whom we were first trained by our parents to fear rather than to know with familiarity. We ought not carry on dogmatically about them, but rather believe our forefathers, who while living in a primitive age, when the world was still young, were able to believe in gods who acted kindly. . . .

---

[1]*Lex Coloniae Genetivae Juliae* 70–71. Translator E. G. Hardy, *Roman Laws and Charters* (Oxford: Clarendon Press, 1912), pp. 31–32.

[2]Minucius Felix, *Octavius* 6, 8. Based on Alexander Roberts and James Donaldson, *The Ante-Nicene Fathers* vol. 4 (Edinburgh: The Christian Literature Company, 1885), pp. 175–177.

So it is that throughout all empires, provinces, and cities, we see that each people has its national rites of worship and adores its own local sets of gods. The Eleusinians [*who lived near Athens*] worship Ceres; the Phrygians [*in modern Turkey*], the Great Mother; the Epidaurians [*in southern Greece*], Aesculapius; the Chaldaeans [*in Iraq*], Bel; the Syrians, Astarte; the Taurians [*in the Crimea*], Diana; the Gauls, Mercury; and the Romans, all divinities. Thus their power and authority has occupied the circuit of the whole world; thus it has advanced the bounds of empire beyond the path of the sun and the frontiers of the Ocean itself. When they fight in the field, they show bravery inspired by religion. At home they fortify their city with sacred rites, with the Vestal Virgins, and with many priestly dignities and titles. When they were besieged [*by the Gauls in 390 B.C.*] and all the city except for the Capitol taken, they still worshipped the gods, although other peoples, when their gods were angry, would have neglected them. . . . When, in turn, they capture a city, they venerate the conquered gods although still full of fury from the struggle. Everywhere they seek the gods of strangers and make them their own. They even build altars to unknown deities and to the spirits of the dead! Thus, while they adopt the rituals of all nations, they have also deservedly won the dominion of all nations. Hence their veneration of the gods has continued without interruption, strengthened rather than impaired by the passage of time. Indeed, antiquity bestows on rituals and temples a holiness proportioned to their age. . . . Therefore, since all nations agree on the existence of the immortal gods, although their nature or their origin may be uncertain, it is intolerable that anyone should have so much audacity or impiety as to strive to undermine or weaken this religion, so ancient, so useful, so wholesome. . . .

8.3   The Divine Emperor

For centuries the peoples of the Eastern Mediterranean honored their kings as the source of blessings and of protection against enemies. As the maintainers of good relations with the gods, the kings ensured the stability of the state. It was natural that these same peoples should look on their new rulers, the Roman emperors, as divine in this sense also. In the West the provincials were encouraged to worship the goddess Roma, the Genius or Fortune of Rome. With Roma was often associated the cult of the deified emperors, that is, those emperors who had been declared divine by decree of the Senate after their death.

The cult of Roma and the deified emperors was entrusted to the upper classes and served the useful function of involving provincial elites in the Roman governmental system. Significantly, it also brought together some of the disparate elements of the provincial upper classes, such as ex-slaves, who had risen to prominence. But, as was typical of all ancient cults, the community as a whole got something tangible from the festivals. Minimally there was some form of entertainment, but in this instance the reward was meat, wine, and incense.

The following is an inscription on a marble altar set up by the people of Narbo (modern Narbonne) in Southern France.[3]

---

[3]H. Dessau, *Inscriptiones Latinae Selectae* (Berlin, 1892), 112.

THE ROMAN TEMPLE: PUTTING PEOPLE IN THEIR PROPER PLACES

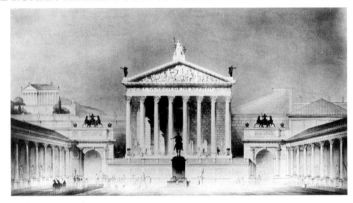

The temple of Venus Genetrix portrayed here dominated the Forum of Caesar in Rome. It was dedicated in 46 B.C. The practice of placing temples at the end of long enclosures was borrowed from the Etruscans by the Romans and eventually became a standard architectural feature of cities throughout the Empire.

The Greek temple was free standing. It was intended to be walked around and taken in by the viewer. By contrast, the Roman temple, following Etruscan models, was placed at the end of a large porticoed enclosure. It had long, overhanging eaves and a high gable. On entering the sacred place the worshipers' attention was immediately focused on the temple. In this arrangement the individual was instantly subordinated to the order and symmetry of the buildings and to the gods of the state who inhabited them.

Unlike the classical Greek arrangement of temples and buildings, where the human being was the accepted measure of things, the Romans early came to locate the individual in an orderly arrangement, symbolizing their belief that all people had preordained places in the scheme of life, places fixed by the gods and interpreted for them by society and the state.

For the Romans hierarchy was normal and good. Correct hierarchy maintained the proper order of things. Rome gave no encouragement to the individual to seek his (and especially, not her) self-fulfillment independently of the norms of society or the state. Individuals were expected to accommodate themselves to society and play whatever role was assigned to them by their birth and social position. In this regard there was little room for kind of liberty treasured in the modern world. For the Romans liberty, of which they regarded themselves as proud champions, had a very different, primarily political, meaning. Freedom was not to do what wanted to do; that was democracy. Freedom was, rather, to do what one ought to do as determined by *mos maiorum*, ancestral custom.

[*Front face of the altar*]:

In the consulship of T. Statilius Taurus and L. Cassius Longinus [A.D. *11*], on the twenty-second day of September, the following perpetual vow to the Divine Spirit (*numen*) of Augustus was made by the people of Narbonese Gaul:

May it be good, favorable, and fortunate for the Imperator Caesar Augustus, son of the divine [*Julius Caesar*], Father of his Country, Chief Priest [*Pontifex Maximus*], holding tribunician power for the 34th time; and also for his wife, children and house [*gens*]; for the Senate and the People of Rome; and for the colonists of Julia Paterna of Narbo Martius who have obligated themselves to worship his spirit forever.

The people of Narbo have set up an altar in the Forum at Narbo. At this altar every year on September 23, the day on which the Good Fortune of the Age produced Augustus as ruler of the world [*i.e., his birthday*], on that day three Roman knights of the plebs and three freedmen shall each sacrifice one animal and at their own expense provide incense and wine for the colonists and residents in order to supplicate his Divine Spirit. Similarly, on September 24, they shall provide incense and wine . . . and on January 1 incense and wine . . . and on January 7, the day on which his command (*imperium*) of the whole world was first initiated, they shall make supplication with incense and wine, and each sacrifice an animal, and provide incense and wine for the colonists and residents of the city. . . .

[*On right side of the altar*]:

The people of Narbo have dedicated this Altar of the Divine Spirit of Augustus . . . in accordance with the laws written below [*the dedication follows*]:

"O Divine Spirit of Augustus, Father of his Country! When I give and dedicate this Altar to you today, I shall give and dedicate it in accordance with the laws and regulations which I will proclaim openly here today . . . . : 'If anyone wishes to clean, decorate, or repair this Altar as a public service, it shall be right and lawful. If anyone makes a sacrifice of an animal without providing the additional offering, it shall nevertheless be regarded as having been done properly. If anyone wishes to give a gift to this Altar and to further embellish it, it shall be allowed; the same regulation applies to the gift as to the Altar. Other laws for this Altar and inscriptions shall be the same as for the altar of Diana on the Aventine [*in Rome*].' 'In accordance with these laws and regulations, just as I have said, I give and dedicate this Altar on behalf of Emperor Caesar Augustus, Father of his Country, Chief Priest, holding the Tribunician Power for the 35th time, and on behalf of his wife, children and house, the Senate and People of Rome, the colonists and inhabitants of the colony of Julia Paterna Narbo Martius, who have bound themselves to worship his Divine Spirit forever. I dedicate this Altar that you may be favorably and propitiously disposed to us.'"

8.4   Rural Religions and Superstitions

The Spanish poet Martial (died ca. A.D. 104), friend of Juvenal and Pliny the Younger, lived in Rome for thirty-five years. He was the author of twelve books of epigrams in which the contemporary life of Rome at every level from high to low is well represented, often salted with mild venom. About to return to Spain toward the end of his life, he commends to his friend Marius the farm at Nomentum, the rural retreat that had made life bearable for him at Rome. Although Martial was no peasant farmer, he refers in this epigram to the gods and goddesses that inhabited the fields and woods of Italy and whose propitiation and honor were the responsibility of the farmer, who acted as a priest to perform these rituals.[4]

Marius, an advocate and sharer of the quiet life, a citizen of whom ancient Atina [*Marius' hometown in Latium*] brags, these twin pines, the decoration of this untilled grove, I commend to you, as well as the holm oaks where the Fauns lived, and the altars of Jupiter the Thunderer and shaggy Silvanus, built by the hand of my rough farm manager, often stained by the blood of lambs and goats. I commend to your care the virgin goddess, mistress of her holy shrine, and him whom you see, the guest of his chaste sister, Mars, who is my birthday god, and the laurel grove of sweet Flora, in which she takes refuge when chased by Priapus. Please say to all these gentle deities of my tiny farm, whether you propitiate them with blood or incense: "Wherever your Martial is, behold he, the absent priest, sacrifices with me by this right hand to you. Reckon him present, and grant to each of us whatever we shall pray for."

8.5   A Holy Man Stops a Plague at Ephesus

The philosopher-sage Apollonius of Tyana led the life of an ascetic, wandering the Mediterranean world during the first century A.D. According to his biographer, Philostratus, he performed miracles, prophesized, and finally ascended bodily into heaven. Despite the legendary aspects of the biography, there is no doubt that Apollonius existed. Nor were the kinds of healings and exorcisms ascribed to him out of character with his lifestyle as a professed holy man, mystic, and magician.

*   Philostratus belonged to the circle of intellectuals around Julia Domna, the wife of the important emperor Septimius Severus (see Section 7.7), and it is possible that it was at her instigation that the Life was composed. Minimally the Life reveals something of the religious interests of the court. The not always dependable Augustan History claimed that Septimius himself had a private chapel where he kept statues of four men: Abraham, Orpheus, Christ, and Apollonius. The parallels in the lives of Apollonius and Christ attracted attention during persecutions of the late Empire, and the biography of Philostratus was used as a source for an anti-Christian tract claiming that Apollonius was the equal of Christ.[5]*

When the plague broke out at Ephesus and there was no stopping it, the Ephesians sent a delegation to Apollonius asking him to heal them. Accordingly, he did not hesitate, but said: "Let's go," and there he was, miraculously, in Ephesus. . . . Calling together the people of Ephesus, he said, "Be brave; today I will stop the plague." Then he led them all to the theater where the statue of the God-Who-Averts-Evil had been set up.

---

[4]Martial, *Epigrams* 10.92.
[5]Philostratus, *Life of Apollonius* 4.10.

In the theater there was what seemed to be an old man begging, his eyes closed, apparently blind. He had a bag and a piece of bread. His clothes were ragged and his appearance was squalid. Apollonius gathered the Ephesians around him and said, "Collect as many stones as you can and throw them at this enemy of the gods." The Ephesians were amazed at what he said and appalled at the idea of killing a stranger so obviously pitiful, for he was beseeching them to have mercy on him. But Apollonius urged them on to attack him and not to let him escape.

When some of the Ephesians began to pitch stones at him, the beggar who had his eyes closed as if blind suddenly opened them and they were filled with fire. At that point the Ephesians realized that he was a demon and proceeded to stone him so that their missiles became a great pile over him. After a little while Apollonius told them to remove the stones and to see the wild animal they had killed. When they uncovered the man they thought they had thrown their stones at, they found he had disappeared, and in his place was a hound who looked like a hunting dog but was as big as the largest lion. He lay there in front of them, crushed by the stones, foaming at the corners of his mouth as mad dogs do. A statue of the God-Who-Averts-Evil, that is, Heracles, stands at the spot where the apparition was stricken.

8.6 Jesus of Nazareth

The exorcisms and miracles of Jesus of Nazareth (died ca. A.D. *30) were of a very different type and purpose from those of Apollonius. In the Gospels Jesus' language and world-view are those of traditional Jewish apocalyptic eschatology of the Hellenistic period. Among the characteristics of this form of Judaism may be found the following beliefs:*

History is not a meaningless cycle of events but a series of steps directed by God to a final, magnificent conclusion, at which time Israel is to be restored, foreigners driven out, and the scattered people of Israel, both living and dead, reunited in a renewed and glorious Jerusalem; all the nations of the earth are to abandon their idolatry and learn to worship the true God at his new Temple in Jerusalem. The Lord either will himself lead the forces of good or will send his Messiah to do so. For some, including Jesus, this definitive intervention of the God included salvation from sin, death, illness, and demoniacal possession. The powers of the cosmos who ruled the world since the sin of Adam were to be overthrown and the Kingdom of God inaugurated.

Signs of the nearness of the Kingdom were the miracles and exorcisms Jesus performed. These events were not mere incidents in his life, but proofs that the Last Days of History were at hand. The plans of God, partially revealed in the past by the prophets of Israel and the events of Israel's history, were on the verge of being completed and made fully clear.

Jesus' message was presented not as a code of ethics or a list of commands, but rather in the form of demands for unconditioned acceptance of all that the rule of God involved. The signs of the Coming of the Kingdom were the casting out of devils, the curing of the blind, the lame, and the sick. The expulsion of the money changers from the Temple was both a challenge to the ruling establishment at Jerusalem and a symbol of the closeness of the End of History: the Temple would be destroyed and replaced in the New Age by a glorious Temple "not made by hands" (Mark 14.58). It may well have been this incident that led to Jesus' final confrontation with the authorities. From among his many disciples Jesus selected an inner core group of twelve (the twelve Apostles) and among them an even more select group consisting of Peter, James, John, and sometimes Andrew. To the apostles was given the command to baptize and preach to all nations.

Signs of the Coming Reign of God

When John the Baptist heard in prison about what Jesus was doing he sent his disciples to ask him, "Are you he who is to come [*i.e., the Messiah*] or should we look for another?" Jesus answered them, "Go tell John what you have heard and seen: the blind see, the lame walk, lepers are cleansed, the deaf hear, the dead are raised up and the poor have the good news preached to them." (Mt. 11.2–6).

The Demands of the Kingdom and the Cost of Discipleship

You have heard that our ancestors were told, "You shall not murder and anyone who commits murder will be subject to judgment." But I say to you that anyone who is angry with his brother will be subject to judgment. . . . You have heard it said, "Do not commit adultery," but I say to you that anyone who so much as looks at a woman with evil desire has already committed adultery with her in his heart . . . You have heard that it was said, "An eye for an eye, and a tooth for a tooth," but I say to you, "Do not resist an evil person. If someone strikes you on the right cheek, turn to him the other as well. . . . You have heard it said, 'You shall love your neighbor and hate your enemy,' but I say to you, 'love your enemies and pray for those who persecute you . . . for if you love only those who love you, what reward do you have? Do not even the tax-collectors do the same' (Mt. 5.21–47) . . . Therefore, whatever you wish that men should do to you, do you also to them, for this is the Law and the Prophets (Mt. 7.12).

"Do not think I came to bring peace to the earth; I came to bring the sword, not peace. I came to set son against father and daughter against mother and daughter-in-law against mother-in-law. The enemies of a man will be his own servants. He who loves father or mother more than me is not worthy of me. Who loves son or daughter above me is not worthy of me. He who does not take up his cross and follow me is not worthy of me. He who saves his life will lose it—and he who loses his life for my sake will find it!" (Mt. 10.37–38).

A scribe came to him and said: "Master, I will follow you wherever you go." Jesus said to him: "The foxes have their holes and the birds of the heaven their nests, but the Son of Man has nowhere to lay his head." One of his disciples said to him: "Master, allow me to go first and bury my father." But Jesus said to him: "Follow me; leave the dead to bury their dead!" (Mt. 8.19–22).

An official asked him: "Good Teacher, what good should I do that I might gain eternal life?" Jesus said to him: "If you wish to enter into life, keep the commandments." He said: "Which do you mean?" Jesus said: "You shall not kill; you shall not commit adultery; you shall not steal; you shall not bear false witness; honor your father and mother, and love your neighbor as yourself." The young man said: "I have kept all these commandments since my youth. What more do I need to do?" Jesus said to him: "There is one thing lacking in you. Go, sell what you have and give it to the poor and you will have treasure in heaven. And come, follow me." When he heard this the young man went away sad because he had many possessions. Jesus said to his disciples: "Truly I say to you, it is difficult for the rich to enter into the Kingdom of Heaven." And again he said: "It is easier for a camel to pass through the eye of a needle than for a rich man to enter heaven!" (Lk. 18.18–25).

Who is My Neighbor? The Good Samaritan

A certain scholar of the law stood up to test him and asked him: "Teacher, what must I do to inherit eternal life?" Jesus said to him, "What is written in the law? How do you read it?" And he answered, "You shall love the Lord your God with your whole heart and your whole soul and with all your strength, and with all your mind; and your neighbor as yourself." Jesus said, "You have answered right; do this and you will live." But wanting to justify himself he asked Jesus, "And who is my neighbor?" Jesus replied, "A man was going down from Jerusalem to Jericho and fell among robbers who stripped him and beat him and went off leaving him half dead. Now by coincidence a priest was likewise going down that road, and when he saw him he passed by on the opposite side. So also a Levite, when he came to the place and saw the man, he also passed by on the other side of the road. But a Samaritan, as he journeyed, came to where the man was and saw him and had compassion for him. He went up to him, poured oil and wine on his wounds and bandaged them up. Then he put him on his own animal and brought him to an inn and took care of him. The next day he took out two denarii [about two days wages] and gave them to the innkeeper saying, 'Take care of him and whatever more you have to spend I will repay you when I come back.' Which of these three, do you think, was neighbor to the robber's victim?" He said, "the one who showed mercy to him." And Jesus said to him, "Go and do the same." (Lk. 10.25–37).

Who is in Good Standing with God?

He told this parable to some who were confident in themselves that they were in good standing with God and despised others. Two men went up to the temple to pray, one of them a Pharisee, the other a tax collector. The Pharisee stood and prayed in this fashion with himself: "I thank God I am not like the rest of men, thieves, rogues, adulterers, like this tax collector here. I fast twice a week, I give tithes of all that I have." But the tax collector, standing afar off, would not so much as lift up his eyes to heaven but beat his breast saying, "God be merciful to me a sinner!" I tell you this man went down to his house forgiven rather than the other. For everyone who exalts himself shall be humbled and he who humbles himself shall be exalted (Lk. 18.9–14).

True Generosity: The Widow's mite

And he sat down opposite the temple treasury and watched the crowd making their contributions. Many rich came and gave large sums, but a poor widow came and gave just two copper coins which together make half a cent. He called his disciples together and said to them, I tell you truly this poor widow has put in more than all those who are giving gifts to the treasury. For they all gave out of their surplus wealth while she out of her poverty has put in everything she had, even her whole livelihood (Mk. 12.41–44).

The Basis of Judgment at the End of the World

"When the Son of Man comes in his majesty and all the angels with him, then he will sit on the throne of his majesty and all the nations will be gathered in front of him and he will separate them from each other as the shepherd separates sheep and goats. He will set the sheep at his right hand and the goats at his left. Then the king will say to those who are at his right: 'Come you blessed of my Father, possess the kingdom prepared for you from the foundation of the world. I was hungry and you gave me to eat; thirsty and you gave me to drink; a stranger and you took me in; naked and you clothed me; sick and you visited me; in prison and you came to visit me.' Then the just will respond and say: 'Lord, when did we see you hungry, and we fed you? thirsty and we gave you drink? when did we see you as a stranger and we took you in, or naked and we clothed you and sick or in prison and we visited you?' And the king answering will say: 'Truly I say to you that as long as you did it to the least of my brethren you did it to me.'" (Mt. 25.31–45).

Cleansing the Temple

And when he entered Jerusalem the whole city was disturbed and people asked: "Who is this?" And the crowd responded: "This is Jesus the prophet from Nazareth in Galilee." And Jesus entered the temple of God and drove out all the sellers and buyers in the temple and the tables of the moneychangers and toppled over the chairs of those selling doves. And he said: "It is written: 'My house will be called a house of prayer'; but you have made it a den of thieves." And the blind and lame came to him in the temple and he cured them. But the leaders of the priests and the scribes saw the wonders he did and heard the young in the temple crying out and saying: "Hosanna to the son of David," and they were enraged and said to him: "Do you not hear what they are saying?" Jesus said to them: "Truly, have you not read: 'Out of the mouths of infants and babes at the breast you have brought perfect praise'?" (Mt. 21.12–16).

The Mission of the Apostles

The eleven disciples went to the mountain in Galilee to which Jesus had told them to come. When they saw him they worshiped him even as some of them doubted.

And Jesus came and said to them: "All authority has been given to me in heaven and on earth. Go therefore and make disciples of all nations, baptizing them in the name of the Father, and of the Son and of the Holy Spirit, teaching them to observe all that I have commanded you. And be assured, I will be with you always, even to the end of the world" (Mt. 28.16–20).

The Keys of the Kingdom: The Role of Peter

It happened that when Jesus was praying by himself and his disciples were with him he asked them: "Who do people say that I am?" They answered: "Some say John the Baptist, others Elijah or Jeremiah or one of the prophets who has come back to life." And he said to them: "But who do you say that I am?" Peter answered: "You are the Christ, the Son of the Living God." Jesus replied: "Blessed are you, Simon Son of Jona because flesh and blood has not revealed this to you, but my Father in heaven. And I say to you, you are Peter [*'Peter' means rock*] and upon this rock I will build my church and the gates of hell will not prevail against it. I will give you the keys of the kingdom of heaven. Whatever you shall bind on earth shall be bound in heaven, and whatever you loose on earth shall be loosed in heaven." (Mt. 16.13–19).

8.7   Paul of Tarsus

Paul of Tarsus (in Asia Minor), a Jew of the diaspora, was educated as a rabbi in Jerusalem and belonged to the sect of the Pharisees. At first opposed to Christianity he experienced a sudden conversion while on a journey to Damascus. Becoming a missionary he preached Christianity in Asia Minor and Greece, first to Jews and then to gentiles. Paul emphasized that Christianity was not for Jews alone, as many Palestinian Christians believed, but for non-Jews as well. Salvation, he preached, comes through belief in Christ, not from observance of the law. This was a crucial step in the expansion of the new religion but one that was at first controversial. Unlike Jesus who left nothing in writing we have Paul's own account of his conversion and the discussion he had with the Christian leadership in Jerusalem regarding the non-observance of the law by gentile converts.[6]

For I want you to know, brothers, that the gospel that was proclaimed by me is not of human origin . . . it came to me through a revelation of Jesus Christ. You have heard of my former way of life in Judaism, how violently I persecuted the church of God and tried to destroy it. I advanced in Judaism beyond many of my peers, for I was more zealous than they for the traditions of my ancestors. But when God, who had set me apart before I was born and called me through his grace, was pleased to reveal his Son to me, so that I might proclaim him among the Gentiles, I did not consult with any human being.

---

[6]Paul, *Letter to the Galatians* 1.11–15; 2.2–3, 7–9.

Paul began his ministry by traveling in Syria and Asia Minor, but after fourteen years went up to Jerusalem to acquaint the leadership there with his version of the gospel and get their approval. He brought with him two companions, Barnabas and Titus.

I went [*to Jerusalem*] in response to a revelation. Then I laid before them (though only privately with the acknowledged leaders) the gospel that I proclaim among the Gentiles, in order to make sure that I was not running, or had not run, in vain. But not even Titus, who was with me, was compelled to be circumcised, though he was a Greek . . . [*the leaders in Jerusalem*] imposed no new requirements on me. On the contrary, when they saw that I had been entrusted with the gospel to the uncircumcised, just as Peter had been entrusted with the gospel for the circumcised . . . and when James and Cephas and John, who were acknowledged pillars of the church, recognized the grace that had been given to me, they gave to Barnabas and me the right hand of fellowship, and agreed that we should go to the Gentiles and they to the circumcised.

8.8   Paul's View of Christian Marriage

Christians were accused by pagans of sexual crimes such as incest and promiscuity. But there were also allegations that Christianity, along with some other Eastern religions, such as Judaism and the mysteries of Isis, gave greater equality to women. In his Letter to the Galatians, Paul, the great theologian and presenter of Christianity to the non-Jewish Greco-Roman world, makes the following radical proclamation of equality: "You are all sons of God through faith in Christ Jesus. . . . There is neither Jew nor Greek, slave nor free, male nor female, for you are all one in Christ Jesus."[7] This and similar statements were at odds with at least the ideology of strict patriarchy and the exhortations of pagan moralists that wives, children, and slaves should accept their position in the established hierarchy of subservience.

In response, Christians defended themselves in their discussion of marriage by adopting the wording of the so-called "Household Codes" of the pagan moralists and giving it a Christian theological interpretation. Whereas the main aim of the pagan household codes was to emphasize the authority of husbands, fathers, and masters over their wives, children, and slaves respectively, Christian writers, such as Paul in this reading, makes the obligations reciprocal. Lurking behind the reworking of pagan moral values there may also be present an attempt on Paul's part to address a more radical form of Christianity which in fact gave greater freedom to women, especially in religious matters.

The following selection is preceded by a general exhortation to moral behavior. The passage begins with the principle of mutual subordination and then goes on to explain how this is supposed to work in the household, that is, how it applies to wives, husbands, children, and slaves, the traditional family unit.[8]

---

[7]Paul, *Letter to the Galatians* 3.26–28.
[8]Paul, *Letter to the Ephesians* 5.6.

[*All of us are*] subject to one another out of reverence for Christ. Therefore:

Wives, be subject to your husbands, as to the Lord, because the husband is head of the wife as also Christ is head of the Church. . . . As the Church is subject to Christ, so also let the wives be subject to their husbands in everything.

Husbands, love your wives, even as also Christ loved the Church and gave himself up for it that he might sanctify it. . . . Even so husbands ought to love their own wives as their own bodies. He who loves his wife loves himself, for no one ever hated his own flesh, but nourishes and cherishes it, even as Christ does the church, for we are members of his body.

Children, obey your parents in the Lord, for this is right. . . .

Fathers, do not provoke your children to anger, but nurture them in the discipline and admonition of the Lord.

Slaves, obey with fear and trembling those who, according to the flesh, are your masters. This is to be done in singleness of heart as to Christ, not by way of eye-service, as pleasing men, but as slaves of Christ, doing the will of God from the soul. Do service with a good attitude as to the Lord, and not to men, knowing that whatsoever good thing each shall have done, this he shall receive again from the Lord, whether he is a slave or free.

Masters, do the same to your slaves and give up threatening, knowing as you do that both their Master and yours is in heaven—and he does not show favors.

8.9 Christian Practice

The actual practice of early Christianity is described in the Apology of Justin Martyr. A convert from paganism, Justin (ca. A.D. *100–165) defends and explains Christian doctrine, ritual, and practice to a hostile readership.[9] For a non-Christian account, essentially confirming what Justin says, see the letter in the next section.*

After we have baptized the person who has been convinced and has assented to our teaching, we bring him to the place where those who are called the brethren are assembled to offer prayers in common, both for ourselves and for him who has been illuminated, and for all people everywhere. We do this so that we may be counted worthy, now that we have learned the truth, to be found good citizens and keepers of the commandments, and that we may be saved with an everlasting salvation.

When we have finished these prayers, we salute one another with a kiss. Then the bread and a cup of wine mixed with water are brought to the president of the brethren. He takes them, gives praise and glory to the Father of the universe through the name of the Son and of the Holy Spirit, and offers thanks at considerable length for our being considered worthy to receive these things at his hands. When he has concluded the prayers and thanksgivings, all the people present

---

[9]Justin, *Apology* 45–46. Based on Roberts and Donaldson, *The Ante-Nicene Fathers*, vol. 1, p. 185.

express their assent by saying *Amen*. This word in Hebrew means "So be it." When the president has given thanks, and all the people have expressed their assent, those who are called by us deacons give to each of those present a portion of the bread and wine mixed with water over which the thanksgiving was pronounced. To those who are absent they carry away a portion.

Among us this food is called the Eucharist. Only those who believe the truth of the things we teach, who have been baptized with the washing for the remission of sins and so regenerated and live as Christ directed, are allowed to partake of it. We do not receive the Eucharist as common bread and drink. As Jesus Christ our Savior, having been made flesh by the Word of God, had both flesh and blood for our salvation, so likewise we have been taught that the food which is blessed by the prayer of his word . . . is the flesh and blood of that Jesus who was made flesh. For the apostles, in the memoirs called "Gospels" composed by them, have thus passed down to us what was enjoined on them, namely, that Jesus broke bread, and when he had given thanks, said, "Do this in remembrance of me; this is my body." In the same manner, having taken the cup and given thanks, he said, "This is my blood" and gave it to them alone. . . .

Afterwards we continually remind each other of these things. And the wealthy among us help the needy, and we visit each other continually. At our meals we bless the maker of all things through his son Jesus Christ and through the Holy Spirit.

On the day called Sunday, all of us who live in cities or in the country gather together in one place. The memoirs of the apostles or the writings of the prophets are read, as long as time permits. Then when the reader has ceased, the president instructs and exhorts us to the imitation of these good things. Next we all rise together and pray, and as we before said, when our prayer is ended, bread and wine and water are brought, and the president in like manner offers prayers and thanksgivings with all his might, and the people assent saying, *Amen*. There is then a distribution to each. . . .

Those who are prosperous and willing give what each thinks fit. What is collected is deposited with the president, who distributes it to orphans and widows and those who, through sickness or any other cause, are in want. This includes those who are in prison, as well as strangers among us, and indeed any who are in need.

8.10　Pliny's Encounter with Christianity

Pliny, the Roman governor of Bithynia-Pontus (in modern Turkey) about A.D. 111–113, appears to have been a genuinely civilized, humanitarian person (see Chapter 7, "Provincial Administration"), yet he casually executed Christians because of their refusal to conform to traditional practice, and he noted with satisfaction the improvement in temple attendance and worship as a result of the executions. The Emperor Trajan, in his response, agrees with Pliny's action but is more sensitive than the complacent Pliny to the role of malice in charges brought against Christians.[10] We begin with Pliny's letter to the emperor.

---

[10]Pliny, *Letters* 10.96–97.

Pliny to the Emperor Trajan

I am in the habit, My Lord, of referring to you all matters regarding which I am in doubt. For who can be a better guide for my indecision or better enlighten my ignorance?

I have never taken part in trials of Christians: hence I do not know for what offense, nor to what extent it is the practice to punish or to investigate. I have been in a lot of doubt as to whether any distinction should be made for age, or whether the very weakest offenders are to be treated exactly like the stronger; whether pardon is to be granted in the case of repentance, or whether a person who was at one time a Christian gains anything by having ceased to be one; whether punishment attaches automatically to the mere name of Christian, even without crimes, or only when the law has been violated.

Meanwhile, this is the course of action I have followed in the case of those denounced to me as Christians. I asked them first whether they were Christians. If they confessed, I asked them a second and third time, along with threats of punishment. If they remained obdurate, I had them executed, for I had no doubt that, whatever it was that they confessed, their stubbornness and their unbending perversity deserve punishment. There were others of similar insanity who, because they were Roman citizens, I have remanded for sending to the City.

Before long, as is often the case, the mere fact that action was taken made the charges commoner, and more cases arose. An anonymous accusation containing many names was circulated. Those who denied that they were or had been Christians, I thought it right to let go since they recited a prayer to the gods at my dictation, made supplication with incense and wine to your image, which I had ordered to be brought for the purpose, together with the statues of the gods, and cursed Christ. Those who are really Christians, it is said, cannot be forced to do any of these things. Others, accused by the informer, said they were Christians but afterwards denied it, explaining that they had been Christians at one time but had ceased to be many years ago, some as much as twenty years before. All these too worshipped your image and the statues of the gods and cursed Christ.

The accused claim that the sum total of their guilt was this: that on a certain fixed day they were accustomed to come together before daylight and to sing by turns a hymn to Christ as to a god, and to bind themselves by oath, not for some criminal purpose, but that they would not commit robbery, theft, or adultery; that they would not betray a trust nor deny a deposit when it was called for. When this was over, their custom was to disperse and to come together again to partake of food of an ordinary and harmless kind. Even this they claimed they had ceased to do after the publication of my edict in which, according to your command, I had forbidden associations. Accordingly, I decided it was all the more necessary to find out the truth by torture from two female servants called deaconesses. I discovered nothing other than a wicked and excessive superstition.

Consequently I have adjourned the case and hastened to consult you. The matter seemed to warrant deliberation, especially on account of the number of those being brought to trial, of every rank and of both sexes. The infection of this superstition has spread not only to the cities but even to the villages and country areas. It seems possible to stop it and bring about reform.

It is plain enough that the temples, which had been almost deserted, have begun to be frequented again, that the sacred rites, which had been neglected for a long time, are being resumed, and that from everywhere sacrificial victims are coming for which until now there were scarcely any purchasers. From this it can be easily supposed that a number of people can be reclaimed if repentance is afforded.

Trajan Replies to Pliny

You have followed the correct procedure, my dear Pliny, in conducting the cases of those who were accused before you of being Christians. No general rule can be laid down with a fixed formula. They ought not, however, to be sought out. If they are brought before you and the charge proved, they ought to be punished. But when someone denies that he is a Christian and proves it by praying to our gods, however much he may have been under suspicion in the past, he should be pardoned as a result of his repentance. Anonymous accusations, however, ought not to be admitted in any charge. They are a very bad example and unworthy of our times.

8.11   Rabbinic Judaism

During the first century A.D. *there were many competing forms of Judaism in Judaea. In Palestine, Sadducees and Pharisees differed over doctrinal issues such as the immortality of the soul and whether there was punishment after death. In interpreting Scripture and the law, Sadducees took a literal approach, insisting that only the written Scriptures were acceptable sources of revelation. Pharisees were more flexible: they claimed that the Torah (the law), came in two forms, one written and the other oral, each necessary and each God-given. The communities of the Diaspora possessed yet another variant of Judaism.*

Of the many traditions of Judaism, Pharisaism proved to be the most vital and capable of responding to the needs of post-revolt Judaism, and it was from this root in particular, though not exclusively, that Rabbinic Judaism developed. In time the oral tradition of the Pharisees was written down and edited, receiving definitive form around A.D. *200. The resulting document, known as the* Mishnah, *is the basis of Rabbinic Judaism. Although the* Mishnah *contains some material going back to the third century* B.C., *the bulk of it, mostly statements of the law and the original commentaries of the rabbis, derives from the first two centuries* A.D. *In the standard English translation it runs to over 1,000 pages. From about* A.D. *200 to 500, loosely organized groups of scholars in Palestine and Babylonia added further commentaries to the* Mishnah *in a process which ultimately led to the production of two other major documents, the Palestinian and Babylonian* Talmuds.

The Mishnah *is essentially a teaching aid, a curriculum for the study of Jewish law, or a method of instruction in how to think about the law. It is structured around six major thematic areas: (1) agriculture, (2) festivals, (3) marriage and property, (4) civil and criminal law, (5) cult and sacrifice, and (6) cultic purity. Both readings given here come from the third area. Typically, first the law is stated and then the comments of selected rabbis are given. The brevity (and sometimes obscurity) of the written form reflects the original oral nature of the* Mishnah, *one of whose aims was to allow for easy memorization.*

The Mishnah

1. In this reading the complex issue of what happens to a widow (or, to be exact, a presumed widow) when her husband reappears is presented for discussion. Various solutions are suggested with the aim, not so much of settling the issues definitively, as of teaching the student how to reason about the subject.[11] *The same problem of disappearing husbands was also addressed in the Code of Hammurapi (ca. 1700 B.C.).*

If a woman's husband has gone overseas and it was told her, "Your husband is dead," and she married again and her husband then returned: (1) her marriage with both of them is annulled; (2) she must receive a bill of divorce from each of them; (3) from neither of them can she lay claim to her Ketubah [*the financial settlement paid at the time of the marriage by the husband to which the wife was entitled if divorced or widowed*]; (4) or to the increase [*of her own property*]; (5) or to alimony; (6) or to indemnity [*for loss suffered to her own property*]. (7) If she has collected anything of (3)–(5) from either one of them, she must restore it. (8) A child conceived by either husband is a bastard. . . .

Rabbi Jose says: "Her Ketubah [*marriage contract*] remains a charge on her first husband's property."

Rabbi Eleazar says: "Her first husband has a claim to anything found by her and to the work of her hands, and the right to set aside her vows. If she was the daughter of an Israelite she becomes ineligible for marriage with a priest. . . .

But if she had married again without the consent of the court [*since the remarriage was null, in view of the first*], she may return to her first husband. If she had married again with the consent of the court [*and her first husband then returned*], the second marriage is annulled. . . ."

2. This reading discusses occupations and the Torah as the way of life.[12] *It too has echoes of earlier readings.*

Rabbi Meir says: "A man should always teach his son a clean and easy trade and let him pray to Him [*i.e., God*] to whom riches and possessions belong, for there is no trade wherein there is not both poverty and wealth; for poverty comes not from a man's trade, nor riches from a man's trade, but all is according to his merit."

---

[11]*M. Yebamot* 10.1, 2. From Herbert Danby, *The Mishnah* (London: Oxford University Press, Geoffrey Cumberlege, 1933), p. 222.

[12]*M. Quiddushin* 4.14. From Danby, *The Mishnah*, p. 329.

Rabbi Simeon ben Eleazar says: "Have you ever seen a wild animal or bird practicing a trade? Yet they sustain themselves without care. And were they not created for nothing else but to serve me? But I was created to serve my Maker—does it not follow that I should sustain myself without trouble? But I have done evil, and so forfeited my right to sustenance without care."

Abba Gorion of Zaidan says in the name of Abba Guria: "A man should not teach his son to be an ass-driver or a camel-driver, or a barber or a sailor, or a herdsman or a shopkeeper, for their craft is the craft of robbers."

Rabbi Judah says in his own name: "Ass-drivers are most of them wicked; camel-drivers are most of them decent; sailors are most of them pious; the best among physicians is destined for Gehenna [*Hell*], and the best of butchers is a partner of Amelek [*ancient enemy of Israel and a stock term for pagans*]."

Rabbi Nehorai says: "I would set aside all the trades of the world and teach my son nothing but the Torah [*the Law*], for a man enjoys its fruits in this world, and the principal remains for the world to come. But with all other trades it is not so. For when a man gets sick or old or has troubles and cannot engage in his trade, lo, he dies of hunger. But with the Torah it is not so. It guards him from all evil when he is young, and in old age it grants him a future and a hope. Of his youth what does it say? 'They who wait upon the Lord shall renew their strength' [*Isaiah* 40: 31]. Of his old age what does it say? 'They shall still bring forth fruit in old age' [*Psalm* 92: 14]."

8.12   Judaism of the Diaspora

Jews living in the cities of the Greco-Roman world were presented with great intellectual, moral, and religious challenges to their way of life. A minimum amount of tolerance toward their religion on the part of Greeks enabled them to survive as separate communities, but this tolerance also opened the way for assimilation and absorption. As the use of Hebrew declined among Diaspora Jews, it became necessary to translate the Scriptures into Greek. This translation in turn introduced into the text of Scripture Greek philosophical ideas, as well as Greek terms that often changed the meaning of the original Hebrew and the thought that lay behind it. There was no equivalent in Greek, for instance, for the sacred name of God, Yahweh, so the translators used the common Greek term of address for pagan gods, kurios, which allowed the possible implication that Yahweh was just one of the many gods of polytheism.

The great intellectual challenge of translating one religious idiom into the language of another, and ultimately of synthesizing two cultures, was taken up by a number of great Jewish scholars. The process was especially successful in Alexandria, where it served the dual purpose of strengthening the Jewish community internally as well as of refuting pagan criticisms and presenting Judaism as a reasonable, philosophical religion. The movement reached its height in the writings of Philo Judaeus (ca. 20 B.C.–A.D. 50) but it had a long afterlife. Christians in their confrontation with the subtle intellectual challenges of Hellenism found the way already prepared for them by the activities of these Jewish scholars, and they borrowed heavily from them.

By mid-second century A.D., however, the vigor of Hellenistic Judaism declined, in part because of assimilation of Jews into the larger pagan population, but also because Christianity was able to press its claims successfully with Gentile proselytes who might otherwise have become Jews. Revolt against Rome among Diaspora Jews in A.D. *115–117 and the rise of Rabbinic Judaism and the consequent Hebraizing of the Greek-speaking synagogues were also major factors in the decline.*

Prologue to the Wisdom of Jesus the Son of Sirach

The difficulty of translating concepts of Hebrew thought into Greek is referred to in this reading, the introduction to the book of Ecclesiasticus or The Wisdom of Sirach.[13] *This work, composed in the second century* B.C., *is the last example of the genre of wisdom literature, such as Proverbs, found in the Hebrew Scriptures. Ecclesiasticus was included in the Greek translation of the Hebrew bible produced in Alexandria, the so-called "Septuagint." The Septuagint in turn was taken over by Greek-speaking Christians as their version of the Bible.*

Since many great teachings have been given to us through the Law and the Prophets and the others who followed after them—for which things' sake we must praise Israel for instruction and wisdom, and since the readers themselves must become adept, and those who love learning must be able to help outsiders [*i.e., non-Jews*] by both speaking and writing, my grandfather Jesus, having given himself much to the reading of the Law and the Prophets and the other books of our fathers, and having acquired considerable familiarity with them, was induced himself to write something pertaining to instruction and wisdom, in order that those who are lovers of learning and instructed in these things might make even more progress by a manner of life lived in accordance with the Law.

You are entreated, therefore, to make your study with good will and attention, and to be indulgent, if in any parts of what we have labored to interpret we may seem to fail in some of the phrases. For what was originally spoken in Hebrew does not have the same meaning when translated into another language. And not only this work, but the Law itself and the Prophecies, and the rest of the books, have no small difference when they are spoken in their original form.

"The Mishnah Is the Holy One's Mystery"

This reading reflects the gradual disengagement with Hellenism that took place in the Greco-Roman Diaspora from the second century A.D. *onward. The rabbis rejected out of hand the claim of Christians that they alone represented the true Israel, placing emphasis in rebuttal on the doctrine that the oral law found in the Mishnah (see above) was the possession of Jews alone.*[14]

---

[13]Cited by M. Avi-Yonah, *The Jews under Roman and Byzantine Rule: A Political History of Palestine from the Bar Kochba War to the Arab Conquest* (Jerusalem: The Magnes Press, 1984), p. 170.
[14]Based on R. H. Charles, ed. *The Apocrypha and Pseudepigrapha of the Old Testament* (Oxford: Clarendon Press, 1913), pp. 316–317.

Thus said Rabbi Judah ben Shalom: "Moses asked for the Mishnah to be also written down, but the Holy One, blessed be He, foresaw that the nations of the world would translate the Torah and read it in Greek, and that they would say 'We also are Israel.' So the Holy one said to him: 'I shall write for you most of my Law . . . but the Mishnah is the Holy One's mystery, and He does not disclose His mystery but to the just.' "

8.13   Divination, Astrology, Magic

As part of his long satire on wives, Juvenal includes the following mocking denunciation of superstitious practices. The picture that emerges is one of widespread use of magic and divination by all classes.[15]

An Armenian or Commagenian seer will promise you a young lover or a huge bequest from a rich and childless man after inspecting the lungs of a dove or the crop of a chicken or the entrails of a puppy or maybe even a child's. But the Chaldaean seers are more trustworthy. These are the ones your wife goes to consult: When will her mother, who has been ill of the jaundice for a long time, finally die? (She asked about *your* departure long ago). And when will she bury her sister or her uncles? Will her lover outlive her? What more could she want?

Don't forget to watch out for one of these women clutching a well-worn calendar like a string of worry beads. She's an expert at giving not taking advice, the sort who, if she wants to take even a short ride out of the city, will have to consult her almanac to find out what is the right hour. If she has an itch in the corner of her eye, she would never think of applying medicine until the horoscope's been consulted. If she's sick in bed, she will take no food till she calculates what is the right time to eat, as Petosiris the Egyptian directs.

Rich women will consult Phrygian or Indian augurs skilled in the study of the stars and the heavens. Plebeian destinies, however, are determined at the Circus or at Servius Tullius' ancient rampart—should they ditch the bar keeper and marry the old-clothes man? These poor women, however, endure the dangers of childbirth and all the labors of nursing that their poverty inflicts on them. How often, by contrast, does a gilded bed see a woman waiting to give birth, so great are the skills and so strong the drugs for inducting sterility or killing mankind in the womb?

The elder Pliny, uncle of Pliny the Younger, gives a straightforward, non-moralizing account of some Roman superstitions.[16]

Why is it on the first day of the year we wish each other with joyful prayers an auspicious and fortunate New Year? Why on days of purification do we select people with lucky names to lead the sacrificial animals? When the dead are mentioned why do we say,

---

[15]Juvenal, *Satires* 6.548–597.
[16]Pliny, *NH* 28.5.22–28.

"May they rest in peace"? We believe that odd numbers are more powerful than even as is proved by the attention we give to critical days when someone is sick with a fever.

Why do we wish "Good health" to people who sneeze? It is possible, supposedly, for absent people to tell when they're being talked about by ringing in their ears. In Africa nobody decides anything without saying "Africa" To calm themselves some people put saliva behind their ears. A proverb tells us that to turn down our thumbs indicates approval. Everyone agrees that lightning is worshipped by clucking the tongue.

It has been noticed that a sudden silence occurs during a meal only when the number of diners is even and that it portends danger to their reputation. Auguries are made from the words or thoughts of diners who drop their food, and the worst omens occur if it is a priest does so at a feast. However, expiation can be achieved by burning the food before the shrine of the Lares [ghosts of the dead]. Many people feel bound to cut their nails in silence on market days at Rome, beginning with the forefinger. To cut one's hair on the seventeenth and twenty-ninth prevents hair falling out as well as headaches.

8.14   Moral Behavior for the Philosophical Pagan

At least a percentage of the educated elites of the Roman world took a tolerant, skeptical view of morality and religion. "It is expedient that there be gods" was an old maxim that held true for many among the ruling elites, if for no other purpose than to help keep the masses in line. But for centuries, at least since the time of Socrates, the creation of a coherent ethical code of behavior, universal for all human beings, was one of the major goals of Greek philosophy. Some of the best minds of the centuries between Plato and the great Stoic Emperor, Marcus Aurelius, devoted themselves to this task.

The major Socratic schools—Platonism, Aristotelianism, and Stoicism—offered a variety of approaches to ethics, ranging from the dogmatic claims of the Stoics, who asserted that truth in ethical matters could be attained with certainty, to the cool flexibility of the Skeptics, who denied this possibility. Epicureanism, following the materialism of Democritus and the Atomists, offered yet another view of the moral universe.

The author of the following reading, Sextus Empiricus, lived at some time in the second century A.D. *Although his aim is philosophical, much of what he has to say reflects a moral attitude prevalent at least among educated members of the Greco-Roman upper and middle classes.*[17]

Moral Relativism

It might not be out of place here . . . to go specifically though briefly into common assumptions about what is shameful and what is not, what constitutes unlawful or lawful behavior, the nature of law and custom, reverence for the gods, proper

---

[17]Sextus Empiricus, *Outlines of Pyrrhonism* 3.198–212.

behavior toward the dead, and so on. In this way we will discover what a great deal of inconsistency there is regarding moral behavior.

Among Greeks, for instance, homosexual relations are regarded more as shameful than illegal, whereas among some Persians they are not considered shameful, but rather as customary. It is said, too, that long ago the Thebans did not think this practice shameful . . . and some [*for example Plato*] think the intense friendship of Achilles and Patroclus was homosexual in nature. . . . To have sex with a woman in public is thought by Greeks to be shameful but not by some Indians. . . . Again, prostitution is held by Greeks to be shameful and disgraceful, but among many Egyptians it is praiseworthy. . . .

For Greeks tattooing is shameful and degrading, but many Egyptians and Sarmatians tattoo their children. Greeks think it is unacceptable for men to wear earrings, but some barbarians, such as the Syrians, regard earrings as symbols of noble birth. Indeed, some, in order to draw attention even further to their noble birth, pierce the noses of their children and hang rings of silver or gold from them!—something no Greek would do. . . .

Cannibalism is outlawed among Greeks, but among whole tribes of barbarians it is considered indifferent . . . and while most of us think it is wrong to pollute an altar with human blood, the Spartans beat themselves furiously over the altar of Artemis so that blood may flow over it. . . . Greek law commands that children should take care of their fathers, but Scythians slit their throats when they get over sixty years. . . . Roman lawmakers put children under their fathers' thumbs—like slaves. Roman children do not have control of their own property, but rather their fathers have until their children are emancipated. Others, however, regard this custom as tyrannical. The law states that murderers should be punished, but when gladiators commit homicide they are often praised. . . .

Moral Dogmatism

A much more dogmatic stance is taken by the famous Stoic philosopher, Musonius Rufus, who was active in Rome during the reign of Nero and exiled by him in A.D. 65. Musonius was a major figure in Roman intellectual life and the teacher of one of the best-known philosophers of the early Empire, Epictetus. He was consulted by such important figures as Seneca, at one point tutor of Nero. Unfortunately his work survives only in the rough-and-ready form of lecture notes made by his students. The following reading is from one of his "diatribes" or popular philosophical lectures. The theory that sexual intercourse was for the purpose of procreation only can be traced to Plato. The idea that to sin is to injure oneself is possibly Musonius' own.[18]

The desire for luxury manifests itself in no small degree in the pleasures of love. This is so because luxury demands a great variety of sexual encounters, not only legitimate,

---

[18]Musonius Rufus, *On Sexual Pleasures* 12.

but also illegitimate, not only with women, but also with men. Those addicted to luxury pursue now this kind of lust, now that, and are not content with what is available at hand but seek for unusual experiences, shameful forms of intercourse—the kinds of behavior that are unacceptable for a human being. Those who are not devoted to pleasure-seeking and not morally corrupt regard sexual intercourse as legitimate only within marriage and only for the intent of procreating children. Only these kinds of sexual relations are moral. However, those who seek only pleasure in sexual intercourse, whether within or out of wedlock, are unrighteous and transgressors of the law. Of sexual relations, those in which adultery is involved are the most illicit.

But not less immoral are homosexual acts between men because they are shameless acts against nature. Setting aside considerations of adultery, all intercourse with women *not* in conformity with custom is also immoral because it offends against continence or self-restraint. Thus, for example, no temperate individual will go to bed with a prostitute or with a free woman outside of marriage, nor, by Zeus, with his own slave. The immorality and indecency of these acts is a matter of great reproach and shame for those who so eagerly perform them. [*This is demonstrated by the fact that*] no one who is capable of blushing even a little can do any of these acts openly; rather, they hide them and do them secretly, showing thereby that they are not completely dissolute. And indeed, trying to avoid being caught while doing one of these acts is to acknowledge having acted immorally.

A person might well argue that while it is true that an adulterer does an injustice to the husband of the woman he seduces, the man who has sex with a prostitute or with an unmarried woman does injury to nobody. The reason for this is that fornication does not destroy a woman's expectation of having children.[19] I, however, continue to insist that whoever commits this kind of sin automatically does an injustice—if not to his neighbor, then to himself—for the offender shows himself to be thoroughly wicked and dishonorable. The offender, to the degree he offends, is the more evil and despicable.

Setting aside the issue of sins of this type as acts of injustice, we must certainly regard those who allow themselves to be overcome by pleasure as lacking in self-control; happily—like pigs—they wallow in the muck. But this kind of behavior is less grievous than the case of the man who has sex with his own slave woman. Now some think this is not really immoral because, after all, the slave-owner is thought to have full liberty to do what he wants with his slave. But to this I have a simple response: If it seems to someone not immoral or shameful for a master to sleep with his slave, especially if she is without a bed-mate, he should reflect how it would appear to him if the situation involved the *mistress* of a slave, his wife, sleeping with her own slave! Wouldn't the matter seem unacceptable, not only in the case of a mistress who had a legitimate husband sleeping with her slave, but also if she did this without being married? Indeed, shouldn't one think men are perhaps worse than women who act that way? Odd that those who are supposed to be stronger in

---

[19]The meaning is, that in the case of adultery the breakup of the marriage results, and the wife loses the chance to have children, a family, and a legitimate place in the community.

judgment than "weak women" are less able to discipline their desires—the governors weaker than the governed! To the extent that it is fitting that men be set over women, so much the more should they be self-controlled. The more un-self-controlled they appear, the more immoral they will be. But when a master sleeps with his slave—isn't this a demonstration of incontinence? What more needs to be said? Everyone knows this is true.

▼▼▼

Questions

1. How were the gladiatorial shows specified in the charter of the Spanish town of Osuna to be funded? (**8.1**)
2. What was the role, according to Minucius Felix, of religion in Rome's conquests? (**8.2**)
3. How did Apollonius of Tyana stop the plague in Ephesus? (**8.5**)
4. What were some of the demands Jesus claimed that the Kingdom of Heaven made on men and women? (**8.6**)
5. On what basis, according to Jesus, was the Last Judgment to be conducted? (**8.6**)
6. Summarize the ritual practices ascribed by Justin to early Christians. (**8.9**)
7. The governor Pliny asked the Emperor Trajan for advice regarding the treatment of Christians. What was Trajan's reply? (**8.10**)
8. What was the answer given in the *Mishnah* to the problem of a husband who disappeared while overseas? (**8.11**)
9. What problems of translation does Jesus Son of Sirach refer to? (**8.12**)
10. What moral rules regarding sexual behavior does Musonius Rufus propose? (**8.15**)

Chapter 9

▾▾▾

Daily Life in the Roman Empire

Roman society, like many other ancient societies, was without many of the institutions we take for granted in modern times. There were no banks, insurance companies or lawyers for hire. People depended on each other for these services. Among the poor loans were provided by kin and neighbors; only in emergencies did they turn to their local "bankers," who were in actuality loan sharks. Most of the rest of society got these services free from their patrons. No cash changed hands, and no cash loans were repaid. Instead these favors or *beneficia*, as they were called, were expected to be repaid in other ways. Daily visits to patrons, the morning *salutatio*, was one way of repaying these loans; erecting inscriptions or statues proclaiming the good deeds of the patron was another since it would have been in bad taste for the patrons themselves to advertise their own good deeds. Favors were concrete expressions of *fides*, the reciprocal relationship of patron and client. Far from being thought of as evil, as we might, patron/client relationships were reinforced by laws and religious practices.

Rural Life

Most people in the Roman Empire lived in villages or scattered farmsteads, not cities. Their lives revolved around agriculture, not trade or industry. The rhythm of everyday activities was dictated by the agricultural cycle of sowing, harvest, orchard maintenance, and food processing. Hard work at particular moments was followed by long periods when there was little or nothing to do. Most people in antiquity were underemployed throughout most of their lives. Unlike modern society life was not dominated by unwearying machines which need attention night and day. An exception to this scenario was the work on slave-run estates, which may have had a more agribusiness character than the average farm owned by free citizens.

The lives of Mediterranean peoples were intensely social. Whether in village or town or city there was constant mutual visitation. Much of life was spent outdoors. Women went to the market, the water fountain, shrines and temples and visited each other's homes. Men spent a great deal of their leisure time hanging out in the marketplace, the baths or other public places. Dancing, singing, gossiping, and storytelling were the main forms of entertainment along with the festivals of the year, which were coordinated with the events of the agricultural cycle and structured daily life even for urban dwelling peoples.

Food in the Mediterranean revolved around olive oil, wine, wheat or barley, and legumes (peas and beans). By necessity most people were vegetarians, enjoying meat only at festivals. A typical dish was *moretum* made of crushed garlic, parsley, coriander and rue, mixed with salt, cheese, oil and vinegar, and kneaded into a ball. Sauces, such as *garum*, a pungent fish sauce, condiments and herbs were used widely in cooking as they are to the present. The diet of Atlantic and northern European peoples included much more meat, milk and milk products. Higher rainfall and the availability of much pasture land allowed the maintenance of large herds of cattle. Northern rivers abounded in salmon and trout. Southerners considered the northern use of butter and the drinking of beer—along with the wearing of trousers—as typically barbarian. Between north and south, however, the main difference lay in the degree of urbanization and the degree to which the various communities were integrated in the Roman state.

Urban Life

In some regions of the Empire such as Britain and France or western Germany, cities were few and far between. By contrast, cities had existed for thousands of years in Mediterranean coastal areas and peasant life was well integrated with them. Correspondingly, in central and western Europe peasants were to a much lesser degree participants in urban affairs and proportionately less integrated in the state.

Only a few cities reached the size of Rome (about a million); most were in the range of 5–30,000. Amenities varied considerably. Temples, baths, porticoes, public toilets, basilicas, gymnasia, libraries, aqueducts, fountains, markets, stoas (covered, colonnaded shopping areas), theatres, and amphitheatres[1] were common. Occasionally, lighted streets were to be found. Even small cities attempted to

---

[1]Theaters in the shape of a "D" were for citizen assemblies, plays, mimes and other entertainment. Amphitheaters were ovals and used for spectacles such as gladiatorial games and animal hunts.

have some of the public facilities found in the larger cities and at times found themselves in bankruptcy as a result of overly ambitious expenditures.

Although the culture of the educated had a bookish, academic quality, Greco-Roman civilization reached out to the masses of the people, especially the city-dwellers, in a number of informal ways. The mere fact of living together in a city had the effect of extending to other classes the high culture of the upper classes. There was a much greater degree of physical proximity between the classes than there is in modern society. To begin with, the cities were designed principally for use by pedestrians, not vehicles, and it was assumed that there would be large population densities in the downtown, forum areas, where most public business was transacted. Here trials were conducted, elections held, and public announcements made. The people met again in the theaters, amphitheaters, gymnasia,[2] and baths and at the formal religious celebrations held periodically throughout the year. Roman imperial officials, town councilors, and magistrates could be easily identified and approached. Merchants and shopkeepers went about their daily business, and life was carried on in a very personal, intimate manner. Gossip and rumor, functioning as the media of ancient town-life, carried tales all over the city, sparing no one.

The cultured and well-to-do classes of the cities of the Empire were not segregated elites who had little contact with the rest of society. The very ideals of urban life demanded an interchange between the classes, and the summit of a man's career was to have himself honored by his fellow citizens as patron and benefactor of his city. The rich were expected to make tangible contributions to the public life of the city by serving, unremunerated, as magistrates, giving festivals, maintaining the food and water supply, erecting public buildings, and generally contributing to the essentials of a civilized life. These services were known as liturgies. The purely private enjoyment of wealth and the gratification of intellectual curiosity or aesthetic tastes were considered aberrations. Although the rich had their country villas, their primary residences were their town houses.

In an even more informal way the culture of the upper classes was passed on through the medium of classical art. New cities were arranged in grid patterns, and markets, temples, basilicas, and theaters were designed according to carefully conceived plans. They conveyed a sense of order and dignity to the town-dwellers and to visitors from the countryside, and some cities such as Timgad in the wilderness of the Algerian Atlas Mountains, were deliberately created as showplaces to impress the barbarians. Hundreds of cities existed in areas where today there are few. Africa had 500, for example, and there were about 300 in Asia Minor

---

[2]Especially in the Greek speaking part of the Empire gymnasia were not just places for physical exercise and training (all kinds of running, wrestling, boxing, javelin throwing), but also intellectual and educational centers with classrooms and libraries. They functioned as secondary schools. In the west the gymnasia were usually associated with the baths (*thermae*).

(modern Turkey). A great deal of cultural diffusion must have occurred even without any formal government plan. The Romans, for the most part, were concerned with the cities as administrative, not cultural, centers.

Urban Life and Romanization

A peculiarity of the Romans (at least to our way of thinking) was their careful gradation of cities in ascending order of importance. In reality, no better way could have been devised to display in very graphic fashion the hierarchical arrangement of Roman society itself and Rome's dominating position in it. Native peoples throughout the Empire could not miss the overt distinctions of rank among cities and the advantages of those near the top of the pyramid.

At the head of the ranks of Roman cities came those that enjoyed the title of Roman colony and at the same time possessed what was called the Italian Right (*jus Italicum*). The latter privilege, in practice not very common, granted immunity from taxation and from the authority of the local Roman governor. All other cities and territories, of whatever status, paid the standard land and poll taxes, the *tributum soli* and *tributum capitis*, respectively. Italy, as the homeland of the Romans, was immune in this period from these taxes.

Below these specially favored colonies came the other Roman colonies, and below them the cities (*municipia*) of Roman and Latin citizenship. Latin municipalities were of two kinds, those whose elected magistrates received Roman citizenship automatically on election (*Latium minus*, or the Lesser Latin Right) and those whose local senators (decurions) automatically received Roman citizenship, regardless of whether they were elected (*Latium maius*, or the Greater Latin Right). Everyone else in these cities was, of course, a Latin citizen and as such barred from the imperial civil service and the Roman magistracies. Practically speaking, this was not a major disadvantage, and Roman law was administered in both Latin and Roman municipalities. Alongside Roman and Latin foundations were the native cities (*civitates*), villages (*vici*), and districts (*pagi*), in which the majority of the non-Roman population continued to live under its own laws and customs.

During the Empire the Romans encouraged their subjects to build and settle in cities, thereby giving up their old rural haunts and inaccessible fortresses on strategic sites. These new foundations were rapidly advanced to first the Latin status and then the Roman, and in this way whole areas of the west were Romanized. The ultimate achievement was the winning of the title of Roman colony, to which great prestige was attached. Leptis Magna, the birthplace of the emperor Septimius Severus, was originally an ordinary non-Roman *civitas*, ruled by Punic magistrates. By the end of the first century A.D. it was a *municipium*, probably with Latin status, and then under Trajan it became a full Roman colony. Finally, under Septimius Severus, its native son, it received the Italian Right. By the end of the second century A.D. cities with un-Roman-sounding names such as

Nisibis in Syria were made titular colonies, and Lebanese Tyre and Heliopolis were given the coveted Italian Right.

In the eastern half of the Empire, where there were few Romans and citizenship was not widely extended to the native population, the pre-Roman system of local and regional government continued to operate. In the Greek areas a great network of cities existed, each with its own carefully defined and often disputed territory, ruled from within by an oligarchic elite according to its own laws, which might date to its foundation. Elsewhere non-Greek cities existed alongside later Greek foundations, as in Palestine, Lebanon, and Syria, or there were Greek cities with large numbers of non-Greeks in their populations.

This complexity was guaranteed to test the flexibility of Roman governors and administrators, who in their careers might at one stage be in contentious Alexandria, which was always ready to erupt into riots between Greeks and Jews, or in peaceful Sicily, where nothing ever happened, or in tribal Britain or Africa. Each region had its own particular set of problems—military, cultural, and social. It was a fine training ground for tolerance or, perhaps more usually, benign neglect.

The Uses of Amusement: Games and Gladiators

At the time of Augustus, the Roman calendar had seventy-seven days of public games honoring the gods; within two centuries the number had risen to 176. The gods had reason to be pleased with the Romans. Good portions of some months were practically given over to such games. April, for instance, had the *Ludi Megalenses* (honoring the Great Mother), April 4–10; the *Ludi Cereales* (for the goddess of cereal grains), April 12–19; and the *Ludi Florales* (for a fertility goddess), April 28–May 3. Another good month was September, with the *Ludi Romani* from the fifth to the nineteenth. At these games people in Rome had a chance to see chariot races in the Circus Maximus or, if they could get tickets, theatrical performances at one of the many theaters that from the first century B.C. sprang up around the city.

The circus races pitted four professional teams, the Red, White, Blue, and Green factions (*factiones*), as they were called, against each other in 4-horse races, although teams of up to eight or ten horses were also known. According to the poet Ovid, the circus was also a good place to meet women because the seating was not segregated the way it was in the theaters and amphitheaters. Nevertheless, the main attraction was the races themselves, especially the spectacular crashes that often occurred as the flimsy chariots careened around the circus, pulled by galloping teams of horses.

More people could cram themselves into the great race track of Rome, the Circus Maximus (capacity 250,000), than into all the other theaters in the city combined, but more days of the games were devoted to the theater than to racing. Theatrical performances in the Empire were gaudy spectacles of music, song, and dance aimed at entertaining mass audiences of up to 10,000 people. Occasionally, plays of the classical period of the Republic were revived or individual scenes from tragedies performed, but the most popular entertainment was a kind of raunchy vaudeville in which mythological scenes were acted out, often grotesquely, on the stage. Sex and violence were staple elements. Understandably, actors in these performances had bad reputations and were regularly banished from the city by emperors trying to exert some kind of control over unruly audiences.

Gladiators

Gladiatorial shows had a different origin than did the *Ludi*, the state festivals honoring the gods. Originally they were staged as funeral games honoring the dead, and as ways of drawing attention to the virtue of the deceased. They were not financed by the state but by the individual who felt he had an obligation (a *munus*; *munera*, pl.) to the dead person. By the first century, although still ostensibly motivated by religion, the *munera* had become an important part of the method by which politicians drew favorable attention to themselves and won votes. In a successful bid for the office of aedile, for example, Julius Caesar presented 320 pairs of gladiators in honor of his father—who had died twenty years earlier! Both Pompey and Caesar put on extravagant wild beast hunts. Pompey's games saw the slaughter of 20 elephants, 600 lions, 410 leopards, and the first rhinoceros ever seen in Rome. Not to be outdone by his rival, Caesar also had masses of animals slaughtered at his games including, for the first time, a giraffe.

Given the political potential of such displays it is understandable why Augustus made a point of monopolizing the spectacles and giving magnificent games himself. From his time onward the gladiatorial *munera* were combined on the same day with wild beast hunts in the morning, the execution of low-status criminals around midday, and gladiatorial shows in the late afternoon. It would be an oversimplification of a complex ritualistic event to argue that all that motivated Augustus and his successors was the desire to retain control of the people through bloody but fascinating entertainment. "Bread and the circuses," Juvenal's famous aphorism, applied to the theater and the chariot races of the *Ludi*, not the *munera*. The motivation was more involved.

As the great benefactor (*euergtes*) of the Roman people the emperor was expected to display his munificence independently of the formal religious festivals of the whole community (the *Ludi*). The tradition of grand display was already well established in the Republic, and it suited the emperors to continue it because by putting on great shows, they could demonstrate both their own power and the power of the Roman people. Through animal hunts the people could see in an impressively visual way how their power extended throughout what seemed to be the whole world. Through their emperor the people of Rome could order distant nations to provide them with their most exotic animals: lions from Libya; hippopotami and crocodiles from Egypt; leopards and giraffes from Africa; tigers and elephants from India; and bears, lynx, and elk from Europe. The wild beast hunts were gaudy celebrations of the immense power and wealth of Rome. Who else but the people of Rome could afford the complete waste of such valuable assets? The slaughter of animals also had symbolic value. In Roman times nature was not as distant as it now seems, nor as well understood. The wilderness was much closer at hand and far from tamed. Wild beasts were seen as cruel and dangerous, not as endangered species, and their slaughter represented the assertion of order over the chaos of wild nature. Even urban populations needed to be reassured that nature was under control, and the arena represented an excellent place to make this point.

The gladiatorial fights were seen in a different light. Gladiators were drawn from the ranks of criminals, slaves, and prisoners of war. They were trained to fight skillfully in stylized forms of combat: the practically naked net-and-trident man was pitted against the man in armor, the "Thracian" against the "Gaul," cavalry against cavalry, charioteers against charioteers. The crowd looked for skill and bravery. They especially looked to see how the gladiators faced death. Sometimes in recognition of a particularly brave performance the crowd declared in favor of a gladiator who had lost, and let the *editor*, the giver of the games (usually the emperor), know how they felt. Drawn from the *perditi homines*, the lost and ruined men of the Empire, gladiators were given a chance to redeem themselves by the display of the most important of all Roman virtues, bravery. By this means they found a way of reintegrating themselves into the society from which they had been ejected by crime, loss in war, or just bad luck.

One final important point about the games must be made. Even though the people of Rome were ruled in the imperial period by emperors, they had not forgotten that they were once sovereign. They expected the rulers to pay attention to them and listen to their grievances and demands. If they lacked free speech as individuals they had no qualms about speaking their mind as a group, and the arena provided an excellent venue for the expression of public opinion. Tiberius, who took a statue for his own enjoyment from a public place, was forced to return it after the people complained. Over the years the emperors were forced to hear demands for reduction of taxes, lower grain prices, as well as complaints about officials. Both Julius Caesar and Marcus Aurelius, who wrote letters and talked to clients and officials during the games, were reminded by the crowd to pay attention. Tiberius, who hated the games and did not attend them, developed a very bad reputation with the people. On the other hand, Claudius and Commodus, whom the elite despised, were much appreciated by the people because they were attentive watchers, or in the case of Commodus, actual participants. The *munera* played an important role in the Romanization of the Empire. In imitation of what went on in Rome, provincial elites spent vast sums of money putting up amphitheaters. Some 272 are known to have existed. Many survive to the present, including the largest of all, the Colosseum.

▼▼▼

9.1   Peasant Life

The Roman poet Ovid provides a romanticized portrayal of peasant life in his story of the couple Baucis and Philemon. The tale begins with Zeus and Hermes in the guise of mortals looking for a place to stay overnight. No one will take them in except the poor peasants Baucis and Philemon. Apart from the picture of agricultural life the story also reveals an important aspect of pagan religion, namely, the awe felt in the presence of unusual natural phenomena such as the double trunked tree which gave rise to the story in the first place.[3]

Once upon a time, long ago Jupiter and Hermes came looking for a place to stay. They knocked for shelter on a thousand doors and had a thousand doors shut against them. At last one received them, a small cottage roofed with straw and marsh reeds. Within its humble walls lived affectionate Baucis and Philemon. Equal in age, they had married in that cottage in youth and now had grown old there. Owning it helped them make light of their poverty which they bore contentedly. There were no masters or servants in that house. The two of them were the whole household and together they served and ruled.

So when the heavenly visitors came and bowing entered the low ceilinged door, Philemon set out a bench and invited them to rest, while Baucis spread a rough rug across it. Then she moved the warm ashes of the dying fire aside, threw leaves and dry bark among the coals and blew them to life. From the rafters she took kindling and twigs and set them under a copper pot that waited near the fire. She trimmed a cabbage that her husband had brought from the well-watered kitchen garden close at hand. Meanwhile the old man raising a forked stick, fetched down a side of smoked bacon which was hanging from the black rafters. From the long hoarded meat he cut off a small piece and tossed it into the steaming water. To pass the time they entertained their guests with small talk. A mattress of soft river grass was smoothed and laid on a couch woven of willow. Over it they draped a cloth which was brought out only on festal days, but even this was poor and old, a good match for the willow couch.

The gods reclined. Then tucking up her skirts and with trembling hands elderly Baucis set out the table. One of its three legs was too short so she propped it up with a piece of broken pottery. Once it was leveled she spread it with green fresh smelling mint. Then the food was served. First came olives, Minerva's fruit, ripe and brown, and September cherries, pickled in sweet wine, fresh lettuce and radishes, creamed cottage cheese, and eggs lightly baked in the ashes. All these were served on plates of country fashioned earthenware. Next an embossed mixing bowl of the same cheap make was set on the table together with small wooded cups, all lined with amber wax. After a short delay the soup prepared at the hearth was served with not long

---

[3]*Metam.* 8.626–677; 712–724.

aged wine. A space was cleared for the next course of nuts, figs, dates, and sweet smelling apples in a flat basket, purple grapes just picked from the vine. In the middle of the table was a comb of clear white honey.

Baucis and Philemon are rewarded for their hospitality. While they watch their modest home is transformed into a temple. Marble columns replace the forked wooden supports, the straw turns yellow and becomes a roof of gold. The gates are richly carved and a marble pavement covers the ground. When asked by the gods what they would like as a reward they requested that they be made priest and priestess of the temple with a final request that they would die at the same time. Years later they are metamorphosed into two trees side by side in front of the temple.

At last in frail old age as they happened to stand before the temple's doors and speak of years gone by, Baucis saw Philemon sprout green leaves and Philemon saw Baucis do the same. As the tree tops formed around their faces and as bark closed their lips they cried out together, "Farewell, good-bye, dear wife, dear husband." In Bithynia the natives show the visitors two trees growing from a single trunk. . . . I myself have seen memorial wreaths hanging from those boughs and have refreshed them with new garlands of flowers saying, "Let those whom the gods love be gods, and those who have worshipped the gods be worshipped themselves."

9.2 City Life: How the Urban Lower Classes Coped

Dignity and social ranking had always been preoccupations of Roman society. Where a person stood in the pecking order was all-important. At the highest level was the Senatorial Order; under it came the Equestrian, and below that assorted other rankings. In the Empire there were further gradations and complications as the elites of Roman colonies and municipalities perpetuated and extended these traditions from one end of the Mediterranean to the other, and in turn non-Romans came to imitate them. Even the lower orders were drawn into this upper-class concern with rank and dignity, as can be seen in the following reading, a charter of a burial society which organized itself in A.D. *133 at Lanuvium near Rome.*

The overt purpose of burial societies (collegia, "colleges," as they were called) was to enable the poor to avoid being buried in the common grave of paupers. In reality these associations, which were open to men and women, slaves and free alike, served a much broader function. Each association, like a miniature municipality, had its own charter, elected officers, and patron deity in whose honor it gathered. Members paid an entrance fee and gathered periodically to eat a meal together or celebrate a festival. Some better-off associations had their own property, had shrines, houses, or gardens where they met. It was considered the civic duty of the upper classes to endow these societies. Such benefactors were then honored by being elected patrons—the usual Roman social trade-off.

The organization of the societies themselves allowed their members to practice a bit of snobbery on each other. Strict precedence was observed at meetings, and donations from patrons were distributed in graded amounts to the members according to their rank in the association. Even the lowliest could be elected to some office or other. In this way the masses of society mimicked *their betters and were drawn into the imperial hierarchical system. In Roman society there was a recognized place for everyone.*[4]

May the Emperor Caesar Trajan Hadrian Augustus, all his household, we ourselves, and our association (*collegium*), enjoy good fortune, happiness, and health. May we well and carefully establish the by-laws of this association that we may suitably discharge our duties regarding the funerals and burials of our dead. Accordingly, having consulted well together we ought to agree unanimously so that our association may endure for a long time.

You who wish to join this association should first read the charter so that, having joined, you do not afterwards complain or cause controversy through your will.

The Laws of the Collegium

Passed unanimously: That whoever wants to join this college should pay an initiation fee of 100 sesterces, an amphora of good wine, and a monthly fee of five *asses*.[5] Likewise passed: If a member has not paid his/her dues for six months in a row and dies, a funeral will not be provided, even if he/she has made a will stipulating the payment of the arrears. On the other hand, if one of our members dies but is paid up, 300 sesterces are to be set aside for his/her funeral. From this amount 50 sesterces is to be paid to those who attend the funeral; it will be divided up at the funeral pyre. The mourners must, however, walk.

Passed: That if a member of the association should die beyond the 20th milestone from this town, and information regarding said death is duly relayed, then three members of the association should go to that place and make arrangements for the funeral. Afterwards they are to render a true and genuine account to the assembled members of the association. If deliberate fraud is demonstrated, they are to be fined fourfold. These representatives of the association are to be reimbursed for the cost of the funeral and be provided with travel expenses to and from in the amount of 20 sesterces each. However, if one of the members dies beyond the 20th milestone from the town and it was not possible to relay the information to the association, then he who saw to his burial should be a witness to this fact in writing, attested to by the seals of seven Roman citizens. When his account is approved, allowing sufficient time for appeal of the costs and provisions, he should be reimbursed in accordance with the rules of the association. Let there be no willful fraud in our association; let there be no suits against us, neither by patron, patroness, proprietor or proprietresses, or creditor—except where someone was named an heir by testament. If a member dies intestate, he/she will be given due funeral rites by the decision of the president and membership of the association.

---

[4]H. Dessau, *Inscriptiones Latinae Selectae* (Berlin, 1881), 7212.
[5]At the time of this inscription a *sestertius* was a brass coin worth a quarter of a silver *denarius*. An *as* was a bronze coin. Sixteen *asses* made a *sestertius*. Soldiers made 225 *denarii* per year.

Passed: Anyone of this association who is a slave and dies, and his/her master or mistress because of their harsh unreasonableness will not hand over his/her body, or if they have not left a will, then the association will celebrate a funeral in their name.

Passed: If anyone belonging to this association, for whatever reason contrives his/her own death, no funeral arrangements will be made.

Passed: If any member of this association who is a slave is manumitted, he/she should donate an amphora of good wine.

Passed: If any member who, in rotating fashion, is Entertainment Director in his/her year, and fails to put on the appointed banquet, he/she will pay 30 sesterces into the treasury and his/her place will be taken by the next person on the list.

Order of Banquets: March 8, the birthday of Caesennius, father of the association's patron; [*a gap in the inscription follows*]; November 27, the birthday of Antinous [*the deified lover of the Emperor Hadrian, in whose temple the association seems to have met on occasion*]; the birthday of the Goddess Diana and of the association itself, August 13; the birthday of Caesennius Silvanus, brother of the patron, August 20; the 4th of [*blank*], birthday of Cornelia Procula, mother of the patron; December 14, the birthday of L. Caesennius Rufus [*the patron of this association; a local big-wig*].

On Entertainment Directors: Entertainment Directors, chosen four at a time in order from the membership list, shall supply the following: one amphora of good wine each, two *asses* worth of bread per member, four pickled fish, a tablecloth, hot water, and a waiter.

On Presidents: Passed: The association's president shall, while president, be exempt from [*it is unclear what this privilege was*] and will receive double servings or divisions in all the distributions to the members. Likewise the scribes and summoners of the association will receive, after the terms of office, one and a half times every division to the membership. Likewise, every president who will have discharged his office with distinction shall receive by way of special honor one and a half times all the divisions made to the members, with the purpose of inspiring others to act in a similar fashion. The club president during his/her term of office on festival days shall, while robed in white, make offerings of incense and wine and, similarly garbed, perform his/her other duties. On the birthdays of Diana and Antinous he/she shall provide oil in the public bath building for the members before they dine.

On Troublemakers: Passed: If anyone has a complaint to make or wishes to bring up a business matter, let it be done at the regular meetings and not at banquets, which should be undisturbed and cheery affairs. Likewise, if any member is the cause of trouble and moves from their place at the meetings, he/she shall be fined 4 sesterces. If any member speaks abusively or causes an uproar, his/her fine will be 12 sesterces. If anyone addresses the president of the association abusively or insultingly during a banquet, his/her fine will be 20 sesterces.

In the late Republic and early Empire large numbers of slaves, especially urban slaves, were manumitted by their masters and mistresses. Since citizenship was conferred at the time of manumission, it was fairly easy for freedmen to blend with the freeborn population, and even easier for their children to do so. In this inscription freedmen parents—whose names, in addition to the appellation "freedman" in the title of the father, indicate that they are ex-slaves—put up a memorial to their son, who "made good" in the town of Capena near Rome. Titus Flavius was aedile, quaestor designate, and a member of the town senate. Unlike his parents, he does not have a giveaway servile name. He possesses the full titulature of a freeborn Roman citizen,[6] a point made with pride by the parents. In the inscription itself, as opposed to the translation given here, Titus' name appears at the very beginning and would be the first item read. The parents, or at least the father, were at one time slaves of the imperial household of the Flavian dynasty (A.D. 69–96) and were clearly well off. Ritual meals were held at burial sites.[7]

T. Flavius Mythus, freedman of Augustus, and Flavia Diogis, parents, have set aside [this burial area] for their most devoted son, T. Flavius Flavianus, son of Flavius, of the Quirinal Tribe, aedile, and quaestor designate of the federate city of Capena. They do this also for themselves, their freedmen and their freedwomen and their descendants. This property, consisting of about four jugera marked off from the Cutulenian farm, comes with a bath house and adjacent buildings on both sides of the road. An aqueduct supplies water from the Cutulenian farm.

9.3   The Upper Classes: Technology and the Good Life

In the following sermonette Seneca, advisor to Nero and a Stoic philosopher, preaches against luxury and praises the simple life. He is arguing against another philosopher by the name of Posidonius, who ascribed the origins of the "arts," that is, technology, to Wise Men or to philosophy itself. Seneca, on the other hand, believes that technology, rather than being the source of progress, is in fact at the root of all modern evils and should not be ascribed to the Wise or to philosophy.

Reading between the lines we can get a pretty good idea of what the life of the well-to-do in Rome was like in terms of creature comforts. We might also note that the debate between primitivists (or naturalists) and those devoted to technology, progress, and development is an old one. Seneca, in fact, was only one of the later contributors to this great debate. The issue of nature versus nurture, civilization versus spontaneity, was a particularly hot issue in the great debates of the classical age.[8]

I do not believe that Philosophy invented these cleverly devised buildings of ours which rise one above the other—where the city's inhabitants are crammed together cheek-and-jowl—any more than Philosophy invented fish ponds for the purpose of sparing gluttons from having to risk storms at sea. No matter how bad the weather, luxury *always* has safe places to raise exotic kinds of fish! What do you say? Was it Philosophy that taught us to use keys and bolts? No, rather the introduction of these security

---

[6]The three names were the *nomen*, *gens*, and *cognomen*: Titus (*nomen*), Flavius (*gens*), Flavianus (*cognomen*) followed by the patronymic, "son of Flavius", and the tribal name, "Quirinal Tribe." Taken together these names and titles offer public proof beyond question of freeborn status.
[7]H. Dessau, *Inscriptiones Latinae Selectae* (Berlin, 1881), 5770.
[8]Seneca, *Epistle* 90.

devices is the consequence of greed. Was it Philosophy that constructed all these dangerous, overhanging tenements? No, it was sufficient for people to provide themselves, happenstance, with any covering, and without art or trouble to provide themselves with some kind of shelter. Believe me! That was a happy age before the age of architects and builders! . . . [*In the good old days*] forked branches at either end propped up their huts. Compact twigs and sloping, thick layers of leaves provided shelter in the heaviest rains. They lived under such dwellings—but they lived in peace! Thatched roofs covered free men, but slavery lives under marble and gold. . . .

I ask you, which of the following is wiser: the person who invents the technique of spraying perfumed saffron to a great height from hidden pipes, who fills and empties canals by sudden gushes of waters and builds a dining room with a ceiling of movable panels that presents one sight after another in coordination with the courses being served? Or is it the one who demonstrates to himself as well as others that nature has not been harsh or difficult when it tells us we can get along *without* the marble cutter or metallurgist; that we can clothe ourselves *without* the silk trade; that we can have everything essential for our needs if we are content with what the earth has placed at hand? If the human race was willing to listen to this kind of advice, it would realize that the chef is as superfluous as the soldier. . . . Essentials are acquired easily enough; it is only luxuries that need effort. If you follow nature, you will not need technology. . . . At birth we're all ready to go! The trouble is we make life difficult for ourselves by disdaining what is easy. Houses, shelter, bodily comforts, food—which are all now a great nuisance—were all available, free and easily acquired.

The proper measure of things is always proportionate to the degree they are needed. It is we that have made all these things valuable and desirable and have caused them to be sought after by intense and complicated techniques. Nature is sufficient for essentials, but luxury has departed from nature. . . . [T]here was a time when everything was offered to the body as to a slave, but now they are offered to it as to a master. Hence it is that we have textile factories and carpenters' shops, the smells of gourmet cooking, the sexual provocativeness of lascivious teachers of dance and song . . . clothing that conceals nothing—see-through clothing which does not provide protection for the body, let alone protection for modesty! . . . For the natural moderation which limits our desires by what is available has vanished; to want only what is enough is regarded as a sign of backwardness and poverty of imagination. . . .

Seneca continues his attack on the theory that most inventions are the work of Wise Men in the distant past:
We know that certain inventions have come into existence only in our lifetime. For example, of recent origin are windows that admit brilliant light through glass tiles; vaulted baths where pipes for hot air are inserted in the walls to diffuse the heat evenly from top to bottom. Do I need to mention the marble with which our temples and our homes glisten? Or the rounded and polished masses of stone by means of which our porticoes are made big enough for whole masses of people? Or our shorthand by which we write down a whole speech no matter how quickly it is pronounced—speed of hand matching speed of tongue?

The Golden Age before science and technology:
When we have done everything, we will possess much; but there was a time when we had everything! The very land was more fertile when it was not worked and yielded enough for people who did not plunder each other's possessions. People found as much pleasure in sharing discoveries of nature as in making the discoveries in the first place. No one could either surpass or fall short of another in possessions. The stronger had not yet begun to impose on the weaker; the greedy had not yet begun to cut off their neighbors from the necessities of life by squirreling away what they could lay their hands on; each cared for the other as much as for himself.

Arms were unused, and the hand, unstained by blood, was turned in all its violence in defense against wild animals. In those days a wood was sufficient to give protection against the sun and the severity of winter rains: under branches men lived and passed peaceful nights without so much as a sigh. We, on the other hand, are vexed in our purple by worries, our sleep is bothered by the sharpest of torments. How soft was the sleep the hard earth gave to the people of ancient times! No fretted and paneled ceilings hung over them as they lay out in the open, and the stars slid quietly above them, and the wonderful pageant of the night passed quickly by, performing in silence its mighty work. By day and by night the vision of this most glorious world lay before them. . . . But you tremble at every creak of your houses; if you hear anything as you sit among your paintings, you flee in terror. They had no homes as huge as cities. The wind blowing free through the open spaces, the gentle shade of rock or tree, pellucid springs and streams unspoiled by man's handiwork, whether pipe or confining channel, but running at will amid fields made beautiful by nature, not by art. In such surroundings they had their rough homes, embellished accordingly. This kind of dwelling was in accordance with nature. There one could live in happiness, fearing neither the home itself nor for its safety. Today our dwellings constitute a large portion of worries.

9.4   Leisure: Gymnasia, the Baths, the Circus, the Arena

Urban life in the Empire offered to rich, poor, and middle classes alike a wide variety of leisure activities. Festivals, scattered at intervals throughout the year, provided everyone with a break from the normal routine of life. They were celebrated with processions, games, public meals, competitions of all kinds (including beauty pageants), and even handouts (see above, the inscription to Pliny and "The Divine Emperor"). Most of the larger cities had libraries (as at Como, see above). No city worthy of the name was without a theater, a proper water supply, public bathing facilities, colonnaded shopping areas, and, in the east, gymnasia.

In the first selection, the orator Dio Chrysostom pokes fun at Greek behavior and love for gymnasia, which formed major focal points of social and educational activity, and not just athletics, throughout the Greek-speaking parts of the Empire.

Baths of every variety from small local dives to huge publicly funded affairs, glorious with marble and heated floors and walls, were also places where people could meet to relax, talk, and, if so inclined, exercise, since most had exercise grounds attached. For the benefit of the culturally inclined some were equipped with libraries, lecture halls, and art galleries.

The circus was perhaps the most popular form of entertainment; whole segments of the population went circus-mad over particular charioteers and teams of horses. By the time of the Empire the theater had lost the elevated character it had in earlier periods and had become a medium of popular entertainment ranging from the harmless to the truly rank. The bloody arena where criminals were executed, gladiators fought, and hunters stalked and were stalked by wild beasts was popular with a certain segment of the population. Gladiatorial fights, being extremely expensive to stage, were not as widespread as the other activities.

Too much emphasis is often attached to the games. It has been estimated, for example, that on the majority of the days of the games only one percent of the population of Rome could have attended the theater. A higher percentage, 20–25 percent, might have been able to attend the horse races since the Circus Maximus had a capacity of 250,000. Even fewer could see gladiatorial fights. The Colosseum, for example, the primary venue for such events, held a maximum of only 50,000. Elsewhere in the Empire, for reasons of cost and the lack of facilities, the attendance figures must have been even lower.

Hanging around the Forum, the law courts, and the shopping colonnades, attending the festivals, visiting the baths and the gymnasia (where they existed) were probably the prime forms of leisure for the urban dwellers of the Empire. For the country people, who must have constituted 90 percent or more of the population, the festivals would have been, as in the past, the primary forms of recreation.

Gymnasia[9]

Anacharsis [*one of the "Seven Wise Men"*] used to say that in each city of the Greeks there is a designated area [*the gymnasium*] where they become mad every day. For when they have gone there and taken off their clothes, they anoint themselves with a drug. This drug, he said, causes their madness, for immediately some are running, some are throwing one another down, while others put up their hands and fight an imaginary opponent, though others are actually beaten up. When they have done these things, they scrape off this drug [*in reality olive oil*] and at once recover their senses and become immediately friendly with each other. . . .

Baths

The second-century author Lucian speaks with admiration of a bath building designed and erected by Hippias, a contemporary of his.[10]

The entrance is high, with a flight of broad steps of which the tread is greater than the pitch, to make them easy to ascend. On entering, one is received into a public hall of good size, with ample accommodations for servants and attendants. On the

---

[9]Dio Chrysostom, *Oration* 32.44; translators Ronald F. Hock and Edward N. O'Neil, *The Chreia in Ancient Rhetoric* (Atlanta: Scholars Press), p. 40. By permission. See note 2 for what went on in a Greek gymnasium.
[10]Lucian, *Hippias* 5–8. Based on the translation of A. M. Harmon, *The Works of Lucian* (London: William Heinemann, 1913), pp. 39–43.

THERMAE: BATHS

Early Romans washed themselves in hip baths into which bathers lowered themselves and sat with knees crooked over the edge and their feet on the floor. Using jugs the bathers could pour warm water over themselves and then emerge relatively clean and at little cost. Overtime these useful but humble hip baths evolved into the gigantic, ornate baths of the Empire period, like the one displayed here. This is a reconstruction of the main hall of the baths of the emperor Diocletian at Rome which was converted by Michelangelo into a church, *Santa Maria degli Angeli*, St. Mary of the Angels, in 1563–66. Other parts of the baths house the National Museum. Although the greatest baths were at Rome virtually all Roman cities had a variety of public and private baths. In the countryside any decent villa had its own bath house which today can be detected in its ruins by the hypocausts or hot air flues that ran under its floors.

Imperial baths (there were 11 of them) were elaborate affairs containing gardens, lecture halls, libraries, art galleries, exercise grounds, and running tracks in addition to the bathing facilities themselves. These latter consisted of a changing room (the *apodyterium*); an unheated *frigidarium* equipped with coldwater basins or pools; a warm room, the *tepidarium*, heated with hot air flues underneath the floor and in the walls and sometimes containing a warm plunge pool; a *caldarium*, the hot room with a hot plunge pool and water basins on stands; and wet and dry *sudatoria* or sweat rooms. The floors of the baths were paved with acres of multicolored marble slabs and the walls glittered with mosaics. Most of these embellishments have been long since stripped away. Except in Santa Maria degli Angeli all that is to be seen now is the brick and concrete framework of the buildings.

Financed by imperial subsidies the under or unemployed citizens of Rome spent long afternoons going slowly from one room to another, socializing with friends, and greeting acquaintances. They passed considerably more of their idle time at the baths than at horse races or gladiatorial shows which were special events, whereas the baths were a permanent feature of everyday life. If the imperial baths did not please there were over 800 private establishments that could be tried, many of them local dives of dubious reputation. Between public and private, the baths of Rome provided ample opportunities for all Romans, men and women, elite and mass alike to relax and while away the hours between the morning stroll in the forum, and the evening supper and stroll.

left are the lounging rooms, also of just the right sort for a bath, attractive, brightly lighted retreats. Then, beside them, a hall, larger than need be for the purposes of a bath, but necessary for the reception of the rich. Next, large locker rooms to undress in, on each side, with a very high and brilliantly lighted hall between them, in which there are three swimming pools of cold water; it is finished in Laconian marble and has two statues of white marble in the ancient technique, one of Hygieia [*the personification of health*], the other of Asclepius [*the god of healing*].

On leaving this hall, you come into another which is slightly warmed instead of meeting you at once with fierce heat; it is oblong and has an apse at each side. Next to it, on the right, is a very bright hall, nicely fitted up for massage, which has on each side an entrance, decorated with Phrygian marble, that receives those who come in from the exercise floor. Then near this is another hall, the most beautiful in the world, in which one can sit or stand with comfort, kill time without fear of criticism, and stroll about with profit. It also gleams in Phrygian marble clear to the roof. Next comes the hot corridor, faced with Numidian marble. The hall beyond it is very beautiful, full of abundant light and aglow with the purple of porphyry. It has three hot tubs.

When you have bathed, you need not go back through the same rooms but can go directly to the cold room through a slightly warmed apartment. Everywhere there is plenty of sunlight. Furthermore, the height of each room is well proportioned and the width corresponds properly to the length. Everywhere great beauty and loveliness prevail. . . . This is probably due in the main to the light and brightness and the windows.

Hippias, being truly ingenious, built the room for the cold baths to the north, though it does not lack a southern exposure, whereas he faced the rooms that needed the most heat to the south, east, and west. Why should I go on and tell you of the exercise floors and of the cloakrooms which have quick and direct communication with the hall containing the basin. . . . [*Hippias' building*] has all the good points of a bath: usefulness, convenience, light, good proportions, fitness to its site, and the fact that it can be used without risk. Moreover, it is adorned with all other marks of thoughtfulness—with two toilets, many exits, and two devices for telling time; a water-clock that bellows like a bull, and a sundial.

Games[11]

Nero put on a huge variety of entertainments: athletic competitions for young men; chariot races; theatrical performances; and gladiatorial shows. . . . Throughout the festival known as the Greatest Games, gifts were distributed to the people: every day a thousand assorted birds and numerous baskets of food, vouchers for grain, clothes, gold, silver, precious stones, pearls, paintings, slaves, horses, mules, and even tame wild animals, and finally vouchers for ships, apartment buildings, and farms. . . . [H]e staged the gladiatorial show in the wooden amphitheater near the Campus Martius . . . but allowed no one to be killed, not even criminals. . . . He put on a naval battle in an artificial salt-water lake which had sea monsters swimming in it.

Tacitus, who disapproved of Nero, also disapproved of his games.

---

[11]Suetonius, *Nero* 11; Tacitus, *Annals* 14.20.

Nero, in his fourth consulship with Cornelius Cossus as his colleague, instituted at Rome games on the Greek model, which were to be held every five years. As is typical with all new things, it received mixed reviews. Some noted that Pompey had been criticized by his older peers for constructing a permanent theater. They said that before its construction, theatrical performances had been given on a temporary stage to an audience on temporary stands, and that even before that the audience stood to watch plays so that people would not learn to spend their time in idleness by sitting in the theater. The old ways ought to be maintained [*so went the criticism; but instead*] our traditional morals have been gradually weakened and finally ruined by imported licentiousness. We thus begin to be able to see in our city everything that can corrupt—or be corrupted. Our youth have been made degenerate by their eagerness for foreign ways, for the gymnasium, for idleness, for perverted sex. . . .

Gladiators: Various Views[12]

You need not imagine that only people of the upper classes have the strength to escape the bonds of human servitude. . . . Men even of the lowest rank have escaped to safety through their own powerful drive. . . . Recently, for example, a German who was slated to be one of the wild animal fighters in the arena was getting ready for the morning show. He withdrew to relieve himself—the only thing he was allowed to do on his own without a guard being present. In the toilet there was a stick with a sponge on the end of it used for wiping away the feces. He rammed the whole thing down his throat, and choked to death. . . . Not a very elegant way to go, it's true, but what is more foolish than to be overly fastidious about our departure? What a brave man!

And in fact, what has Norbanus ever done for us? He produced a show with gladiators worth about a sesterce apiece, so decrepit that one puff and they would have all fallen flat on their faces. The mounted infantry fought like characters on a jug. . . . One, a Thracian, had a bit of spunk in him, but he too fought lackadaisically. At the end of the show they were all flogged while the crowd shouted: Hit them! Hit them! Clearly a bunch of losers. "Still," said Norbanus, "I gave you a show, didn't I?"

[*Inscription at Rome*]:
To the shades of M. Antonius Niger, a Thracian-style fighter, who lived to be 38 and fought 18 times. Put up by his wife, Flavia Diogenis, to her well-deserving husband from her own resources.

[*Inscription at Rome*]:
To the shades of M. Ulpius Felix, veteran myrmillion [*a gladiator who usually fought against the net-man or the Thracian type of gladiator*], who lived forty-five years. By nationality a Tungrian [*modern Belgium*]. . . . His wife, the freedwoman Ulpia Syntyche, and their son Justus erected this inscription to her beloved and well-deserving husband.

---

[12]Seneca, *Letters* 70; Petronius, *Satyricon* 45; Dessau, *Inscriptiones Latinae Selectae* (Berlin, 1888), 5090; 5106; 5142A.

[*Graffito at Pompeii*]:
Heartthrob of the girls, Celadus, Thracian-style fighter; fought three times, won three times.

A Charioteer[13]

[*Inscription at Rome*]:
To the shades of Diversus Pompeius Musclosus, driver of the Red Faction, born in the Tuscus neighborhood of Rome. He won first place a total of 682 times; three times as charioteer of the Whites, five times with the Greens, twice with the Blues, and 672 with the Reds; put up by his wife Apuleia Verecunda in honor of his memory.

9.5   Daily Life as Seen Through the Law Codes

From the Roman law codes we get a somewhat different view of daily life in the Roman world. One of Rome's greatest achievements was the development of a uniform law code for the whole Empire along with the scientific study of law itself. The idea that the same law could be applied everywhere regardless of time, culture, language, religion, or ethnicity was original to the Romans. While the development of Roman law took place over centuries, the process of collecting and updating it occurred late in Roman history. Some legal collections appeared in the third century, but it was not until the Emperor Justinian published the Digest of Roman Law in A.D. 533 that the definitive codification occurred.

Roman law has been described as "organized common sense," a characteristic that may be seen in the following selections from the Digest. The Lex Aquila, to which reference is made in the first selection, dates from the period of the Republic; it was the basic law covering claims of negligence. Alfenus was a legal expert of the late Republic; Ulpian, Mela, Proculus, Pomponius, and Marcellus belong to the Empire period.

"If, While Several Persons Are Playing Ball . . ."[14]

Ulpian, *On the Edict, Book 8:* Mela also says that if, while several persons are playing ball, the ball having been struck too violently should hit the hand of a barber who is shaving a slave at the time, in such a way that the throat of the latter is cut by the razor, the party responsible for negligence is liable under the *Lex Aquila*. Proculus thinks that the barber is to blame, and, indeed, if he had the habit of shaving persons in a place where it is customary to play ball or where there was much activity, he is in a certain degree responsible, although it may not improperly be held that where anyone seats himself in a barber's chair in a dangerous place, he has only himself to blame. . . .

---

[13]Dessau, *Inscriptiones Latinae Selectae* (Berlin, 1888), 5281.
[14]From S. P. Scott, *The Civil Law in 17 Volumes*, vol. 3 (Cincinnati, OH: Central Trust Co. 1932), p. 327, 345.

"Mules were Hauling Two Loaded Wagons..."

Alfenus, *Digest, Book 2*: Mules were hauling two loaded wagons up the Capitoline Hill [*at Rome*], and the drivers were pushing the first wagon, which was inclined to one side, in order that the mules might haul it more easily. In the meantime the upper wagon began to go back, and as the drivers were caught between the two wagons they jumped out of the way and the last wagon was struck by the first. The second wagon then moved back, crushing a slave boy who belonged to someone.

The owner of the boy asked me against whom ought he to bring an action? I answered that it depended on circumstances, for if the drivers who had hold of the first wagon voluntarily got out of the way, and the result was that the mules could not hold the wagon and were pulled back by its weight, then no action would lie against the owner of the mules, but an action under the *Lex Aquila* could be brought against the men who held the wagon; for if a party, while he was supporting something, by voluntarily releasing his hold enabled it to strike someone, he nevertheless committed damage, as for instance, where anyone was driving an ass and did not restrain it, or where anyone were to discharge a weapon or throw some other object out of his hand.

But if the mules gave way because they were frightened, and the drivers, actuated by fear of being crushed, released their hold on the wagon, then no action can be brought against the men, but one could be brought against the owner of the mules. And if neither the mules nor the men were the cause of the accident, but the mules could not hold the load, or while striving to do so slipped and fell and this caused the wagon to go back, and the men were unable to support the weight when the wagon was inclined to one side, then no action could be brought against the owner of the mules or the men. This, however, is certain, that no matter what the circumstances were, no action would lie against the owner of the mules that were in the rear, as they did not go back voluntarily, but because they were struck. . . .

Bequests: "She Afterwards Disposed of the Pearls..."[15]

Marcellus, Opinions: Seia charged her heir, Publius Maevius, with a bequest as follows: "I give and bequeath to Antonia Tertylla such-and-such a weight of gold, and my large pearls set with hyacinths." She afterwards disposed of the pearls, and at the time of her death did not leave any among her jewels. I ask whether the heir will, under the terms of the trust, be compelled to furnish the value of the property which does not form part of the estate. Marcellus answers that he will not be required to do so. I also ask, if it can be proved that Seia converted her necklace of pearls and hyacinths into some other kind of ornament which afterwards became

---

[15]From S. P. Scott, *The Civil Law in 17 Volumes*, vol. 7 (Cincinnati, OH: Central Trust Co. 1932), p. 250.

more valuable through the addition of other jewels and small pearls, whether the legatee can demand the said pearls and hyacinths, and whether the heir will be compelled to remove them from the other jewelry and deliver them. Marcellus answers that the demand cannot be made. For how can a legacy or a trust be held to exist when what is given by a will does not retain its original character? For the bequest is, as it were, extinguished, so that in the meantime it is lost sight of, and hence by this dismemberment and change the intention of the bequestor also appears to have been altered. . . .

"Wolves Carried Away Some Hogs . . ."[16]

Ulpian, On the Edict, *Book 19*: Pomponius discusses the following point. Wolves carried away some hogs from my shepherds; the tenant of an adjoining farm, having pursued the wolves with strong and powerful dogs, which he kept for the protection of his flocks, took the hogs away from the wolves, or the dogs compelled them to abandon them. When my shepherd claimed the hogs, the question arose whether they had become the property of him who recovered them or whether they were still mine, for they had been obtained by a certain kind of hunting.

The opinion was advanced that, as where animals were captured on sea or land and regained their natural freedom, they ceased to belong to those who took them, so, where marine or terrestrial animals deprive us of property, it ceases to be ours when the said animals have escaped beyond our pursuit. In fact, who can say that anything which a bird flying across my courtyard or my field carries away still belongs to me? If, therefore, it ceases to be mine and is dropped from the mouth of the animal, it will belong to the first occupant; just as when a fish, a wild boar, or a bird escapes from our control and is taken by another it becomes the property of the latter.

Pomponius inclines to the opinion that the property continues to be ours as long as it can be recovered, although what he states with reference to birds, fishes, and wild beasts is true. He also says that if anything is lost by shipwreck, it does not immediately cease to be ours, and that anyone who removes it will be liable for quadruple its value. And, indeed, it is better to hold that anything which is taken away by a wolf will continue to be ours as long as it can be recovered. Therefore, if it still remains ours, I think that an action on the ground of theft will lie. For if the tenant pursued the wolves, not with the intention of stealing the property (although he might have had such an intention), but admitting that he did not pursue them with this object in view, still, as he did not restore the hogs to my shepherd when he demanded them, he is held to have suppressed and concealed them, and therefore I think that he will be liable to an action on the ground of theft, as well as one to produce the property in court; and after this has been done, the hogs can be recovered from him.

---

[16]From S. P. Scott, *The Civil Law in 17 Volumes*, vol. 9 (Cincinnati, OH: Central Trust Co. 1932), p. 171.

9.6   Family Life

An Affectionate Paterfamilias

The poet Horace honors his father, a former slave, whose occupation was that of a tax collector. The family lived in out-of-the-way Apulia in southern Italy so that the decision to educate Horace in Rome involved considerable sacrifice on the father's part. The reading draws attention to the potential for social mobility in Rome—at least if one had as much talent as Horace—and the support of sensible and ambitious parents.[17]

If my character, while generally sound, is only flawed in a minor way—like moles on an otherwise good looking person—if no one can charge me with avarice or meanness or sexual excess, if (pardon my self-praise) I live a decent life and am a friend to my friends—I owe it all to my father.

Although he was just a poor farmer he would not send me to the local school with the tough sons of tough centurions, their slates and school bags slung over their shoulders, each with his eight cents of tuition due on the Ides. No, he had the courage to send me off to Rome to be taught what sons of senators and knights were taught. If anyone in that bustling city saw my clothes and slave retinue he would have thought my support came from ancestral wealth. But in point of fact my father was my attendant [*i.e., instead of having slaves accompany him as slaves did the rich, Horace's father served in their place*]. He was my incorruptible guardian among my teachers Need I say more? He kept me chaste, the first grace of virtue, free from shameful deeds as well as their reputation. He wasn't afraid that some day I might end up in some lowly occupations like an auctioneer or a tax collector like himself, and earn a wage. I would not have complained. But as it is I owe him my praise and thanks. Never—at least as long as I am sane—would I be ashamed of such a father, and so I will not defend myself as many like me do, who say its no fault of theirs that they have not free-born, famous parents.

A Satirist's View of Marriage

If we were to believe the satirist Juvenal, Roman family values, especially among the upper classes and the well-to-do middle classes, were hopelessly corrupt. (For a different view see "Musonius Rufus".) Spoiled rich women abused their slaves and their weak husbands. But if we set aside the rhetoric and Juvenal's venom, it is possible to get a somewhat different view of the relationship between husband and wife. Juvenal's women are clearly not passive—despite the supposed nearly dictatorial power possessed by the Roman paterfamilias. Their own resources give them a degree of freedom—at least in their private lives. Many were also educated. The presence of slaves in the household is taken for granted, along with the easy and, from a modern viewpoint, incredibly exploitative sexual power both husband and wife had over them.[18]

---

[17]Horace, *Satires* 1.6.65–92.
[18]Juvenal, *Satires* 6.206–223; 457–494; 434–456.

If you are determined to be monogamous then you might as well bow your head and accept the yoke. No wife spares the man who loves her, for though she may be passionate she gets her real pleasure from tormenting and putting down her spouse. The better the husband and the man the less good it will do him. He will never give a present unless she approves. If she objects there will be nothing, I repeat, nothing, that you can buy or sell. She will decide who your friends are going to be. You will find that long time friends are banished. Pimps and gladiatorial trainers are free to make their wills as they please, even gladiators, but you will find among your heirs more than one of your own rivals.

"Crucify that slave!" orders your wife. "But what capital crime has he committed?" you reply, "Who is the witness? Who is his accuser? Stop and listen. No delay can be too long when a man's life is at stake!" "What, you fool," she says, "you think a slave is a human being? He did nothing? True, but it's my wish, my command— my desire is sufficient reason". . . . If you have turned your back on your wife at night, the woman who cards the wool is done for as is the woman in charge of her wardrobe. The man with the litter will be accused of coming late—he'll have to pay for your sin. One will have a rod broken over his shoulders, another will bleed from the strap, the third from the lash. Some wives engage their torturers by the year; it's cheaper. While the flogging is going on the lady will be making up her face, listening to her friends, or examining a gold-embroidered robe. . . . If she wants to be turned out more nicely than usual the unfortunate maid, her own hair a mess and her clothes falling off will hear, "Why is this curl standing up," and down comes the leather thong to inflict punishment for the offending hair. . . .

Worst of all is the woman who has barely sat down to dinner when she starts to praise Vergil, forgives the dying Dido [*the Carthaginian queen whom Aeneas jilts in Vergil's masterwork the* Aeneid], pits the poets against each other, setting up Vergil on one side of the scales and Homer on the other. The scholars yield, the professors are vanquished, the whole dinner crowd is shut up. No one, not even a lawyer or an auctioneer, can get a word in edgewise—no, not even another woman! She sets down definitions and like a philosopher talks of morals, dying to be both learned and eloquent. How I hate women who are for ever consulting Palaemon's grammar! They insist on keeping all the rules and laws of language. Like pedants they quote verses I never heard of and correct their unlettered friends' speech. You would think husbands could at least be allowed to make slips in grammar!

A Moralist's View of Marriage

Just how accurately Juvenal's satire mirrors husband–wife relations in Roman society at large is hard to estimate. Was the kind of behavior described above typical of upper-class society as a whole or only of a part of it? What of the middle and lower classes? Was Juvenal's hectic lifestyle common only in Rome? What about Italy and provinces? Other types of evidence— though it is equally difficult to determine how much they reflect actual practice—are epitaphs found on tombstones (e.g., the Turia Inscription in Chapter 4) and the moral codes of the great philosophies of the Empire. The following reading from Musonius Rufus discusses the purpose of marriage.[19] *The philosophical belief that marriage existed for the sake of a shared life and the procreation of children goes back to Aristotle.*

The main purpose of marriage is twofold: a shared life and the procreation of children. Musonius says that those entering a marriage should be united with each other with the intent of: (1) having a common life together, and (2) begetting and raising children. Indeed, while holding their material goods in common, spouses should consider nothing to be their own, not even their individual bodies. The raising of children is a matter of the greatest importance; indeed, marriage exists for this purpose. While it is possible to achieve the same result outside marriage—just as animals do—this is not fitting. For in marriage there must be full community of life between husband and wife, real love for each other, whether in health or illness, indeed, in all circumstances, since it was for this purpose, as well as for having children, that they married in the first place.

When the love of husband and wife for each other is perfect, and when they share it fully, each spouse seeking to outdo the other, then this is what a marriage ought to be and is indeed enviable. Such a union is fine and good. But when each spouse seeks just his or her interest without concern for the other or when, by Zeus, one feels this way and although living in the same house has his or her heart fixed elsewhere, and has no wish to unite his efforts or his sentiments with his yoke-mate, by necessity this union is finished. Spouses who live in a situation like this have a terrible relationship. In the end they separate entirely; their life together is worse than being alone.

An Affectionate Marriage

Pliny, an important Roman senator, seems to have had a deeply affectionate relationship with his wife.[20]

You cannot begin to imagine how much I miss you! This is because I love you so much and we are not used to being separated. And so I lay awake most of the night thinking of you. During the day I find that my feet lead me, they really do, to your room at the time I used to visit you. Finding it empty I leave, as sick at heart and sad as a lover locked out by his loved one. The only time I manage to escape these miseries is when I am in court and wearing myself out pleading my friends' lawsuits. You can judge for yourself what a state I'm in when I find relaxation in work, and distraction in troubles and anxieties!

An Epitaph for a Wife

Thousands of grave monuments put up by husbands and wives to each other survive. The inscriptions on them are often formulaic and it is difficult to know just how much genuine

---

[19]Musonius Rufus, *The Purpose of Marriage* 13a.
[20]Pliny, *Letters* 7.5.

sentiment is to be inferred from them. They come from all over the Empire. The following was put up in Britain by a Syrian to his freedwoman wife, a native Celt. It is in Latin and Syriac. The monument shows Regina seated wearing a long sleeved robe reaching to her feet. She wears a necklace and bracelets and holds an open jewelry box in her right hand. On her lap are a distaff and spindle. Beside here is a work-basket with balls of wool.[21]

To the spirits of the dead. To Regina, his freedwoman and wife, a Catuvallaunian by tribe. She was aged thirty years. Barates of Palmyra set this up.

In Palmyrene script under the Latin text appears the following:
Regina, the freedwoman of Baratas, alas.

Epitaphs for Children

Many, perhaps most, children never survived childhood, and were mourned by their grieving parents. The monument to Hateria Superba who is commemorated in this inscription depicts her holding in her hands a dove and some fruit, while hovering putti place a crown on her head. By her side are her pet dog and crow. The second reading is by the poet Martial (ca. A.D. 40–104), a friend of Juvenal and Pliny. Martial commends the soul of a little girl by the name of Erotion, possibly his slave, to the care of his already deceased parents.

To the spirits of the departed and to Hateria Superba who lived one year, six months and twenty-five days. Her inconsolable parents, Q. Haterius Ephebus and Julia Sosima, set up this monument for their daughter, for themselves and their household.[22]

To you my father Fronto, and to you my mother Flaccilla, I commend this little girl, my darling sweetheart. In your care may little Erotion not be terrified by the dark shades and the monstrous gaping jaws of Hades' hound. She would have completed six years—less six days—the midwinter winter day she died. In your protection, now her guardians, may she continue her playful childhood, chattering about me, lisping my name.

Gentle earth weigh lightly on her small bones as she, when living, lightly trod on you.[23]

Friendship Among Wives: A Birthday Invitation

During the excavation of the Roman fort at Vindolanda near Hadrian's Wall in England, hundreds of wooden writing tablets, some with the writing still legible, were found. They date from about A.D. 90 to 120 when the fort was occupied by Cohors I Tungrorum and later by Cohors IX Batavorum, auxiliary units in the Roman army from Germany and the Netherlands

---

[21]R. G. Collingwood and R. P. Wright, *The Roman Inscriptions of Britain* (Oxford, 1965), no. 1065.
[22]Dessau, *Inscriptiones Latinae Selectae*, 8005.
[23]Martial, *Epigrams* 5.34.

respectively. The officers of the units were Romans (or at least Roman citizens). The wives of several of these officers lived in the fort and the reading that follows is a birthday invitation from Claudia Severa, the wife of an officer, to her friend Lepidina, the wife of Flavius Cerialis, prefect of one of the cohorts at the fort. The words "Sister I shall expect you . . . hail," which are in Claudia's own hand, are the oldest known example of a woman's handwriting in Latin.[24]

Claudia Severa sends greetings to her friend Lepidina. Sister, I happily invite you to be sure to come to our house on my birthday, the third day before the Ides of March [*March 12*], for if you are present you will make the day more enjoyable for me. Say hello to your Cerialis. My Aelius and my little son send their greetings. Sister, I shall expect you. Be well, sister, dearest soul, as I hope to be well, and hail. To Sulpicia Lepidina, wife of Cerialis, from Severa.

Abortion and Infanticide

Abortion and infanticide were practiced throughout the Roman Empire, though to what extent is uncertain. Life expectancy at birth in antiquity was extremely low and parents at all levels of society needed children to carry on the family name and traditions and to look after them in old age. While too many children could be a serious problem for the poor, there were also frivolous reasons for abortion. For the most part abortion was a resort of the elite since only they could afford the medical costs involved. Exposure was an alternative for the rest of society and for those among the upper-class who wished to avoid the dangers and pain of an abortion. Under Roman law the paterfamilias *had extensive rights over his offspring and could choose to raise his infants or not. The Emperor Augustus, for instance, would not allow the child of his granddaughter Julia to be raised after she had been condemned for adultery (Suet. Aug. 65). Fathers of illegitimate children, on the other hand, had no right to expose their children.*

Opinion about abortion and infanticide was divided. Aristotle wrote that abortion was legitimate only before the quickening of the fetus, i.e., before it showed signs of sensation. The well known Hippocratic Oath forbade doctors to administer abortifacients, and the orator Cicero deplored abortion on the grounds that it reduced the citizen population and made the continuity of families impossible.

Legally abortion was not a crime because in Roman law the fetus was not a person. Until the baby was born it had no legal standing. On the other hand it was not just an inanimate object either, and could be afforded protections as witnessed by the opinion of the jurist Julian who said: "In practically the whole of civil law the child in the womb is regarded as having real existence" (Julian, Digest 1.5.26). Accordingly, in Roman law, pregnant women condemned to torture or death could not be executed or tortured until after they had delivered. Exposed children were sometimes brought up as slaves by their finders although if they could later prove they were freeborn, they had to be liberated. The law also protected the rights of birth parents even if they chose not to raise their child. Such parents could later claim the child although there was probably an obligation to reimburse the foster parents for the costs of raising it.

---

[24]Tab. Vindol. II.291.

The family consilium *or council, which included the mother and advised the father on many issues, probably also advised on this subject. Philo, the great Jewish philosopher from Alexandria, regarded exposure as the equivalent of murder. The* Didache (The Teachings of the Apostles, ca. A.D. 100), *one of the oldest Christian documents outside the New Testament, is the first text to mention abortion explicitly. It condemns the practice. By the later Empire exposure came to be regarded as murder. Infanticide was proscribed in* A.D. 374. *In the sixth century the Emperor Justinian enacted that exposed children were to be deemed free. The following readings are from the first century* A.D. *Roman poet Ovid. The first reading is a fantasy from his work, the* Metamorphoses.[25]

Once upon a time, near the royal city of Knossos in Crete, there lived a man named Ligdus. He was freeborn, but lower class and from a poor family. Nevertheless, although he was poor he was a decent and honorable person. One evening he told his wife, who was pregnant and approaching the time for her baby to be delivered, "I pray for two things. One, that you have an easy labor, and second, that the baby be a boy. A daughter is more trouble and fortune hasn't given us the wherewithal to raise her. I hate to say this, but if it's a girl . . . we'll have to let her die." They both wept. . . . His wife, Telethusa, begged her husband again and again to change his mind, but he wouldn't and stubbornly resisted his wife's appeals.

As her time neared Telethusa had a dream and in her dream she saw the goddess Isis walking towards her bed with a procession of sacred beings. Upon her forehead shone the crescent moon and a wheat yellow garland of glittering gold surrounded her head, a sight of royal beauty. . . . Isis spoke: "O Telethusa, dear child of mine, forget your troubles and do not obey your husband's mistaken command . . . protect and nurse your child, boy or girl. I'm the goddess who answers the prayers of those who love me; you have not worshipped a thankless deity." Joyfully Telethusa rose from her bed and raising her innocent hands in prayer to the stars, she begged that her vision might come true.

The story goes on to tell how the child—a girl—was born and how Telethusa, pretending it was a boy, raised it. Iphis, as the child was called, grew up healthy and beautiful. Complications arose when it came time for the arrangement of a betrothal. At the intercession of Telethusa Isis intervened to solve the impasse and metamorphose Iphis into a male.

In this next reading Ovid addresses his girlfriend, Corinna, complaining that she is contemplating an abortion just to avoid stretch marks. He uses the metaphor of war and gladiatorial combat to describe the contemplated abortion.[26]

The woman who first tore her tender baby from her womb should have died in the butchery on that battlefield herself. And are you now ready to enter that same sad arena and make a similar slaughter just so that your stomach will be free of wrinkles? If this practice had been engaged in by the mothers of olden times, their crime would

---

[25]Ovid, *Metamorphoses* 9.669–703.
[26]Ovid, *Amores* 2.14.5f.

have rendered the human race extinct . . . Had the mother of Romulus and Remus ripped the twins from her swollen womb there would have been no Rome . . . Had your own mother tried to do what you are now planning, you yourself would have perished, your beauty embryonic!. . . . No tigress in Armenia would do a thing like this, no lioness dares to destroy her own cubs. But frail young girls do!

▼▼▼

Questions

1. How did the gods reward Baucis and Philemon for their hospitality? (**9.1**)
2. What provisions did the Laws of the Collegium at Lanuvium make for a member of the college who died while away from home? (**9.2**)
3. What kinds of luxuries were enjoyed by the elite according to Seneca, and what was his view of them? (**9.3**)
4. Figure out the stages bathers could have gone through in their afternoon at the bath. What other activities besides bathing was available to them? (**9.4**)
5. What was the case against the barber and the owner of the mules in the suits cited in **9.5**?
6. What was Juvenal's complaint against wives in his satire? (**9.6**)
7. Musonius Rufus says marriage existed for two purposes. What were these? (**9.6**)
8. What was unusual about the find of Claudia Severa's invitation to her friend to attend a birthday party? (**9.6**)
9. Abortion and infanticide generated different responses among Greeks and Romans. What were the positions of Aristotle, the author of the Hippocratic Oath, Cicero, Philo, the author of the *Didache*, and, finally, Ovid? (**9.6**)

Chapter 10

The Transformed Empire

The Geographical Shift

By the fourth century (A.D. 300–400) the axis of the Roman world had shifted away from the Mediterranean. Italy had become a backwater. Rome itself was rarely visited by the emperors, who now needed bases closer to the danger spots on the frontiers 10.4. Trier on the Moselle (in present-day Germany) was the Western capital. Milan in northern Italy, Sirmium on the Danube, Byzantium (soon to be renamed Constantinople), Caesarea in Turkey, and Antioch in Syria were all major administrative centers or regional capitals.

Political, Military and Administrative Transformations

But the shift of the axis was more than geographical: there was also a shift in the political, military, social, and especially the cultural life of the Empire. The army was enlarged and rearmed to cope with the threat of Persia in the east and the Germans in the north and west. In turn a large bureaucracy grew to generate the necessary taxes and round up the recruits needed for the expanded military 10.2. The command and administrative structure was revised, and the Empire divided into eastern and western halves. The imperial office itself was surrounded with pageant and ceremony and became more remote and authoritarian.

But the military and administrative reforms were incomplete and inadequate. The army tended to grow on paper while the actual number of available front-line troops declined. Much of the additional revenue that was supposed to go to increasing the size of the army went instead to corrupt officials 10.4. Bribery, which had always been an endemic aspect of the Roman system, was now given huge opportunities for growth, on a scale not dreamed of in the past. The traditions of *polis* society, especially in the realm of religion and municipal service, were undermined by the increasing burdens of taxation, administration, and corruption and by the rise of Christianity as an alternative value system.

At the most basic level, the central administration was never able to persuade reluctant municipal elites and even more reluctant peasants in the peaceful parts of the Empire that defending the remote Rhine or Danube frontier or northern England was in their self-interest. The Empire held together only when the external pressures were not too great and the demands on its inhabitants not too heavy. But at some point the demands began to be seen as outweighing the benefits, and then the decay began in earnest.

Oddly, in these years some of the most devoted "Romans" were Germans or other barbarians serving in the army. The key to the future, particularly in the vulnerable western half of the Empire, lay in Rome's relationship with the Germans, and it was in this area that the imperial system ultimately broke down, leading to the rise of multiple, independent German kingdoms in the old western and central European provinces. Paradoxically it was the Church that now became the most vital mediator between the barbarians and the classical, *polis* past.

In the east the Empire had a much stronger base. More populous and more deeply urbanized, richer, and with a long tradition of submission to autocracy, the East was more receptive to the reforms of Diocletian and Constantine. The Empire survived there to the time of the Arab invasions in the seventh century, and in a more reduced form until the fall of Constantinople to the Turks in A.D. 1453.

Christianity and Classical Traditions

The most significant cultural challenge of the age was the task of coming to terms with Christianity 10.6. This took place at many levels of society and in many places, but from a purely intellectual viewpoint the most serious challenge for Christianity was to present itself in a form acceptable—and intelligible—to the traditionally educated middle and upper classes of the Empire. Although people from these strata of society were attracted to many aspects of Christianity, the cultural context in which it evolved was alien and in some instances repugnant to classical sensibilities. The Hebrew theological concept of sacred history, of God as the Lord of History acting in such events as the Exodus or through the prophets and bringing about salvation through a new Exodus in the death and resurrection of Jesus, was simply outside the ken of people educated in the old fashion. Miracles and prophecies did not present much of a problem, nor did the belief that Jesus was the Son of God, but what of such themes as the suffering servant of Isaiah, the radical call to holiness, the hope of the Second Coming, and other peculiarities of late Judeo-Christian eschatology? It was impossible to accept Christianity without in some way coming to terms with its cultural origins. The scriptures, both the Hebrew scriptures and the New Testament, in all their bewildering (from a Greco-Roman viewpoint) complexity, had to be dealt with. It is a tribute to the integrity and vitality of Greco-Roman culture—supposedly in decline—that it accepted the challenge. Some of the best minds of the age devoted themselves to this task. Such people as Irenaeus of Lyons; Clement and Origen of Alexandria; the two Cappadocians Basil, Gregory of Nazianze, and Gregory of Nyssa; Ambrose of Milan; Tertullian and Augustine from Africa; and many others would have made their mark in an earlier age in the secular world of politics, the army, and literature. Now they devoted themselves to understanding this alien religion, translating it into a language intelligible to Greeks and Latins, and, equally challenging, devising an organizational structure for the scattered Christian communities of the Empire. By any estimate it was a formidable undertaking.

The New Religious Environment: The Democratization of Excellence

At times the areas of agreement between pagan and Christian seem more significant than their differences. Christianity offered no radical challenges to commonly accepted Greek and Roman views of society, and there was no head-on collision over such fundamental questions as the ownership and use of property—including slaves—or the hierarchical arrangement of Roman society, which set one person above another and loaded privileges on some while denying them to others. Pagans and Christians often shared common views on such different ethical issues as slavery, abortion, the exposure of infants, astrology, prostitution, the immorality of the pagan gods, and the often frivolous and materialistic character of urban life. They even shared much the same views of the material world around them.

Since the fourth century B.C. it had been generally held that the cosmos consisted of a series of concentric spheres that revolved around one another in a fixed hierarchy, with the earth at the center. These spheres were composed of matter of differing grades of fineness. At the highest and purest level were the stars; then in descending order came the spheres of the sun, the planets, the moon, and finally, at the lowest and poorest level, the earth. Despite such an assumption that the earth was at the bottom of the cosmic hierarchy, the average Christian or pagan did not believe that the world of matter was wholly or intrinsically evil. For the Christian there was the irrefutable endorsement of matter in the belief in the resurrection of the body at the end of the world and in the assumption of human form by God's Son (known in theological terms as the mystery of the Incarnation). Pagans hardly needed to demonstrate their acceptance of the material world. Alongside this mainstream view, however, there lurked in both groups a suspicion of matter and the belief that the body was a weight that dragged down the soul, the purer element, whose natural tendency was to strive upward toward heavenly things. Thus the great pagan philosopher Plotinus could declare that he was ashamed to possess a body and wondered what deterioration had reduced man to his present state, and Saint Anthony, the Christian hermit, said he blushed when he had to perform any of the normal bodily functions. The body, it was imagined, needed to be subdued and brought under the control of the soul by ascetic practices, which ranged from the intellectual exercises of the Neoplatonists to the fantastic mortifications imposed on themselves by the Syrian and Egyptian ascetics, such as Saint Simeon the Stylite, who sat for forty years on his pillar outside Antioch without descending.

Yet at the same time there was a growing feeling among many that it was possible for the individual to realize a new self and rise to previously impossible heights of moral excellence. In the past, it was thought that moral worth was the preserve of those who could, by reason of birth or wealth, achieve high military or civil office and that it was in the performance of the functions attached to these positions that an individual achieved true goodness and the fullest development of human potential. To a lesser extent the practice and study of rhetoric and philosophy could also be a source of this excellence, and in the third century the mystical philosophy of Plotinus held out yet a higher ideal of human achievement through intellectual union with God. On the other hand, the lower classes, engaged in time-consuming menial tasks, were automatically excluded by their occupations from the possession of moral goodness. However, with the advent of Christianity, even the ordinary man or woman could aspire to high levels of moral achievement without holding exalted civil or military rank or without the expense of a classical education. By a simple act of conversion or initiation, a person could begin to lead a new life of moral enlightenment. The knowledge that was acquired in this conversion or initiation was not mere information about God and the cosmos but a special kind of understanding or insight that affected the whole person, transforming mind and emotions alike. It penetrated into the person's innermost being, converting and radically altering his or her life. Thus were the traditional concept of culture and the moral excellence it was assumed to entail transformed, democratized, and extended in religious form to the masses of the Empire.

Being All Things to All Men

A revolutionary aspect of third and fourth century religious development was the comprehensive attempt of Christians to reach as wide an audience as possible. By the time of Constantine, Christianity was on its way to becoming a mass religion, and its organizational structure was well equipped to handle its new role. It was no longer restricted to the small fervent cells of the past, and following Saint Paul's maxim, it tried to be all things to all people. To the intellectuals and educated classes it presented the learned apologies of its philosophers from Clement of Alexandria to Augustine, couched in the language and style of argument that these classes would recognize. To the masses it presented the same message in less abstruse fashion, and to all it extended the same hope of immortality, freedom from slavery to fate, the stars, the demons, sin, and even death itself, as well as the possibility of overcoming human weakness and vice in the here and now.

Religious Enthusiasts: A Problem for the Authorities

Of course, some people felt more deeply moved by these religious currents than others, and the third and fourth centuries abounded with religious enthusiasts of all kinds. Some felt that they were the intermediaries of the gods who had been selected to convey a special message to humankind.

Such emperors as Aurelian, who made the sun god the preeminent deity of the Empire; Constantine, who made Christianity the supreme religion; and Julian, who tried to turn the Empire back to paganism, felt the tug of religious conviction profoundly. Often the visionaries were regarded as heretics, and the establishment, whether Christian or pagan, tried to suppress them. In the second century the Phrygian Montanus proclaimed that a new Jerusalem would soon be revealed, and people poured out of the towns and villages to await with him the coming of Christ. A council of bishops promptly condemned him, but the movement lingered for centuries, and the problem of holy men, whether prophets, martyrs, or ascetics, was a difficult one for the authorities. The riotous monks of Egypt were a well-known menace to both the ecclesiastical and the civil establishments, and in Africa, Constantine attempted to suppress the rigorous Donatists, who had split the Church because of the orthodox clergy's alleged indulgence of those who had shown weakness during the Great Persecution of Diocletian.

For the average person, whose visionary capacities were limited, it was important to cling as closely as possible to favored beings who seemed to have been especially chosen by God to perform great spiritual deeds and whose charisma contrasted shatteringly with the ordinariness of the usual ministers of religion. Quite spontaneously, the practice of honoring the memory of the saints sprang up. Relics were treasured and circulated, and the churches and monuments built to enshrine their remains quickly became places of pilgrimage. Feasts were established in their honor and grew to occupy an increasingly important place in the annual cycle of religious celebrations. A new kind of literature, hagiography—the study of the lives of the saints—became one of the most common forms of popular reading for the next millennium and a half.

Self-Realization: Pagan and Christian Ways

Among educated pagans it was commonly accepted that the traditional gods were mediating spirits or demons but that God himself was infinitely removed from human beings, uncontaminated by matter and revealed only through his creations, which emanated from him in a descending series. According to Plotinus and the Neoplatonists, he could be reached by intellectual contemplation because the soul had a natural tendency toward union with God and sought completeness by identifying with him. This was not a matter of technique or ritual, and there were no special exercises or sacraments. Union could be achieved only by intellectual asceticism and contemplation, which required long years of training and education, especially of a literary kind. Understandably, this kind of rarefied Neoplatonism was accessible only to the few, but in watered-down forms it became the most popular type of religion practiced by the educated classes of the late Empire.

Christians agreed that the universe was peopled by invisible powers, the demons, and that God was indeed accessible to humankind, but whereas pagans feared the demons and struggled on their own to reach the Divine, Christians triumphantly declared that the demonic world had been overwhelmed by the intervention of God in the historical person of Jesus. All that remained was a mopping-up operation, part of which, unfortunately, involved the dismantling of demon-ridden pagan society and the building of a new community in its place. With many pagans, Christians shared the belief in the possibility of the individual realizing a new self through revealed knowledge and achieving liberation from the spirits and demons of the world. Although the mystery religions and the theosophies of the educated claimed to be able to transmit this knowledge, they lacked a coherent theology and an organization to do this effectively. For the Christian, access to the source of power over the unseen world was easy and secure, and did not depend on the maintenance of enthusiasm over long periods. A person was indeed converted to the new way of life, but that life was as regular and well organized as city life itself. The Christian could turn for help to the rituals and sacraments of the Church or to the clergy, the holy men, the angels, or the saints, as well as to the local church community itself. This support was comprehensive, for it was economic and social as well as spiritual. And it was worldwide. By the fourth century a Christian could move just about anywhere in the Empire and expect to find the same organization, ritual, and beliefs. Letters of introduction from the home church eased entry into the new community, where spiritual life could continue as before.

Faith and Reason

To the upper-class pagans who took the trouble to observe them, the early Christians seemed to be a supremely irrational group of fanatics. Marcus Aurelius and Galen the doctor were appalled at their uncritical assumptions, their lack of logic, and their stubbornness. The critic Celsus thought they were a dangerous sect, a people who considered themselves apart from the state and whose loyalties lay to another organization altogether. In the third century, however, the gap between educated Christians and pagans was narrowed by the development of a sophisticated Christian apologetic. By the time of Constantine a bridge of understanding, if not toleration, had been built between the two worlds by a succession of brilliant philosopher-theologians 10.10.

Clement of Alexandria (ca. A.D. 150–ca. 215) was the first to go beyond the early apologists and attempt a thoroughgoing reconciliation of faith and reason. Christians, he argued, had no reason to fear philosophy, for just as the Law was the tutor or guide of the Jews leading to Christ, so God had made philosophy the guide of the pagans. It, like reason, was a gift of God. Hence, he could argue, philosophizing was synonymous with being a Christian. Clement's brilliant disciple Origen also happened to be a pupil of Plotinus' master, Ammonius Saccas. For Origen the best in the pagan world had been nourished by God's providence before the appearance of Christianity, and a Christian could therefore not completely reject either Greek culture or the Roman Empire without refusing to accept part of God's providential plan for humankind. However, Christianity was the true education (*paideia*), and Christ the True Philosopher would lead human beings to the truth. The historical personality of Jesus was played down by these theologians, who instead emphasized Jesus as the Divine *Logos*, or Word, who was God's agent in creating and ruling the cosmos, a concept that would be familiar to the Neoplatonists, who believed in a whole series of beings mediating between God and humankind.

Both Christians and pagans placed great emphasis on prophecies and miracles, and in the eyes of Christians one of the most compelling arguments in favor of their beliefs was the fact that the coming of Christ had been foretold in the Hebrew scriptures. This line of argument was considered particularly cogent in antiquity because of the great reverence for the written word and the wisdom of the past. Miracles were used as arguments because Christians were not debating rationalists or nonbelievers but only believers of a different kind. The argument usually went along the lines that pagan miracles were worked by demons or that the miracles of Jesus were of a superior, moral kind. Origen borrowed the method of allegorical interpretation, which had been used by generations of scholars to avoid the obvious meanings of classical texts and to find new truths in them. In the absence of the tools of higher criticism it enabled both Christians and pagans to explain away the more awkward problems in their respective bodies of literature. Until the development of modern historical techniques in the nineteenth century, the cultural worlds of the Hebrew scriptures, late Judaism and early Christianity remained a lost, unintelligible world. Its place was taken by a set of doctrines and ethical prescriptions formulated in Greco-Roman terminology.

The Empire and the Church Come to Terms

The emergence of the Church as a major institution and the attempt of the government to bring it within the framework of the state were the most important developments of the third and fourth centuries. By themselves, the administrative and military reforms of Diocletian and Constantine and the artistic and architectural revivals of the fourth century would have been an interesting epilogue to the end of the classical world, but it was the emergence of the institutional Church that provided the connecting link between this world and the later stages of the development of Western history 10.7.

The life of the Church revolved around a series of rituals, of which baptism and the Eucharist were the most important, and the day-to-day contact of the average Christian with the Church was through these events rather than through any more personal or formal contacts with the clergy. The message of Christianity was deeply embedded in ritual, and the incidental education that derived therefrom was probably a good deal more important than exhortations and explanations from the pulpit.

The Christian liturgy borrowed heavily from Judaism. The calendar of feasts followed by the Church was Jewish, with the principal feasts of the year, Easter and the Descent of the Holy Spirit, occurring at the same time as Passover and Pentecost, respectively. It was only after much bitter debate that the date for Easter was changed and given its present position in the calendar. Sunday soon displaced Saturday as the most important day for Christians, and each week they gathered to celebrate the resurrection of Jesus and wait for his Second Coming.

Baptism, a Jewish ceremony of washing, was required for initiation into Christianity. Although at the beginning all that was necessary was a profession of faith, the practice of giving instructions in the essentials of the religion soon became common. A succinct expression of these essentials was found in the Symbol or Creed of the Apostles. Hence, from an early date, in addition to a moral conversion and the performance of ritual acts, Christian converts were expected also to think correctly and to know the essential doctrinal beliefs of their religion.

The principal—and most original—act of the Christian community was the celebration of the Eucharist. This ritual consisted of two parts, the first borrowed from the synagogue service and consisting of prayers, readings, homilies, and hymns to which candidates for baptism were admitted. The second and most mysterious part, to which only the fully initiated were admitted, was a simple meal revolving around the blessing of an offering of bread and wine and then its ritual consumption by the participants. In origin it was a common Jewish domestic ritual to which Jesus had given special meaning at the Last Supper. It was seen by early Christians in a number of ways—as an anticipation of the Messianic banquet to be enjoyed with Jesus in the Heavenly Kingdom, a symbolic repetition of the sacrifice on Calvary, and as a mysterious reenactment of the Last Supper itself.

The liturgy had a dynamic of its own and made certain demands on the celebrant and congregation alike. Because its principal act, the Eucharist, consisted of a number of parts, of which the first was a series of readings and a homily, or sermon, the celebrant had to be literate and possess some degree of education to be able to comment on the readings and expound the essentials of Christian beliefs. The scriptures of the new religion were enshrined in its rituals, so that for the first time the masses were exposed to a literature not composed exclusively for an educated elite. The rituals themselves were powerful educational tools, so that even without any explicit inculcation by the clergy (or even in the face of it), certain points were emphasized again and again and thus sank imperceptibly into the consciousness of the congregations. Year after year the liturgy celebrated the birth, death, and resurrection of Jesus and other events of his life. A whole history and prehistory, beginning with Adam and passing through the events of the scriptures, was taken for granted, as were suppositions about the movement of current history toward a grand finale, the Second Coming of the Lord. Local barriers were dissolved in the celebration of the liturgy, and the Christian community was seen not as an isolated entity but as part of a larger body that extended everywhere in the world, embracing all peoples. Paradoxically, this development occurred just as the secular state was beginning to disintegrate and other forms of communication were disappearing.

It was in the liturgy that the wider, organizational Church and the local communities made contact because the rituals could be performed only by a properly appointed celebrant. The bishop (or his representative) had a powerful position in the community. One element of his strength lay in the fact that he represented the outside world to his particular church because his mandate came from there, not from the people. He was an accepted member of the community, however, and, whether popular or not, was viewed as the means through which the grace to live a spiritual life would come. He was present at all the main events in the lives of his people from birth to death, strengthening, consoling, educating. His power was not political or even religious in the old sense. It was something quite new, and around the person of the bishop a new community began to form that was unlike anything that had existed before.

▼▼▼

10.1   "Now Declining into Old Age": A Review of Roman History from a Late Empire Viewpoint

The author of this reading (and a number of others in this chapter) is a Greek army officer, Ammianus Marcellinus of Antioch in Syria, who published a history of Rome in the A.D. 390s. A pagan and admirer of the Emperor Julian, who had been the champion of the old religion during his brief reign, Ammianus lived at the time when Christianity consolidated its hold on the Empire. That he chose to retire to Rome and write his great work in Latin rather than his native Greek says something about the continuing power of Rome to attract provincials into its service. He subscribes to conventional moral values and the belief that Providence lay behind Rome's rise to greatness. Within ten to fifteen years of the publication of his history Rome would be sacked by a Gothic warrior-band under its chief Alaric, and half a century or so later the last emperor, Romulus Augustulus, would be replaced by a German warlord, but those events should not obscure the general validity of his belief that the reputation of Rome had an extraordinarily high standing among peoples outside as well as within the Empire.[1]

At the time when Rome first rose to world greatness—that Rome which was destined to last as long as the human race—bravery and fortune, though commonly at

---

[1]Ammianus Marcellinus, *Roman History* 14.6. All selections from Ammianus are adapted from the translation of C. D. Yonge, *The Roman History of Ammianus Marcellinus* (London: Henry G. Bohn, 1862).

variance, agreed upon a treaty of eternal peace to assist its rise to glory. If either had been missing, Rome would never have reached its heights of greatness. Its people, from their earliest infancy to the latest moment of their youth, a period which extended over 300 years, carried on a variety of wars with the peoples around its walls. Then, when it arrived at adolescence, after many and various labors in war, it crossed the Alps and the sea, until as youth and adult, it had carried the triumphs of victory into every country in the world.

And now that it is declining into old age, and often owes its victories to its mere reputation, it has come to a more tranquil time of life. Therefore, the venerable city, after having bowed down the haughty necks of fierce nations, and given laws to the world to be the foundations and eternal anchors of liberty, like a thrifty parent, prudent and rich, entrusted to the Caesars as to its own children, the right of governing its ancestral inheritance. And although the Tribes and Centuries [*i.e., the voting assemblies of Rome*] are no longer active, and the contests for votes have been replaced by a calm recalling of the age of King Numa [*second king of Rome after its founder Romulus*], nevertheless, in every quarter of the world, Rome is still looked up to as the mistress and queen of the earth, and the name of the Roman people is respected and venerated.

10.2   New Founders of Rome: Diocletian and Constantine

During the third century it seemed as though the Empire was certain to break up, but a vigorous new dynasty of emperors from Illyria (modern Yugoslavia) managed to reestablish the Empire on a new footing. The first of these great emperors was Diocletian. Building on the reforms of previous regimes, Diocletian consolidated them into a coherent new program that enabled Rome to cope with the immediate challenges of civil war and barbarian invasions. His successor, Constantine, took the step of embracing Christianity and building a new capital, Constantinople, on the site of the ancient Greek city of Byzantium.

The following extremely hostile (and highly rhetorical) account of the reforms of Diocletian was written by Lactantius, a Christian professor of Latin at Nicomedia, the emperor's capital. Understandably prejudiced against the emperor who launched the last bloody persecution of the Church, Lactantius nevertheless distorts the great accomplishments of Diocletian. In order to cope with the problem of the frontiers, the army had to be significantly increased in size. This increase could be accomplished only by major "revenue enhancements" (taxes). Increased taxes required tighter administration—more bureaucrats—and generally more sacrifice all around. Not everyone was pleased, particularly large property owners, on whom the burden was principally supposed to fall. The reading is useful insofar as it accurately describes both Diocletian's reforms and the reaction to them of a segment of the population.[2]

---

[2]Lactantius, *The Death of the Persecutors* 7.

Diocletian was the instigator of crimes and the contriver of evils. He despoiled everything; he could not even keep his hands off God himself! Through greed and anxiety he managed to turn the whole world inside out.

He made three men partners in his rule and divided the Empire into four parts. Correspondingly, he increased the armies since each of the four partners strove to have a much larger number of troops than previous emperors did when the state (*res publica*) was ruled by a single emperor. Naturally, the number of tax recipients began to exceed the number of taxpayers—to such an extent that the farmers' resources were overwhelmed by the enormous size of the state's assessments. Fields were abandoned and cultivated areas were turned into wilderness.

To be sure that everyone was properly terrorized, provinces were chopped up into pieces. Many governors and even more sub-governors were imposed on individual districts, and even on individual cities. Along with them came numerous account-ants, administrators, and deputy prefects [*local representatives of the now civilian Praeto-rian Prefects*]. The actions of these individuals, however, was rarely civil! In fact, they were involved mainly with condemnations and repeated confiscations; to be exact, their demands were not just frequent, but constant, and involved intolerable wrongs.

The methods of raising troops was also intolerable. With insatiable greed, Dio-cletian would never allow the treasury to be depleted but always piled up surplus resources and funds so as to preserve intact what he had already collected. Likewise, when as a result of his blunders he had generated tremendous shortages, he tried to legislate the prices of goods [*by edict*]. Much blood was then shed over worthless items, and because of fear nothing was offered for sale. Prices rose until, following many deaths, necessity led to the law's repeal.

To all of this was added an unbounded passion for building. This created more pressure on the provinces, more exactions for workers, craftsmen, wagons, and all the other essentials for building. Here basilicas [*large buildings used for public business*], there a circus; here a mint, there an arms factory; here a house for his wife, there one for his daughter. Suddenly a great part of the city would be torn down. Everyone fled, with wives and children, as though the city had been assaulted by an enemy. When the new buildings were all up—and the provinces wiped out in the process—he would say, "No good; they must be done another way." Down they came again, were remodeled and often rebuilt yet again. He was always crazily trying to make Nicomedia [*his capital in Turkey*] the equal of Rome.

10.3   Constantine and Christianity

Constantine took the fateful step of abandoning the ancestral religion of Rome for the new, eastern religion of Christianity. For many pagans of the time this act was the immediate cause of the decline of the Empire, and there is no doubt that it had a dramatic impact on the history of Rome as well as of the Church. Nevertheless, Constantine's decision recognized the need for some kind of accommodation with the upstart religion, and in fact there were some precedents already at hand. Fifty years earlier the Emperor Gallienus had stopped the persecution of the

Church that had been initiated by his predecessors, restored confiscated property, and in effect extended recognition to Christianity. Constantine's own involvement was gradual, and in reality the triumph of Christianity was not complete for another half century.

Constantine's first step in recognizing Christianity was the so-called Edict of Milan published in February A.D. 313. Jointly issued with his co-emperor Licinius, the decree recognized Christianity as a legitimate religion and extended toleration to all religions (which in Roman eyes meant just about any religion that did not subvert the existing social or political order). As in all matters concerning religion, the first objective of the Roman government was to maintain the goodwill of the gods, or, as the Edict puts it: "That whatever Divinity there may be in the heavens may be appeased and look kindly on us and all under our rule."[3]

I, Constantine Augustus, and I, Licinius Augustus, having met by Fortune at Milan, we thought in the course of our discussions regarding public well-being and security, that our first regulations which would benefit many should concern the respect due to the Divinity: We therefore grant Christians and all others full permission to observe whatever religion they wish, with the intent that whatever Divinity there may be in the heavens may be appeased and look kindly on us and all under our rule. By this wholesome counsel and just purpose we thought to ensure that no one whosoever should be denied the opportunity to give himself to the observance of the Christian religion—or to whatever religion he should think best for himself. Again, our intent is that the Supreme Deity, to whose worship we freely yield our minds, may show in everything his usual favor and goodwill.

Therefore, your Excellency should know that we have decided to remove all the conditions whatsoever which were in the previous ordinances handed down to you officially concerning the Christians; regulations that are inappropriate and alien to our clemency are abolished. Henceforth, anyone who wishes to observe the Christian religion may do so freely and openly, without any anxiety or interference. We thought it right to commend these decisions most fully to your care that you may know that we have given to those Christians free and unrestricted opportunity to practice their religion. When you see that we have granted them this favor, your Excellency will understand that we have also granted to other religions the right of open and free observance of their own cult. We have done this for the sake of peace in our times, that each individual may have the freedom to worship as he pleases and that no cult or religion may be impaired.

10.4   The Majesty of Emperors: Desires and Realities

From the time of the crisis of the third century, the central government tried to cope with the pressures of barbarian invasions by increasing the power of the central government. The pageantry and pomp of the imperial court was designed to impress the people of the Empire with

---

[3]Lactantius, *The Death of the Persecutors* 48.

the power of the emperors, thereby encouraging morale while discouraging rebellion. Provinces were divided into more manageable units and taxes were collected with greater efficiency. Nevertheless these reforms, especially in the western half of the Empire, did not produce a proportionate increase in the real power of the emperors.

The pageantry of the court—as manifested, for example, in Constantius' entry into Rome (first reading below)—was coolly received by the blasé inhabitants of the Eternal City; it was the emperor himself who was impressed by Rome's glories. In the second reading we see how even well-intentioned emperors could be frustrated by corrupt officials. The third reading shows what could happen when an Emperor, in this case Valens (A.D. 364–378), made a disastrous policy error.[4]

The Entry of Constantius into Rome: A.D. 357

Constantius [*A.D. 351–361, the son and successor of Constantine*] . . . developed a strong desire to visit Rome and celebrate there his triumph over [*the rebel leader*] Magnentius. . . . Accordingly, after long and expensive preparations . . . the emperor passed through Ocricoli with his army in battle order, attracting the astonished gaze of all who gathered to watch. . . .

Preceded by standards on both sides of the road, he sat alone in a golden chariot brilliant with precious stones which seemed to spread a flickering light all around. His chief officers went before him surrounded by purple banners woven in the form of dragons and attached to the golden or jeweled points of spears. The wind blew through the dragons' gaping mouths and hissed as though inflamed with anger, while the coils of their tails streamed behind them. After these marched a double row of heavy-armed soldiers, with shields and crested helmets glittering and shining, their breast-plates reflecting the sunlight. Among these were scattered heavily armored cavalry protected by cuirasses and belts of steel whom you would think of as statues polished by the hand of the sculptor Praxiteles rather than as human beings. The light circular plates of steel that surrounded their bodies and covered their limbs were so well articulated that however they moved the joints of their mail adapted themselves accordingly.

The emperor as he moved along was cheered, and the hills and the shores reechoed the shouts of the people. Despite all the noise, he showed no emotion and kept the same impassive appearance he was accustomed to display when traveling through the provinces. Although he was very short, he stooped when passing through high gates, and he looked straight before him as though his neck was in a vice, statue-like, turning neither to the right nor to the left. When the carriage shook, his head did not nod, nor was he seen to spit or wipe his face or his nose or even move a hand. While this calmness was no doubt an affectation, yet there was other evidence in his personal life of extraordinary patience which one might have thought to have been his alone. . . .

When he entered Rome, that home of empire and all virtues, he mounted the Rostra [*the orators' platform in the Forum*]. From there he gazed with amazed awe on the Forum, the most renowned monument of ancient power. Wherever he turned he

---

[4]Ammianus Marcellinus 16.10.

was bewildered by the number of wonders on every side. After addressing the nobles in the Senate house and the people from the tribune, he retired with the goodwill of all to the palace, where he enjoyed the pleasures he had anticipated. On a number of occasions, when he celebrated the races in the Circus, he was entertained by the talkativeness of the common people, who maintained their freedom of speech without disrespect. He himself observed a proper moderation. He did not, for example, as was usually done in other cities, allow the length of the gladiatorial games to depend on his caprice but left it to be decided as local customs suggested.

Then he surveyed the summits of the seven hills and the different quarters of the city, whether located on the slopes of the hills or on the level ground. He visited the suburbs as well, and whatever he first saw he thought the most impressive of all. Thus he admired the Temple of Tarpeian Jupiter, which is as much superior to other temples as divine things are superior to human; then it was the baths the size of provinces or the vast mass of the Colosseum, so solidly erected of Tibertine stone, to the top of which human vision can scarcely reach. Or it might have been the Pantheon with its vast extent that caught his eye, its imposing height, and the solid magnificence of its arches and lofty niches rising one above the other like stairs, decorated with the images of former emperors; or the temple of Rome, the Forum of Peace, the theater of Pompey, the Odeum or the race course or any of the other sights of the Eternal City.

But when he came to the Forum of Trajan, the most exquisite structure, in my opinion, under the canopy of heaven, which even the gods admired, he stood transfixed with wonder, casting his mind over the gigantic proportions of the place, beyond the power of mortals to describe, and beyond the reasonable hope of mortals to rival. Therefore, giving up all hope of attempting anything of this kind, he contented himself with saying that he would and could imitate the statue of Trajan's horse which stands in the middle of the hall bearing the emperor on his back.

The Emperor, the Truth, and Corruption

One of the greatest problems faced by the rulers of the late Empire was their inability to control corruption within their own vastly enlarged administrative system. As the following reading shows, they had enormous difficulty just finding out the truth. Pay that was supposed to reach troops in the field was often siphoned off en route. The unpaid soldiers then resorted to barefaced shakedowns of the locals, the worst being refusal to help civilians in moments of real crisis. Then, when complaints were made by the local population to the emperor, there were cover-ups. The investigators themselves were frequently in collusion and returned to the emperor with false reports.

The story of the unhappy people of Tripoli (modern Libya) was one that appealed to Ammianus, although he had many from which to select. The incident, even though it had a quasi-happy ending, reveals the critical inability of the late Empire to provide what every government is supposed to provide: basic security and protection for its citizens from violence. It was ultimately this failure that undermined provincial support for the imperial administration in the west.[5]

---

[5]Ammianus Marcellinus 28.6.

From here let us move, as though to another part of the world, to the sorrows of the African province of Tripoli, sorrows over which, in my opinion, Justice herself must have wept. . . .

The Austorians are barbarians who live on the frontiers of this province, always ready for a quick attack and accustomed to live by plunder and bloodshed. Although subdued for a time, they relapsed into their natural state of disorder, claiming the following as the cause of their actions. One of their countrymen, a man named Stachao, while wandering freely in our territories during peacetime, broke the law on a number of occasions. His most serious violation was his effort to subvert the province. . . . Since the evidence against him was undeniable, he was burned to death at the stake.

To avenge his death, the Austorians, claiming that he was their countryman and that he had been unjustly executed, sallied out of their own territory like wild beasts. . . . Fearing to approach close to Leptis, a city with a large population and fortified by strong walls, they occupied the fertile district around it for three days. They massacred the peasants, whom fear at their sudden attack had deprived of all courage or had driven to take refuge in caves. They burned the household goods they could not take with them and returned home with vast plunder, taking with them Silva, the most prominent local magistrate, who happened to be with his family at his country house.

The people of Leptis were terrified at this sudden disaster and, to forestall further incursions by the barbarians, implored the protection of Count Romanus, who had recently been appointed to the command of Africa. When he arrived at the head of his army and received their request to come to their immediate assistance, he said he would not start a campaign without new supplies and 4,000 camels. The unhappy citizens were stupefied by this demand and declared that after the looting and fires it was impossible for them to provide such supplies, even if it were to help them recoup their losses. After fooling them for forty days and attempting nothing militarily, the count marched off with his army. Disappointed and fearing the worst, the people of Tripoli at their next annual meeting appointed Severus and Flaccianus as ambassadors to the Emperor Valentinian. They were to take some golden images of victory in honor of his accession to the Empire and to set before him fearlessly the miserable situation in the province.

When Romanus heard of this move, he sent a swift messenger to the master of the office, Remigius, his own kinsman and his partner in his shake-downs, warning him to make sure that the affair was referred by imperial decree to himself and his own deputy for investigation. The ambassadors from Tripoli arrived at the court and, having obtained access to the emperor, they laid the matter before him in a set speech and presented him with a decree of their council in which the whole affair was fully described. The emperor read it but trusted neither the report of the master of the offices, who tried to give Romanus' actions a favorable spin, nor the ambassadors' version, which tried to accomplish just the opposite. Instead, a full investigation was promised; typically, however, the investigation was deferred, as frequently happens at high levels of government where the press of more important matters is used [*by collusive officials*] to deceive those in power.

While waiting in suspense and anxiety for some relief from the emperor's military headquarters, the citizens of Tripoli were again attacked by the same barbarians, now elated by their previous success. They ravaged the whole territory of Leptis and Oea, spreading total ruin and desolation everywhere. At last, loaded with enormous quantities of spoil, they withdrew, having killed many of the local magistrates, the most distinguished of whom were Rusticanus, one of the priests, and the aedile Nicasius. . . . A new messenger was sent to Gaul with an account of this fresh disaster and this report roused the emperor to great anger. Palladius, his secretary, who also had the rank of tribune, was sent at once to pay the wages that were due the troops stationed in Africa and to investigate and give a truthful report of what had happened in Tripoli.

This marks the second effort to get to the bottom of the matter, but despite his genuine concern for the province, the emperor is once again frustrated.

When Palladius arrived in Africa, Count Romanus, who knew why the imperial secretary had come and who had been warned to take measures for his own safety, sent orders to his officers through confidential messengers to hand over to Palladius the greater part of the pay he had brought. . . .

This was a blatant attempt to buy the influence of the emperor's confidant. Apparently, however, Palladius was unaware of the source of the money and, although he seems to have had a conscience, found himself trapped, as we shall see, by the wily Romanus.

This was done, and the suddenly enriched Palladius arrived in Tripoli.

In order to get at the facts of the case, he took with him to the districts that had been devastated Erechthius and Aristomenes, two eloquent and distinguished citizens of Tripoli. They freely demonstrated to him the distress that their fellow citizens and the inhabitants of the adjacent districts had suffered. When Palladius got back to the city, he criticized Romanus for his inactivity and threatened to make a true report of the situation to the emperor. Romanus retorted angrily that he too would send a report, pointing out that the man who had been sent as the emperor's incorruptible secretary had diverted to his own use the money that had been intended for the soldiers. Palladius recognized that he had been cornered and proceeded henceforth in concert with Romanus. When he returned to the court, he deceived Valentinian with atrocious lies and declared that the citizens of Tripoli had no grounds for complaint.

The story goes on for several chapters more as the cover-up developed a momentum of its own and the case became more complex. Lies were piled on lies. At one point the emperor, in a rage, thinking he had finally gotten to the bottom of the mess, ordered that tongues of the two whistle-blowers, Erechthius and Aristomenes, should be cut out for supposedly deceiving Palladius. They immediately went into hiding. Gradually, however, the truth emerged. Palladius and Remigius committed suicide and Erechthius and Aristomenes were rehabilitated. The sure-footed Romanus, however, escaped punishment.

10.5   The Emperor and the Barbarians

One of the keys of Roman military success throughout its history was its ability to integrate non-Roman auxiliaries into its armies (see for instance, the speech of Calgacus in Section 7.2 in which he claims that the Roman army was a motley collection of peoples from all over the Empire). *In the late fourth-century Rome's ability to do this broke down in the west. In effect the Empire in that region was overwhelmed by the sheer magnitude of the invasions and the inadequacy of its own resources. In response, whole barbarian war-bands and immigrating peoples were given land inside the Empire. Militarily, the effect of this policy was that instead of contributing individual units to fight under Roman officers the barbarians now fought under their own tribal commanders as federates. For Ammianus this was a fatal mistake and led to the end of the Empire.*

The particular incident described here came about when the Germanic Visigoths were driven into the Roman Empire by the advance of the Huns from Central Asia. Ammianus' gloomy forebodings were born out a generation later when this same people sacked Rome in A.D. 410.[6]

Accordingly, under the command of their leader Alavivus, the Goths occupied the banks of the Danube. They sent envoys to the Emperor Valens and humbly asked to be received by him as subjects, promising to live quietly and to furnish a body of auxiliary troops if any necessity for such a force should arise. . . .

The affair caused more joy than fear. The practiced flatterers around the emperor praised his good fortune. They congratulated him that an embassy had come unexpectedly from the furthest corner of the earth offering him a large body of recruits. By combining these foreign forces with his own resources, he would have an absolutely invincible army. Further, they pointed out that by their substituting cash for recruits from the provinces, a vast amount of money could be accumulated.

Filled with this hope, Valens sent forth officers to bring this ferocious people and their wagons into our territory. And such great pains were taken to gratify this nation which was destined to overthrow the Empire of Rome that not one was left behind, not even of those who were stricken with mortal diseases. Having obtained permission of the emperor to cross the Danube and to cultivate some districts in Thrace, they crossed the river day and night without ceasing, embarking in crowds aboard ships and rafts and canoes made of the hollow trunks of trees. In this endeavor, as the Danube is the most difficult of all rivers to navigate and was at that time swollen with continual rains, a great many were drowned. . . .

Thus, through the misguided zeal of the advisers who pushed the project, the ruin of the Roman world was brought on. . . .

10.6 Christianity Rome and Classical Culture: A Different Vision

That there was an intrinsic incompatibility between Christianity and classical values was apparent from the time Romans became aware of the presence of the new religion. Christians were criticized on a variety of grounds, but principally because they had rejected the gods of their ancestors

---

[6]Ammianus Marcellinus 31.4.

and the civic values of Greco-Roman world. Their religion was new; they had turned away from the traditions of their immediate ancestors, the Jews. Because of their refusal to attend the festivals, they were atheists and misanthropists. In popular belief they even practiced incest and cannibalism. In short, they did not fit into the system that had been sanctioned by centuries of classical use.

In some respects the charges were true. Christians, indeed, had other goals than civic life. But in this they were not unlike many in the Empire. The difference was that the Christian viewpoint was articulated as part of an organized religion. The highest honors of civic life, the consulship, the Senate, municipal office, and the command of armies, were not of primary importance for Christians, at least in their ideology. Their kingdom, as they claimed, did indeed seem to lie elsewhere.

In self-defense Christians attempted to justify their way of life, claiming that they, not the Jews, were the true inheritors of the Hebrew religious tradition; that their values were compatible with traditional Greco-Roman values; that their religion was the true philosophy of life, and because it was revealed by God rather than devised by men it was therefore more certain. Naturally, what was popularly said about them, they claimed, was false. From the second century onward one apology followed another. The anonymous Epistle to Diognetus belongs in this tradition but is presented here because, in a burst of eloquence, its author actually concedes the main charge against Christianity, though he tries to give his admission a favorable spin. In the end, however, it is clear that Christianity did represent a different, and indeed a new, set of values.[7]

Christians are distinguished from other men neither by nationality, language, nor custom. They do not live separately in cities of their own, have their own special language, or lead a life that is peculiar in any way. The way of life they follow has not been devised by human speculation or deliberation. Indeed, Christians do not, like some, proclaim themselves the advocates of any merely human doctrines. Rather, while inhabiting Greek as well as barbarian cities, according as the lot of each of them has determined, and following the customs of the natives in respect to clothing, food, and the rest of their ordinary conduct, they display to us their wonderful and admittedly striking way of life.

They dwell in their own lands—but simply as sojourners. As citizens they share in all things with others, and yet endure all things as if foreigners. Every foreign land is to them as their homeland, and every homeland as a land of strangers. They marry, as do all others; they beget children; but they do not commit infanticide. They share a common table, but not a common bed. They are in the flesh, but they do not live after the flesh. They pass their days on earth, but their citizenship is in the heavens. They obey the prescribed laws and at the same time surpass the laws by their lives. They love all men and are persecuted by all. They are misunderstood and condemned; they are put to death and yet restored to life. They are poor yet make many rich. Lacking all things, they have everything in abundance. They are dishonored but are glorified in their dishonor; slandered, yet vindicated. They are reviled yet

---

[7] *Epistle to Diognetus* 5–6. Based on Alexander Roberts and James Donaldson, *The Ante-Nicene Fathers* (Edinburgh: The Ante-Nicene Christian Library, 1867), pp. 26–27.

they bless, insulted but repay insult with honor. They do good but are punished as evil-doers. When castigated they rejoice like men revived to a new life. . . .

To sum up all in a word—what the soul is to the body, that are Christians to the world. The soul is dispersed through all the members of the body, and Christians are scattered through all the cities of the world. The soul dwells in the body yet is not *of* the body; Christians dwell in the world yet are not *of* the world. The invisible soul is guarded by the visible body, and Christians are known indeed to be in the world, but their holiness remains invisible.

The flesh hates the soul and wars against it because it is prevented from enjoying its pleasures, though itself suffering no injury. The world similarly hates Christians because they are opposed to its pleasures, though it is in no wise injured by them. Despite this, the soul loves the flesh that hates it, and also its members. Christians, too, love those that hate them. The soul is imprisoned in the body yet preserves that very body. Christians are confined in the world as in a prison, and yet they are the preservers of the world. The immortal soul lives in a moral tabernacle; Christians live as sojourners in corruptible bodies, looking for an incorruptible dwelling in heaven. Finally, Christians, although subjected day-by-day to punishment, increase in number, just as the soul when poorly provided with food and drink becomes better. God has assigned them this high position, which it is unlawful for them to abandon.

10.7 Organization and Ideology

Christians possessed not only a different vision of life and a set of values that was at variance with the traditions of polis society, they also possessed a new organizational structure and a sophisticated ideology to back it up. In the first reading below, the great church historian and apologist Bishop Eusebius of Caesarea (in Palestine, ca. A.D. 260–340) casually describes how the bishops of some of the regions in the western Mediterranean dealt with a disciplinary and doctrinal problem. In the process, he reveals much about how the Church was organized as early as the mid-third century. There were problems of ambition and office-seeking within the Church. A great debate raged over Christians who fell away in times of persecution and then wanted to return to the Church. Should they be readmitted? The prestige and authority of the confessors, that is, those who had suffered under the persecution, had the potential to undermine institutional Church authority. Most important of all was the problem of how dissidents within the Church were to be dealt with.

Eusebius takes for granted that an effective communications network allowed different church communities to coordinate their activities with each other. The citation of official, authoritative documents from key councils and important bishoprics is a characteristic of the process by which Church discipline was established, maintained, and extended.[8]

---

[8]Based on the translation of A. C. McGiffert and E. C. Richardson in Philip Schaff and Henry Wace, *A Select Library of Nicene and Post-Nicene Father of the Christian Church* (New York: Post-Nicene Library of the Christian Fathers, 1890), pp. 286–290.

THE BASILICA: FROM CITY OF MAN TO CITY OF GOD

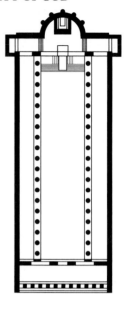

Despite considerable decorative changes over the centuries, the great Basilica of St. Mary Major in Rome has remained structurally unaltered since its construction around A.D. 440. Flanked by two aisles, the majestically proportioned nave suggests the grandeur of the basilican style of architecture.

For both Greeks and Romans temples were buildings whose primary purposes were to honor the gods and goddesses by providing suitable dwelling places for them. The exterior was emphasized, and the interior, cramped and dimly lit, was much less important. The temple was intended to be looked at and walked around. By contrast the worship needs of the new faith created a demand for fresh architectural forms. Its churches were not principally the dwelling places of a god, and what Christians needed most were large interior spaces where the people could gather to celebrate their rituals, preferably with unblocked views of the altar and the celebrant. Conveniently, the model for this kind of building was readily available in the secular basilica.

The rectangular basilica was an old Italian architectural form designed to serve the civic community's social, commercial, and legal needs. Every Italian city had one or more basilicas, located in or near the forum, the town's business area. Their purpose was to provide shelter from bad weather for large numbers of people, so special emphasis was given to the interior; the outer form was of secondary importance. Barrel and cross vaults provided the essential structural elements of the building, and light was supplied by clerestory windows high above the floor. The results were impressive, and in the hands of the new secular and religious authorities, all the potential of this ancient architectural form was realized. New visual and spatial dimensions were opened up. With illumination coming from high above, mysterious effects of light and shade became possible. A riot of colored pavements, mosaics, wall decorations, and coffered ceilings confronted the eye in all directions, yet all the elements were integrated and a focus was provided by the structure's axial lines, which drew the gaze immediately to the apse at the end where the altar and the seat of the bishop was located.

Novatus, a priest of the church at Rome, was lifted up in arrogance against those who had fallen away during the persecution [*the first empire-wide persecution initiated by the Emperor Decius in* A.D. *250*] but had subsequently repented. There was no hope of salvation for them, he held, even if they did everything to prove their conversion was genuine and pure. Novatus became the leader of the heresy of those who, in the pride of their hearts, called themselves "The Pure Ones."

To settle the matter, a very large synod was called at Rome. It consisted of sixty bishops and a much larger number of priests and deacons. In the provinces of the Empire the other bishops and pastors debated privately what ought to be done. The upshot was a decree which unanimously declared that Novatus and those who joined with him and approved of his hatred and inhumanity toward his fellow Christians should be considered to be outside the Church. On the other hand, those brothers who had, through misfortune, fallen during the persecutions should be treated and healed with the medicines of repentance.

We have received letters from Cornelius, the bishop of Rome, to Fabius, bishop of Antioch, telling him what had happened at the Synod of Rome and what the local representatives in Italy, Tunisia, and the surrounding areas had decided. There are other letters in Latin from Cyprian [*bishop of Carthage*] and those associated with him which make it clear that they agreed as to the necessity of helping those who had been tempted in the persecutions, and that it was right to cut off from the Catholic Church the leader of the heresy and all who had joined with him. Attached to these was another letter of Cornelius regarding the resolutions of the Synod and others on the conduct of Novatus. It is appropriate that I make selections from these so that any one who reads this work may know the facts about the case. Cornelius tells Fabius what kind of person Novatus was:

"You should know that for a long time this incredible fellow wanted to become a bishop. He kept his ambitions to himself and used as a cloak for his plot those confessors [*i.e., those who had suffered during the persecutions and not fallen away*] who had adhered to him from the beginning. I speak of Maximus, one of our priests, and Urban, who twice gained the highest honor by confessing their faith; along with Sidonius and Celerinus, a man who, by the grace of God, most heroically endured all kinds of torture and by the strength of his faith overcame the weakness of the flesh—these men found him out and detected his unscrupulousness and duplicity, his perjuries and falsehood, his self-preoccupation and false friendship. They returned to the Holy Church and denounced his craftiness and wickedness in the presence of many bishops and priests and laypeople . . .

"How remarkable, dear brother, the change and transformation which we have since seen take place in this man and in so short a space of time! This most illustrious man, who bound himself with terrible oaths not to seek to become a bishop, suddenly appears a bishop as if dropped into our midst by some machine [*Cornelius means machines like those that were used to make wild animals suddenly pop up in the arena*]. This doctrinal purist, this champion of the Church's discipline, in attempting to grasp and seize the episcopate which had not been given him from above, chose two of his companions who had given up their own salvation. He sent them to an obscure and insignificant corner of Italy to deceive three bishops of the region who were rustic and very simple men. He asserted positively and strongly that it was essential that they come quickly to Rome in order that all the dissension which had arisen there might be worked out through their mediation, along with that of the other bishops. When they came, being, as we have stated, very simple in the craft and artifice of the wicked, they were shut up with certain selected men like himself. By the late afternoon, when they had become drunk and sick, he compelled them by force to consecrate him a bishop through a counterfeit and vain imposition of hands. Because it had not come to him [*as he thought it should*], he avenged himself by craft and treachery. One of these bishops shortly came back to the Church, lamenting and confessing his transgression. We admitted him back as a layman since all the people present interceded for him. We consecrated successors of the other bishops and sent them to the places where they had been.

"This great defender of the Gospel [*i.e., Novatus*] then did not know that there should be only one bishop per Catholic church! Yet he was not ignorant (for how could he be?) that at Rome there were 46 priests; 7 deacons; 7 subdeacons; 42 acolytes; 52 exorcists, readers, and janitors; over 1,500 widows and persons in distress, all of whom the grace and kindness of the Master nourish [*but only one bishop*]. Yet not even this great multitude . . . together with the very many, even innumerable people, could turn him from such desperation and presumption and recall him to the Church. . . .

"You will be glad to know that he has lost support and is abandoned. Every day the brothers leave him and return to the Church. When Moses, the blessed martyr, who late suffered among us a glorious and admirable martyrdom, while yet alive, saw Novatus' insane arrogance, he broke off communion with him and the five priests who along with him had separated themselves from the Church."

At the close of the letter Cornelius gives a list of the bishops who came to Rome and condemned the foolishness of Novatus, together with their names and the sees over which each of them presided. He mentions also those who did not come to Rome but who expressed by letters to these bishops their agreement with the vote, giving their names and the cities from which they individually wrote.

10.8   Determining Church Doctrine

The theory of Church doctrine and how it is to be determined is proclaimed succinctly by Irenaeus, bishop of Lyons in France, writing some time between about A.D. 180 and 200. The way to end doctrinal confusion, he says, is to consult the traditions of the churches founded by the apostles. But since doing this would be a very tedious process, he proposes a simple test: It is sufficient to check the traditions of the Church of Rome; Rome is the guarantor of orthodoxy.[9]

Since, however, it would be very tedious in such a volume as this to reckon up the successions of all the churches, we confound all those who, in whatever manner, whether for evil self-pleasing, or vain glory, or blindness, or perverse opinion, assemble in unauthorized meetings. This we do: (1) by pointing to the faith preached to men, which comes down to our time by means of the succession of the bishops; and (2) by

---

[9]Irenaeus, *Against the Heretics* 3.3. Based on Roberts and Donaldson, *The Ante-Nicene Fathers*, vol. 1, p. 415.

pointing to that tradition derived from the apostles, of the very great, very ancient, and universally known Church founded and organized at Rome by the two most glorious apostles, Peter and Paul. For it is a matter of necessity that every church should agree with *this* Church, on account of its preeminent authority . . . for in it the apostolic tradition has been preserved. . . . [*A list of the bishops of Rome from Peter onward is next given, ending with*] Eleutherius, who now holds the see of Rome in the twelfth place from the apostles. In this order, and by this succession, the ecclesiastical tradition from the apostles, and the preaching of the truth, have come down to us. And this is the most abundant proof that there is one and the same vivifying faith, which has been preserved in the Church from the apostles until now and handed down in truth.

10.9   The Pagan Response

Logically enough, the official response to Christianity was often repression. The new religion had none of the characteristics that would have given it an approved status. The following, from an apology called The Octavius, sums up the official view neatly: "Why do Christians endeavor with such pains to conceal and to cloak whatever they worship, since honorable things always rejoice in publicity while crimes are kept secret? Why have they no altars, no temples, no acknowledged images? Why do they never speak openly, never congregate freely, unless for the reason that what they adore and conceal is either worthy of punishment, or something to be ashamed of?"[10]

From the Roman viewpoint Christianity had one of the most dangerous characteristics a religion could possess: It was new; it had no track record on which it could be judged. What they did see, they did not like. Christians not only did not participate in the festivals and rituals of the gods, they actively refused to do so, and they vilified the civic religion as the worship of demons. Understandably, the authorities regarded this attitude as threatening the stability of the state. The neglect of the all-important duty of honoring the gods might lead to disaster.

Early acts of repression tended to be sporadic and localized, as, for example, in the activities of Pliny (Chapter 8). Sometimes persecution was the result of simple malice: neighbors settling grudges against each other. Some persecutions were the result of natural disaster. The second century Christian apologist Tertullian claimed rhetorically that "If the Tiber rises as high as the city walls; if the Nile does not rise and flood the fields; if the weather is awful; if there is an earthquake, a famine, a plague—immediately we hear the cry: 'Christians to the lions!'" (Apology, 40).

Repression

Of the many accounts of martyrdom in Christian literature, The Acts of the Scillitan Martyrs are among the closest to the original Roman court records. The date of the hearing referred to here was July 17, A.D. 180. The martyrs were from Scili in Tunisia (North Africa). Despite

[10]Based on Roberts and Donaldson, *The Ante-Nicene Fathers*, vol. 4, p. 178.

the apparent simplicity of the account, it still has a strong rhetorical flavor. Note the reluctance of the judge.[11]

When Praesens, for the second time, and Claudian were the consuls, on the seventeenth day of July, at Carthage, there were arraigned in the judgment hall the following: Speratus; Nartzalus; Cittinus; Veturius; Felix; Aquilinus; Laetantius; Januaria; Generosa; Donata; Secunda, and Vestia [*seven men and five women*].

The proconsul Saturninus said: "You can obtain the forgiveness of our Lord the Emperor if you return to your senses."

Speratus: "We have never done ill; we have not lent ourselves to wrong; we have never spoken ill, but when ill-treated we have given thanks, for we pay heed to our Emperor."

Saturninus: "We too are religious, and our religion is simple. We swear by the Genius of our Lord the Emperor, and pray for his welfare, as you also ought to do."

Speratus: "If you will give me a peaceful hearing, I can tell you the real truth of simplicity."

Saturninus: "I will not listen to you when you begin to speak evil of our sacred rites; rather, swear by the Genius of our Lord the Emperor."

Speratus: "I do not recognize the Empire of this world, but rather I serve that God 'Whom no man has seen, nor with these eyes can be seen.' I have committed no theft; but if I have bought anything I pay the tax, for I acknowledge my Lord, the King of Kings, and Emperor of all nations."

Saturninus (to all the accused): "Cease to be of this persuasion."

Speratus: "An ill persuasion is to do murder, to speak false witness."

Saturninus (ignoring Speratus, addresses the others): "Be no partakers in his folly!"

Cittinus: "We have none other to fear, save only our Lord God, who is in heaven."

Donata: "Honor Caesar as Caesar; but it is God we fear."

Vestia: "I am a Christian."

Secunda: "What I am, that I wish to be."

Saturninus (to Speratus): "Do you persist in being a Christian?"

Speratus: "I am a Christian." (*And all agreed with him.*)

Saturninus: "Do you want time to reconsider?"

Speratus: "In a matter so straightforward, there is no need for consideration."

Saturninus: "What are the things in your case?"

Speratus: "Books and letters of Paul, a just man."

Saturninus: "You are granted a reprieve of thirty days to think it over."

Speratus: "I am a Christian." (*And all the others agreed with him.*)

Then Saturninus the proconsul read out his decision from a tablet:

"Whereas Speratus, Nartzalus, Cittinus, Donata, Vestia, Secunda, and the others have confessed that they live according to the Christian rite; and since after opportunity was offered them of returning to the custom of the Romans, they have obstinately persisted; it is determined that they be put to the sword."

---

[11]*Acts of the Scillitan Martyrs* (entire text).

Speratus: "We give thanks to God."

Nartzalus: "Today we are martyrs in heaven; thanks be to God."

Saturninus the proconsul ordered the following to be declared by the herald:

"Speratus, Nartzalus, Cittinus, Veturius, Felix, Aquilinus, Laetantius, Januaria, Generosa, Vestia, Donata, and Secunda, I have ordered to be executed."

They said: "Thanks be to God." Immediately they were all beheaded for the name of Christ.

Reform

Another approach, reform of paganism, was tried by the Emperor Julian as a way of recovering lost ground. A former Christian, Julian borrowed liberally from Christian ideals and organizational principles and attempted to reform the civic religion of the Empire. He articulated a Christian-sounding value system, a justifying ideology, and an organization that was supposed to match that of the Christians. Julian wrote in the 360s, after Christianity had made great progress toward acceptability, and his efforts tell as much about why Christianity succeeded as about Julian's own mind-set. Raised a Christian, he was never quite able to erase the impact of his early training. Julian writes as Pontifex Maximus, Chief Priest of the State Religion.[12]

The religion of the Greeks does not yet prosper as I would wish, on account of those who profess it. But the gifts of the gods are great and splendid, better than any prayer or any hope. . . . Indeed, a little while ago no one would have dared even to pray for such a change, and so complete a one in so short a space of time [*i.e., the arrival of Julian himself, a reforming traditionalist, on the throne*]. Why then do we think that this is sufficient and do not observe how the kindness of Christians to strangers, their care for the burial of their dead, and the sobriety of their lifestyle has done the most to advance their cause? Each of these things, I think, ought really to be practiced by us. It is not sufficient for you alone to practice them, but so must all the priests in Galatia [*in modern Turkey*] without exception. Either make these men good by shaming them, persuade them to become so—or fire them. . . . Secondly, exhort the priests neither to approach a theater nor to drink in a tavern, nor to profess any base or infamous trade. Honor those who obey, and expel those who disobey.

Erect many hostels, one in each city, in order that strangers may enjoy my kindness, not only those of our own faith but also of others whosoever is in want of money. I have just been devising a plan by which you will be able to get supplies. For I have ordered that every year throughout all Galatia 30,000 modii of grain and 60,000 pints of wine shall be provided. The fifth part of these I order to be expended on the poor who serve the priests, and the rest must be distributed from me to strangers and beggars. For it is disgraceful when no Jew is a beggar and the impious Galileans [*the name given by Julian to Christians*] support our poor in addition to their own; everyone is able to see that our co-religionists are

[12]Julian, *Letter to Arsacius, High Priest of Galatia; Letter to a Priest*. Based on the translation of Edward J. Chinnock, *A Few Notes on Julian and a Translation of his Public Letters* (London: David Nutt, 1901), pp. 75–78.

in want of aid from us. Teach also those who profess the Greek religion to contribute to such services, and the villages of the Greek religion to offer the first-fruits to the gods. Accustom those of the Greek religion to such benevolence, teaching them that this has been our work from ancient times. Homer, at any rate, made Eumaeus say: "O Stranger, it is not lawful for me, even if one poorer than you should come, to dishonor a stranger. For all strangers and beggars are from Zeus. The gift is small, but it is precious." [*Julian is quoting from the* Odyssey, *14.53*]. Do not therefore let others outdo us in good deeds while we ourselves are disgraced by laziness; rather, let us not quite abandon our piety toward the gods. . . .

While proper behavior in accordance with the laws of the city will obviously be the concern of the governors of the cities, you for your part [*as a priest*] must take care to encourage people not to violate the laws of the gods since they are holy. . . . Above all you must exercise philanthropy. From it result many other goods, and indeed that which is the greatest blessing of all, the goodwill of the gods. . . . We ought to share our goods with all men, but most of all with the respectable, the helpless, and the poor, so that they have at least the essentials of life. I claim, even though it may seem paradoxical, that it is a holy deed to share our clothes and food with the wicked: we give, not to their moral character but to their human character. Therefore I believe that even prisoners deserve the same kind of care. This type of kindness will not interfere with the process of justice, for among the many imprisoned and awaiting trial some will be found guilty, some innocent. It would be cruel indeed if out of consideration for the innocent we should not allow some pity for the guilty, or on account of the guilty we should behave without mercy and humanity to those who have done no wrong. . . . How can the man who, while worshipping Zeus the God of Companions, sees his neighbors in need and does not give them a dime—how can he think he is worshipping Zeus properly? . . .

Priests ought to make a point of not doing impure or shameful deeds or saying words or hearing talk of this type. We must therefore get rid of all offensive jokes and licentious associations. What I mean is this: no priest is to read Archilochus or Hipponax or anyone else who writes poetry as they do. They should stay away from the same kind of stuff in Old Comedy. Philosophy alone is appropriate for us priests. Of the philosophers, however, only those who put the gods before them as guides of their intellectual life are acceptable, like Pythagoras, Plato, Aristotle, and the Stoics . . . only those who make people reverent . . . not the works of Pyrrho and Epicurus. . . . We ought to pray often to the gods in private and in public, about three times a day, but if not that often, at least in the morning and at night. No priest is anywhere to attend shameful theatrical shows or to have one performed at his own house; it is in no way appropriate. Indeed, if it were possible to get rid of such shows altogether from the theater and restore the theaters, purified, to Dionysus as in the olden days, I would certainly have tried to bring this about. But since I thought that this was out of the question, and even if possible would for other reasons be inexpedient, I did not even try. But I do insist that priests stay away from the licentiousness of the theaters and leave them to the people. No priest is to enter a theater, have an actor or a chariot driver as a friend, or allow a dancer or mime into his house. I allow to attend the sacred games those who want to, that is, they may attend only those games from which women are forbidden to attend not only as participants but even as spectators.

When the Shoe Was on the Other Foot

After Constantine, Christianity gradually secured its hold on almost all aspects of the Empire. Pockets of resistance, however, remained. One of these was the ancient Senate at Rome. In this reading the pagan historian Zosimus describes the dramatic confrontation between the senators and the Emperor Theodosius I (A.D. 375–395). One of the interesting points that emerges is the connection between the poor financial condition of the Empire and the cost of pagan rituals, which could be performed only, so the senators claimed, at public expense. There are echoes here of the speech of Camillus to the Romans urging them not to move from the sacred site of Rome to Veii after the sack of the Gauls in 390 B.C. (Chapter 2), and of Ammianus Marcellinus' condemnation of Valens' policy of admitting whole peoples into the Empire (above, "The Emperor and the Barbarians"). Theodosius banned paganism in A.D. 391.[13]

Theodosius' success having reached this point, he journeyed to Rome and declared his son Honorius emperor. At the same time he made Stilicho [*an able German*] commander of the legions there and left him in charge as his son's guardian. Then he convened the Senate. The Senators had remained faithful to their long-standing ancestral rites and would not be moved to agree with those who condemned the gods. Theodosius delivered a speech to them in which he exhorted them to recant their "error" (as he called it) and to embrace the Christian faith because it promised forgiveness of every sin and every kind of impiety. None was persuaded by this harangue or was willing to give up the rites which had been passed on from generation to generation since the City's founding, in favor of an absurd belief. For, the Senators said, by preserving the former rites they had inhabited a city unconquered for almost 1,200 years, while they did not know what would happen if they exchanged these rituals for something different.

In turn Theodosius said that the treasury was burdened by the expense of the rites and the sacrifices; that he wanted to abolish them; that he did not approve of them and, furthermore, that military necessities called for additional funds. The Senators replied that the ceremonies could not be performed except at public expense. Nevertheless, a law abolishing them was laid down and, as other things which had been handed down from ancestral times lay neglected, the Empire of the Romans was gradually diminished and became a domicile of barbarians. . . .

---

[13]James T. Buchanan and Harold T. Davis, translators, *Zosimus: Historia Nova. The Decline of Rome* (San Antonio, TX: Trinity University Press), pp. 191–192. By permission.

10.10   The Hellenization and Romanization of Christianity

Christianity had the advantages as well as disadvantages of springing from a highly literate tradition. Its Jewish origins supplied it with sacred writings of great complexity and depth as well as a long apologetic tradition of justification to gentile readers. Greeks and Romans were also highly literate, though their "bible" was much less formalized. Still, there was clearly a canon of classical literature and a developed educational system—so much so that the Emperor Julian felt it necessary to prohibit Christians from teaching the classics. Christian professors were not to be allowed to teach authors such as Hesiod and Homer because in their hearts they felt something else: "I think it absurd that those who expound the works of these writers should dishonor the gods who are honored by them."[14] *In fact, the challenge of Christianity nudged Greeks to the last great intellectual effort of the ancient world, the adaptation of Christianity to Greco-Roman culture. The amalgam produced in the centuries between approximately* A.D. *200 and 450 has not been replaced to the present.*

Of course the amalgam was never entirely satisfactory to all members of the Church. One viewpoint, represented by Tertullian, felt paganism and Christianity were incompatible: "What does Athens have to do with Jerusalem? What is there in common between [Plato's] Academy and the Church? . . . Away with all attempts to produce a 'Stoic,' a 'Platonic,' a dialectical Christianity! After possessing Jesus we want no subtle theories, no clever inquiries after the Gospel. With our faith we desire no further belief" (*Against Heretics*, 7).

The opposite viewpoint was expressed by Synesius of Cyrene, who agreed to become a bishop only on the condition that while he spoke "myths" in church he was allowed to "think as a philosopher" in private. Perhaps the commonest position was the one stated by Clement of Alexandria: "Philosophy," *he said,* "is the 'school master' or teacher to bring the Greeks to Christ, just as the Law brought the Hebrews to him. Thus philosophy is a preparation, paving the way towards perfection in Christ" (*Stromateis,* 1.5.28).

In the following reading Eusebius is quoting from a book, The Little Labyrinth, *written against a second-century heretic and still circulating in his time.*[15]

They have treated the Divine Scriptures recklessly and without fear. They have set aside the standard of the ancient faith. They have not known Christ. They do not endeavor to learn what the Divine Scriptures declare but strive laboriously after any form of syllogism [*a form of linguistic argument used in Greek philosophy, especially among the followers of Aristotle*] which may be devised to sustain their impiety. And if anyone brings before them a passage of Divine Scripture, they examine it to see whether a conjunctive or disjunctive form of syllogism can be made from it.

---

[14]*Rescript on Christian Teachers,* in Chinnock, *A Few Notes on Julian,* p. 61.
[15]Eusebius, *Church History* 5.28. Based on the translation of McGiffert and Richardson in Schaff and Wace, *A Select Library of Nicene and Post-Nicene Fathers of the Christian Church,* p. 248.

Since they are of the earth and speak from the earth, they abandon the holy writings of God and devote themselves to geometry. Some of them laboriously study the geometry of Euclid and admire Aristotle and Theophrastus. Some of them even worship Galen [*famous physician and scientist*]. But those who use the arts of unbelievers for their heretical opinions and adulterate the simple faith of the Divine Scriptures by the craft of the godless, need I say, are far from the faith. . . . Either they do not believe that the Holy Scriptures were spoken by the Holy Spirit, and they are thus unbelievers, or else they think themselves wiser than the Holy Spirit, and in that case what else are they than possessed?

Justin Martyr represents an increasingly common type of second-century convert. Born in Palestine around A.D. *114 to a well-off family, he traveled widely and studied philosophy. The constancy of the Christian martyrs impressed him, and he took up the study of the new religion and was baptized. He moved to Rome, where he set up a Christian school. His teaching and writing apparently generated a pagan backlash, and he was martyred in* A.D. *165. In his* Apologies *Justin claimed that Christianity was true philosophy, the end and goal of all philosophic endeavor, and that in fact Greek philosophers, insofar as they had discovered the truth, could be said to be "Christians." He attempted to show that contemporary philosophy, especially Platonism, could be harmonized with Christianity.*[16]

Lest some should claim with the intent of turning people from our teaching that we say that Christ was born 150 years ago under Cyrenius, and taught what we say he taught under Pontius Pilate, and then go on to accuse us of saying that everyone who lived *before* him were worthless—let us anticipate and solve this difficulty.

We are taught that Christ is the firstborn of God, and we have demonstrated above that he is the Divine Reason [*Logos* or *Word*] in whom every race of men are partakers. Thus, those who live according to reason are Christians even though they have been thought to be atheists. Such were Socrates and Heraclitus among the Greeks. . . .

I declare that I prayed and strove with all my strength to be found to be a Christian, not because the teachings of Plato are contrary to those of Christ, but because they are not in all respects like them. The same is true of the doctrines of the Stoics, the poets, and prose writers. For each discoursed rightly, seeing that which was akin to Christianity through a share in the Divine Reason. But those who have uttered contrary opinions seem not to have had the invisible knowledge and irrefutable wisdom. Whatever has been uttered aright by any men in any place belongs to us Christians, for next to God, we worship and love the Reason which is from the unbegotten and ineffable God. . . . All the authors were able to see the truth darkly, through the implanted seed of Reason dwelling in them.

---

[16]Justin, *Apology* 1.46; 2.13.

10.11   Monasticism

Christianity introduced a novel form of life, one that in some respects represents the most extreme departure that can be imagined from the old polis tradition of civic involvement as the fulfillment of the highest goals of human endeavor. This was monasticism. Open to both men and women, monasticism provided a truly radical alternative to contemporary lifestyles. In monasteries both men and women could find a new kind of autonomy that included spiritual, economic, social, and even, in some sense, political dimensions. In their developed forms monasteries were self-sufficient economically, and often strong enough to defend themselves against all but the most powerful marauders. They represented attractive alternatives to the growing chaos of society in the West, and the over sophistication of the more urbanized East. From a spiritual viewpoint the monasteries offered their members a means of reaching the highest levels of spirituality. At a more mundane level monasteries provided women with an alternative never available to them before: escape from marriage and their parental families.

Jerome, a native of Illyricum, translator of the Bible into Latin, voluminous correspondent, satirist, and irascible polemicist, writes in A.D. 374 to a friend, encouraging him to join him in his monastery in Bethlehem, where the Gospels, in all their literalness, could be practiced. The letter is full of biblical illusions and quotations. Reading between the lines we also get an inside look at life in a comfortable Roman household in the late Empire.[17]

Pampered soldier, why are you wasting time in your father's house? Where is the rampart, the ditch, the winter campaign under canvas? Behold the trumpet sounds—from heaven! Our General, fully armed, comes amid the clouds to overcome the world. From our King's mouth comes the double-edged sword that cuts down all in its path. Are you going to remain in your chamber and not come out to join in the battle? . . . Listen to your King's proclamation: "He who is not with me is against me, and he who does not gather with me scatters."

Remember when you joined up as a recruit, when buried with Christ in baptism, you took the oath of allegiance to him, declaring that you would spare neither your father nor your mother? But now the adversary in your own heart is trying to kill Christ! Now the enemy's camp has its sights on your loyalty! Though your little nephew twine his arms around your neck; though your mother, with disheveled hair and tearing her robe asunder, point to the breast with which she nourished you; though your father fall down on the threshold before you— trample on his body and go your way! Fly with tearless eyes to the standard of the Cross. In this matter cruelty is your duty. . . .

I know well the chains which you will say hinder you. Indeed, my breast is not made of iron, nor my heart of stone. I was not born from a rock or raised by Hyrcanian tigers. I have been through this experience too. Your widowed sister may throw her gentle arms around you. The household slaves, in whose company you grew up, will cry, "To what master are you abandoning us?" Your old nurse and her husband,

---

[17]Jerome, *Letter* 14.

who, after your own natural father, have the next claim to your devotion, say, "Wait awhile until we die so you can bury us!" Perhaps your foster mother, with sagging breasts and wrinkled face, will sing you your old childhood lullaby! . . . But the love of Christ and the fear of Gehenna will easily break such bonds.

You will claim that the Scriptures command us to obey our parents. On the contrary, whoever loves his parents more than Christ, loses his own soul. If my enemy takes up a sword to kill me, will I be held back by my mother's tears? Should I desert from the army because of my father, to whom in the cause of Christ I owe no burial because in his cause I owe burial to everyone? . . . You may claim that all your fellow citizens are Christians. But your case is not the same as everyone else. Hear what the Lord has to say: "If you would be perfect, go and sell what you have and follow me." You promised to be perfect.

When you resigned from the army and "made yourself a eunuch for the kingdom of Christ," what else had you in mind besides a perfect life? A perfect servant of Christ has nothing besides Christ. Indeed, if he has anything besides Christ, he is not perfect. . . . If you are perfect, why do you pine for your father's property? But if you are not perfect, you have failed the Lord. The Gospel thunders the divine words: "You cannot serve two masters." Does anyone dare to make Christ a liar by serving Mammon *and* the Lord at the same time? Does he not say often, "If anyone will come after me, let him deny himself, take up his cross and follow me"? If I load myself with gold, do I imagine I am following Christ? . . .

O desert, green with the flowers of Christ! O solitude in which the stones of the Great City of the King mentioned in the *Apocalypse* are found! O wilderness rejoicing in the presence of God! Brother, what are you doing in the world when you are so much more important than the world? How long are the shadows of a roof going to hold you back? How long will the smoky dungeon of these cities imprison you? . . . How refreshing to fling off the burdens of the flesh and fly to the sparkling aether? . . . You are spoiled indeed, dear friend, if you wish to rejoice here on earth—and afterwards reign with Christ!

10.12   The Fall of Rome

When Jerome in his monastery in Bethlehem heard of the sack of Rome by Alaric and his band of Goths in A.D. 410, he gave vent to the following lament on the collapse of the Empire in the West. It is inspired as much by Hebrew poetry and the dirges of the prophets over Jerusalem as by Jerome's own classical training. As history it probably does not tell us very much, but it has importance insofar as it helped lodge the impression of a ghastly catastrophe, the Fall of the Roman Empire, in the Western historical tradition.[18] *Six years after the sack of Rome, the poet*

---

[18]Jerome, *Letter to Ageruchia; Commentary on Ezechiel, Preface to Book 3*. Translator James Harvey Robison, *Readings in European History*, vol. 1 (New York: Ginn and Company, 1904), pp. 44–45.

Rutilius Namatianus writes of the city as though it were still as glorious as ever. The real destruction was to come later.

Nations innumerable and most savage have invaded all Gaul. The whole region between the Alps and the Pyrenees, the ocean and the Rhine, has been devastated by the Quadi, the Vandals, the Sarmati, the Alani, the Gepidae, the hostile Heruli, the Saxons, the Burgundians, the Alamanni and the Pannonians. O wretched Empire! Mayence, formerly so noble a city, has been taken and ruined, and in the church many thousands of men have been massacred. Worms has been destroyed after a long siege. Rheims, that powerful city, Amiens, Arras, Speyer, Strasburg—all have seen their citizens led away captive into Germany. Aquitaine and the provinces of Lyons and Narbonne, all save a few towns, have been depopulated; and these the sword threatens without, while hunger ravages within. I cannot speak without tears of Toulouse, which the merits of the holy Bishop Exuperius have prevailed so far to save from destruction. Spain, even, is in daily terror lest it perish, remembering the invasion of the Cimbri; and whatsoever the other provinces have suffered once, they continue to suffer in their fear.

I will keep silence concerning the rest, lest I seem to despair of the mercy of God. For a long time, from the Black Sea to the Julian Alps, those things which are ours have not been ours; and for thirty years, since the Danube boundary was broken, war has been waged in the very midst of the Roman Empire. Our tears are dried by old age. Except a few old men, all were born in captivity and siege and do not desire the liberty they never knew. Who could believe this? How could the whole tale be worthily told? How Rome has fought within her own bosom not for glory, but for preservation—nay, how she has not even fought, but with gold and all her precious things has ransomed her life. . . .

Who could believe [*Jerome exclaims in another passage*] that Rome, built upon the conquest of the whole world, would fall to the ground? that the mother herself would become the tomb of her peoples? that all the regions of the East, of Africa and Egypt, once ruled by the queenly city, would be filled with troops of slaves and handmaidens? that today holy Bethlehem should shelter men and women of noble birth, who once abounded in wealth and are now beggars?

▼▼▼

Questions

1. According to Ammianus Marcellinus, what two factors allowed Rome to rise to greatness? (10.1)
2. What was Lactantius' explanation for Diocletian's division of the Empire into many provinces? (10.2)
3. What did Constantine decree in the Edict of Milan? (10.3)
4. Ammianus Marcellinus regarded what building in Rome as "the most exquisite under the canopy of heaven?" (10.4)

5. What problems did the Emperor Valentinian encounter in trying to help the people of Tripoli in Libya? (10.4)
6. In what way, according to the author of the *Epistle to Diognetus*, were Christians different from their neighbors? (10.6)
7. Eusebius describes how disciplinary problems in the Christian church were handled. Explain what steps were taken to discipline the errant priest Novatus. (10.7)
8. Describe the attitude of the proconsul Saturninus towards the Christians brought before him for trial. (10.9)
9. What reforms of paganism did the Emperor Julian propose? (10.9)
10. What was Justin's view of Greek philosophy? (10.10)